Dedication

To my wife, Kathryn, my partner and the love of my life.

Published by Hereditea
Brentwood, Tennessee
Cover Design by Sandy Perry
Brentwood, Tennessee
ISBN (13): 978-0-9796029-1-7; ISBN (10): 0-9796029-1-2

Forward

I learned of my relationship to Commodore Robert Field Stockton five years ago when I inherited a book that belonged to my 101 year old grandmother, Catherine Augusta Dod. Inside the four inch thick book was documented family genealogy going back several hundred years, including information about Commodore Robert Field Stockton, my third great-grandfather. To my astonishment the book documented my direct descent from a signer of the Declaration of Independence and several Kings and notables of Scotland. I never knew about this book or my ancestors, and at age 58 it changed my life.

As a retired naval officer, with 24 years of service, I was eager to learn about the Commodore. I looked through history books for information about him, and unfortunately I found very little. Recently while looking through the history section at a local book store, I picked up a current book on American history. The paragraph describing the War with Mexico and the military action in California was a character assassination of Commodore Stockton and Colonel Fremont and a glorification of General Kearney (incorrectly listed as Colonel); unfortunately this has been the case in several American history books I have lately reviewed. It seems the writing of American history is getting out of hand as names and events are twisted until they hardly resemble the history of the actual events.

During my research on the Commodore I found this book, '*A Sketch in the Life of Commodore Robert Field Stockton*' that I believe captures the true character of the Commodore and what he did for America. I kept the book exactly as it was printed in 1856 making it a little difficult to read and perhaps not 'politically correct' today, but that is why I believe the book should be kept exactly as it was written, capturing the events that shaped American history. The author, Samuel Bayard, wrote about the Commodore based on his personal knowledge of the Commodore and those who knew him, along with the letters, documents, speeches, and hearings of the events as they occurred; the truth by those that were there to witness and write about the actual events.

I hope you enjoy the book and it allows you to learn about this American naval hero, Commodore Robert Field Stockton, who deserves our admiration and thanks for helping make American what it is today…a great nation.

A grateful great grandson,

Lieutenant Commander John C. Glynn, Jr. USN
Brentwood, Tennessee

iii

Introduction

The Commodore's first ancestor to arrive on American shores was Richard Stockton, known in the family as 'the immigrant'. He arrived from Cheshire, England in 1655, and with his wife and son, Richard settled on Long Island, near the city of New York. In 1691 he became a member of the Society of Friends or Quakers as they were known. In 1701 his son, Richard, bought 5,500 acres of land from William Penn and the family moved to the colony of New Jersey. The land that was purchased sits nearly in the center of Princeton, New Jersey. Richard's son, Judge John Stockton, gave money and land to establish the College of New Jersey in Princeton (now Princeton University).

Judge John Stockton's eldest son was Judge Richard Stockton (the Commodore's grandfather), a signer of the Declaration of Independence from New Jersey. Judge Richard Stockton was the only signer to be captured, locked in irons, starved and brutally treated as a common criminal by the British in the notorious Provost Prison in New York City. After three years of research on his life and imprisonment, my wife Kathryn and I wrote '***His Sacred Honor, Judge Richard Stockton a signer of the Declaration of Independence***'. Judge Richard Stockton's wife, Annis Boudinot Stockton, was one of America's first female published poets and was a close friend and favorite correspondent of General George Washington.

The Commodore's father, a Richard Stockton, the signer's eldest son, personally experienced the hardships of the Revolutionary War after his father was imprisoned by the British and their home burned and pillaged. He became an eminent lawyer, served as a Senator from New Jersey in 1796, in Congress during the war of 1812, and was affectionately known as 'the Duke'.

Commodore Robert Field Stockton was the second son of Richard 'Duke' Stockton. He departed the College of New Jersey at the age of 16 to join the Navy (against his father's wishes). He fought in the War of 1812, alongside Commodore Rogers defending Baltimore from the British and was promoted to Lieutenant for his gallantry. He earned the nickname 'Fighting Bob' from the sailors while fighting at Baltimore.

He distinguished himself under the command of Commodore Stephen Decatur in the war with Algiers, and fought duels in honor of America. He became the first United States naval officer to act against the foreign slave trade conducting anti-slavery patrols off the coast of West Africa, and captured four slave ships on one voyage. After meeting with Francis Scott Key and other officials of the American Colonization Society, and at great personal risk to himself, he acquired the land that became the Republic of Liberia.

In 1823 he married Harriet Maria Potter, of Charleston, South Carolina. Her father, John Potter, my 4th great-grandfather, is a direct descendant of King Robert I (Robert the Bruce), King Robert II (Robert Stewart, the first Stewart King), and other notable Scottish families. Harriet Maria's mother, Catherine Fuller, shared a great-grandfather, Captain Nicolas Martiau, of Yorktown, Virginia with General George Washington. Therefore, Washington is my cousin and interestingly so is Queen Elizabeth II of Great Britain, linked to me through both Captain Martiau, her great-grandfather also, and the Royal Stewarts.

The Commodore brought Harriet Maria to Princeton, New Jersey and her father (John), mother (Catherine) and two brothers soon followed, building some of the finest homes in Princeton, many still in use today. The Commodore and Harriet Maria had nine children and I descend from their first born daughter Catherine Elizabeth Stockton. The Commodore along with John Ericsson developed the first propeller driven warship for the United States Navy. In New Jersey he pioneered the project of the canal that linked the Raritan River with the Delaware River and along with the Stevens brothers constructed the Camden and Amboy railroad in New Jersey that eventually became part of the main line of the Pennsylvania Railroad.

The Commodore could have been the Secretary of the Navy under President Tyler, but declined the honor. As a naval Captain he delivered the Annexation papers, annexing Texas into the United States, to Sam Houston in Texas from President Polk. Fort Stockton Texas is named in his honor.

In October 1845, with the new rank of Commodore, Robert Field Stockton as the Commander of the Navy's Pacific Squadron set sail on the *USS Congress* on a voyage that would place his name in history alongside Zachary Taylor and Winfield Scott in a war that carried the boundaries of the United States to the Rio Grande and the Pacific Ocean. As Commander of the Navy's Pacific Squadron, he bravely led his small band of sailors and marines and with the aid of Col. Fremont conquered California during the Mexican War. He became California's first military Governor. Stockton California is named for him as well as a major street in San Francisco, an African river, and a bay in Puerto Rico.

After 40 years of naval service he retired and in 1852 he became a United States Senator for New Jersey and passed legislation banishing flogging in the Navy. And if the circumstances would have suited him, he could have been a Presidential candidate for the Democratic Party. He died October 7, 1866 in Princeton, New Jersey at the family home 'Morven', built by his grandfather the signer of the Declaration of Independence.

These Stockton's: the Signer, the Duke, and the Commodore all served this country and helped in the formation of what it is today, a great nation. They all took their first and last breaths at 'Morven' and it is fitting that their home would become the New Jersey Governor's Mansion from 1954 to 1981 and is now a state owned museum honoring the Stockton family.

Yours truly

R. B. Stockton

A SKETCH

OF THE

LIFE

OF

COM. ROBERT F. STOCKTON;

WITH

AN APPENDIX,

, COMPRISING

HIS CORRESPONDENCE WITH THE NAVY DEPARTMENT

RESPECTING HIS CONQUEST OF CALIFORNIA;

AND

EXTRACTS FROM THE DEFENCE OF COL. J. C. FREMONT,

IN RELATION TO THE SAME SUBJECT;

TOGETHER WITH HIS

Speeches in the Senate of the United States,

AND HIS

POLITICAL LETTERS.

—————

NEW YORK:

DERBY & JACKSON, 119 NASSAU ST.

1856.

W. H. TINSON, STEREOTYPER.   GEO. RUSSELL & CO., PRINTERS.

CONTENTS.

APPENDIX.

INTRODUCTION.

If great achievements, important public services, and a life devoted to conferring benefits on his country and race, can render the biography of a living man, interesting to his cotemporaries,—if modest reluctance to trumpet his own fame, or even vindicate himself from injustice or detraction, impose on his friends an obligation to perform that duty for him,—then we need offer no apology for this sketch of the life and services of Commodore Stockton.

We esteem it one of the most happy events in our life to have known Commodore Stockton intimately from his youth. Educated and brought up in the same village and academic institutions,—though often separated from him during some of the most active years of his life,—we never lost sight of him, nor failed to observe, with the greatest interest, every incident of moment in his varied and remarkable career.

It is therefore from our own knowledge from time to time, as the chief events of his life took place, as well as from information obtained from his companions on sea and shore, and from official documents, that we have derived the materials for the following narrative.

7

We present it to the public, not without confidence that, although imperfect and deficient, as it doubtless is, they will nevertheless find in it something worthy to be recorded and remembered,—a contribution to American history which justice to a patriotic and meritorious fellow-citizen has long demanded.

A SKETCH

OF THE

LIFE OF COMMODORE STOCKTON.

CHAPTER I.

ANCESTORS—RICHARD STOCKTON, THE SIGNER OF THE DECLARATION OF INDEPEND-
ENCE—RICHARD STOCKTON, FATHER OF THE COMMODORE—AN EMINENT LAWYER—
BOYHOOD—ENTERS COLLEGE—CHARACTER AND STANDING IN COLLEGE—HIS SELF-
EDUCATION—ENTERS THE NAVY IN 1811—HABITS OF TEMPERANCE.

MORE than a hundred years previous to the Declaration of Independence, the ancestors of Commodore Robert F. Stockton emigrated
from England, and purchased a large tract of land, on which they
settled, in the central part of New Jersey. They belonged to the
Society of Friends (or Quakers, as they are often called), and left
their fatherland to escape from the persecution which all dissenters
experienced from the restored dynasty of the Stuarts. They obtained a deed from the Pennsylvania lawgiver for all that land
bounded by the Province line of New Jersey on the west, the Mill-
ston on the east, and Rocky Hill on the north, embracing the present borough of Princeton and about six thousand acres. Upon
this tract the Stocktons for several generations have continued to
reside, and here the subject of our narrative was born and now lives.
The great-grandfather of the commodore was John Stockton, one
of the first Presiding Judges of the Court of Common Pleas of the
County of Somerset. He was a man of education and influence in
the early history of New Jersey, and universally respected. His
eldest son Richard (grandfather of Commodore Stockton), who
was educated with great care, was still more distinguished.* He
adopted the profession of the law, and soon became successful in
its pursuit. He married a sister of Elias Boudinot, one of the

---

* See Fields's Provincial History, p. 190.

Presidents of Congress under the old Confederation. The Boudinots were of Huguenot extraction. Thus, in the commodore's lineage was blended the blood of the Friends and the Huguenots, who were alike voluntary exiles from the land of their nativity for conscience' sake—fugitives from the tyranny and oppression of the old country—pioneers of religion and liberty in the forest wilds of America. Richard Stockton attained the highest eminence as a lawyer in New Jersey. He was a Judge of the Supreme Court before the Revolution, and a member of the King's Council for New Jersey. He was one of the principal benefactors of the College of New Jersey; and it was through his instrumentality, while on a visit to England and Scotland, that Dr. Witherspoon was induced to accept the presidency of that institution, and emigrate to New Jersey. The commanding talents and virtues of Mr. Stockton gave him great influence in the colony, and were exerted from the first in stern resistance to the tyranny of the mother country. He and all his family friends zealously united in defence of American liberty. Among these were Elias Boudinot, his brother-in-law, and the celebrated Dr. Benjamin Rush, of Philadelphia, his son-in-law. Mr. Stockton was elected to Congress in 1776, and had the honour, together with his son-in-law, Dr. Rush, of subscribing the immortal Declaration of Independence of the 4th of July of that year. His life was shortened by the cruel treatment he received from the British in 1781, by whom he was captured and thrown into prison. From the hardships and sufferings to which he was then subjected he never recovered, but in a few months prematurely ended his brilliant career, universally lamented. Had he survived the Revolutionary War, his great abilities, purity of character, and patriotic services, would have given him a high position in the new republic. He was a devoted friend of Washington, and enjoyed his confidence in a high degree.*

The father of the commodore was Richard Stockton, the eldest son of the signer of the Declaration of Independence. At twenty-five years of age he stood at the head of the New Jersey Bar, and maintained that position for forty years, and until his death in 1828. He ranked among the foremost lawyers of the United States. For profound learning, sound judgment, weight of character, and unblemished integrity, his memory will long be cherished in New Jersey. Despising the arts of the politician and the demagogue, he stood aloof from all personal strifes for office or popular favour,

---

* Fields's Provincial Courts.

preferring the independence of the private citizen to any official post. In politics, he was a Federalist of the Washington and Hamilton school; but no one more freely condemned the factious and ultra designs of the Eastern or Hartford Convention Federalists than he. He was elected to the Senate of the United States during the administration of Washington, and, after a short period of service there, retired altogether from public life, which he re-entered again only to serve a single term in the House of Representatives of Congress during the war of 1812. It was as a great common-law lawyer, however, that he was chiefly distinguished: as such, his reputation was co-extensive with the country, and his opinion constantly sought and consulted by eminent counsel from other states.

Such were the immediate ancestors of Robert F. Stockton. Those who are best acquainted with him, and who have most frequently witnessed his grasp of mind when brought in conflict with subjects of importance, say that he much resembles his father in the vigour of his intellectual faculties, and in that strong practical common sense for which he was so remarkable. His boyhood furnished strong indications of the character by which he has since been distinguished. All its principal features were displayed in his early youth. Personal courage, a high sense of honour, an intolerable hatred of injustice, united with unbounded generosity and devoted attachment to his friends, were traits of disposition which marked him as an original and decided character while at school. Magnanimous and chivalric, he was always the champion of the weaker party, and the foe of every species of school-boy tyranny. Respectful and courteous to all, his high sense of honour was prompt to repel and punish insult or aggression. The legends of his youthful prowess and victorious encounters while a school-boy constitute a part of the traditions of the Princeton schools, and are still often recited for the entertainment of his juvenile successors. Intrepidity, an intuitive perception of right and wrong in every difficulty, however unexpected—decision of character, and a cool and wary self-possession, by which he was always master of his own resources—characterized the boy as they now characterize the man. These qualities bore him triumphantly through all the conflicts and difficulties of boyhood, with a reputation increased by every test to which he was subjected.

He entered college in the freshman class when in his thirteenth year, and was soon distinguished for his industry and proficiency. He stood among the first in his class, exhibiting much aptitude both for the languages and the mathematics. In elocution he particularly excelled; and had he remained at college until he graduated, would probably have received the highest honours of his class. In a year and a half he would have completed his whole collegiate course, when the impending war with Great Britain excited his patriotic sensibilities and inspired him with the desire to seek glory in the path of danger. The fame of Nelson was then in its zenith, and Stockton's young heart was fired with the hope of emulating the exploits of the great British Captain. Though fond of literary pursuits, and with talents which would have enabled him to take a high rank at the bar, yet such was the ardour of his patriotism that he relinquished all the advantages which he enjoyed for the acquisition of a finished education, and earnestly sought a position in the navy. His application for a midshipman's warrant was forwarded to Washington in the summer of 1811, and in due time he received his commission, bearing date September, 1811.

Considering the immature age at which he ceased his academic studies, and the fertility and resources of his mind, as exhibited so soon as it was directed to civil and political affairs, it must be seen that Mr. Stockton should be classed with those who are called *self-made men*. Aided by the little elementary training which he enjoyed, his mind directed itself in its development. Guided by the instincts of good sense and a sound judgment, he pursued, at all intervals of leisure from active duty, such a course of reading and such studies as were calculated to be of the greatest practical utility. Moral and ethical philosophy, the law of nations, and history, constituted the principal subjects of his attention. The Bible, Cicero, Shakspeare, and Lord Bacon were his favourite studies. Whatever subjects he investigated, he did so thoroughly. Not so much the details as the principles of knowledge engaged his attention. An eminent professor of Princeton College* a few years ago remarked to us, that Mr. Stockton, in some respects, was the most extraordinary and best informed man he had ever met; that there was no subject which could be started for discussion in his presence, whether of law, religion, morals, science or philosophy, on which he would not throw light by whatever he said, and hold a successful controversy with any one who had made the particular subject in dispute the chief object of his study.

There can be no doubt that, as soon as he entered the navy, Mr. Stockton formed for himself a very high standard of excellence, the attainment of which he persisted in reaching, without being diverted from his object by any obstacle or exigency. He saw and

---

* Professor Albert B. Dod.

appreciated the defects as well as the merits of his superiors in command, and soon learned that the cultivation and training of the intellectual faculties were the only proper means of insuring invariable success. His energy and force of character enabled him, notwithstanding a keen relish for pleasure and those amusements which so often entirely engross the time of the young officer, to persevere in the line of conduct which he had prescribed for himself. His love of pleasure or society never tempted him to neglect his duty, nor to trespass upon the rules of sobriety. To his habitual temperance, notwithstanding the seductions of naval life, he is indebted for a sound constitution and an adolescence of spirit and *physique* characteristic of a man of thirty-five or forty years of age. Though now approaching his grand climacteric, his capacity for enduring fatigue and labour, whether of mind or body, was perhaps never greater at any period of his life than at present.

CHAPTER II.

SOON after receiving his commission, Mr. Stockton was ordered
to join the frigate President, in command of Commodore Rodgers.
He left his paternal residence at Princeton, February 14th, 1812,
and repaired to his ship, then lying at Newport, Rhode Island. The
President soon afterwards sailed on a cruise along the coast, where
a number of British frigates were arrogantly hovering. She remained at sea during the spring, giving protection to our commerce,
and returned to New York about the 1st of June.

On the 21st of June, three days after the declaration of war with
Great Britain, Commodore Rodgers sailed from New York in command of a squadron consisting of the frigates President and Congress, the ship-of-war Hornet, and the brig Argus. On the second
day after getting to sea, the President fell in with the British frigate
Belvidera, Captain Byron. The President, by superiority of sailing, got within gunshot of the Belvidera between four and five
o'clock, P. M., when, finding the breeze moderating, Commodore
Rodgers commenced firing with his bow-chase guns, with the design
of crippling the enemy, and by this means retarding her and bringing on an action. His very first shots killed several seamen on the
Belvidera and wounded the captain. The enemy kept up a brisk
discharge with her stern guns, and resorted to all the usual means
of increasing her speed for the purpose of escape, by throwing overboard anchors, yawl and jolly boats, and starting water-casks; and
by this means her flight was accelerated, and she gained on her
opponent. The President then bore up and fired her broadsides,
but, owing to the distance, without much effect, except on the sails
and rigging of the Belvidera. The running action between the two
frigates continued for three or four hours after night; and during
the darkness the Belvidera succeeded in eluding her adversary.

Three men on the President were killed by the shot of the Belvidere, and four by the bursting of a gun, and nineteen were wounded, principally by the accident. The enemy's loss, according to his own account, was two killed and four or five wounded, though it is believed that his loss was much greater. Thus, young Stockton had hardly breathed the salt-water air before he heard the whistle of the enemy's cannon-shot. During the action, his coolness and his fine military deportment attracted the particular attention of the Commodore. The sagacious old sea-captain saw in the manly bearing of his young midshipman the true sort of stuff,—the enthusiasm which kindled with the roar of guns and the undaunted self-possession which the tumult of battle only concentrated.

One of the duties of the youngest aid (when the men were called to quarters or to man the batteries) was to bring the Commodore's belt and pistols. In performing this duty soon after his appointment, the young aid, on one occasion, was not so expert and ready as the Commodore desired. On reproving him slightly for his deficiency, Stockton said he had "never before been accustomed to perform such services for a gentleman." The Commodore, pleased with the frankness of his manner, laughed heartily and let it pass. Rodgers entertained the most favourable opinion of Stockton's good qualities, and considered him an officer of the highest promise.

His promptness to perform every duty, his alacrity to anticipate its requisitions, his fine spirits and joyous temper, his courteous and respectful but manly deportment, and his daring courage, made him the general favourite of the ship's crew, from the old Commodore to the common sailor. The enjoyment which he seemed to derive from the perils of battle, as well as the ardent hopes he evidently cherished of soon again participating in its excitement, won for him the significant *sobriquet* of "*Fighting Bob;*" an appellation by which he is yet remembered by many an *old salt*.

The President and Congress continued their cruise for eighty or ninety days, capturing many British vessels, passing over a space of not less than eight thousand miles, and hunting for an enemy wherever he was most likely to be found. In relation to this cruise, the editor of Niles's Register (vol. iii. p. 300) says:—"For such a cruise as this, were Rodgers and Smith" (captain of the Congress) "Frenchmen, Bonaparte would have made them members of the Legion of Honour."

After refitting with the utmost despatch, during a short stay in port, Commodore Rodgers again put to sea in search of a foe. He ran down near the outer line of the Gulf Stream, with the intention of intercepting the convoy of the West Indian fleet, then supposed to be on its way to England. Failing to come up with them, he crossed over to the Banks of Newfoundland. Thence he shaped his course for the North Sea, cruising in the vicinity of the Shetland Isles and Orkneys, and almost within the "chops of the British Channel." It was reported in the English papers that he had landed for water and provision in Scotland; and the frightened islanders began to fear that another Paul Jones would pounce on their coast and burn their towns.

The dismay and consternation with which this bold captain struck the British Isles may be seen by perusing the contemporary newspaper chronicles.

Niles's Register of October 9, 1813, says:—"The British papers call Commodore Rodgers the Julius Cæsar of America; and, on its being reported that he was captured by a seventy-four, say (and we believe truly) that few events would give more satisfaction than a visit from the Commodore."

The Register quotes also the following from the London Courier of July 20, 1813, to show what efforts to capture Rodgers were made by the enemy:—"Several small squadrons have been detached in search of Commodore Rodgers. Lord A. Beauclerk sailed from St. Helens, on Thursday, with the *Royal Oak* and *Sea Horse;* the Hon. Captain Paget is gone from Plymouth with the *Superb, Menelaus,* and *Fly;* and Admiral Young has detached *several frigates* to go north about."

It will be observed that, although it was known, from the numerous captures made by the President, that she was cruising in the neighbourhood alone, the British frigates detached in pursuit of her sailed in companies of two or more, and appeared by no means willing to encounter Rodgers, unless with a force decidedly superior.

Though diligently scouring the seas for five months, and frequently sailing in sight of the shores of Great Britain and Ireland, the President could not succeed in bringing any British frigate to action. Wherever such a vessel was seen, she was always found under the protection of a seventy-four.*

The President, on the 5th of December, after a few weeks' visit in port, again spread her sails on a winter's cruise to the West Indies. She was again unable to meet an adversary willing to engage her. Impatient and chafing with his ill luck, the Commodore, as he was entering the harbour of New York, came across the

---

* Commodore Rodgers's letter to Secretary of Navy, September 27, 1813.

British seventy-four-gun ship Plantagenet, and offered her battle for five consecutive hours, often approaching so near that an engagement seemed inevitable.*

During the exciting preparations for the expected action, Mr. Stockton was stationed in the maintop, in command of twenty men, with rifles and two howitzers; and at a period when the guns were ordered to be manned, and the Commodore supposed the engagement was about to commence, he hailed the maintop, saying, "Mr. Stockton, I expect a great deal from your maintop to-day." Stockton replied, "Only get near enough, Commodore, and we will give a good account of ourselves."

The excuse subsequently made by the British Commodore for declining to fight an American frigate was, that his crew had shown symptoms of mutiny. This excuse must be considered altogether unsatisfactory, when it is known that a British frigate was within sight, though not observed, at first, from the President. As soon as this additional enemy was discovered, Commodore Rodgers, having taken a pilot, thought it his duty to enter the harbour of New York.†

Notwithstanding Commodore Rodgers was not so fortunate as to enjoy a fair encounter with a British frigate, no naval commander stood higher in the esteem and confidence of his countrymen. The

---

* Niles's Register, March 12, 1814; August 13, 1814.

† "The Saucy President." Extract of a letter dated February 22, inside the light, Sandy Hook, from an officer of the frigate President to his friend in Providence.

"Situations in which we have been placed, this cruise, will, I think, add lustre to the well-established character of Commodore Rodgers.

"After passing the light, saw several sail,— one large sail to the windward. Backed our maintopsail and cleared for action. The strange sail came down within gunshot; hauled her wind on the larboard tack. We continued with our maintopsail to the mast three hours; and, seeing no probability of the seventy-four-gun ship's bearing down to engage the President, gave her a shot to windward and hoisted our colours, when she bore up for us reluctantly. When within half-gunshot, backed his maintopsail. At this moment all hands were called to muster aft, and the Commodore said a few but impressive words, though it was unnecessary; for what other stimulant could true Americans want than fighting gloriously in sight of their native shore, where hundreds were assembled to witness the engagement? Wore ship to engage, but, at this moment, the cutter being discovered off, backed again to take in the pilot; and, the British seventy-four (strange as it may appear) making sail to the southward and eastward, orders were given to haul aboard the fore and main tacks, to run in, there being then in sight from our deck a frigate and a gun-brig.

"The commander of the seventy-four had it in his power, for five hours, to bring us at any moment to an engagement,—our maintopsail to the mast during that time." —*Niles's Register, March* 12, 1814.

terror with which he inspired the enemy proved his renown as a brave and skilful captain. Had the British commanders been as desirous as he was of a meeting on equal terms, he would doubtless have given them a reception worthy of his fame.

To have won the esteem and affection of such a commander is evidence of good conduct and youthful promise in Stockton.

Commodore Rodgers was soon afterwards ordered to the new frigate Guerriere constructed at Philadelphia and nearly ready to proceed to sea.

The war-cloud, however, which had so often threatened, now burst with fury upon our coasts. Immense fleets with Wellington's invincibles, released by the fall of Napoleon Bonaparte from European campaigns, hovered along the Atlantic shores, blockading our ports, and prepared to attack the most defenceless. Washington had been taken, the public buildings burned, and Alexandria and Baltimore were both in danger. Alarm and apprehension pervaded the entire seaboard. Commodore Rodgers and his crew were summoned to the defence of Baltimore, and thither they repaired with the utmost promptitude. After his arrival at Baltimore, no immediate attack being apprehended, the Commodore went to Washington to advise with the Secretary, Mr. Jones, and took his young aid Stockton along with him. Being thrown for several days much in the company of the Secretary, Stockton became so much of a favourite with him that he insisted on retaining him as his aid. While acting in this capacity, he was on one occasion summoned from his bed at Crawford's Hotel in Georgetown at midnight, in consequence of a brisk cannonade in the direction of Alexandria. When coming into the presence of the Secretary and a number of officers, who were astonished at what they heard and at a loss to assign a cause for it, Stockton at once remarked, "We make no discoveries by remaining here; give me a horse and I will soon let you know what is going on down below." A horse was furnished him, and he rode that night into Alexandria, which was in possession of the enemy.

Returning from Alexandria, he asked to be relieved from his attendance as aid to the Secretary, and resumed his post with Commodore Rodgers, where he expected more active service.

Commodore Rodgers was immediately despatched to Alexandria, in the vicinity of which several British frigates were anchored, and from which they had already exacted large contributions. Immediately on his arrival there he fitted out a flotilla of small vessels, some of which were prepared as fire-ships, for the purpose of being floated down in contact with the enemy's ships. Barges were manned likewise, with the design of boarding and capturing in a hand-to-hand fight the British frigate. The gallant manner in which Rodgers and his crew defended Alexandria, and protected her from experiencing the fate of Hampton and Havre de Grace, may be seen in detail in his correspondence with the Navy Department, September 9, 1814.* We insert the following extracts, to show the conspicuous part which young Stockton bore in this expedition:—

"Having reconnoitred the enemy, getting my cutters hauled up, placing the lighter in an advantageous position and my musket-men on the top of the cliff overlooking the river, I was at 1 P. M. attacked by all the enemy's barges; but, by the cool intrepidity of Lieutenant Newcomb, having charge of the lighter, assisted by Lieutenant Gaunt, S. Master Ramage, and Master's Mate Stockton, and forty-five seamen, the enemy were not only repulsed, but in less than twenty minutes thrown into the utmost confusion and driven back to their ships."

In another part of the same letter, Commodore Rodgers says:—

"Permit me at the same time to recommend to your attention Mr. Stockton, master's mate, who not only rendered me essential service as acting aid-de-camp, but in every other situation manifested a zeal and intrepidity not to be shaken."

Baltimore was now threatened by the force under General Ross, flushed with his successful and Gothic foray on Washington. The most serious apprehensions of the expected attack were generally entertained. Rodgers was directed to co-operate with the militia hastily collected for the defence of that city. The authorities in command received the Commodore and his crew with the greatest cordiality, and posts of danger and honour were generously assigned them.

The important part performed by the officers and men of Commodore Rodgers, in repelling the combined attack of the British land and naval force on Baltimore, is recorded in contemporary documents.† In the report of the Assistant Adjutant-General to Major-General Smith, he says:—

"It is with peculiar satisfaction the commanding general seizes the opportunity of acknowledging the very great assistance he has received from the counsel and active exertions of Commodore Rodgers. His exertions and those of his brave officers and seamen

---

* Niles's Register, vol. xvii. p. 36.
† Niles's Register, September 24, 1814, vol. vii.

have contributed in a very eminent degree to the safety of the city, and should be remembered with lively emotions of gratitude by every citizen."

In Commodore Rodgers's despatch to the Naval Department of the 23d September, 1814, (Niles's Reg., vol. vii.,) he sets forth in detail the services of his officers and men on that occasion. In this letter he says, "Much praise is also due to Major Randal, commanding a battalion of Pennsylvania riflemen, who was also placed under my command, and whom I despatched, with my aid, Mr. Stockton to dislodge a party of men in the enemy's boats which it was supposed intended landing near the Lazaretto to take possession of our little three-gun battery. Mr. Stockton, on his return, reported to me in very high terms the zeal and gallantry displayed by the major and his corps on the occasion."

In another part of the same official despatch, Commodore Rodgers says:—

"*To Master's Mate Stockton, my aid, I am greatly indebted for the zeal and promptitude with which he conveyed my orders from post to post, and wherever I had occasion to communicate, although in some instances he had to pass through showers of shells and rockets.*"

It may not be without interest to give some of the details respecting young Stockton's participation in the defence of Baltimore, such as we heard them when the particulars were current.

Stockton, with three hundred men, had marched down below the city to assist in repelling the attack of the British on the Lazaretto. After the enemy had failed in their attempt, he found himself on a narrow neck of land, with no boats with which to cross the bay, and an English force exceeding his own in numbers so posted as to be able to intercept his retreat. He made a forced march, and, before the enemy could take advantage of the ground to cut off his communication, extricated himself from that danger and took a position between the British and American force. He then rested, and sent a messenger to the Commodore, informing him of his situation. His letter was returned to him with an endorsement by the Commodore to this purport:—"It is desirable that the enemy should be induced to make his attack before nightfall. Meet them, and bring them on behind you."

As soon as he received these instructions, he stationed about two hundred of his men on each side of the road on which he intended to retreat, with directions not to fire a shot until they had the enemy between them, and, taking the other hundred, proceeded to reconnoitre his opponents. On approaching, he discovered the British encampment flanked by a thick swamp. As he was proceeding quietly and cautiously in advance of his men, he was unexpectedly fired upon from one of the enemy's outposts. Looking in the direction of the shot, he saw a British soldier reloading his musket for another trial. Stockton gave him a chance to exchange shots, and when they had both fired it was supposed to be the last shot which the Englishman ever made. This drew out the British, and a general skirmish took place. Stockton, retreating on his ambush, was followed by the enemy until they came within sight of the sailors, who, having heard the frequent reports of their comrades' rifles, could not repress their excitement. Shouting and hurraing "Stockton has got them—he'll bring them along!" disclosed themselves, when the enemy, suspecting a stratagem, prudently checked their advance and concluded to return. Stockton remained watching their movements till after night, and until he became satisfied that they meditated a retreat to their ships. As soon as he had formed this opinion, he sought the Commodore and told him that he believed the enemy intended to retreat that night, and requested to have the command of the sailors and marines, and "he would board them in their camp." The Commodore was much pleased with Stockton's conduct, and took him to the head-quarters of General Smith, the commander-in-chief, to whom he repeated the expression of the opinion that the enemy would go to their ships that night, and offered, if the general would give him one thousand men, to lead a night-attack upon the retreating foe. But the general said there was an ancient saying, "Make a bridge for a retreating enemy," in which he thought there was much wisdom; and that if the enemy were disposed to retreat, he would not interpose any obstacle to such a movement.

Cooper, in his naval history, says of Stockton in his California campaigns that he seemed to be everywhere. The same ubiquity seems to have characterized his service on the waters of the Chesapeake during the war of 1812, although acting in a subordinate capacity. On his first arrival at Baltimore, his first service was at night, lying down on the wharf watching the enemy's motions. Then he went with Commodore Rodgers to Washington, who was summoned there for consultation with the Secretary of the Navy. There, for a few days, we find Stockton acting as aid to the secretary; then riding at night to Alexandria, and returning to give the government intelligence of the enemy's attack on that city. Next we hear of him engaging the enemy and aiding to repulse them on the banks of the Potomac; then we find him soon after at Baltimore, towing vessels and sinking them in the channel near the fort, the enemy firing shot and shell over his head all the time. We next learn that he is in Fort McHenry, consulting with Colonel Armstead; then he is found down on the marine battery, aiding in driving the British ships from their mooring. He then is seen as an express rider conveying information from the fort to the general over ground literally ploughed by the enemy's shells. For three days and three nights, including the time when the principal attack on Baltimore was made, he had no repose. When he first arrived at Baltimore he wore a straw hat, blue jacket, and linen trousers. When the enemy had retired, Commodore Rodgers ordered him to the city for food, rest, and refreshment; some one loaned him a hat, Commodore Perry furnished him an overcoat, and from another he obtained a decent garment for the remainder of his person.

These details, imperfect as they are, nevertheless show the ardour, spirit, and gallantry of young Stockton in the performance of his duty. They show, too, how well he improved every opportunity which offered for obtaining distinction. Though one of the youngest midshipmen under the Commodore, he was still thought worthy of being made his *aid-de-camp*. In this responsible position his good conduct justified the discernment which induced the Commodore to make the appointment, and drew from him the most decided commendation. He soon received from the government that evidence of its consideration always the most grateful to the young officer,—promotion. On the 9th of December, 1814, Mr. Stockton was commissioned as a lieutenant.

The war terminated, and the navy having covered itself with laurels in every sea, and wherever an enemy could be met, without a single defeat involving the slightest diminution of its glory, the most favourable disposition was manifested towards it by the people and the government. Whatever may be thought of the few victories achieved by the army and the militia, there can be no question that our naval achievements inflicted the most poignant wounds upon our adversary. They touched the chords of his most exquisite sensibilities; they broke the charm of Old England's naval invincibility; they humbled her national pride and destroyed her boasted claim to wield the Trident of the seas.

As it is within the scope of this narrative to vindicate the claims of the navy to some of the most brilliant achievements of the Mexican war, it may be excused if we here quote from the enemy, to show what were the effects of our naval exploits in the war of 1812.

In the London Times of December 30, 1814, immediately after the preliminary articles of the Treaty of Ghent were signed, appeared an article of doleful tenor, from which we quote :*

"The state of the funds may be said to afford a most striking comment on the text of those who have the front to call the Treaty of Ghent *honourable* to this country. The peace is like that of Amiens,—a peace of *necessity;* and upon what grounds ? '*A leaning to certain points,*' it seems, has been '*hinted*' at the Congress of Vienna. Russia or Austria or Prussia has avowed an inclination to support the innovations on public law which Mr. Madison asserts. If any of the powers who have received our subsidies, or have been rescued from destruction by our courage or example, have had the baseness to turn against us, it is morally certain that the Treaty of Ghent will confirm them in their resolution. They will reflect that we have endeavoured to force our principles on America, and have failed; nay, that we have retired from the combat with *the stripes yet bleeding on our backs.* Even yet, however, if we *could but close the war with some great naval triumph, the reputation of our maritime greatness might be partially restored.* But to say that it has not hitherto suffered in the estimation of all Europe, and, what is worse, of America herself, is to belie common sense and universal experience. 'Two or three of our ships have struck to a force vastly inferior !' *No; not two or three, but many on the ocean, and whole squadrons on the lakes;* and the numbers are to be viewed with relation to the comparative magnitude of the two navies.

"*Scarcely is there an American ship of war which has not to boast a victory over the British flag.* Scarcely one British ship in thirty or forty that has beaten an American. With the bravest seamen and the most powerful navy in the world, we retire from the contest when the balance of defeat is so heavy against us. From that fatal moment when the flag of the Guerriere was struck, there has been quite a rage for building ships of war in the United States. Their navy has been nearly doubled, and their vessels are of extraordinary magnitude. The people, naturally vain and boastful, have been filled with an absolute contempt for our maritime power and furious eagerness to beat down our maritime pretensions."

These passages from the oracle of the British public show how humiliating to British arrogance were our naval victories during the war of 1812. And they prove also how deserved was that popu-

---

* Niles's Register, February 18, 1815, vol. vii.

larity of our naval heroes, which was universal when their triumphs were still fresh in the remembrance of men. But when the army began to furnish Presidents, the glory of the American navy insensibly faded in the memories of a new generation.

The whole policy of the country was, however, revolutionized by the success of the navy in the second war with Great Britain. It was looked upon as the primary means of defence with any maritime power. The people, with general unanimity, demanded that it should be placed upon a footing of greater efficiency. The government promptly responded to the national wishes, by making liberal appropriations for the gradual increase of the navy. One of the first results of this change of policy was the maintenance of a respectable squadron in the Mediterranean.

CHAPTER III.

STOCKTON SAILS WITH COMMODORE DECATUR TO CHASTISE THE ALGERINES—AFFAIR WITH ALGERINE FRIGATE—CAPTURE OF ALGERINE BRIG—RETURNS TO THE UNITED STATES—APPLIES FOR SERVICE IN MEDITERRANEAN SQUADRON—SAILS WITH COMMODORE CHAUNCEY—TRANSFERRED TO SLOOP-OF-WAR ERIE—AFFAIR WITH A MIDSHIPMAN—INSOLENCE OF BRITISH OFFICERS—STOCKTON RESENTS IT—MEETING AT NAPLES—DIFFICULTIES AT GIBRALTAR—NARROW ESCAPE OF STOCKTON—RETURNS IN CHARGE OF ARRESTED CAPTAINS—ENCOUNTER WITH SPANISH FRIGATE—TREATMENT OF HIS PASSENGERS.

SOON after the restoration of peace with Great Britain, war was declared by the United States against the Dey of Algiers. In conformity with the policy which governed the relations of the chief maritime nations of Europe with the Barbary powers, the United States had formed treaties with them providing for the annual payment of subsidies in consideration of their forbearing to prey on the commerce of American citizens. No sooner had war between the United States and Great Britain commenced, than the Dey of Algiers, well knowing that our national ships would be fully employed with the British, violated the subsisting treaty, and proceeded to capture American vessels and reduce to slavery those American captives who had been taken prisoners. The United States had discovered that it was the policy of the larger maritime states of Europe, especially of England, to tolerate the Barbary powers, for the purpose of checking the growth of the commercial enterprise of the smaller European states. In Lord Sheffield's work entitled "Observations on the Commerce of the American States," he recommends this policy without disguise. He says, (p. 204,) "*It is not probable the American States will have a very free trade in the Mediterranean; it will not be the interest of any of the great maritime powers to protect them from the Barbary States. If they know their interests, they will not encourage the Americans to be carriers. That the Barbary States are advantageous to the maritime powers is certain. If they were suppressed, the little States of Italy, &c. would have much more of the carrying trade.*" "*The armed neutrality would be as hurtful to the great maritime powers as the Barbary States are useful. The Americans cannot protect themselves from the latter; they cannot pretend to a navy.*"

This language, held by a prominent British statesman, did not escape the attention of the American government. The ratification of the Treaty of Ghent had not been exchanged when, on the 2d of March, 1815, Congress declared war against Algiers.

On the 18th of May following, Commodore Decatur sailed for the Mediterranean with a squadron composed of the frigates Guerriere, (the flag-ship,) Macedonian, Constitution, sloop-of-war Ontario, brigs Epervier, Firefly, Flambeau, Spark, and schooners Spitfire and Torch.

Mr. Stockton sailed in this squadron as junior lieutenant, on the Guerriere, but was transferred soon after to the Spitfire, Commander Dallas, in which vessel he acted as first lieutenant. The squadron had been but a few days in the Mediterranean, when the Guerriere, in company with the Spitfire, fell in with the Algerine frigate Mishouri, of forty-four guns. In the chase, the Spitfire, being an excellent sailer, kept side-by-side with the Guerriere as she approached the corsair; when, to avoid getting between the Guerriere and the enemy, the Spitfire ran close up under the stern of the Algerine. While the Guerriere was ranging up broadside and broadside, at the moment when the action was commencing, Lieutenant Stockton suggested to Captain Dallas that they would never, perhaps, have so good an opportunity to observe the effect of a frigate's broadside, and asked leave, before the Spitfire took part in the action, to go out on the bowsprit and watch the effect of the Guerriere's first broadside. He immediately went out on the extremity of the bowsprit, and, after the second broadside of the Guerriere, returned, and said to Dallas, "The Guerriere is shooting very wild; let us go to work and knock in the cabin-windows of the pirate." During the remainder of the action, which lasted a half hour, the Spitfire, with her long thirty-two-pound gun, poured in a raking fire until the enemy's guns were silenced, and her men, after striking their flag, ran below. She proved to be the flag-ship of the Algerine admiral, who was killed, together with thirty of his crew. No one on the Spitfire was injured, and the only damage sustained by the Guerriere was four men wounded. The commodore put a prize crew on the Algerine frigate, and sent her into Carthagena.

Two days afterwards, the American squadron fell in with an Algerine brig of twenty-two guns and two hundred men, which, in the chase, ran ashore on the coast of Spain, in such shallow water that none but the smaller vessels of the squadron could approach her. The Spitfire was among the first to commence the action; but, while it was raging, some of the other smaller vessels got in between the Spitfire and the enemy. Immediately on perceiving this, Lieutenant Stockton asked permission of Captain Dallas to take the boats and go in and board the pirate, as the only chance of having an equal share in the victory. Leave being granted, Stockton put off for the stranded vessel. As soon as this movement was perceived, boats were manned from the other vessels and followed the crew of the Spitfire. Stockton kept ahead, and first led his men on the enemy's deck, through the port-holes. They found the deck of the Algerine brig literally covered with the dead and dying. The brig was subsequently lightened and got off-shore, and sent into a Spanish port.

Commodore Decatur now sailed for Algiers, and dictated peace to the humbled Dey. Full reparation was exacted for previous depredations, and the treaty expressly provided, that thenceforward the United States commerce should suffer no molestation, without any tribute of any sort being paid for such exemption. From Algiers the Commodore went to Tunis and Tripoli, and obtained from those powers compensation for injuries sustained.

Commodore Decatur was soon after relieved by Commodore Bainbridge, who took command of the squadron, Commodore Decatur returning home.

The following year, Commodore Bainbridge, with his squadron, returned to the United States. Lieutenant Stockton, in the Spitfire, accompanied him.

Another squadron, under Commodore Chauncey, was soon despatched to the Mediterranean. The Spitfire being ordered to be laid up, Lieutenant Stockton applied to be detached from her and to be transferred to the squadron of Commodore Chauncey. He was ordered to join the flag-ship of the Commodore, and sailed as seventh lieutenant on the Washington, seventy-four guns, for the Mediterranean, in February, 1816.

The cruise of this squadron, which continued several years, was memorable on many accounts, and will long be celebrated in our naval annals.

In a period of profound peace, occasions do not often happen when naval officers of subordinate rank can increase their reputation. Their duties, when on service, consist of an ordinary routine with little variety of circumstance or action. Any failure to observe the rules prescribed for the government of the navy, may prove fatal to the young officer; while scarcely any opportunity is offered for the display of talents, however brilliant. It could hardly be expected, therefore, that Lieutenant Stockton, during his four years' cruise in the Mediterranean, would have been able to augment to any great extent his rising reputation.

But it is the property of genius to create opportunities in which to acquire fame, as well as to use them to the best advantage. Lieutenant Stockton, during these few years of service in the Mediterranean, not only augmented his high standing as a naval officer, but acquired a reputation for chivalry and courage which gave him a name throughout Europe as well as America.

Among the occurrences which will always make the cruise of the squadron at this time stationed in the Mediterranean deserving of note in our naval history, were those many serious difficulties which grew out of the extraordinary powers claimed and exercised by the commanders of the different vessels over their crews and officers.

During this cruise it was that Commodore Perry struck Captain Heath, and a duel ensued between them. Then, too, the first effort for reform in the discipline of the navy may be said to have commenced with the famous memorial subscribed by the junior officers of the squadron, denouncing in manly but respectful language the arbitrary assumptions, tyranny, and injustice of the commanders.

During all these exciting events, Lieutenant Stockton still maintained his standing as a cool, reflecting, dispassionate, but firm reformer. He signed the celebrated memorial to Congress of the junior officers of the fleet, and placed himself as a firm, unyielding opponent of the indiscriminate use of the CAT, and of the unofficerlike and harsh and unjust treatment of subaltern officers of all grades.

In the course of this cruise, on the application of the commander of the Erie, Captain Gamble, Lieutenant Stockton was ordered as second lieutenant to that ship. A short time afterwards, the first lieutenant of the Erie having obtained leave to return home, Stockton became the first lieutenant.

It was on board of the Erie, while Lieutenant Stockton occupied this position, that an event took place which, perhaps, as much as any other event of his life, marks the decided character of the man. Owing to the difficulties to which we have referred, the discipline of the squadron had by this time become seriously demoralized. Many of the superior officers were held in contempt by the subaltern officers, who did not hesitate to express frequently, in unguarded language, their hostile feelings and opinions. The Erie was officered by a high-spirited, gallant set of young gentlemen, jealous of their rights and as inflammable as gunpowder.

Captain Gamble was a good officer and disciplinarian, and Lieutenant Stockton was determined to do his part in reforming the discipline of the squadron, and teaching the junior officers the first principle of military life,—that of respect for and obedience to their superiors in command. He has always held, however, that it was obligatory on the commander to inspire his officers not only with a sense of deference to his official dignity, but to impress them likewise with a conviction of his own high sense of honour and his punctilious regard for the principles of justice in all his intercourse with them; in fact, that it is his duty to convince his officers that he is a gentleman who will neither do wrong himself, or suffer it to be done by others with impunity. One of the first lessons which he endeavoured to teach those under his command was that of remaining cool and preserving their self-possession under all circumstances. He would say, (to use his own words, which we have often heard repeated,) "Remember, gentlemen, that there is always time enough to fight; keep cool; never get in a passion, under the grossest provocation."

These principles and views being entertained by him, it is quite natural that he should consider the event which we are now about to relate as one of the most trying and difficult of all others which on any occasion happened to him while he was in the service of the country. He was undoubtedly governed in his conduct in this affair by a sense of duty to the service, and not by personal considerations. Indeed, from the best information we have been able to obtain, he never had a serious personal altercation on his own account with any officer of the navy. All the difficulties in which he was ever involved were produced by his devotion to the country and the honour of the service. And in all cases of personal difference between others, whether officers or citizens, in which he was induced as a friend to act for one of the parties, never in any one instance did he permit them to proceed to the final resort, but invariably succeeded in effecting an amicable arrangement.

Returning one evening to his state-room, Lieutenant Stockton overheard one of the midshipmen of the Erie in the steerage, which was only separated by a thin partition from the state-room, say, among other unpleasant things, that "Lieutenant Stockton would not have dared do" what he had been referring to before, (but which was not heard,) "unless he had taken advantage of his superior rank."

Stockton retired without any notice of the remark. In the morning, however, he communicated what he had heard to a marine officer. The marine officer said to him "that he was under no obligation to take any notice of the midshipman's observation, because he was not supposed to have heard it."

Stockton replied, "that it was a very easy thing to get out of the difficulty if he could reconcile himself to consider it only as a personal matter." But he said, "That is a clever young man: I entertain a high opinion of him as a good and gallant officer; and if he really believes that I am that sort of person, as his remark imports me to be, he will impress others with the same opinion, and my usefulness in the service will be at an end. I see no way to prevent the evil consequences of such impressions among the officers but to offer myself a sacrifice, to check the disposition on the part of the young officers to speak disparagingly of their superiors without cause."

He then told the marine officer that he wished him to invite the midshipman on shore, and there say to him that "Lieutenant Stockton understands that you consider yourself as having been grossly insulted by him, and that you have said that he would not have dared to have acted as you allege he did had he not taken advantage of his rank." Stockton told the marine officer that he had no idea how or when he had insulted the midshipman. "But if he asks whether I intended to insult him, you must consider your lips sealed on that subject, and reply that you have considered yourself insulted, which constrains Lieutenant Stockton to direct me to inform you that you have very much mistaken his character, and that he wishes you, as well as all others, to understand that his rank need never stand between him and the just indignation of any honourable man."

The result was, that the midshipman challenged the lieutenant; that they went on shore and stood at eight paces, and were to fire as they pleased after the word "FIRE" had been given. As soon as the word was given, the young midshipman fired and missed. Stockton then said that "perhaps that was a mistake, and that the opposite party had better reload, as Lieutenant Stockton waived his right to take deadly aim and fire at an unarmed man." But with great gallantry the young midshipman said that he had had his fire, and that if Lieutenant Stockton would shoot, and he was able afterwards, he would reload. Whereupon Stockton discharged his pistol in the air. The young officer, however, refused to consider that as the fire which Stockton had the right to make, and persisted, together with his friend, in refusing to load again until Stockton had shot at him.

Thus the parties stood in an attitude towards each other which it seemed at first very difficult to alter. The seconds, after a short consultation, referred to the principals. Lieutenant Stockton said he thought " there was no difficulty in the case; that he had come to give those gentleman satisfaction, and if they were satisfied, he was—perfectly." The second of the midshipman, as chivalrous as any man, observed that they must be satisfied; and thus the affair terminated. And all those gentlemen, principal and seconds, became and continued ever afterwards firm and admiring friends of Stockton. The midshipman remained on the Erie precisely as if nothing had occurred, only there was no one aboard more zealous and prompt to preserve the discipline of the ship than he.

During the four years which Lieutenant Stockton spent on the Erie, many changes took place in her *personnel*. At last there was no ship in the squadron which could boast a superior company of officers. They were all gentlemen of a high sense of honour, courteous, hospitable, intellectual, and brave, and were in fact the *élite* of our service, if any could be so called. The leisure time of the officers of the Erie was not devoted to dissipation or wasted in idleness. Lieutenant Stockton particularly applied himself with assiduity to his nautical studies. He esteemed it to be one of his first duties to become perfect master of his profession. The law of nations likewise, as well as the common law and the law martial, were objects of his special study.

His aptitude for questions of law, and the forensic talents which he displayed, induced his brother officers to call on him to act as their counsel before courts-martial; and we have been told that, whether owing to the justice of his causes or to his own ingenuity and ability in such efforts, he was invariably successful.

On the first appearance of the American squadron in the Mediterranean as part of our regular peace establishment, the American uniform was a comparative stranger in the principal ports of that sea. The British naval gentlemen had been long accustomed to the assertion of superiority or precedence over the officers of other flags. They hectored and bullied the officers of other nations with impunity; at places of public resort, on public occasions, at hotels, and even at private entertainments, their arrogance and insolence were displayed without restraint. Chafed and mortified by the brilliant naval victories of the United States during the recent war, they seemed disposed to manifest a particular animosity towards the American uniform. Notwithstanding this bad state of feeling, the American officers were determined to give no just cause of offence; nor did they ever do so.

It will be observed, therefore, that the provocation which led to the celebrated encounters in which Stockton was engaged in the Mediterranean were national in their origin. Their object was not the gratification of personal pique or resentment, but the discharge of a patriotic duty, implicating the defence of American honour.

On the arrival of the squadron on one occasion in the Bay of Naples, while a British fleet was at anchor there, the following occurrence took place:—

It is the custom at that rendezvous of the fleets of different nations, for the officers who employ the natives on shore to work for them or to supply them with fresh provisions, to give them certificates in a book carried by them, and which they exhibit as evidence of their honesty and skill. On the arrival of the Erie, she was boarded by one of these Neapolitans, who exhibited his book of certificates and solicited employment. On opening the book, Mr. Stockton observed a recommendation given in the usual form by an American officer, who had returned to the United States, and immediately under it a remark, subscribed by a British officer, expressing in very insulting language a contemptuous reflection on the "Yankees." The author of this needless insult was known to be on a British ship of the line then at anchor in the bay. The insult was addressed to every American, and liable to the observation of the officers of every flag which might visit Naples. Lieutenant Stockton accordingly determined to exact an apology or a fight from the offender. He despatched a friend with a note addressed to the British officer who had been guilty of the offence, demanding an apology or satisfaction. The latter alternative was conceded, and a meeting agreed on. After some delay the parties met on shore. The Americans found that the Englishmen were very shy of exchanging shots at close quarters. They desired to fight at long distances, and would only consent to the combatants shooting in the time that a handkerchief held to the chin of one of the seconds, on being dropped, would reach the ground. They desired to fight duels without any risk of being hit. Stockton, however, shot his opponent on the first trial in the leg, when, picking up his wounded limb in his hand, he commenced crying, "I am hit! I am hit! Are you satisfied? are you satisfied?" Stockton replied that he was not satisfied, and demanded another trial. But nothing could induce the Englishman to make another such experiment.

The next affair of this nature occurred at Gibraltar, and originated in the circumstances which we shall now briefly narrate.

The Erie arrived at Gibraltar, on one occasion, alone, no other American ship-of-war being in company. As soon as she arrived, a very respectable captain of a Boston merchantman came aboard and complained of the outrageous treatment to which he had been recently subjected. The captain was evidently a gentleman keenly susceptible of any indignity, personal or national, which could be offered to him. It appeared that it was a regulation at Gibraltar that every one in the streets after a certain hour at night should carry a light in a lantern with him. The American captain was ignorant of this regulation, and, returning home after the prescribed hour from supper with a friend, only a few doors from his boarding-house was arrested by the guard. He offered to satisfy the guard who he was if he would only go with him a few doors to his boarding-house. The guard refused this reasonable request, and conducted him to the officer of the station. To him the American captain repeated his excuse. The officer affected to discredit his story, and ordered him to be detained. The American captain remonstrated, and the British officer abused him in opprobrious terms, and finally thrust him in a dungeon in which the vilest criminals were confined. He was there detained until liberated at the instance of the American consul, but no redress was tendered. The American captain then challenged the British officer of the station, who received his challenge with the contemptuous inquiry whether he was fool enough to suppose that a British officer would fight the captain of a "damned Yankee merchantman."

After satisfying himself of the facts of the case, every effort was made to obtain some redress from the British captain by Lieutenant Stockton; but every such attempt was repelled in such a manner as aggravated the original offence. In consequence of this outrage upon an American citizen, a hostile meeting was arranged to take place between Lieutenant Stockton and the captain of the guard, with the express stipulation that, whatever might be the result, the American officers should have a free passage to their ship.

The meeting took place, and much dispute arose respecting the terms and distances to be agreed upon. The British officers desired to fight at long distances, and on the dropping of a handkerchief. The Americans wanted the distance shortened, and to fire when they pleased. The British officer was wounded, and his second would not permit another exchange of shots at that time. Lieutenant Stockton told them pretty plainly that he did not approve their conduct,.

3

which indicated, in his opinion, nothing but cowardice. They then said that, unless the affair was soon settled, Stockton would have to fight all the captains of the regiment. Assuming this communication to be a challenge from all the captains of the regiment, Stockton promptly accepted it, adding that, as they had differed about the distance, they might choose it for themselves at any point between eight paces and two inches. The difficulties increased with every negotiation; and, after several meetings, the governor of Gibraltar interposed, and, at his suggestion, the Commodore of the American squadron forbid the officers of the Erie to go ashore.

The particulars of these hostile meetings we have never been able to obtain; or, if we have heard them, it has been so long ago that we cannot trust our memory for a correct description.

But there was a meeting between Stockton and a British officer of the garrison of Gibraltar, the account of which, at the time, made such a lively impression that we shall venture to relate it according to our remembrance.

Some time after the first affair at Gibraltar referred to on the previous page, the Erie returned from a cruise of a month or two, to Gibraltar. Soon after her arrival, Lieutenant Stockton received a message from the British captain with whom the unsettled difficulty was pending, that he was ready to give Stockton the meeting agreed upon at the neutral ground, and that he might depend upon their not being molested by the military police.

At the appointed time, Stockton, accompanied by Purser Bowen and Dr. Peaco, proceeded to the ground at 12 o'clock. The British parties were again unwilling to fight on the terms and at the distance proposed by the Americans, and would only fight on their own terms. So many difficulties were raised by them that at last Stockton told them they only wanted to prolong the negotiations until they should be discovered by the authorities of Gibraltar and interrupted. He had hardly made this remark when a guard was seen coming out of Gibraltar in the direction of the neutral ground, and it became apparent that the guarantee by which they had been lured ashore was worthless, and that, unless the terms dictated by the Englishmen were accepted, no conflict would take place. Stockton told his second to have done with negotiation, and let him fight on the terms of his adversary. Having wounded his opponent, upon going up to him to inquire into his condition, the British officer advised him to save himself, by immediately leaving the ground, if he wished to escape being arrested. After denouncing their treachery, and defying them for any future encounter they might dare to risk, Stockton turned into the road leading to the shore, where his boat was awaiting his arrival. The road was rough and strewn with rocks, and at the foot of the hill could be seen a strong detachment approaching for his arrest. In descending the eminence, the road forked, and Stockton took the route on which he saw the guard consisted of but two men. In his descent he fell, and rose with his eyes filled with dust, and his face streaming with blood from the wounds received in his fall. He was in his shirt sleeves, and had his head bound up in a red bandanna handkerchief, and could see out of the corner of but one eye. In this plight, covered with dust and blood, he pushed on, visible to all the inhabitants of Gibraltar, who soon became apprised of what was going on, and who covered the tops of the houses to witness the scene. As he approached the guard of two men, they presented their bayonets and ordered him to stand. He approached them, apparently with the intention of surrendering, until they had shouldered their guns; when, seizing each of them by the collar, he dashed them to the ground, and rushed on with all the speed he could make. After proceeding about one hundred yards farther, he met a man on horseback, whom he surprised, and, pitching him from his saddle, mounted his horse, and, on full gallop through the main street of Gibraltar, eluding every attempt to stop him, held his way until he reached the spot where his sailors were anxiously waiting his appearance. They received him in their arms with a shout which sounded over the whole bay, and which was responded to with three cheers from the American squadron, as well as the vessels of many other flags, whose crews had been spectators of the exciting scenes which we have endeavoured to relate.

Governor Don now issued his proclamation forbidding any intercourse, for hostile purposes, between the American and British officers, and applied himself seriously to the task of effecting a final settlement of all differences between them. He had frequent conferences for that end with Commodore Stewart, the commander-in-chief of the American squadron. Through these exertions of the governor and the Commodore, terms of amity were agreed upon; and some months afterwards, upon the return of the Erie, proposals for peace were accepted and a general pacification concluded. Governor Don gave a grand ball, in celebration of the treaty of peace, at which the English and American officers came together with good-will and complete harmony.

It would be unjust to Stockton for the reader to infer, from these personal rencontres in the first years of his naval life, that he is what is called a professional duellist. So far is this from being the case, that it is well known that he has uniformly discouraged the practice among those over whom he exercised any influence, and that he has been the means of compromising more difficulties between officers in the American service, and of averting more duels, than any other officer in the navy. No one, while he was in the service, was more frequently called upon to arbitrate personal difficulties, and no one's advice on affairs of honour was more generally approved.

We have been told that he has been often heard to express the opinion that a case can rarely happen in which it is necessary for gentlemen to fight a duel; because the aggressor, if a gentleman, will always be willing to make proper explanations, and the offending party, if likewise a gentleman, will be equally disposed to accept as satisfactory such honourable atonement. We believe that Mr. Stockton, except on the single occasion which we have before related, was never engaged, as principal or second, in any duel between American officers.

The personal combats in the Mediterranean, fortunately, were attended with no loss of life. Their effects, however, were very important and useful. They taught the British naval and military gentlemen a salutary lesson. Their deportment thenceforward was extremely circumspect and respectful towards all Americans. The American character for courage, sensibility, and honour, was established. Since this period, no difficulties of a personal nature have ever occurred of any serious importance between the American and British officers.

Soon after this, some unfortunate difficulties took place in the squadron, which led to numerous courts-martial. Several post-captains were suspended from their commands and placed under arrest by Commodore Stewart, for the purpose of being sent home. Mr. Stockton, having command of the Erie in consequence of the arrest of the captain, was selected for the performance of this delicate duty. He was one of the youngest lieutenants in the squadron; and his appointment to this charge may properly be considered as evidence of his high standing, and of the confidence reposed in his discretion by the commander-in-chief.

On his way home he ran down the African coast, with the view of falling in with some of the numerous vessels then engaged, under the American flag, in the slave-trade, which he was instructed to capture if possible. While in the track of those vessels prosecuting this illegal traffic, a vessel resembling those usually engaged in this trade made her appearance. When first discovered, her course was nearly at right angles to that of the Erie. Instead of pursuing her course, she lay to in the path of the Erie, and acted so suspiciously that Stockton took her to be a pirate. Towards evening she altered her course several points, so as to keep the Erie in sight. Stockton determined to overhaul her and ascertain her character. Late at night, which was quite dark, he got within hearing distance and hailed her. The strange vessel made no reply, though repeatedly hailed, but was evidently preparing for action, and in appearance seemed to be much larger than the Erie. Stockton now called his boarders, had his guns loaded and primed, and ran under the stern of the stranger, directing his men at the proper signal to grapple and make fast both vessels together. He now hailed again: "What ship is that?" and repeated the words "What ship is that?" three times. On the third interrogatory, the stranger replied, in good English, "What ship is that?" At this moment one of the arrested captains came to Stockton, and, presuming on his seniority, said, "Mr. Stockton, we have consulted together, and see no impropriety in your replying to the stranger and informing him of the character of your vessel." Stockton replied to him:— "Sir, if you desire to take part in the action which may now occur, you can furnish yourselves with arms; otherwise, you can retire below. No vessel on the high seas can threaten any ship under my command without disclosing her name, character, and purpose." He then ordered the covers to be removed from the lights, and revealed his crew of boarders armed to the teeth, their sabres reflecting the blazing torches, and every thing prepared to board his adversary. He then hailed him for the last time, and said that unless he immediately disclosed his character he would board him and ascertain it for himself. This brought the stranger to his senses, and he immediately stated that the strange vessel was a Spanish frigate. She carried an armament nearly double that of the Erie. Stockton sent Lieutenant McCawley aboard of her to verify this report, with directions, if he found it to be true, that he need not be *very particular* in his examination. The report was ascertained to be true, and the Erie pursued her way unmolested.

On his way home with the arrested captains, the commander of the Erie extended to them every mark of respect. He gave up to them his cabin, and messed with his own officers, excepting at dinner.

His instructions directed him to take them to the United States and report them to the Secretary of the Navy. As they came near their destination, he found that the captains expected to go ashore

as passengers, free from all restraint.   In the most respectful manner he informed them that they were mistaken; that he had no objections to their going ashore, but that they must give their word
of honour to hold themselves subject to respond to the summons of
the Navy Department at some specified place.   The captains received this information with apparent astonishment, and bristled
up with great indignation, and declared their determination to land
when they pleased and go where they thought proper.   Stockton
again, in a mild but resolute manner, gave them to understand that
they should not go unless on the terms prescribed.   He promptly
told them that any attempt on their part to leave the ship without
his permission should be frustrated at all hazards, even to death.
The captains ultimately acquiesced, and they parted from the young
lieutenant with feelings of augmented respect.

CHAPTER IV.

STOCKTON SOLICITED BY THE FRIENDS OF THE COLONIZATION SOCIETY TO AID THEM—
APPLIES FOR ONE OF THE NEW SCHOONERS—SAILS IN THE ALLIGATOR FOR THE
WESTERN COAST OF AFRICA—INTERVIEW WITH SIR GEORGE M^cCARTY—VISIT TO
CAPE MESURADO—INTERCOURSE WITH NATIVES—KING PETER AGREES TO TREAT—
DANGEROUS PALAVER—A CESSION OF TERRITORY OBTAINED BY TREATY—LIBERIAN
REPUBLIC.

SOON after the arrival of Lieutenant Stockton at New York, he visited Washington on official business. While there, several of the prominent friends of the American Colonization Society—particularly Judge Washington, president of the Society, and Francis Key, Esq., one of the managers—called upon him to express their wishes that, in case he could procure a suitable vessel, he would consent, with permission from the government, to make an effort to obtain for the Society some territory on the western coast of Africa better adapted to the purposes of colonization than that which they had previously obtained. He agreed, provided he could obtain one of the new schooners then being built, that he would endeavour, with the approbation of the Navy Department, to do something for the Colonization Society.

Lieutenant Stockton had now (1821) been ten years in the service without any furlough, leave of absence, or relaxation on shore. It might be supposed that he would feel some inclination for a little repose from the privations and fatigues of the service, and some disposition to enjoy the society of his friends and family at home. But, while the path of honourable service was open, such enjoyment did not come within the scope of his ambition. Accordingly, he applied for one of the new schooners. At first he was informed that it was impossible to accede to his request, because many of his senior officers were also applying for these vessels. But, having set his heart on obtaining one of them, he stuck to the Secretary (Thompson) with such pertinacity, and assigned so many good reasons why his application should be granted, that the Secretary at last yielded to his importunities, and gave him the command of the Alligator.

Having obtained a vessel, Lieutenant Stockton now held several conferences with Judge Washington and the managers of the Colonization Society in relation to his proposed mission to Africa in their behalf. Their colony at Sherbro, where first located, had proved unfortunate: it was an unhealthy part of the coast, and the first colonists had nearly all perished from the effects of the deleterious climate, the few survivors having returned to the United States or sought refuge elsewhere. Unless some more favourable country could be obtained, the plan of African colonization would have to be relinquished, and the benevolent designs of the founders of the Society altogether abandoned. Lieutenant Stockton, with the consent of the Navy Department, cordially acceded to the wishes of the Colonization Society, and agreed to undertake the acquisition of some more eligible site on the African coast better adapted to the settlement of colonists from America. But he stipulated with the managers of the Society that he should be left to the exercise of his best discretion, without being embarrassed and controlled by minute instructions; and, with this understanding, amounting to a *carte blanche* to pursue his own course, he sailed on this expedition in the fall of 1821.

We may here remark that Stockton remained several years in command of the schooner Alligator, cruising during that time on different coasts, and performing a variety of important duties in the service; and, while no vessel was under better discipline and no crew more obedient, the use of the lash was altogether abolished. Stockton had always maintained that the lash was not necessary to enforce good government on a vessel when the commander was properly qualified to govern men. He determined to make a practical experiment of his opinions on this subject on the first suitable occasion. For this purpose, while the Alligator was still in sight of shore, he ordered the "CAT" pitched overboard, and informed his men that he intended to exact obedience from them by other means. The records of the Navy Department will show that the lash was never used by order of the commander of the Alligator while she sailed under Stockton. His experience on the Alligator confirmed him in the opinions which he had previously entertained respecting the inutility of the lash on a man-of-war, and he has been ever since the uniform advocate of its abolition.

Mr. Stockton was a sincere believer in the practicability and importance of the scheme of colonizing Africa with colonists from America—the educated and civilized descendants of the ignorant barbarians originally torn by rapine and piracy from their native country. He had a high respect for Dr. Samuel Finley, the original founder and projector of the American Colonization Society, under whose tuition he spent some time at Baskingridge, in New Jersey, and with whom he had frequently discussed the subject. He entered with zeal into the objects of the Society, and devoted all his energies to the successful accomplishment of the expedition. Dr. Ayres, the agent of the Colonization Society, was a passenger on the Alligator; and to his pen we are indebted for the only narrative of Stockton's exertions to carry out the objects of this mission with which the public has been favoured.

It was thought expedient in the first instance to visit Sierra Leone, the British colony on the western coast of Africa, to obtain what information could be had there respecting that coast. Upon his arrival at that place, Mr. Stockton sought an interview with Sir George McCarty, the governor of the colony, and apprised him of his objects, and was received in a friendly and hospitable manner. The governor informed him that, several hundred miles from Sierra Leone, there was a fine country, high and healthy, and better adapted than any other known portion of the coast for purposes of colonization. But the governor declared that he thought it would be impossible to obtain it by peaceable cession from the natives. They were among the most ferocious, warlike, and depraved, of all the tribes on the coast. They subsisted entirely on the slave-trade and its incidents. They were constantly engaged in wars of rapine and invasion with the feeble nations of the interior, from whom the captives were obtained with which they supplied the slave-ships. Many efforts had been made during the previous century, both by the British, French, and Portuguese, to purchase this country from the chiefs and head-men; but they had uniformly refused to negotiate for a sale of any part of it, or listen to any propositions for such a purpose from any quarter. Messrs. Andrews and Bacon, former agents of the Colonization Society, were repulsed with severity a year previous, in their efforts to enter into negotiations with the savage chiefs.

These representations were not very flattering; but Stockton determined he would take a look at this desirable region, and judge for himself whether it was worth the apparently-hopeless task of making an attempt for its acquisition. If it were what it was represented to be, the difficulties to be encountered were not so appalling as to deter him from some exertion to overcome them. He thought it best not to permit his national character to be known on the coast, lest the native chiefs should suppose that he entertained some designs of establishing an American station in the neighbourhood, and thus distrust his overtures. Accordingly, a small vessel, called the Augusta, was hired, and Mr. Stockton and Dr. Ayres sailed on a voyage of exploration, and ostensibly for the purposes of traffic. As soon as Stockton and Dr. Ayres came in the vicinity of Cape Mesurado, they saw that this was the country which they had heard described; and that it was admirably suited for the purposes of the Colonization Society. The surface of the territory was high and undulating, the soil evidently fertile and well-watered, and every appearance indicated a salubrious climate for that latitude.

Having resolved to make an effort for the purchase of this country, Stockton determined to proceed with caution, and become acquainted with the inhabitants and their chiefs, and, if possible, acquire their confidence before he disclosed the object of his visit. He went ashore, and proposed to trade with them; he exchanged tobacco and other articles of traffic with them, and soon ingratiated himself with their head-men by his judicious and prudent deportment. Availing himself of the aid of interpreters, he conversed freely with all, and established himself upon terms of familiar social intercourse with them. On every suitable opportunity, he descanted on the advantages they would derive from a settlement of civilized Africans on their coast,—the important commerce which would spring up, the arts which would be introduced among them, and the improved cultivation of the soil which would be the certain result of such a colony. Gradually he unfolded the scheme of the Colonization Society, and all the benefits which would be conferred on the native tribes by its success. Without alluding to the suppression of the slave-trade, he at last created in the minds of many of their chiefs a sincere desire to realize all the advantages which he had enumerated.

After thus preparing the minds of the principal men among them, and especially of King Peter, as he was called,—the chief who exercised the greatest influence over them,—Stockton at last proposed directly to King Peter the cession of a certain district of country around Cape Mesurado. The proposition was not pressed at first with much effort, lest, by the exhibition of any eagerness on his part, the savages might suppose that he had come there at first for the purpose of purchasing their land. He let it operate on their cupidity for some time, apparently indifferent whether they agreed to sell or not. At last King Peter, completely won over by the attentions and frank, open deportment of Stockton, agreed to the proposition as made. A day was appointed when the treaty should be consummated, and a place designated where they would meet.

At the appointed time, Stockton, accompanied by Dr. Ayres, a Croo interpreter, and one seaman, Mr. Nicholson, of New Jersey, all apparently unarmed, repaired to the ground selected for the interview. But when they arrived no Peter was visible; not a trace of him could be discovered in the neighbourhood, nor any of his people. Finally, it was ascertained that he had gone, with all his people, twenty miles into the interior. This failure to keep his appointment, and his abrupt departure, wore the appearance of King Peter's having been operated upon by some malign influence, and that his views had been entirely changed. A mulatto, who had seen Stockton at Sierra Leone, was suspected to be the agent who had thus influenced Peter. The mulatto was a professional slave-trader, and had the sagacity to see that if the Colonization Society succeeded in purchasing the country, it would break up his traffic in slaves. The mulatto, it was understood, had recently been with Peter, and followed him into the interior. After some deliberation, Stockton resolved to pursue Peter and hold him to his agreement at all hazards. Unless he succeeded now, by reason of Peter's previous agreement to sell, he foresaw that it would be impossible at any future time to acquire any hold upon him. The adventurous Anglo-Saxon, when he obtains a foothold, seldom takes "any step backwards."

Peter had left word for Stockton to follow him to his retreat in the interior "if he dare." It was doubtless an enterprise of great risk. The route to it lay through swamps and jungles, where the white man had never penetrated before, where wild beasts frequented, and where savages more dangerous, habituated to every atrocity, were the only inhabitants. There was no absolute certainty that their reception would be friendly, or that it would lead to any useful result. They would place themselves completely in the power of a savage noted for his treachery, ferocity, and hatred of white men. Notwithstanding these obvious suggestions of the peril and objections to the excursion, Stockton thought it was his duty to proceed while there existed the least hope of success.

Accordingly they struck boldly into the wilderness, and, after a tedious and fatiguing march, came to the village where, from the numbers collected, they believed that Peter would be found. Numerous groups of naked negroes, generally pretty well armed, were lounging in the shade of the palm-trees, or collected in groups, and apparently discussing the subject which had brought them together. They gazed on the strangers with evident indications of surprise, as if astonished at their presumption and temerity, and seemed undetermined whether to greet them as friends or foes. The principal men were soon apprised, however, of the object of the new comers and their desire to confer with the king in council. After some senseless ceremonials, the concourse of negroes, exceeding five hundred in number, upon a signal assembled in a large palaver-hall, which seemed appropriated for the use of such convocations. Places were assigned and mats spread for the strangers. After they were seated, one of the head-men came forward and shook them by the hands formally. But when Peter entered, he took no notice of them, but proceeded to a seat farthest removed from them and sat down—frowning and scowling, and evidently prepared to treat the intruding negotiators with indignity, if not outrage.

After an interval, one of the chiefs, with whom Stockton had been previously acquainted, arose and formally presented Stockton to Peter. His reception was the reverse of being cordial or gracious. Nevertheless he assumed the appearance of being much pleased, and with great coolness seated himself on the throne alongside of Peter. Peter seemed, however, much disturbed, and was evidently in an ill humour. At last, unable to contain himself longer, he demanded, in an angry tone, the business of the strangers, and how they dared penetrate thus far into his dominions, where white men had never before been seen. Stockton was now convinced that Peter had been incensed against him by some enemy, and, seeing the mulatto in the crowd to whom we have before referred, was satisfied that he was the calumniator. Through the mulatto, Peter must have ascertained all about the object of his visit. He therefore determined boldly to avow his real character and design, and convince Peter that he had not deceived him. Peter, he supposed, had been told by the mulatto that Stockton was an officer of the United States, and he naturally concluded that, in purchasing land in Africa, the United States intended to establish a colonial station similar to that in Sierra Leone, and that the cession of land was not sought for the humane purposes represented by Stockton, but for those of national aggrandizement.

In a calm but decided manner he admitted that he was a naval officer, but insisted that, notwithstanding the suspicions which this fact might excite, his real objects were such as he originally represented. He was proceeding to explain the advantages which the natives would gain by such a settlement of their civilized country, in their neighbourhood, as he had frequently before described, when the mulatto suddenly rushed up, and, clenching his fist before him, denounced him as an enemy of the slave-trade, and as having already captured several slave-traders. At this instant the whole multitude of armed negroes rose, and with an awful yell clanged their instruments of war together, and seemed prepared, with any encouragement from their chiefs, to rush upon Stockton and his party and cut them to pieces. It appeared to Dr. Ayres that the hour for martyrdom had arrived, and he meekly prepared in his own mind to submit to the fate which menaced them, and in silent prayer lifted up his thoughts to heaven. But a few seconds elapsed while the hostile demonstrations were made which it has required so much longer to relate. But instantly thereafter, almost with the celerity of intuition, Stockton, appreciating the danger which encompassed them, decided on the action necessary to avert the impending catastrophe. With that clear, ringing, and overpowering tone of voice for which, it is said, he is singularly remarkable,* he commanded silence. The trumpet-sound of his voice rose ascendant over the tumult around. The multitude were hushed as if by a thunderbolt

---

* We are indebted to the late Professor ALBERT B. DOD, of Princeton College, for the following anecdote, illustrative of the peculiar and commanding tones of Commodore Stockton's voice:—

A serious quarrel existed between the students of the college and the mechanics and labouring young men of Princeton. One evening, after twilight, a collision took place between some of the parties, which called out the entire force on both sides. They were marshalled in opposing ranks in the public highway, in front of the college edifice, and, in a high state of excitement, were preparing for a desperate battle. The civil authorities and the college faculty in vain interposed to restore peace and avert the apparently-inevitable conflict, which must have had a bloody issue, as many on each side were armed with pistols, guns, and dirks. The numbers about to engage in the fight were not less than one hundred and fifty on each side. Their passions were roused, and the most implacable and deadly animosity was manifested towards each other. As the riot had reached that point when blows were about to be exchanged, the Commodore appeared on the ground, (having been sent for by the Professors.) The combatants were drawn up on each side of the turnpike, and were stretched along a space of about eighty yards. The roar of three hundred angry voices produced a confused clamour, which seemed to defy all possibility of any single voice rising so predominant in sound as to be audible. Yet suddenly the well-known clarion tones of the Commodore's voice were heard, piercing with startling pungency every ear and commanding the attention of every hearer. He seemed to throw his voice to the farthest extremity of the crowd with as much distinctness as to those close by him. Every man on the ground seemed to hear it as addressed to himself. It arrested at once the parties on both sides, and brought them to a parley. The Commodore passed down through the file of young men, remonstrating with each one personally on his conduct, and insisting upon the preservation of peace. With that happy faculty which he possesses of influencing others whenever he makes a serious effort for that purpose, he soon succeeded, after ascertaining the original cause of the quarrel, in persuading them to settle and compromise their whole difficulties on terms honourable and acceptable to each party.

falling among them, and every eye was turned upon the speaker. Deliberately drawing a pistol from his breast and cocking it, he gave it to Dr. Ayres, saying, while he pointed to the mulatto, "Shoot that villain if he opens his lips again!" Then, with the same deliberation, drawing another pistol and levelling it at the head of King Peter, and directing him to sit silent until he heard what was to be said, he proceeded to say, in the most solemn manner, appealing with uplifted hand to God in heaven to witness the truth of what he said, that in all the previous conferences with King Peter and the other chiefs he had told them nothing but the truth; that they came there as their benefactors, and not as their enemies, to do them good and not evil; that their mission was not to defraud or cheat them, but to confer on them and their country inestimable blessings; that King Peter might now murder them, but that, if he did so, God on high, who was now looking down on them, would punish their guilt with almighty vengeance;* that the price demanded for their cession of territory had been conceded without abatement; that they had entered into a treaty already; its particulars were agreed upon, and the *form* of its execution only remained to be complied with; that, well knowing, from the dispositions manifested, that if they did not agree to execute the treaty that they intended to kill him and his party, he had determined that King Peter himself should be the first victim, and that unless he agreed to execute the treaty on the following day his fate was fixed; and, moreover, if he again agreed to ratify the treaty and failed to perform his duty, he might expect the worst punishment which an angry God could inflict on him and his people.

During this harangue, delivered through an interpreter, the whole throng, horror-struck with the danger of their king and awed by the majesty of an ascendant mind, sunk gradually, cowering prostrate to the ground. If they had believed Stockton to be an immediate messenger from heaven, they could not have quailed and shrunk and humbled themselves to more humiliating postures, nor have seemed more imploringly submissive. Like true savages, the transition in their minds from ferocity to abject cowardice was sudden and involuntary. King Peter was quite as much overcome with fear as any of the crowd; and Stockton, as he perceived the effect

---

* At this instant, when the reference to God was made, the sun, which had previously been veiled with a dark cloud, burst forth in full radiance; and, we are told, as the savages observed it, they appeared to be convinced that Stockton was really invested with divine authority.

of his own intrepidity, pressed the yielding mood of the king only with more sternness and vehemence.

King Peter, with all the chiefs and head-men, agreed and pledged themselves, with the utmost sincerity, that they would repair to the place originally designated for the execution of the treaty, on the following day, and execute it.

This time the negroes were as good as their word. At the appointed time and place the treaty was duly executed, with all the usual formalities.

The territory thus acquired by Lieutenant Stockton is now the flourishing republic of Liberia. The American Colonization Society, as soon as practicable after the cession, took possession of the country, and established their settlement of colonists near the Cape Mesurado, on St. Paul's River. The colony, under the discreet management of the parent society, has annually increased by immigration, and spread over additional territory several hundred miles along the coast. The ultimate success of the scheme can no longer be questioned. The republic of Liberia—the offspring of the infant colony at Mesurado—now embraces a population of 200,000 people subject to its free and Christianizing influences.

The dark and hidden mysteries of the vast continent of Africa may yet, through the agency of the Liberians, be revealed, and the blessings of true religion and civilization be extended to the benighted millions known to swarm in primeval ignorance and barbarity throughout its sequestered interior.

The name of Stockton will be associated in history with the names of the founders of this prosperous State, for to his courage, prudence, and valour, its original acquisition must be ascribed.*

---

* See speeches of Commodore Stockton on Colonization, Appendix E.

CHAPTER V.

SOON after the purchase of the territory of Liberia, Lieutenant Stockton sailed for the United States.

While on the coast of Africa, or going from or returning home, he captured several vessels. As important principles of the law of nations were involved in the justification of these captures, and as they well illustrate the moral intrepidity, sagacity, and other distinguishing traits of Stockton, they will merit the careful consideration of the reader. On the 5th of November, 1821, as the Alligator was pursuing her course with a favourable breeze, a strange sail was observed, whose course when first seen, if continued, would have crossed that of the Alligator nearly at right angles, long before the Alligator had arrived at the point of intersection. The stranger, instead of continuing her course, lay to at that point, and awaited the approach of the American schooner. She showed no national colours, but had a flag hoisted in the usual position of signals of distress. Stockton, supposing the stranger to be some merchant-man short of water or provisions, or else desirous of comparing longitude, directed a barrel of pork and several casks of water to be got up in readiness, so that no unnecessary delay might be incurred. Having given these orders, he went below to the cabin and sat down to work up his longitude to that moment of time. While thus engaged, he heard a shot pass through his mainsail. Immediately dropping his pen, he returned to his deck, and found the Alligator within gunshot of a vessel evidently larger, and, judging from the size of the shot which had perforated the mainsail, carrying a much heavier armament than the Alligator.

Stockton told his men to put the provisions and water they had on deck below, and bring up the shot, which he said was better adapted to the occasion, and then ordered them to quarters. The Alligator's guns were of no use at the distance at which she was when the stranger commenced the attack. Stockton, having shotted his guns, to avoid the raking shot of the enemy made all his men lie flat on deck. Having thus secured his men, Stockton, in full uniform, took his seat on the hammock-cloths and guided the vessel, and in this manner approached his adversary without firing a shot.

The wind was light and baffling, sometimes entirely dying away and then again slightly breezing up. For several hours he was thus the target of the stranger, who kept up an uninterrupted fire, cutting the sails and rigging of the Alligator and wounding several men.

Just as the Alligator had got within pistol-shot, the purser of the ship ran up to Stockton, and said that the strange vessel had hoisted Portuguese colours. "Very well," said Stockton; "then we'll make her haul them down again." And now, having got sufficiently near for the guns of the Alligator to do the required work, and having reached a position in which they could rake the enemy's deck, they poured forth a volley which swept out of sight every living object on the stranger's upper-works,—her men who were unhurt quitting their guns and running below. The Alligator then, luffing round, delivered her whole broadside, repeating broadside after broadside, until, after twenty minutes, the flag of the stranger was struck.

On being hailed, her captain came on deck and informed Stockton that his prize was the Portuguese letter-of-marque Marrianna Flora, of twenty-two guns. Being ordered aboard the Alligator, he said, in excuse for his attack, that he supposed her to be a pirate. Stockton asked him why he had not taken the trouble to inform himself of the character of the Alligator, and why he showed colours of distress? To these questions the Portuguese captain could give no satisfactory reply. Stockton was of opinion, upon a full consideration of all the circumstances, that the Portuguese had intended to commit an act of piracy, and that if the Alligator had been an unarmed merchantman she would have been captured and plundered. He determined, therefore, to put a prize crew on the Marrianna Flora and send her to the United States.

We may here state that, when the case came before the District Court of the United States at Boston, Stockton not being there to give the suit his attention, the capture was declared illegal, the Marrianna Flora ordered to be surrendered to the representatives of her owner, and damages awarded, to a large amount. As soon as Stockton heard of this result, he appealed to the Circuit Court of the United States, and engaged Mr. Webster to conduct his cause. The judgment of the District Court was reversed. The case was then taken up to the Supreme Court of the United States, and the decision of the Circuit Court sustained. The report of the case will be found in 11 Wheaton. The Marrianna Flora was, however, ultimately given up on application from the Portuguese government. She was surrendered from comity, and not on the ground that her capture was not legal or proper.

Judge Story, delivering the opinion of the Supreme Court in relation to the case of the Marrianna Flora, says, (11 Wheaton, p. 50,) "Upon the whole, we are of opinion that the conduct of Lieutenant Stockton, in approaching and ultimately in subduing the Marrianna Flora, was entirely justifiable. The first wrong was done by her; and his own subsequent acts were a just defence and vindication of the rights and honour of his country." "If, (p. 52,) Lieutenant Stockton had acted with gross negligence or malignity, and with a wanton abuse of power, there might be strong grounds on which to rest this claim of damages. But it is conceded on all sides, and in this opinion the court concurs, that he acted with honourable motives and from a sense of duty to his government. He thought the aggression was piratical, and that it was an indignity to the national flag utterly inexcusable.

"We are then to consider the real difficulties of Lieutenant Stockton's situation. An attack had been made upon a national ship under his command, without cause. It was a hostile act,—an indignity to the nation and trespass upon its rights and sovereignty. It was not an accidental, but a meditated act, not necessarily carrying its own excuse along with it, but susceptible of different interpretations. It was not an affair in which he was at liberty to consult his own wishes or honour merely; although a brave and distinguished officer might naturally feel some solicitude to preserve his high reputation untarnished in the eyes of his government. He was bound to look to the rights of his country. He might well hesitate in assuming the arbitration of national wrongs. He might well feel a scrupulous delicacy in undertaking to waive any claim which the government had authority to enforce; or to defeat any redress which it might choose to seek; or to prevent any inquiries which, through its established tribunals, it might think fit to institute in respect to his conduct or that of the offending vessel. Considerations of this nature could not but weigh heavily upon the mind of a gallant officer; and they are not unfit to be entertained by this court in forming its own judgment.

" It is, also, further to be observed that the case was confessedly new in its character and circumstances. The researches of counsel, throughout the progress of this protracted controversy, have not discovered any case which, in point of law, can govern this. If it is new here, it may well be deemed to have been new and embarrassing to Lieutenant Stockton. In such a case, it is not matter of surprise that he should come to the conclusion that it was not proper to take upon himself the responsibility of a final decision, but to confide the honour of the nation, as well as the rights of the other party, to judicial decision. No inference is attempted to be drawn that his acts were intentionally oppressive and harsh; and it would be going a great way to declare that an exercise of honest discretion, in a case of wrong on the other side, ought to draw after it the penalty of damages."

On a subsequent cruise in the Alligator on the coast of Africa, Stockton captured the *Jeune Eugenie*, a French slaver. His instructions directed him to capture all vessels, sailing under the American flag, found engaged in prosecuting the slave-trade. But he discovered that, if he confined himself to the letter of his instructions, his presence there was of no sort of use; as every slaver, as soon as the Alligator was seen, was sure to exhibit any other colour but the American. Upon full reflection, he came to the conclusion that slaves on that coast, found on any vessel bound to the several slave-markets, could not be lawfully claimed as property by those who held them in custody. They were held in durance in violation of the law of nature and of the civilized world; and the vessel which held them could be protected by the flag of no country which had prohibited the slave-trade. A vessel with white men in their situation, forcibly torn from their country, and, against their consent, being transported to be sold as slaves, no matter by what flag covered, would, in his estimation, be lawful prize to any ship-of-war belonging to any civilized nation which cherished or respected the laws of God and humanity. The fact of the slaves on this coast, thus borne away by rapine and violence, being African negroes, in no degree modified the fundamental principles of justice applicable to the circumstances of the case. Firmly believing the soundness of these principles, he was determined that they should be tested in the courts of the United States. The *Jeune Eugenie* was captured, therefore, though not sailing under the American flag. She was captured on the ground that her cargo and her voyage made her, *ipso facto*, a pirate. The nation whose flag she bore had interdicted the slave-trade; and that flag, therefore, could not

protect her in a trade declared to be illegal by the government of
the country to which she belonged. At the time he sent the *Jeune
Eugenie* to the United States, Stockton wrote a letter to Mr. Webster, in which he set forth briefly the principles of law by virtue
of which he believed the capture justifiable. We have been informed
that Mr. Webster has said that he argued the case of the Jeune Eugenie from this letter as his brief. The opinion of the Circuit
Court of the United States, sustaining the capture of this vessel,
has long been celebrated for the broad and enlightened doctrines of
humanity and justice which it declared and vindicated. It will be
found in 2 Mason's C. C. Reports. Judge Story, who delivered the
opinion of the court, thus enunciates those broad principles of national law on which Lieutenant Stockton justified the capture of the
Jeune Eugenie:—   ·

"Now, in respect to the African slave-trade,—such as it has been
described to be, and in fact is, in its origin, progress, and consummation,—it cannot admit of serious question that it is founded in
a violation of some of the first principles which ought to govern
nations. It is repugnant to the great principles of Christian duty,
the dictates of natural religion, the obligations of good faith and
morality, and the eternal maxims of social justice. When any
trade can be truly said to have these ingredients, it is impossible
that it can be consistent with any system of law that purports to
rest on the authority of reason or revelation; and it is sufficient to
stamp any trade as interdicted by public law, when it can be justly
affirmed that it is repugnant to the general principles of justice and
humanity.

"It is of this traffic, thus carried on and necessarily carried on,
beginning in lawless wars and rapine and kidnapping, and ending
in disease and death and slavery—it is of this traffic, in the aggre-
gate of its accumulated wrongs, that I would ask if it be consistent
with the law of nations. It is not by breaking up the elements of
the case into fragments, and detaching them one from another, that
we are to be asked of each separately if the law of nations prohibits
it. We are not to be told that war is lawful, and slavery lawful,
and plunder lawful, and the taking away of life is lawful, and the
selling of human beings is lawful. Assuming that they are so under
circumstances, it establishes nothing; it does not advance one jot
to the support of the proposition that a traffic that involves them
all, that is unnecessary, unjust and inhuman, is countenanced by
the eternal law of nature on which rests the law of nations.

"I think, therefore, that I am justified in saying that at the present moment the traffic is vindicated by no nation, and is admitted by almost all commercial nations as incurably unjust and inhuman. It appears to me, therefore, that, in an American court of judicature, I am bound to consider the trade an offence against the universal law of society, and, in all cases where it is not protected by a foreign government, to deal with it as an offence carrying with it the penalty of confiscation.

"After listening to the very able, eloquent, and learned arguments delivered at the bar on this occasion,—after weighing the authorities which bear on the case with mature deliberation,—after reflecting anxiously and carefully upon the general principles which may be drawn from the law of nations to illustrate or confirm them, I have come to the conclusion that the slave-trade is a trade prohibited by universal law and by the law of France; and that, therefore, the claim of the asserted French owners must be rejected."

Lieutenant Stockton was the first in the United States who ever asserted and acted upon these broad and fundamental principles of natural law. It was a bold and decided assumption of responsibility, which was as creditable to his moral courage as to the accuracy of his perceptions of justice.

On his return from his second cruise on the coast of Africa, Stockton was ordered to the West Indies, to check the depredations of the numerous pirates then cruising in the neighbouring seas. This duty he performed with all the ardour, vigour, and enterprise by which his character was distinguished.

The pirates, whose residence was on the coast of Cuba, would lie in wait along-shore for their prey, and, whenever a vessel was discovered upon which they could bring to bear superior numbers, they would put off in their boats, surprise and murder the crew, and take possession of the ship. Stockton believed that the only true course to contend with such outlaws was to pursue them on shore and extirpate them wherever found. If the Spanish authorities were unable to restrain the inhabitants of Cuba from such atrocities, they had no reason to complain if, in hot pursuit, their shores were invaded for the purpose of chastising the enemies of all mankind.

Stockton, accordingly, whenever he discovered a piracy to be committed, and had made pursuit of the perpetrators, invariably followed them ashore, and hunted them down to their dens and hiding-places. In this way he gave a serious check to their nefarious depredations, and inspired them with a salutary terror of American retribution.

Returning to the United States, he was ordered South, with a party to survey the Southern Coast, in 1823–4. While thus engaged, he was married, at Charleston, South Carolina, to Miss Maria Potter, only daughter of the late John Potter.

In 1826, after continuing in service for near sixteen years without furlough or leave of absence, he considered himself entitled to some repose. He accordingly settled at Princeton, New Jersey, and, in consideration of his long-continued and arduous services, was suffered by the Department to remain at home for some time, though not actually on furlough.

One of his first acts upon his return to New Jersey was the organization of the New Jersey Colonization Society, of which he was the first president. This Society still exists in flourishing condition, and has been the means of great usefulness to the colony of Liberia. It has recently received liberal assistance from the Legislature of the State; and it may be said, without exaggeration, that there is no State in which the colonization cause has warmer friends, or where it is more popular.

At this period of his life Captain Stockton indulged in the pleasures of the turf. He imported from England some of the finest stock of blooded horses which have been introduced into the country. Their progeny still maintain by their general success the reputation and value of their sires. Among the most celebrated of his importations, it is only necessary to name Trustee, Langford, and Diana. Captain Stockton is supposed to have been quite successful on the turf.

Langford, one of his favourite horses, won a produce-stake of ten thousand dollars, on the Washington course, over a good field of horses, among which was said to be a famous racer of General Jackson while he was President, though he was known as the owner only to a few of the initiated.

The sportsmen, familiar with the merits of General Jackson's horse, were confident of success, and bet high in his favour. A few days before the race, Captain Stockton's trainer fell sick, and, unable to supply his place, the captain came on himself and took the place of the trainer, superintending minutely the grooming of his horse until the day of the race. A day or two before the race, Langford had the ill luck to fall lame suddenly while galloping around the course. These incidents inspired the friends of his competitors with additional confidence; and, though the lameness disappeared immediately after its cause was ascertained, (a piece of gravel,) and was removed, the jockeys pretty generally bet on the General's horse.

An immense concourse of people assembled on the race-course on the day of trial. The President's horse was the general favourite, and odds were freely given by those who bet on the field. So confident were those who bet on the General's horse of his success, that the floor of the ballroom, where the annual ball of the season was given, was ornamented with a full-length portrait of the horse. To the astonishment of the crowd, however, Captain Stockton's horse proved to be the winner.

After Stockton's sudden and unexpected departure for the Pacific in 1845, and during his absence in California, his stud was broken up and all his racers sold, and, we believe, ever since he has entirely relinquished the sports of the turf.

CHAPTER VI.

REORGANIZATION OF PARTIES IN 1826–7—INDEPENDENT ACTION OF MR. STOCKTON—
HIS RECTITUDE AS A POLITICIAN—THE FEDERALISTS—HIS OPINIONS OF THEIR PRO-
SCRIPTION—MR. ADAMS PLEDGES NOT TO PROSCRIBE—GENERAL JACKSON'S ADVICE
TO MR. MONROE—STATE OF PARTIES IN NEW JERSEY—STATE DEMOCRATIC CONVEN-
TION—MR. STOCKTON APPOINTED A DELEGATE—HIS PROMPT PUNISHMENT OF AN
INSULT—CONVENTION DISSOLVED—SUCCESS OF THE ADAMS TICKET—MR. ADAMS'S
VIOLATION OF HIS PLEDGES—MR. STOCKTON DENOUNCES HIM—SUPPORTS GENERAL
JACKSON IN 1828—CONSTRUCTION OF DELAWARE AND RARITAN CANAL—FINANCIAL
DIFFICULTIES—MR. STOCKTON GOES TO LONDON AND SECURES A LOAN—MR. STOCK-
TON AN ANTI-MONOPOLIST—CANAL COMPLETED—ITS NATIONAL IMPORTANCE—NEW
JERSEY INTERNAL IMPROVEMENTS—TRANSIT DUTIES—NO TAX ON CITIZENS OF OTHER
STATES—PARALLEL BETWEEN MR. STOCKTON AND DE WITT CLINTON—LETTER ON
PUBLIC WORKS.

THE years 1826–7 were distinguished by the incipient reorganization of parties on a basis somewhat different from that on which
they had previously stood. A new era in the political history of
the United States now commenced. From the administration of
General Washington to the Treaty of Ghent, the Federal and Democratic parties were at issue chiefly in relation to our foreign policy.
But, after the restoration of peace in 1815, new questions arose, and
in a few years the old lines of political difference were in a great measure obliterated. As it respects these new questions—relating to
the encouragement of domestic manufactures and the prosecution
of internal improvements—Federalists and Democrats concurred or
differed without reference to party. The representatives of the
commercial interests of the North acted in co-operation with the
South; while the great body of politicians who represented the interior districts of the Northern and Middle States, together with
those from the West, sustained the policy of protection and that of
the prosecution of internal improvements. During the whole of
Mr. Monroe's eight years' administration, notwithstanding this state
of things, and notwithstanding the Federal party had ceased all
opposition to the government, and had entirely relinquished its
national organization, nevertheless Federalists continued to be excluded from office, and were as rigidly proscribed by the State
governments which were controlled by the Democrats, as if they
were still acting in open hostility to the Democratic party.

The consequence of the dissolution of national parties then was the same as that which has followed the dissolution of national parties in our own times. Geographical preferences and sectional animosities soon divided politicians who had before acted in concert.

The succession to the Presidency, in the latter part of Mr. Monroe's administration, became the absorbing subject of political attention. The candidates for the Presidency in 1824 were all members of the Democratic party, distinguished for talents and their public services; but they were all candidates supported principally by that section of country in which they had resided. The presidential contest of 1824 was, with some slight exceptions, a sectional contest, in which the recent differences between Federalists and Democrats were totally disregarded. The North presented Mr. Adams; the South brought forward Mr. Crawford and Mr. Calhoun, though the latter soon retired from the controversy in favour of General Jackson, who was a native of the same State as Mr. Calhoun. The Southwest and West were divided between General Jackson and Mr. Clay. The proneness of the people to geographical divisions is, therefore, strikingly illustrated by this portion of our political history.

Mr. Adams, although extremely obnoxious to the Federal party, which he left soon after it fell into the minority, notwithstanding, derived his chief support from those very States of New England in which the Federal party had always been most powerful; and the caucus nomination of the Democratic party, though made in strict conformity with Democratic usages, was treated with contempt by a large majority of those who had always been recognised as the leaders and oracles of that party. The caucus nominee, Mr. Crawford, received the smallest number of votes of any candidate who was returned to Congress to be voted for by that body. The sectional preferences of the people over rode all other considerations, and entirely ignored the obligations of party. As we have observed, we are witnessing this political phenomenon in our day.

Mr. Adams received in the New England States the united support of Federalists and Democrats. In the Middle States, however, especially in New Jersey, a large number of Federalists supported General Jackson. The grounds for this preference of the Federalists (there being no candidate for the Presidency residing in any of those States) was the celebrated letter of General Jackson to Mr. Monroe, advising him to appoint a Federalist as a member of his cabinet, and, as the Federalists were no longer organized as an opposition party, to receive into his confidence meritorious statesmen who had formerly belonged to the Federal party. This advice of

General Jackson, far in advance of the public sentiment of his party, was dictated by those enlarged, patriotic, and magnanimous feelings which have contributed quite as much as his achievements in the field to exalt our estimate of his abilities and virtues.

In order to secure his election by the House of Representatives, it became necessary for Mr. Adams to give pledges that he would abolish the proscription of the Federalists. The balance of power in Congress was held in the representation of three States by Federalists. The votes of these gentlemen could have elected General Jackson as well as Mr. Adams. Mr. Adams, it is charged, gave the necessary pledges, and was elected.

An opposition was immediately organized against the administration of Mr. Adams, and a disposition manifested to oppose it without regard to its measures or principles.

It became obvious to all who were acquainted with Captain Stockton, as he was then called, that a man of his activity of mind, decision, and force of character, would soon obtain weight and consideration among the people when he became known to them. Efforts were very naturally made, therefore, by leading politicians, to enlist him in their respective parties.

The conduct of Stockton at this period of his life, when called upon for the first time to act with reference to politics by the solicitations of distinguished politicians, strikingly illustrates one remarkable feature of his character, and that is, his complete independence. If there is a man who invariably decides all important questions respecting his own course of action for himself, it is Commodore Stockton. He is influenced neither by friend nor foe, nor by his interests, and much less by his fear of consequences, in making up his mind to do what he considers proper. When called upon to act, he is only solicitous to know what is right, what is consistent with honour, duty, and patriotism, and he decides without reference to the consequences as they may affect himself, whether for good or for evil.

He had never participated in the fierce conflicts so acrimoniously conducted between the Federalists and Democrats. He had entered the navy at a period of life which precluded the indulgence of any sympathy with political parties. When he returned to his country, he found that, although the Federalists had ceased all opposition to successive Democratic administrations, they were still proscribed as if they were aliens; all offices of distinction were closed upon them. In New Jersey, the effect was the proscription of the most talented and patriotic men in the State. In the State of New

Jersey, the course of the Federalists during the war of 1812 had not been factious. Many of them had volunteered and nobly stepped into the ranks of the army or militia at the first appearance of danger. He thought that the continued proscription of such men was unjust and injurious to the country. Accordingly, when solicited to espouse the cause of Mr. Adams, his first response was that he would support no administration which would not raise the ban of that odious proscription which ostracized from the public service the men who were among the founders and fathers of the republic. He was informed by gentlemen in the confidence of the President that it was his intention no longer to recognise the distinction of Federalist and Democrat. Mr. Adams, he was informed, owed his election to his having given such a distinct pledge. It was said in the cotemporary papers that a letter containing in black and white that pledge* of Mr. Adams was submitted to Captain Stockton.

He had the sagacity, however, to perceive that, though Mr. Adams had given such a pledge, it was by no means certain that he had the moral courage to redeem it. He had called no Federalist into his cabinet, nor had he in any way given any evidence of his disposition to observe it by any of his appointments. It was evident that parties were in a state of transition, and no peculiar principles had yet (in the spring of 1826) been developed, either by the administration of Mr. Adams or by his opponents, which would justify, in the opinion of Stockton, his attaching himself to one or the other prematurely. He would not, therefore, enlist in favour of Mr. Adams's re-election nor for the election of General Jackson. He took the position that Mr. Adams's administration should be tested by its merits, and explicitly protested that any support he might give his administration should not preclude his opposing the re-election of the incumbent if his measures or principles should prove justly obnoxious to censure.

In order that his peculiar position might be vindicated, if necessary, he established a newspaper at Princeton, in the columns of which he declared that his support of Mr. Adams was contingent on his good behaviour in office. Many of the leading editorial articles in that paper were written by Captain Stockton, and exercised an important influence on public opinion in New Jersey.

For many years a Democratic State convention had assembled biennially at Trenton, for the purpose of nominating candidates for

---

* See National Gazette, edited by Robert Walsh, for the fall of 1826.

Congress, to be voted for on a general ticket. The ticket thus nominated was always sure to be elected, such was the decided preponderance of the Democratic party.

In the year 1826, this convention assembled in August, and the supporters of Adams and of Jackson respectively made great exertions to elect delegates to it. Whichever party obtained control of this convention would have ostensibly the prestige of the Democratic party in its favour. The effort was, in the first instance, to acquire the ascendency in the Democratic county conventions, which selected the delegates to the State convention. In some of the counties, double delegations were returned, each claiming to be the pure Democratic representatives. They assembled at Trenton on the 20th day of September. The Adams and the Jackson party were both nearly equal in strength.

Captain Stockton was elected a delegate from the county of Somerset, in which he resided. On the evening previous to the convention, an informal meeting of the Adams delegates was held. At that meeting it became apparent to the Adams men that they had in Stockton a leader in whom entire confidence could be placed, and it was agreed that he should be supported, in every move, with the whole strength of the party. He perceived, from the spirit of overbearing and impetuous determination exhibited by the Jackson party, that they would probably put all rules and precedents at defiance, and attempt to carry their measures by mere numerical force, without regard to justice or usage. He therefore determined to give them every facility for the indulgence of this spirit, well knowing that it would result either in breaking up the convention in confusion, or else in a reaction among the people fatal to those who should violate the usages of the Democratic party.

As soon as the convention assembled, Captain Stockton nominated as president of the convention a leading Jackson delegate, and subsequently another Jackson delegate as secretary, who were elected without opposition. This rather surprised the Adams men who were not in the secret. Stockton voted also in favour of receiving the Jackson delegates, whose seats were disputed, from several counties, until the reception of the delegates from Cumberland became the question.

The Adams delegates from this county, according to Democratic usage, were the regularly-appointed delegates, and should have been received. But the Jackson men, now feeling strong enough to defy their opponents without any respect for their rights, rejected the

Adams delegation from Cumberland and received the Jackson delegates.

A flagrant act of injustice had now been perpetrated; and Captain Stockton determined that upon this act he would make a case for the dissolution of the convention which the people would justify and vindicate, or that he would compel his opponents to rescind their vote and retrace their steps. He accordingly proceeded to address them in a bold and exciting manner, denouncing their violation of Democratic usages, and stigmatizing their exercise of power as arbitrary and tyrannical.

Several of the most prominent Jackson leaders were in the lobby, at this time, and some of them said audibly to their partisans that Stockton must be stopped and put down, or that he would break up the convention. While he was thus haranguing the convention, he saw one of the delegates who had been in conference with the Jackson leaders in the lobby leave them and enter the area in front of the President's chair, immediately opposite his own position. This delegate had, on the previous day, used offensive language in presence of Captain Stockton, which he did not resent at the time, partly because the offender was visibly intoxicated, and partly because he was ignorant that Captain Stockton was present. The delegate approached, as we said, the speaker, until within a few feet of him, and then, in a loud and violent tone, said, "What right has that damned rascal here with the government's commission in his pocket? Turn him out."

With that intuitive sagacity for which he is so distinguished on emergencies of importance, Captain Stockton saw that this public insult was designed to confuse and arrest him. Those who had prompted it calculated that Stockton would sit down and wait till after the convention should call the offender to account; in the mean time, having silenced the chief champion of the Adams men, they would have every thing their own way. But they were entirely ignorant of the man upon whom they experimented. He seized upon the occurrence as the consummation of violence and aggression which he had predicted would hurry his opponents to the commission of some great offence which would justify the dissolution of the convention. He determined, with that promptitude and decision of character which belongs to him, to punish a public insult in a public manner, on the spot and at the moment when it was offered. Without the hesitation of a second, he stepped across the intervening platform, and with a single blow prostrated the offender to the floor; then, quickly resuming his place, in a voice which commanded the atten-

tion of the now tumultuous crowd, he proceeded to vindicate what he
had done. But no sooner had he thus punished his assailant than
the whole convention of delegates sprang to their feet, the lobby
rushed in upon the floor of the delegates,—some struggling, apparently, to assail Stockton personally, others to ascertain the facts.

Stockton's friends crowded around him, resolved to defend him
to the last. One of them offered him a dirk, but he put it aside,
saying, " It is brains, not arms, which are required now." At one
time several orators were speaking together, and a Babel of excitement, uproar, and agitation was exhibited, perfectly indescribable.
All this occurred in a few moments of time; when Stockton, perceiving that he could not be heard from the floor, sprang on a table
and continued his address. He spoke with regret of the necessity
which devolved upon him to punish such an insult as that which he
had received immediately, and he appealed to his hearers, as
Jerseymen and men of honour, if it was possible for him without dis-
gracing his uniform to have done otherwise. His hearers were
gradually softened and mollified; and, as their temper cooled, Stockton concluded by a motion that the convention should adjourn *sine
die*, which was carried by acclamation. He then gave notice of a
place and the time of the day when the Adams delegates would
meet and form a ticket.

It is to be regretted that the speech delivered on this occasion by
Captain Stockton has not been preserved. It was undoubtedly one
of the most powerful addresses ever made to a popular assembly in
New Jersey, and raised him at once to the foremost rank among the
political men of the State.

Thus, owing to his tact and presence of mind, his political opponents were balked of their expected triumph,—they lost the prestige
of making their nomination under the forms of the old Democratic
party; while the friends of Stockton were saved from an ignominious
defeat, and entered the field upon equal terms with their adversaries.
The election came on the second Tuesday of October, and resulted in
the election of the Adams candidates for Congress by a decided
majority.

An occasion now happened by which Mr. Adams's fidelity to his
pledges respecting the Federalists could be effectually tested. The
office of District Judge of the United States for New Jersey became
vacant by death, and an appointment was required to fill the
vacancy. The names of three candidates who had been Federalists,
and whose qualifications were of the highest order, were forwarded
to the President.

At the head of the list was the name of Richard Stockton, who, for a whole generation, had stood unrivalled, the foremost lawyer at the bar of New Jersey. Chief Justice Kirkpatrick, who for twenty-one years had sat as Chief-Justice of the Supreme Court of New Jersey, was also pressed upon Mr. Adams for this appointment. Aaron Ogden, also a distinguished lawyer, and a soldier of the Revolution, was a candidate likewise. But the gentleman preferred for the honourable post of District Judge of the United States had never been professionally educated as a lawyer, and on that ground Mr. Monroe, several years previously, had refused to appoint him to the same office, but conferred it on Judge Pennington. The appointee of Mr. Adams was the only candidate notoriously destitute of the proper qualifications for this office. But he had for many years been the leader of the old Democratic party; and Mr. Adams, unfortunately for himself, seemed more desirous of making political capital by means of this appointment than of properly administering the trust with which the Constitution invested him of dispensing his official patronage for the benefit of the people. Mr. Rossell was appointed. Mr. Adams's pledges were violated, palpably, without excuse or justification.

Immediately after the New Jersey appointment, the vacancy in the Southern District of New York was filled by Judge Betts; and the friends of Chancellor Kent, and D. B. Ogden, and Josiah Hoffman,—all eminent lawyers and Federalists,—were chagrined and disgusted by the evident determination of Mr. Adams to continue the proscription of the Federalists, though his administration had been indebted for its existence to them. Other appointments were made soon after, showing "*a foregone conclusion*" that Mr. Adams, instead of adapting himself to the new order of things, which indicated the total disruption and dissolution of both the old parties, was vainly attempting to preserve their vitality by courting one at the expense of the other, in utter contempt of his pledges to his friends and his duty to the country.

Captain Stockton, having originally supported Mr. Adams's administration upon the principle that it would cease to proscribe the Federalists who were meritorious and were true to the Constitution and the Union, now perceiving that he had been deceived, promptly and abruptly did as he originally said he would do whenever he had reason to doubt the honesty or condemn the acts of Mr. Adams. He ceased, therefore, to render any aid or assistance to the Adams administration.

As the measures and principles of Mr. Adams were developed, his

latitudinarian views in relation to the construction of the Constitution, to internal improvements and State rights, Stockton soon perceived the necessity of resisting his re-election. In 1827, the sectional strife of 1823–4 had entirely ceased. The people were again
divided into only two parties,—the one supporting the administration of Adams and advocating his re-election, the other opposing
his policy and measures and united in favour of General Jackson.
Stockton soon became one of the most decided supporters of the
General, and continued so throughout his whole term of service.
Between them the most cordial and friendly intercourse subsisted.
The principles of the Democratic party as it was reorganized by
General Jackson, and as those principles were then understood,
he approved; and they still constitute in the main his political
creed, as will be seen by reference to his speeches. The doctrine of
State rights as expounded by the Virginia and Kentucky resolutions
of 1798–9,* of a strict construction of the Constitution, of a simple
and economical government, of opposition to all foreign entangling
alliances, and the sentiment of devotion to the Union and implicit
observance of the obligations of the Constitution, he has always
consistently advocated and maintained. Nor, in the exercise of
that independence which is an element of his character, has he
failed to denounce any disregard of these principles, whether exhibited by political friends or opponents.

   Some have thought that he was not sufficiently observant of the
obligations of party. Such persons have not been aware of the
uniform language which he has always held from youth up in
relation to party. The country and its welfare, he has uniformly
asserted, were the only legitimate objects of party action; and when
the safety, honour, or happiness of the country conflicted with the
success of parties, it has been his doctrine that the claims of patriotism were paramount to those of party. The truth is that Stockton, in the political field, is the same man, with the same identical
characteristics, as Stockton in the field of war. Bold, chivalric, and
adventurous, whether it be an enemy to be encountered—thundering
on his advance, or a principle of political action to be attacked or
defended, he displays the same fearless intrepidity, and marches
onward with the same unfaltering steps. There is a chivalry in
politics as well as in war; but, unfortunately, while the one is ad-
mired and extolled by the multitude, they often deride and depre-

---

* See his speech on harbour defences, for a eulogium on these resolutions.

ciate the other. It is only history, and the FEW good and wise, who appreciate the honest politician.

In 1828-9, public attention in New Jersey was attracted with much interest to the subject of internal improvements. The benefits conferred on the people and State of New York by the construction of the Erie Canal had given a great impulse to the public mind in relation to roads and canals. Believing the construction of a canal to connect the waters of the Delaware and Hudson Rivers to be a work of national importance, the citizens of New Jersey had made frequent applications to Congress for aid towards the accomplishment of that work; but no aid from that quarter could be obtained. The State of New Jersey, in 1826, conferred a charter on a New York company to construct the Delaware and Raritan Canal, with very liberal privileges; but, after a year spent in fruitless efforts to dispose of the stock, the New Yorkers abandoned the enterprise.

In 1830, another charter was granted by the Legislature for a canal company at the same time that the Camden and Amboy Railroad Company was incorporated. Mr. Stockton was absent from New Jersey at this time, and took no part in the popular action which led to the enactment of the charter for the canal. Upon his return from the South, in the summer of 1830, he found that the books of subscription to the stock of the canal company had been opened, and but a small portion of the stock had been taken. He was originally in favour of the State's constructing the canal, and predicted that it would eventually become a source of emolument.

By the action of the Legislature it now became settled that the State would not undertake the work; and it was a question between having no canal or obtaining its construction through the instrumentality of a chartered company. Mr. Stockton was strenuously urged to undertake the enterprise. After due deliberation, he subscribed the necessary number of shares to secure the charter. He at once endeavoured to enlist the New York and Philadelphia capitalists in the work; but, though it was apparent that those cities would derive the chief benefit from the canal when completed, he obtained little or no material aid from those quarters. They doubted whether so short a canal could be made profitable, and considered the enterprise too hazardous to contribute to its prosecution. He was compelled to rely chiefly upon his own resources and those of his immediate family friends. The work was commenced with vigour, and prosecuted with all his energy. He embarked his whole fortune and that of his family in the enterprise. He manifested a remarkable liberality in letting the contracts for the canal and

locks, by directing that no contracts should be given at a price below the estimates of the engineer.   He knew that they were as low
as any man could honourably afford to do the work, and he would
suffer no temptation to be offered to contractors to cheat the company or the labourers employed by them.

During the progress of the work, a severe financial crisis occurred
in the United States.   It became evident that the original stock
subscribed would not be sufficient to complete the canal, and a loan
could not be obtained upon any reasonable terms at home.   The
credit of the United States had been somewhat strained in Europe,
and Mr. Stockton was told by the New York and Philadelphia
brokers that he could not negotiate such a loan as was required in
London.   He, however, determined to make the experiment, and
accordingly proceeded to Europe.   Avoiding the intermediate assistance of the money-dealers, he applied directly to the great capitalists themselves, and soon convinced them of the sufficiency of the
Delaware and Raritan Canal as a security for the loan proposed.
His success was deemed at that time a financial operation of no
ordinary character.

While the canal was thus in progress, the Camden and Amboy
Railroad was likewise in process of construction, under the direction
of his friends, the Messrs. Stevens, so renowned for their enterprise
and sagacity.   It became quite plain that the railroad would carry
all the passengers and the greater part of the most valuable freight.
Mr. Stockton, with the people in the central counties of New Jersey,
considered the canal as really the most important work of the two to
the State.   In order to protect the canal, they therefore applied for
liberty to construct a railroad through the central parts of New
Jersey, from Trenton to New Brunswick.   There was nothing in the
Camden and Amboy charter which rendered such a grant an infringe-
ment of their privileges.   It was, however, strenuously opposed by
the railroad company and its friends.   Mr. Stockton took the ground
that, unless their application were conceded, the Camden and Amboy
Company would be a monopoly.   Much has been said about monopoly and anti-monopoly in New Jersey: it will appear from these
facts that Mr. Stockton was among the first of the anti-monopolists.

The Legislature terminated the controversy which threatened to
agitate the State, and consolidated the companies, with authority to
construct the Trenton and New Brunswick Railroad.   A railroad
already had been constructed from Trenton and Philadelphia, and
also another connecting New Brunswick and Jersey City.   The
joint companies thus secured to New Jersey two distinct thorough-

fares through the State by railroads, as well as the successful completion of the canal. They likewise gave the State $200,000 of their stock, guaranteed that the transit duties accruing to the State for passengers and freight should never be less than $30,000 per annum, and submitted to important reductions in the fares which they were originally permitted by their charters to collect.

Much outcry has been raised because of these transit duties, by citizens of other States who imperfectly understand their nature. Notwithstanding New York and Pennsylvania, and every State which has constructed public works, exact a revenue from them in the shape of tolls and charges for freight, New Jersey, having constructed her public works without incurring any public debt through the instrumentality of chartered companies, is vehemently censured because she has been provident enough to reserve some revenue to herself from the business done upon the works she has authorized.

The mistake of the citizens of other States, who censure New Jersey for this cause, is, that they consider the transit duties as a *tax* levied upon *them*. If it were such, there could be no doubt of the right of New Jersey to exact it. But it is a tax on the business of the companies, and not upon individuals. It is a substitute for taxation of the capital of the companies. The State foresaw that, while the capital remained stationary, the business of the companies would augment annually. While granting important privileges, the State therefore wisely protected her own interests. The entire income which she derives from the companies is now about $150,000 per annum. The tolls and charges of the companies are, however, in no manner affected by these duties. Were they entirely abolished the companies would charge the same as they do now.

Much clamour has been raised in the newspapers also respecting the monopoly enjoyed by these companies. It is obvious that these works could not have been constructed unless exclusive privileges had been originally conferred, as an inducement and protection to those who made them. These privileges are the price paid for these works at a time when there was no certainty that they would ever remunerate their projectors. Notwithstanding the value of these great works, the proprietors have several times offered to surrender them to the State upon their being paid the actual value, or the cost and interest thereon, of their original construction. But public opinion, with few exceptions, is satisfied that they can be managed better and more economically by chartered companies than by the State herself.

The Delaware and Raritan Canal is a work of great value and

importance. Its business promises to exceed the most sanguine expectations of its projectors. When the coal-fields of Pennsylvania are more fully developed, this canal will be supplied with freight to its utmost capacity. Vessels of five hundred tons now pass through it from the Delaware to the Hudson. In time of war with any maritime nation, the whole coasting trade afloat will seek this channel. No other work of similar importance in the United States has yet been constructed through the energy and exertions of any single individual. Mr. Clinton, indeed, is celebrated as one of the most powerful projectors of the construction of the Erie Canal. But he was assisted by many associates, who shared the responsibility and the honour of that work; and he was sustained by the credit of the State of New York, which alone contributed the financial means. Mr. Stockton was aided by the credit of no State. No debt was incurred by New Jersey for that object. But there it is, a magnificent and enduring benefit not only to the people of New Jersey, but to the people of the adjacent States particularly and the commerce of the whole country generally.*

The following letter of Commodore Stockton, reviewing the whole subject of internal improvement in New Jersey, will be a useful auxiliary to the reader in enabling him to understand better this portion of our history :—

REPLY OF COMMODORE R. F. STOCKTON TO THE LETTER FROM CITIZENS OF TOM'S RIVER.

To Messrs. F. J. Speer, W. I. James, James Gulick, Benjamin L. Irons, and others, citizens of the county of Ocean.

GENTLEMEN :—In consequence of my absence from Princeton, I did not see your letter until it was published in the *Monmouth Democrat.*

It would, nevertheless, have been sooner acknowledged had not numerous engagements prevented. The act to which you refer, I assure you, gave me no annoyance. If in the exercise of the "largest liberty" any of my fellow-citizens see fit to recreate themselves by executing effigies which they please to designate "Commodore Stockton," they are welcome to all the enjoyment and glory they can derive from amusements so harmless. While conscious of the rectitude of my own actions and intentions, malicious denunciations move me not.

---

* See Address of R. F. Stockton to the people of New Jersey, *Appendix.*

It is now nearly a quarter of a century since I devoted my mind, my means, and those of co-operating friends whom I could influence, to the cause of internal improvement in New Jersey. When I consider the inadequacy of my experience and abilities to the vast enterprise in which I then engaged, the difficulties to be encountered, and the slender resources which at first were within my control, and then advert to the realization of my proudest hopes, and more especially when I survey the benefits which, in part through my instrumentality, have been conferred upon New Jersey by this system of internal improvements, which I have advocated and defended, I can well tolerate with indifference any abuse which my success and my fidelity to the true interests and welfare of my native State may provoke.

Gentlemen, you say that "a majority of the people here are opposed to the measures of the party with which you co-operate, and to the State policy of which you are an able advocate." With regard to "party measures," I do not care a rush; but in relation to the improvement of New Jersey I do feel deeply concerned, and will hope that the time is not far distant when there will be little or no difference of opinion between us. No doubt the time has been, when a formidable opposition existed in New Jersey to the system of internal improvements with which I have been identified. The papers teemed with abuse of me, and a powerful party threatened the extinction of private rights and the violation of public honour. I placed myself in the breach on those occasions; but I never deprecated abuse, nor retorted the intemperate fulminations of political adversaries. I chose rather to let results speak for me. To their verdict I always confidently appeal. I was willing to stand or fall with the success or failure of the system which I recommended. Now that these results have proved eminently fortunate—now that triumphant success vindicates my system, though I may continue to treat defamation with silence and calumny with contempt, I shall on no fitting occasion like the present fail to remind my fellow-citizens that they owe the present prosperity of New Jersey, under God, first, to the system of internal improvement now subsisting, and, second, to the adherence by the State and the joint companies to the principles of plighted good faith and honour.

Interposing between the two great commercial emporiums of the continent—the natural bridge for all internal intercourse between the North and the South,—her commerce absorbed and diverted from her own harbours, New Jersey was bound by every dictate of political sagacity to make the most of her territorial advantages, and to compensate herself therefrom for the injuries inflicted by the overshadowing rivalship of New York and Philadelphia. The first great desideratum for the accomplishment of this object was the construction of the Delaware and Raritan Canal. The success of the Hudson and Erie Canal inspired many with a desire that New Jersey should make the Delaware and Raritan Canal a State work.

The State wisely (as events have shown) shrunk from the danger of encumbering herself with debt. She was not possessed of the vast resources of New York, and, judging from the analogy furnished by State prosecution and management of public works elsewhere, it is quite probable that, had this State commenced the construction of the Delaware and Raritan Canal, she would have abandoned it before its completion, and, instead of pouring its contributions (as at present) into her treasury, the debt incurred for its commencement would hang like an incubus on her prosperity.

For more than ten years subsequent to the completion of the canal, the receipts of the joint companies for toll hardly paid its expenses. How would the State have sustained herself under such a result, even if she had completed the construction of the canal? She would probably have been compelled by public clamour to have sacrificed it to speculators, who would assume only half of her indebtedness, just as Pennsylvania is now endeavouring to dispose of her public works. The State of New Jersey pursued a more cautious policy; she conferred a liberal charter on a company for the construction of the canal. The company which have completed it were secured against ruinous competition, and have been thereby enabled patiently to await the growth of business on that great work.

Contemporaneous with the incorporation of the Canal Company, the State incorporated also the Camden and Amboy Railroad and Transportation Company. At that time the nature and uses of railroads were but little known or understood, and no one was aware of the mighty capacity of the steam locomotive. I foresaw that the Delaware and Raritan Canal could not be constructed while menaced with the rivalship of a railroad. The public men of New Jersey and the people soon became impressed with the same views; they saw in *competition* none of those benign influences which its over-zealous friends attribute to it. They were not willing to risk the defeat of the canal for the sake of encouraging a ruinous competition, principally for the benefit of the inhabitants of other

States. They established, then, after careful deliberation, the policy and the system which have continued to this day,—a system which, whether called a monopoly or any thing else, has vindicated itself. That system insured the construction of the Delaware and Raritan Canal; it insured also two other railroad thoroughfares across the State; adequate accommodations, at reasonable fares, for the transit of all freight and passengers over the State; it insured, too, just compensation to the State for the privileges conferred, yielding an abundant and increasing revenue, and, in the progress of time and the development of the system, it secured likewise the construction of all local roads which may be needed in the southern and western parts of the State, when, without it, they would hardly be made in the lifetime of the present generation. And lastly, that system, after all doubt about the productiveness of the canal and railroads shall have been dispelled, and after experience shall have demonstrated the most judicious and economical method of managing them, invests the State with the right to take them at their appraised value. Should she do so at the time when by law she is authorized to exercise her option so to do, and should she conduct them wisely and economically, there can be no doubt they will make New Jersey, in proportion to her population, the most opulent and flourishing State in America or elsewhere.

Now, in contrast with the results of this system of New Jersey, cast your eyes over our sister States, where State construction and management of public works, and boundless competition, have prevailed. In one case you perceive powerful States crippled with debt and tormented with vexatious taxation, oppressing industry and depreciating the value of the property of the people. In the other case you see gigantic corporations tottering on the verge of bankruptcy, and threatening, in their fall, to cover the land with desolation, impoverishing widows and orphans—the rich and those who are not rich.

Unrestricted competition, when applied to railroad constructions, is an enormous and delusive fraud; it is a fraud because it promises advantages which it cannot confer; it allures into a snare the unwary, the ignorant, and the helpless, and involves them all in one fatal catastrophe.

It is far better for the public to have one good railroad than two inferior railroads. The real interests of the people of the whole country are not promoted by railroads transporting freight and passengers at a loss. The interest of no class can be permanently promoted by the industry of any other class being underpaid. Unrestricted competition in the construction of railroads, by producing inadequate compensation for railroad services, has a tendency to destroy capital. The destruction of capital is a calamity to the whole community. It checks enterprise and deprives labour of employment. There is another reason why such unrestricted competition is a fraud. It eventually places the weaker competitor in the power of the stronger,—making the rich richer, and the powerful more powerful, and finally terminates in a more inexorable and omnipotent monopoly than otherwise could be possible.

When, under the sanction of legislative enactment, a large capital is invested in such a work as a great railroad or canal, the objects of which are the promotion of the public interests as well as those of individuals,—when that capital is unalterably fixed, and converted into such a public improvement, and in the shape of stock-shares diffused throughout the community in the hands of men of limited means, held in part by the comparatively poor—by widows and orphans—by executors and administrators—eleemosynary institutions,—it ought to be considered as under the ægis of the public protection.

Were an incendiary to fire the shop and stations of such a railroad company, to tear up its rails, destroy its bridges, or in any way wantonly injure its structures, he would be deemed worthy of condign punishment, and the condemnation of all men would make him infamous. Yet, under the plausible pretext of competition, still more destructive and pernicious injuries are inflicted upon the enterprising capitalist and his helpless and confiding friends, who may have embarked their whole worldly substance in a railroad or a canal.

I care not what circumstances furnish the occasion for such unrighteous legislation; when such wrongs are perpetrated, they are equivalent to robbery; they have no foundation in justice; they are exertions of despotic power, irrespective of the principles of honour or justice. It is impossible for the interests of any community to be advanced by the violation of the eternal principles of justice.

These conclusions are established by experience, as exhibited in the consequences of unrestricted railroad competition in New England, in New York, and in Great Britain. New Jersey has wisely repudiated the fraud and folly of a reckless and destructive competition. And the public enjoys the benefit of her wisdom and prudence, in the most ample accommodations, upon fair terms, of the facilities offered by her public works. The proprietors of these works, controlled by no sordid or circumscribed view of their duties and obligations, strong in the confidence of the people, and grateful for the good faith and support which have always been manifested towards them by the State and their fellow-citizens, feel an abiding disposition to comply with all the just requisitions of an enlightened public, and will ultimately be able, from the abundance of their resources and their strength, to transport both passengers and freight at lower rates than any ill-judged competition could ever have compelled.

Next in importance to the adoption of the present system of internal improvement in New Jersey, in estimating the causes of her prosperity, may be ranked the firmness and consistency with which the joint companies and the State have adhered, through all the phases of monetary and political affairs, to the principles of honour and plighted faith.

There has been no time within the last twenty years when the joint companies, by the simple relinquishment of all opposition to efforts for the establishment of competing railroads, could not have rid themselves of all contributions to the State Treasury, and vastly augmented their profits and income, while at the same time they could have defeated any actual competition. They have, however, turned a deaf ear to all overtures contemplating such results, even when the madness of party seemed to create a necessity for such action. They have stood at the portals of the State Treasury, its protector and defender, when others have sought the destruction of the State revenue and credit. I do not exaggerate when I say that it has always been considered by the joint companies a paramount obligation to consult the interest of the State.

And now, after having devoted the best portion of my life to the promotion of the interests, the happiness, and prosperity of New Jersey,—after having been so long in contact with her public men, her legislators, and her most intelligent citizens in all parts of the State,—if there be a man whom I have deceived or misled, whose confidence I have abused, or who can justly charge me with any violation of the strictest principles of honour and integrity in my intercourse with him, I am yet to know him.

It is because my fellow-citizens know that I have been thus governed by the severest principles of honour that they have stood by me to baffle and defeat those who, no matter under what pretence or profession, sought to endanger the State revenue. Demagogues have in vain attempted, by all the acts of political chicanery, to corrupt their principles or excite their cupidity. There never has been a year or a day, in spite of all the lavish expenditure of foreign adventurers or the marshalled array of faction, when any man could stand up in the Legislature of New Jersey and propose the violation of the State's compact with the joint companies, without incurring the doom of universal execration and contempt.

Vindictively as I have been assailed for my connection with these companies,—identical as their prostration has been sought to be made with the triumph first of one party and then of another,—ingeniously as astute lawyers and politicians have proved the infraction of the public faith to be compatible with law and justice,—there has been no time when any of these attacks, or propositions, or sophisms, have made any serious impression on the public mind. That public mind has been too honest and too sagacious to cherish error, or to be led, even by its passions or its prejudices, to the commission of injustice.

There is no State in the Union—there is, in my opinion, no State in the world—in which public faith and the rights and property of men are more secure than in New Jersey. There is no State in which stronger temptations have been offered to violate the sanctity of State obligations than here; but there is no State in which such temptations have been more contemptuously spurned or more universally despised. To live in such a State, to be citizens of such a commonwealth, is a great satisfaction. To die in such a community, with the consoling reflection that our children will enjoy the shelter of its protection and all the benefits of its just laws and free and noble institutions, divests even death itself, in some measure, of apprehension. In the natural course of human life, there are but a few more years allotted to me. I am withdrawn from public life, and never expect or desire to reappear on its surface. My chief desire and solicitude with respect to public affairs are concentrated in New Jersey. My chief ambition is to be remembered as one of her sons, who honestly and assiduously devoted himself to her welfare. There is a monitor within my breast which assures me that, whatever may be the views of any of my fellow-citizens in relation to me now, however harsh their judgment, however unrelenting and unforgiving their enmity and hostile their attitude, the time will come, when, after my poor remains shall repose beneath the sods of New Jersey with those of my ancestors, that my memory will be cherished with respect, and that my name will stand on the page of New Jersey's history, associated forever with those whose chief ambition was the promotion of her prosperity, happiness, and glory.

Gentlemen, I thank you for the letter which you have addressed to me. I will long remember it as a flattering evidence of true regard from my fellow-citizens at Tom's River.

Very faithfully,

Your friend and obedient servant,

R. F. STOCKTON.

CHAPTER VII.

In 1838, having received orders, Mr. Stockton left all his great
interests in New Jersey without delay, and repaired to the post
assigned him.

It may here be remarked that during his whole period of
service he never refused or declined to obey a single order of the
Navy Department, nor did he ever ask to have any order modified or withdrawn, but always promptly obeyed, whatever might
be the personal sacrifice; nor was he in one single instance ever
reprimanded by a superior in rank, or subjected to a court-
martial for any acts, official or otherwise. His history will show
that this exemption from such incidents to a long period of service
in the navy was not owing to any reluctance on his part to the
assumption of responsibility. Not General Jackson, or any other
officer, military or naval, took upon himself responsibility, when
the welfare of the service required it, more fearlessly than Stockton.

He sailed for the Mediterranean as Flag or Executive officer of
the Ohio, (seventy-four,) flag-ship of Commodore Hull. He was likewise bearer of despatches from the administration to our minister in
England. While there, he devoted much time and incurred great
expense in visiting and inspecting the naval depôts, and yards,
and shops, and marine armaments of Great Britain, and investi-
gating the improvements in naval architecture. At this time he
conceived the idea of constructing a formidable steamship-of-war,
with all her machinery below water-line, and capable of carrying
such an armament as would make her invincible for defence and
the most destructive of all known instruments of war. He had the

model of such a ship prepared and forwarded to the United States, and subsequently, as will be hereafter related, on a reduced scale, tested its practical value by the successful construction of the Princeton.

Mr. Stockton did not remain long in the Mediterranean, having been promoted in 1839 to be a post-captain and recalled. He returned at a period of great political excitement. The suspension of specie payments had disturbed the financial condition of the country, and commerce and industry generally were embarrassed or paralyzed.

Mr. Van Buren's administration, confiding in the strength of the Jackson Democratic party, by whom it was created, was characterized by a reckless defiance of public opinion. Relying on the coherence of party attachments, it rather defied than conciliated the people. The enormous corruption and expenditures of the Florida war, the numerous cases of peculation by government officers tolerated with impunity, the proposition recommended by Mr. Van Buren to establish an immense standing army and substantially to withdraw from State control the militia, and, above all, in (New Jersey) the contemptuous treatment of the Broad Seal of the State, by the refusal to receive, in violation of precedents, the members of Congress who were certified by the Governor to be elected, had arrayed against Mr. Van Buren's re-election a formidable opposition, including in almost every State many leading men previously attached to the Democratic party.

Having no political aspirations, but anxious for the prosperity of the country, Mr. Stockton had acted with the Democratic party because he agreed with them as to the principles best adapted to promote the welfare of the people and protect the rights of the States. But when he saw those principles disregarded or violated by the administration, and when, as in the case of the New Jersey members, he saw State rights assailed and the sovereignty of New Jersey insulted, he determined to act independently and in accordance with his own patriotic feelings. The trammels of party could not compel him to support an administration which he disapproved. Measures inconsistent with Democratic principles he was unwilling to consider Democratic merely because supported by the party. A party, he believed, could be false to its own professions. The course of events has fully justified his political action in 1840. The House of Representatives of Congress solemnly reversed the principles of the decision which then excluded the Jersey members. And Mr. Van Buren by his apostasy in 1848 justified the opinion which Mr. Stockton entertained of his merits in 1840. He only anticipated the judgment of condemnation which the whole party have since unanimously awarded him.

After having made up his mind to oppose the re-election of Mr. Van Buren, Mr. Stockton took the field, and addressed the people of New Jersey in almost every county in the State. No correct reports were ever given by the press of his efforts on these occasions. Many garbled misrepresentations of them were, however, published, which, with Mr. Stockton's usual disregard of fame, he never thought it worth while to notice. The author of these pages was so fortunate as to hear him address the people several times during this political campaign, and we have a distinct recollection of many of his speeches, which all bore a general resemblance to each other.

In his exordium he defined his position, and uniformly avowed himself an unchanged Democrat, and, *because* he was such, he opposed Mr. Van Buren's re-election. He stigmatized Mr. Van Buren's administration as false to Democratic principles, measures, and policy, and, in all his speeches, invariably said that, should General Harrison, if elected, become obnoxious to any of the charges which he now made against Mr. Van Buren, he should be found as strenuous an opponent of him as he was of Mr. Van Buren. He declared that he had himself no political objects to gain by a change of administration; that all he desired was to see the country prosperous and happy, State rights properly regarded, and correct principles and measures maintained.

The novelty of a young officer of the navy appearing in the political arena, boldly arraigning a President at whose will his commission was held, excited much remark, while the ability and eloquence which he displayed astonished and electrified his hearers. An immense concourse attended whenever he was invited to address the people; and all, whether friend or foe, united in conceding him a high rank among the most popular orators of the day. His power and resources as a political speaker took the people by surprise. The wonder was, how and when and in what school were these oratorical faculties cultivated? Were they natural, or inherited, or acquired? A clear head, a sound judgment, confidence in his own rectitude, and a moral intrepidity that quails not in the presence of living man, are distinguishing characteristics of Mr. Stockton. These enable him, no matter with whom confronted, however refined or exalted the persons or multitudinous the assemblage, always to retain his self-possession and exert his intellect to the extent which the occasion requires.

As a popular speaker, Mr. Stockton enjoys a high reputation. But those who know him best say that his strength is felt to be greatest in the discussion of affairs of business. Then his penetrating sagacity, strong practical common sense, and clearness of perception, give him superior weight in all deliberative councils.

We believe that many entertain the opinion that Stockton is a man of impulse,—that he is rash and impatient, and decides without due reflection. No opinion is more groundless and erroneous. No one more patiently and carefully deliberates before he attempts to act. Every circumstance is duly weighed, every obstacle considered, and every chance of defeat canvassed, before he determines upon action. But, when he has determined, no one acts with more impetuous promptness or vehemence: to conquer difficulties then becomes in him a passion. Whether in public speaking or private council, the perfect honesty and sincerity of his character always give to his opinion an intrinsic force and weight which at all times command respect.

With popular manners and address, courteous to all who approach him, devotedly attached to his native State, of which he was beginning to be appreciated as a benefactor, it is not remarkable that his political exertions produced a decided influence on the result. New Jersey gave a large majority of votes in favour of General Harrison, and the Van Buren party was defeated.

Mr. Tyler, who, being Vice-President, succeeded to the Presidency on the death of General Harrison, soon found himself opposed by the bulk of the party which elected him. He, too, had always previously acted with the Democratic party until 1840; but, disgusted with the measures and principles of Mr. Van Buren, he refused to support his renomination for the Presidency. Though he would not go with his party for this purpose, nevertheless he had never disavowed his former principles and opinions. When, therefore, the triumphant leaders of the administration which General Harrison formed endeavoured to seduce Mr. Tyler to approve the creation of a national bank, he refused to become their instrument for that purpose. This produced an irreparable breach between them. Mr. Stockton, approving Mr. Tyler's consistency, and the moral courage with which he defied the difficulties in which he was involved, came out openly in his favour. He thought Mr. Tyler right, and he sustained him without any regard for his own popularity or personal interests. The disinterestedness of his support of President Tyler was proved by his refusal of the office of Secretary of the Navy, which was pressed upon him not only by the President, but which numerous

friends, confident in his abilities to discharge the duties of that station, earnestly solicited him to accept.* He was determined, however, that his motives for differing with friends with whom he had
so long acted should not be impeached by being supposed to be influenced by ambition. He knew them to be patriotic, and he would
not permit them to be tainted by any such imputation.

For several years previous to this period, Mr. Stockton had given
much attention to gunnery and the construction of steam-engines,
and also to naval architecture. The steamboats and locomotives
constructed by his friends, the Messrs. Stevens, (so celebrated as
civil engineers and for their scientific attainments,) for the railroad
and canal companies, gave him favourable opportunities to obtain
experience and knowledge in that branch of the arts. Their boats
were then, as they continue to be, models of beauty, power, and
celerity.

At his earnest solicitation, Mr. Stockton was now permitted by
the Navy Department to construct a steamship-of-war,—not exactly
of the dimensions which he recommended, but on a reduced model.
There were at this time no national steam-vessels in the navy.
The government had entirely neglected to avail itself of that wonderful agent which had been already appropriated to warlike purposes by other maritime nations. There never had been any ship-
of-war at this period constructed by the United States to which
steam-power had been successfully applied. The Fulton and other
previous attempts were miserable failures. Stockton had for several
years urged upon the Department the importance of keeping up
with other nations in all improvements in naval architecture. His
advice to the Navy Department was, that every ship-of-war thenceforward built should be larger and more effective than the best and
most powerful vessels constructed by the British or French. Thus,
in case of a war with either of those powers, we might reasonably
hope to win some laurels. He advised the Navy Department to
apply steam-power to all our vessels already built, and to build
hereafter none but war-steamers of the largest size, adapted to the
largest known guns.

The head of the Navy Department is generally a politician, more
solicitous to obtain popularity among the officers than competent to
discharge judiciously the functions of his office. He listens, therefore, to the advice of the superannuated officers, who, with pro-

* The office was suffered to remain vacant several weeks by the President, with
the hope that Captain Stockton would be prevailed on to accept it.

fessional dogmatism, denounce all novelties and pronounce all innovations dangerous. The application of steam to national ships-of-war from the first was resisted by many naval officers, and had to encounter many prejudices and much opposition. It was confidently asserted by the old captains that sailing-vessels would never be superseded by steam-vessels, and that the latter would be worthless except for purposes of transportation.

Notwithstanding the prevalence of these opinions at Washington, the urgency of Stockton's advice was such that he finally obtained the consent of the Department to his construction of a steam-frigate, though very inferior in dimensions to the plan which he had originally proposed. The steamer Princeton was commenced in Philadelphia, accordingly, in 1842, and completed in 1844. The construction of the Princeton confuted the ignorance and antiquated dogmas of the Washington Naval Bureau. Her speed and sailing qualities, her admirable model, the impregnable security of her motive-power, (being placed below water-line,) and her powerful armament, made her an object of universal admiration. Wherever she appeared, immense crowds gathered to witness her evolutions and inspect her machinery. She was kept in continual service from the time she was launched until the antipathy of the blundering incapables who controlled the Bureau of Construction at Washington directed her to be broken up. On her visit to the Mediterranean she attracted the attention of the curious and of the skilful engineers of every European naval power; and, while the United States neglected to multiply such cheap and efficient auxiliaries of naval defence after her model, England and France profited by the experiment, and their navies are now crowded with powerful steamers, many of them built on the model, and possessing all the peculiar characteristics, of the Princeton.

The following letter of Captain Stockton, descriptive of his noble ship, will be read with interest by those who remember the sensation produced by the Princeton on her first appearance in our waters :—

"UNITED STATES SHIP PRINCETON,
"PHILADELPHIA, February 5, 1844.

"SIR :—The United States ship Princeton having received her armament on board, and being nearly ready for sea, I have the honour to transmit to you the following account of her equipment, &c.

"The Princeton is a 'full-rigged ship,' of great speed and power, able to perform any service that can be expected from a ship-of-war. Constructed upon the most approved principles of naval architecture, she is believed to be at least equal to any ship of her class, *with her sails.* She has an auxiliary power of steam, and can make greater speed than any sea-going steamer or other vessel heretofore built. Her engines lie snug in the bottom of the vessel, out of reach of an enemy's shot, and do not at all interfere with the use of the sails, but can at any time be made auxiliary thereto. She shows no chimney and makes no smoke, and there is nothing in her external appearance to indicate that she is propelled by steam.

"The advantages of the Princeton over both sailing-ships and steamers propelled in the usual way are great and obvious. She can go in and out of port at pleasure, without regard to the force or direction of the wind or tide, or the thickness of the ice. She can ride safely with her anchors in the most open roadstead, and may lie to in the severest gale of wind with safety. She can not only save herself, but will be able to tow a squadron from the dangers of a lee-shore. Using ordinarily the power of the wind, and reserving her fuel for emergencies, she can remain at sea the same length of time as other sailing-ships. Making no noise, smoke, or agitation of the water, (and, if she chooses, showing no sail,) she can surprise an enemy. She can at pleasure take her own position and her own distance from the enemy. Her engines and water-wheel being below the surface of the water, safe from an enemy's shot, she is in no danger of being disabled, even if her masts should be destroyed. She will not be at a daily expense for fuel, as other steamships are. The engines, being seldom used, will probably out-last two such ships. These advantages make the Princeton, in my opinion, the cheapest, fastest, and most certain ship-of-war in the world. The equipments of this ship are of the plainest and most substantial kind,—the furniture of the cabins being made of white pine boards, painted white, with mahogany chairs, table, and side-board, and an American-manufactured oil-cloth on the floor. To economize room, and that the ship may be better ventilated, curtains of American-manufactured linen are substituted for the usual and more cumbrous and expensive wooden bulkheads, by which arrangement the apartments of the men and officers may in an instant be thrown into one, and a degree of spaciousness and comfort is attained unusual in a ship of her class. The Princeton is armed with two long 225-pound wrought-iron guns and twelve 42-pound carronades, all of which may be used at once on either side of the ship. She can consequently throw a greater weight of metal at one broadside than most frigates. The big guns of the Princeton can be fired with an effect terrific and almost incredible, and with a certainty heretofore unknown. The extraordinary effects of the shot were proved by firing at a target, which was made to represent a section of the two sides and deck of a seventy-four-gun ship, and timbered, kneed, planked, and bolted, in the same manner. This target was five hundred and sixty yards from the gun. With the smaller charges of powder the shot passed through these immense masses of timber, (being fifty-seven inches thick,) tearing it away and splintering it for several feet on each side, and covering the whole surface of the ground for a hundred yards square with fragments of wood and iron. The accuracy with which these guns throw their immense shot (which are three feet in circumference) may be judged by this:—that six shot fired in succession at the same elevation struck the same horizontal plank in a target more than half a mile distant. By the application of the various arts to the purposes of war on board the Princeton, it is believed that the art of gunnery for sea-service has, for the first time, been reduced to something like mathematical certainty. The distance to which these guns can throw their shot, at every necessary angle of elevation, has been ascertained by a series of careful experiments. The distance from the ship to any object is readily ascertained with an instrument on board, contrived for that purpose, by an observation which it requires but an instant to make, and by inspection without calculation. By self-acting locks, the guns can be fired accurately at the necessary elevation, no matter what the motion of the ship may be. It is confidently believed that this small ship will be able to battle with any vessel, however large, if she is not invincible against any foe. The improvements in the art of war adopted on board the Princeton, may be productive of more important results than any thing that has occurred since the invention of gunpowder. The numerical force of other navies, so long boasted, may be set at naught. The ocean may again become neutral ground, and the rights of the smallest as well as the greatest nations may once more be respected.

"All of which, for the honour and defence of every inch of our territory, is most respectfully submitted to the honourable Secretary of the Navy, for the information of the President and Congress of the United States,

"By your obedient and faithful servant,

"R. F. STOCKTON,

"*Captain U. S. Navy.*

"To Hon. DAVID HENSHAW,

"*Secretary of the Navy.*"

The enthusiasm produced by the appearance of the Princeton wherever she went, will appear from the following extracts from a letter dated Washington, February 20, 1844, published in the *Ohio Statesman :—*

"*House of Representatives on board the Steamship Princeton— Excursion down the Potomac and back—Captain Stockton and his Ship—Coronation dinner on board.*

"Washington, Tuesday, February 20, 1844.

"When the Queen of Sheba visited King Solomon, who, it is said, was somewhat partial to ladies, she declared upon her sacred honour that not the half had been told her of the power and glory and gallantry of the illustrious philosopher-king, the mighty successor of the minstrel-monarch of the Golden city of Zion ; so it is impossible to tell you the half that we saw and heard and enjoyed in the excursion given to the House of Representatives by Captain Stockton, of the steam-frigate Princeton, this day.

"The morning was propitious, auspicious, and tolerably delicious. The atmosphere, it is true, was rather misty and overclouded, but the wind was from the right quarter; the golden angel upon the steeple of the Rev. O. B. Brown's church held her trumpet steadfastly to the south.   At half-past ten, in company with two of our Representatives—Messrs. Morris and M'Causlen—of the House, we set out on foot for Greenleaf's Point, at the southern extremity of the city, distant about two miles ; but the mud was impassable, and so we accepted the offer of a passing hackman and rode it.   Had the constituents of our friends seen them sitting with their hats off in an aristocratic-looking coach, on the way to the landing, we doubt not they would have been chalked down on the blackboard for future accountability.

"Arrived at the landing, we discovered the Princeton, with her graceful keel, her tall and tapering spars, lying out a mile off in the stream.   Several boats and a 'broadhorn' were kept plying to and fro between ship and shore for nearly an hour, in the transportation of most of the honourable members of the House, and some of the Senate, and not a few of the honourable fraternity of reporters, among which was your faithful ambassador at Washington in *propria persona.*

"The marines were discovered drawn up in line on the upper deck as we mounted through the port-hole.   When the whole company of visitors were aboard, (some three hundred persons,) the ship was put in motion by her invisible and almost noiseless machinery in the hold. We found the Princeton armed with twelve 42-pounders and two tremendous pieces of ten tons' weight each, (of wrought iron, carrying a ball of two hundred and thirty pounds for two miles with the precision of a rifle,) all on the upper deck. The two great guns are fixed at the bow and stern of the ship, and are called the 'Peacemaker' and the 'Oregon.' These two 'bursters' are as bright as Aunt Peggy's pewter plates on Saturday evening, shining all in a row on the top shelf of the kitchen-cupboard. When the ship was fairly under way, Captain Stockton, mounting one of the guns, said, 'Now, gentlemen of the House of Representatives, fellow-citizens, and shipmates, we are going to give a salute to the wisdom of this mighty republic, (God bless her!) in Congress assembled. Stand firm, and you will see how it feels!' In rapid succession the pieces were fired, the ship thrilling and the distant hills reverberating with the thunder-peals. The instantaneous combustion of forty pounds of gunpowder in a discharge from the 'Peacemaker' closed the round of twenty-six guns. The deck of the ship was enveloped in smoke. We came near falling over the venerable Ex-President Adams in the momentary darkness. Captain Stockton's voice rose high amid the din of the battle. 'It's nothing but honest gunpowder, gentlemen; it has a strong smell of the Declaration of Independence, but it's none the worse for that. That's the kind of music when negotiations fail. It has a little of the ring of the earthquake, but it tells handsomely on salt water.' Some one asked Mr. Speaker Jones what was the main question before the House. The Speaker promptly rejoined that 'the main question was the Navy, and that it had been carried by the casting vote of the Peacemaker.'

"In due season the deputation of visitation were called to dinner in the cabin on the middle deck, extending the whole length of the ship. Captain Stockton is a man of wealth; and the scruples of the friends of retrenchment will be appeased when they learn that the magnificent feast prepared for the occasion was drawn, to the extent of the 'extras,' from the Captain's private resources. It was a feast of substantials and delicacies worthy the coronation-day of a South American Emperor. Ducks and chickens, turkeys and hams, beef a-la-mode, and partridges, &c.; ice creams, oranges, apples, raisins, almonds, &c.; champagne, sherry, cognac, and——but we forbear to trespass upon the feelings of the Washingtonian tee-totallers.

"The ship passed below Alexandria, till the Hill of Mount Vernon and the sacred residence of Washington loomed into view on the right, and the frowning battlements of Fort Washington on the left, when she turned about and returned. Several experimental shots were made from the 'Peacemaker' during the trip; and those solid balls of two hundred and thirty pounds skimmed the surface of the water for several miles with the lightness of an arrow.

"Nearly the whole of the Ohio delegation were on board, and we were gratified to learn that General Moore was sufficiently restored to be present. Captain Stockton goes for Oregon. He says if the question is brought to the tug of war, he will undertake to defend the mouth of the Columbia with his single ship. A nobler and a hardier man—a man whose appearance more favourably impresses you with his qualifications as a man and a sailor—is not to be found than Captain Stockton.

"The ship returned by three o'clock, having steamed it part of the way at twelve knots an hour. The river was filled with floating ice, and an occasional canvas-back duck. It was a great trip; and, if any thing would have mitigated Mr. Cave Johnson's determination to retrench, it would have been this excursion; but it is better, perhaps, for the long purse of the people that he was not of this Congressional deputation of visitation."

The following is from the Washington correspondent of the *New York Herald*:—

"Although particularly requested not to particularize individuals, yet I shall transgress so far as to mention the name of Captain Stockton, who made his first appearance here at the levee. He was attended by a crowd wherever he moved, and again and again was he obliged to recount the exploits of the Princeton, especially in coming up through the ice of the Potomac. The utter astonishment and amazement which she created among the inhabitants upon the banks of the river is not easily conceived, as they beheld this fairy phantom-ship, without a patch of sail spread upon her spars, or a living soul upon her decks,—without the slightest evidence of steam, fire, light, or life, on board, still plowing her onward way through the immense thickness of ice, ripping, tearing, breaking, crushing it with irresistible power,—*mirabile dictu!* The Messrs. Harpers will please issue proposals for a new edition of the 'Arabian Nights,' and Irving must retouch his legends of the 'Flying Dutchman;' for the age of romance is come again.

"To-day the Captain invigorates, advises, and prepares; and to-morrow the President and *suite*—a private party—will visit the Princeton. It will be a select party, but I think you will get a report of it."

Undoubtedly the *éclat* which Mr. Stockton obtained by his successful construction of the Princeton provoked the jealousy of some petty spirits in the navy; and soon after her return from the Mediterranean, and immediately following the resignation of his commission in the navy by Mr. Stockton, she was directed to be broken up, on the pretence that her timbers were so rotten as to render her repair impracticable; but immediately upon the election of Commodore Stockton to the Senate of the United States, she was ordered to be rebuilt. But her model was spoiled and her machinery changed, so that she in no way resembled herself as she came from the hands of her original architect. In a speech in the Senate on the navy, Commodore Stockton pronounced her, as rebuilt, "an abortion in the service."*

No vessel, during the Mexican war, was more useful than the Princeton in the Gulf of Mexico. The records of the Navy Department will show that she performed more service than all the rest of the Gulf squadron put together.

On the 28th of February, the President, Cabinet, and a large number of members of Congress, and distinguished strangers in Washington, went on board the Princeton for an experimental excursion. The beauty and the chivalry of the United States assembled at the seat of government were also present. A more gay, joyous, or delighted company seldom before were ever gathered together on the deck of any one of our national ships. It was a beautiful, bright day, and the resplendent sun blazed upon the firmament without a cloud to threaten his effulgence. The Potomac was unruffled by a breeze, its glassy surface presenting the lustre and serenity of a perfect mirror. As the Princeton, without the aid of wind or current, smoothly pursued her way as if moved by some unseen agency, no cloud of smoke marked her progress, no uncouth sounds of jarring machinery mingled with the voice of festivity which rose in pleasant harmony from the deck of the gallant vessel. There were grave matrons, mothers of the naval and army heroes of the country; there were illustrious senators and curious statesmen; and there were youth and beauty, light-hearted and joyous. There, too, were gallant post-captains, generals, distinguished engineers, and men of science, come to feast their eyes upon this nautical wonder, this gem of the ocean, this last effort of American genius, skill, and architectural ingenuity.

It is not possible to suppose that the heart of the gallant commander did not throb with patriotic exultation, or that he did not consider all his risks in past years, his toils, his hardships, the

---

* See Appendix.

sneers of enemies and the derision of the ignorant, (which had so often, within a short time previous, lightly esteemed his experiment in the construction of this ship,) more than compensated by the universal homage which rewarded his success. The grateful tribute of general popular admiration and applause now flowed upon him in torrents. "He was the observed of all observers." We have been informed that he has himself said that on that day he felt perfectly happy. He had attained the acme of his hopes for the navy and his country; yet, from that lofty height of honourable exaltation, in a single instant, with the flash of a gun, he was plunged into wo unutterable, and prostrated to the earth with the groans of the dying and the lamentation of the living vibrating with agonizing poignancy through every avenue of consciousness.

During her progress down the Potomac, the great guns on the Princeton had been again and again discharged, until public curiosity appeared to be satiated. The company had returned below, and at the festive board the voice of hilarity resounded through the decks of the proud ship. Toasts were given appropriate to the occasion, and all went merry as the sound of marriage-bells. The feast of reason and the flow of soul was nearly spent. Some of the guests had commenced retiring from the board and renewing their scrutiny on the different parts of the ship. Captain Stockton had risen to offer a toast complimentary to the chief magistrate of the republic. As he rose, with his wine-glass filled in his hand, an officer entered and informed him that some of the company desired one of the great guns to be again discharged. Captain S. shook his head, and saying "No more guns to-night," dismissed the officer. He soon again returned, while Captain S. was speaking on the subject of his toast, with a message from the Secretary of the Navy expressive of his desire to see one of the big guns fired once more. This message Captain Stockton considered equivalent to an order, and immediately went on deck to obey it. He placed himself upon the breech of the gun, aimed, and fired. Feeling a sensible shock, stunned and enveloped in a cloud of smoke, for an instant he could not account for his sensations. But, in a few seconds, as the smoke cleared, and the groans of the wounded and the shrieks of the bystanders who were unhurt resounded over the decks, the terrible catastrophe which had happened was revealed. But, in that appalling hour, when other men in similar circumstances would have been utterly paralyzed, if not crushed into utter imbecility, he, of all the crowd around, alone seemed to retain possession of his faculties. He was severely hurt, but the strength of his intellectual powers, now intensely concentrated, sustained him. Calmly but clearly his voice pealed over the elements of confusion and disturbance; and a few brief orders, recalling his men to a sense of duty, were given, the dead and the wounded ascertained, and all proper dispositions respecting both being made, when, as he turned to leave the sad scene, he fell into the arms of his men exhausted physically, and was borne insensible to his bed.

The unfortunate sufferers by the explosion who were killed were the Hon. Abel P. Upshur, Secretary of State; the Hon. Thomas W. Gilmer, Secretary of the Navy; Captain Beverley Kennon, United States Navy; Hon. Virgil Maxey, of Maryland; and the Hon. David Gardiner, father-in-law of the President.

We need not say that none among the friends of the deceased were more sorrow-stricken by their untimely fate than Captain Stockton. But every generous and susceptible heart in the nation, acquainted with the man, felt and knew that he was entitled to a full proportion of their commiseration.

Every disposition was manifested, by the press and the public, to consider the catastrophe temperately and justly.

The following is an extract from one of the cotemporary New York papers, which, with the Report of the Court of Inquiry, belongs to the history of this event:—

"UNITED STATES STEAMSHIP PRINCETON.

" This noble ship left the Potomac on Tuesday for Philadelphia. Captain Stockton, though yet much indisposed from the effects of the recent accident, is on board the ship.

" We copy from the Washington papers of yesterday the annexed Official Report of the Naval Court of Inquiry—composed of Captains Bolton, McKeever, and Aulick—appointed to investigate and report upon the circumstances connected with the late disastrous explosion on board the Princeton. The result of the investigation, carefully and fairly made, shows that the occurrence in question was one of those which sometimes take place notwithstanding the exercise of the utmost human care and precaution combined with thorough skill and science. The perfect success achieved by Captain Stockton in the construction of the Princeton constitutes a triumph in the art of naval defence of which the country has just reason to be proud, and the melancholy catastrophe under consideration no more detracts from the praise due to Captain Stockton than did the event—strikingly parallel in its character—of the death of Mr. Huskisson, the British statesman, at the memorable original trial of locomotive steam-power on the Liverpool and Manchester Railroad, take from the merits of Ericsson and others, whose inventive genius has since led to such astonishing results.

"OFFICIAL REPORT.

" The Naval Court of Inquiry convened by order of the Secretary of the Navy, by a precept under his hand, bearing date the 6th day of March instant, for the purpose of inquiring into the conduct of Captain Robert F. Stockton and officers, in relation to the experiments and proofs which preceded the construction and the proof and subsequent explosion of one of the great guns of the Princeton, occasioning the awful and distressing catastrophe which has recently occurred on board the said ship, and to report the opinion of said court on the matters thus referred to it, respectfully submit to the consideration of the Honourable the Secretary of the Navy the evidence which has been laid before it in relation to the premises.

" In further performance of the duty imposed on it, the court would respectfully report :—

" That, in pursuing the investigation with which it has been charged, the court was limited to the facts and circumstances immediately connected with the captain and officers of the Princeton anterior to and immediately attending the explosion of one of the large guns on board that vessel on the 28th February last. This investigation has satisfied the court.

" That, in the year 1839, Captain Stockton being in England, his attention was attracted to the extraordinary and important improvements which had recently been introduced into the manufacture of large masses of wrought-iron, as a substitute for cast-iron, for objects which required a combination of strength and adhesiveness or toughness. Large shafts for steam-engines had been thus fabricated, which experience had demonstrated to be superior, in those qualities which were desirable, to the same articles manufactured of cast-iron.

" These circumstances appear to have led Captain Stockton to consider the question how far the same material might be employed in the construction of cannon of a large calibre. He appears to have been animated by motives the most patriotic, stimulated by the laudable desire of being himself instrumental in promoting the honour of his country and of elevating that branch of the service with which he was personally connected. To what extent his inquiries were carried the court has not been advised; but it is in evidence that he did advise and consult with three gentlemen possessing, from their scientific acquirements and practical experience on such subjects, very superior qualifications in questions of this character, and whose opinions were entitled to high respect:—Mr. William Young, Captain Ericsson, and Francis B. Ogden, Esq., are the gentlemen to whom allusion is made.

"After much deliberation, and several consultations, with calculations furnished from the same quarter, Captain Stockton determined upon the construction of a gun of the proposed dimensions, for the purpose of testing the opinions of scientific men by the results of experience. A cannon was accordingly made at the Mersey Works, of Yorkshire iron, which, being approved of, was shipped to the United States. Having been properly prepared for the purpose, this gun was carried to Sandy Hook and subjected to what was deemed the proper test. After the first firing, preparations were made to mount the gun. In doing this a crack was perceived opposite the chamber, which induced Captain Stockton to have the breech strengthened by putting bands around it. These bands are represented as being three and a half inches in thickness. With this additional strength given to the defective part of the gun, the experiments were renewed, and the result was a decided conviction upon the minds of all connected with them, that, in general, the anticipations of Captain Stockton were perfectly realized; and, secondly, that if a gun of this construction should yield to the force of the trial, it would be by a simple opening, and not, as in cast-iron, a violent disruption and scattering of the fragments.

"The success of these experiments was such as to decide Captain Stockton forthwith to direct the construction of another gun of a similar character, to be made of American iron, which is usually regarded as superior in strength and tenacity to the English iron. This second gun—the same which exploded on board the Princeton—was constructed with a chamber similar to that of the first gun, with an additional thickness of twelve inches at the breech,—a difference, even if the metal were only of equal goodness, far more than sufficient to compensate for the bands by which the first had been fortified.

"Application was made to Colonel Bomford, of the Ordnance Department of the Army, who, it is well known, has been professionally occupied in experimenting upon guns of a large calibre, and his opinion requested as to the proper proof to which such a gun ought to be subjected. The proof suggested by Colonel Bomford as a suitable one will be found in his letter of November 25, 1840, appended to the record. The new gun constructed by order of Captain Stockton exceeded in dimensions and weight, consequently should also have surpassed in strength, that contemplated by Colonel Bomford, they being of the same calibre; and the proof to which this cannon was subjected was much more severe than what was proposed as sufficient by that experienced officer.

" In view of all the circumstances briefly adverted to, but minutely detailed in the evidence which is spread upon the record, the court entertains a distinct and confident opinion that, in originally forming the plan for the construction of large guns, Captain Stockton proceeded on well-established practical facts; that, in coming to a decision upon the feasibility of the contemplated project, he did not rely upon his own theoretical opinions, but resorted to men of science and practical skill for advice, and that he was fully sustained by their judgment in every particular; that a series of experiments and trials with the two guns fully sustained the deductions of the gentlemen whose advice was sought, and justified the most assured confidence in the durability and efficiency of the gun.

" In regard to the mode of loading and firing on every occasion, and emphatically that which was followed by the explosion, it is established by the fullest proof, to the entire satisfaction of the court, that every care and attention which prudence and professional capacity could dictate was observed. No shadow of censure in this respect can be attached to any officer or any of the crew of the Princeton.

" In regard to the conduct and deportment of the captain and officers of the Princeton on the occasion of the deplorable catastrophe which occurred on the 28th of February last, the court feels itself bound to express its opinion that in all respects they were such as were to be expected from gallant and well-trained officers, sustaining their own personal character and that of the service:—marked with the most perfect order, subordination, and steadiness.

" In conclusion, the court is also decidedly of opinion that not only was every precaution taken which skill, regulated by prudence and animated by the loftiest motives, could devise to guard against accident, but that Captain Stockton, Lieutenant Hunt, and Mr. King, the gunner, who had attended to and directed all the experiments and trials of these guns, exhibited only a due confidence in what they had witnessed, in placing themselves on every occasion, and particularly on that of the explosion, almost in contact with the gun, and in a position apparently not only more dangerous than any other, but that which might rationally have been deemed the only perilous situation on board the vessel.

"The court, having thus completed its business, adjourned *sine die.*

"(Signed)   W. C. BOLTON, *President.*

"RICHARD S. COXE, *Judge-Advocate.*"

Captain Stockton was selected by President Tyler, at the close of his administration, as the bearer of the celebrated annexation resolutions to the government of Texas. Immediately on the adoption of the resolutions by Congress, he sailed on this mission, in the steamer Princeton, for Galveston. The delicate and important duties with which he was charged he performed in such a manner as to obtain the entire approval of the new administration of Mr. Polk.

While in Texas, his prescient eye foresaw the coming conflict with Mexico; and on his return to Washington he communicated to Mr. Polk the grounds of his belief that war would soon commence. He also expressed an earnest desire, in that event, for some command which would enable him to take an active part in the anticipated contest.

CHAPTER VIII.

MR. POLK concurred with Captain Stockton in his opinion respecting the probability of a war with Mexico; and, looking upon California as the proper theatre on the Pacific coast for the prosecution of hostilities against Mexico in the event of a war, he displayed his confidence in the discretion of Captain Stockton by appointing him to reinforce our squadron in that quarter. The reports from the emigrants who had been allured to California by promises of liberal grants of land were beginning to excite much interest in the United States for that country; and some indications of a growing cupidity for its acquisition may be discovered in the newspapers of 1844–5, as well as in the debates of Congress. After the declaration of war, the avidity of the government for the conquest of California was manifested in its instructions to both naval and military officers; and, in its eagerness for the acquisition, instructions were indiscriminately given to both arms of the service in such a manner as created a conflict of authority.

At this time, however, Captain Stockton supposed, from the unsettled question of the Oregon boundary, that there was about the same probability of war with England as with Mexico. He would therefore have preferred service in a quarter where he would be more likely to meet an enemy on his own element, whose immense resources and powerful marine would test to its utmost capacity the skill and valour of the American navy.

The Baltimore National Democratic Convention had pledged the new administration to the boundary of 54° 40′, and Captain Stockton believed that the administration were disposed to redeem that pledge; they probably would have been compelled to do so had not the difficulty with Mexico intervened.

The frigate Constellation was first designated as the ship to the command of which he would be appointed; but, subsequently, he was ordered to hoist his broad pennant on the Congress, which could be got ready for sea in less time, and in her he was instructed to convey the commissioner, Mr. Ten Eycke, to the Sandwich Islands, with *sealed orders* respecting his future destination.

His letter to the Secretary of the Navy, dated on the Congress, at Norfolk, and written on the eve of sailing, (and which we annex,) details graphically the history of his appointment to that ship. It likewise affords striking evidence of the avidity with which he sought a post where danger threatened and glory might be achieved. It shows also how keenly sensitive he was (in the possible event of a war with Great Britain) of being supposed "a volunteer" on service remote from danger. The concluding paragraph of this letter, breathing a lofty and self-sacrificing spirit of devoted patriotism, is a fitting prologue to the grand drama of the California campaign :—

"UNITED STATES FRIGATE CONGRESS,
NORFOLK, VA., October 24, 1845.

"SIR,—I have the honour to acknowledge the receipt of your letter of the 17th, ordering me to proceed in the Congress to the Sandwich Islands, &c. &c. ; and also the 'sealed orders' which I am not to open till I am 'beyond the capes of Virginia.'

"The following expression in your letter of the 17th—'So soon as the United States frigate of which you have *volunteered to take command*, in connection with the "*sealed package*," '—has given rise in my mind to some reflections that prompt me to recall to your remembrance, in the most humble and respectful manner, the circumstances under which I felt constrained, by every principle of patriotism and personal honour, to accept or volunteer for the command of the Congress.

"Having performed, in the best way I could, the duty assigned to me in Texas, I returned to the United States, to bring the glad tidings of annexation, and to explain to you my views (the importance of which I no doubt overrated) in regard to our relations with Mexico. During those conversations I stated to you that I thought Mexico would probably, when ready, commence hostilities. You suggested that it was important to have the Princeton back in the Gulf as soon as possible, that a constant and certain communication might be kept up with Vera Cruz; and mentioned Commander Engle as the officer whom you thought of ordering to command her, and ordered me to make the necessary arrangements to fit out the Constellation. My only desire was to do as you wished, and to be ready, with a good ship under me, to take part—any part—in the expected conflict in the Gulf. I was satisfied with the Princeton; I applied for no change; I suggested none. But, as you wanted the Princeton as a tender to Commodore Conner, and offered me the Constellation in her place, I was still better pleased, because I thought I was pleasing you and at the same time would have a ship larger, stronger, and more effective even, than the Princeton, and that I would then be ready for war, come from where it might. You changed your notions, and ordered me to proceed no farther with the Constellation. The Princeton had gone to the Gulf, and I was a volunteer idler on shore, having left a cruising ship at a time of threatened hostilities. To relieve myself from this painful situation you offered me no facility, and I saw no way open but to apply to fit out the Congress or some other ship. If you had time to give to my poor character and position a few moments' consideration, I am sure you would appreciate the feelings which prompted me to ask to fit out the Congress, and would not suppose for one moment that I could have volunteered to command the Congress as she now is, with 'sealed orders' and *twelve passengers—men, women, and children.* My great object in the first place was to be prepared, in the event of a war with Mexico, to try to do something creditable to the navy. If Mexico did not make war, I wanted then to get a ship ready for England, that might be able to keep the station to which she was ordered, and not to go cruising about with passengers in time of peace, and in war to run away (as the Congress must necessarily do) from the English squadron in the Pacific. They not only have a much larger squadron, led by an eighty-gun-ship, but have means of communication which will enable them to receive their despatches months before we can.

"But here I am; and, whatever that ominous-looking package may contain, and wherever I am ordered to go, or whatever I am ordered to do, by the leave of Providence there I will go, and that I will do, in the best way I can.

"Faithfully, your obedient servant,

"R. F. STOCKTON.

"To the Hon. GEORGE BANCROFT,
  "*Secretary of the Navy.*"

On the 25th of October, the Congress heaved anchor and proceeded with a light breeze towards sea. On reaching Hampton Roads, the wind out ahead, the anchors were reluctantly dropped. There, for five weary days, lay the gallant vessel, like a hound in leash, impatient to bound over the mighty plain of waters on her destined mission. On the 28th, to while away the time and relieve the disappointment which clouded every countenance, on account of the unfavourable breeze which detained her, a mimic battle was performed, *sola cum sola*. The guns were fired, the boarders called, and all the forms of a naval engagement took place. The enthusiasm and excitement of the performance were well adapted to display the characteristics of the men, and enable the officers to form some estimate of the materials of which the ship's crew was composed.

The Rev. Walter Colton was chaplain to the Congress, and to his diary kept on this voyage, and published subsequently under the title of DECK AND PORT, we are indebted for many interesting details respecting the Congress. Page 17 of "Deck and Port," Mr. Colton says :—"The sailors are proud of our frigate—and well they may be; she is a splendid specimen of naval architecture. For capacity, strength, and harmony of proportions, she stands in her class without a rival in the world. She is so much a favourite in the service that one old sailor travelled all the way from Pensacola to Norfolk in the mail-stage, and at his own expense, to join her. We had our complement of seamen, but his was so strong a case he could not be denied.

"We number about two hundred souls, all told; have laid in provisions and fuel for five months, with fifty thousand gallons of water, and sails and rigging sufficient to replace what is now in use, should emergency demand.

"*October* 29.—I have been occupied to-day in arranging in suitable cases the library of the crew,—a library comprising between three and four hundred volumes. For many of the miscellaneous and religious books I am indebted to the Presbyterian Board of Publication, to the Sunday-school Union, to the American Tract Society, and to the liberality of Commodore Stockton.

"*Thursday, October* 30.—The long-looked-for breeze came at last. It was a southwester, and at daylight this morning we weighed anchor and got under way. When we had cleared the capes of old Virginia, all hands were called, and Commodore Stockton delivered the following brief and appropriate address to the officers and crew :—

'Captain Dupont, (executive officer of the ship,) and Officers :— Your reputation in the service is a sufficient guarantee that the cruise before us will enlist your highest energies and zeal.

"Men :—Your conduct since you have been on board the ship justifies the strongest confidence in your fidelity. Above us floats the

7

flag of our country; to your patriotism and undaunted valour I intrust its honour, dearer to me than life. We now sail for California and Oregon; and then where it may please Heaven.

"Then, turning to the chaplain, he said, 'You will offer up prayers to Almighty God for his protection.'

"This service performed, the broad pennant was saluted, the ship cheered, and the band struck up 'Hail Columbia.'

"The whole ceremony was well calculated to inspire a jealous regard for the honour of our flag and impress sentiments of dependence on the divine protection, so well becoming those who 'go down to the sea in ships, and who see the wonders of the Lord in the deep.'"*

The following extract from the Rev. Mr. Colton's diary will illustrate the kind interest manifested by Commodore Stockton in those under his command:—

"*Wednesday, Nov. 19.*—We have three sailors in the *sick bay* to-day, in a very critical condition. They are all good men, so far at least as ship-duty is concerned. Their death would make a serious breach in the crew. Our intelligent surgeon and his faithful assistants are devoted to them. They are not left, night or day, for an hour without a medical attendant. Commodore Stockton went into the sick bay to-day to see them. He never forgets the sailor; he pities when others might reproach, forgives when others might denounce, and never abandons him even though he should abandon himself, and yet he exacts prompt obedience. His discipline and that of Captain Dupont is derived, in a great measure, from moral influence, the power of correct example, and the pressure of circumstance.†"

The Congress arrived at Rio de Janeiro on the 21st December, and, after a short stay required for some necessary repairs, proceeded on her voyage. Cape Horn was soon doubled, with the usual vicissitudes of storms and gales.

On the 6th of May, the good ship anchored at Valparaiso, whence, after receiving fresh supplies of water and provisions, she proceeded down the coast to Callao, where the Commodore expected he should hear from the Expresses from the United States, which he had arranged to meet him there.

While the Congress was at Callao, an incident happened which will show in what manner Commodore Stockton believes American citizens should be protected in foreign ports from unjust treatment.

---

* "Deck and Port," pp. 19, 20.   † "Deck and Port," p. 44.

One morning he received a note from the captain of an American merchantman, informing him that the writer had been arrested suddenly in the streets, without just cause, and thrown into prison, and urgently requesting that a United States officer might be sent to inquire into the circumstances of the affair. Stockton immediately ordered a boat and went ashore himself to prosecute the inquiry. On landing, he went to the prison, saw the captain, and learned from him the facts of the case, which he found likewise corroborated by the concurring statements of all present on the occasion.

The captain of the American ship was coming ashore in his barge, when he was purposely run into by the boat of a Peruvian man-of-war. This led to a quarrel between the Peruvian and American men as soon as they reached the shore. The American captain, who had left the wharf before the quarrel commenced, returned as soon as he heard of it, in order to assist in quelling the affray. While thus engaged, he was seized, and, without any opportunity of defending himself, thrown into prison.

After ascertaining these facts, Commodore Stockton presented himself before the civil authorities, and, in polite and courteous terms, requested the release of his countryman. This was refused without hesitation, in a peremptory manner. Stockton then, assuming a different tone, demanded the immediate liberation of the American, or he would undertake himself to release him. The authorities, now seeing that he was in earnest, asked for time to send to Lima to know the pleasure of the government on the case. Stockton would grant them no such accommodation; but, pulling out his watch, said he would give them fifteen minutes to determine whether they would surrender the American peaceably, and if he were not given up in that time, he would lay the United States ship-of-war Congress where her guns would soon open the prison-doors. The prisoner was released at once.*

On the 9th day of May the Congress sailed from Callao, and, turning westward, directed her course to the far-distant isles to which she was bound. No adventures or occurrences of a novel character diversified the usual monotony of a voyage across the Pacific.

The Rev. Mr. Colton, in his diary, remarks frequently on the strict observance of Sunday on board the Congress. Officers and crew all united in attendance on divine service.

The following passage from " Deck and Port" will exhibit the

---

* The Captain, on his return to the United States, did not fail to make this incident known.

Commodore in a new character, and well illustrates his versatility of talent and his respect for religion :—

"*Sunday, June* 7.—Commodore Stockton, who has always taken an interest in our religious exercises, having occasion to speak to the crew to-day, I induced him to extend his remarks to topics more sacred than those which lay within his original purpose. He spoke of the Bible as that crowning revelation which God has made of himself to man, of its elevating influences on the human soul, of the priceless counsels which it conveys, and the immortal hopes which it awakens.

"He contrasted the gloomy condition of those tribes and nations which were without it with that of those where its steady light shone, and found in this contrast a vindication of its divinity which none could gainsay or resist.

"He commended its habitual study to the officers and crew as our only infallible rule of duty,—as our only safe guiding-light in the mental and moral twilight of our being here.

"He rebuked the idea that religion was out of its element among sailors, and told them that of all classes of men they were the one that most needed its restraining influences and glorious promises, and denounced as insane a disposition to trifle with its precepts.

"He commended the good conduct of the crew on the Sabbath, and expressed the earnest hope that they would continue, in the event of a probable separation from them, the same respectful and earnest regard for the duties of religion.

"Such remarks as these, coming from the commander of a ship or squadron, will do more to sustain a chaplain in the discharge of his difficult duties than any privileges which can be conferred upon him through the provisions of law. They honour the heart from which they flow, and their influence will be felt in the moral well-being of hundreds when that heart shall have ceased to beat. The tree you have planted will grow, and its fruit come to maturity, though you see it not."

In another place, Mr. Colton says, with reference to the observance of religious duties by the crew:—

"The effect of this on the discipline of the ship is too marked to escape observation. There is no disobedience and no punishment. Each performs with alacrity the duties of his station. It would seem as if we might throw every instrument of correction and coercion overboard; their requirement for the present, at least, has ceased. Give me the religious sentiment in a crew, and you may sink your handcuffs, cats, and Colts, in the depths of the ocean."

On the 9th of June the Congress let go her anchors in the port of Honolulu, after making one of the shortest runs on record from Callao, having left the latter port on the 9th of May.

The Commodore found on his arrival that all intercourse between the King's government and the American Commissioner, Mr. Brown, (superseded by Mr. Ten Eycke,) had been suspended, and that the most unfriendly feelings existed between them. The American flag had been hauled down by Mr. Brown and his functions suspended. He was much irritated with the King and his ministry, and made grievous complaints to the Commodore of the manner in which he had been treated.

Mr. Brown unfortunately had, with or without cause, in imitation of the British and French, assumed a dictatorial attitude that, after long discussions, terminated in a complete rupture. The English and French commanders of squadrons which had visited Honolulu a short time previous, with powerful fleets to back them, had bullied and hectored the King, and extorted at the cannon's mouth their unjust and exorbitant demands. Mr. Brown, with no such auxiliaries, had attempted likewise to act the dictator. His demands were rejected, and he expected to use the first American ship-of-war which visited the Sandwich Isles for the purpose of punishing the refractory King and his subjects.

Commodore Stockton was fully informed by Mr. Ten Eycke of the history of these difficulties, and saw very soon that there were faults on both sides, and that Mr. Brown's temper and spirit, together with the part taken in the affair by the foreign residents, had complicated the dispute until it was beyond his control. The course of Mr. Brown had so incensed the King and his ministers that no disposition to receive Mr. Ten Eycke was manifested. Mr. Ten Eycke felt embarrassed by the difficulties which presented themselves, and in this disagreeable state of affairs applied to Commodore Stockton to extricate him from the dilemma, and, if possible, to effect such a reconciliation as would enable him to enter upon the discharge of the duties of his office.

In reply to Mr. Ten Eycke's invitation that he should act the part of mediator, Commodore Stockton said to him that, if he would leave the whole matter to his discretion, without any interference whatever, he would undertake it. Mr. Ten Eycke having assented, the Commodore immediately wrote a note to the Minister of Foreign Affairs, and informed him that, the duty of negotiating with the government having been devolved upon him, (Stockton,) he would suggest that an informal meeting, which might save writing and misunderstanding, would probably facilitate the objects of both. The minister consented to the interview, and the Commodore called the next day and had two hours' conversation with him. The Commodore told him that he much regretted the existing misunderstanding, but thought there was nothing in it which should permanently estrange the two governments; that he had not come there to use force or intimidation, as others had done; that he had no authority to exert force except for the protection of citizens of the United States unjustly assailed; and that he desired to know how and in what manner he could best aid in the restoration of good feelings between the King's government and the representatives of the United States. The interview finally resulted in a thorough and complete amicable understanding. The minister on the following day called on the Commodore and expressed himself gratified and surprised at his unlooked-for and friendly interposition, and said that he had been directed by the King to express the high sense which the government entertained of the Commodore's liberality and justice.

Mr. Brown was indignant at first with this advance of Commodore Stockton, and in conversation with him spoke of the King in such contemptuous terms—as a tawny red-skin—that the Commodore felt constrained to tell him that such disrespectful language, applied to the chief magistrate of the country to which he had been appointed to represent the United States, was altogether inconsistent with his position; that, if the King were actually as ignorant and degraded as a barbarian African chief, it would still be the duty of the representative of the United States at his court to exhibit towards him the most respectful deportment; that, for his part, he would treat the King with the same respect that he would Queen Victoria or the Emperor Nicholas.

Finally, Mr. Brown, convinced by the remonstrances of Commodore Stockton of the impolicy of his course, modified his views, and even consented to be present at the first audience of his successor by the King.

Mr. Ten Eycke presented his credentials on the 18th of June, when he was received by the King in state; he accompanied their presentment with a few appropriate remarks, which were followed by a brief address from Commodore Stockton, who expressed his earnest hope that uninterrupted amity might prevail between the two countries. He assured the King of the lively interest felt in the United States for the successful issue of all his majesty's plans and purposes for the benefit of his people, and pledged the cordial support of our government in any aggressive emergencies which might threaten the tranquillity and integrity of his realm.*

The following interesting scene, as described by the Rev. Mr. Colton, will, we are sure, be perused with pleasure by all who feel an interest in the subject of our narrative:—

"*Sunday, June* 21.—I exchanged with Mr. Duncan this morning,—he officiating on board the Congress, while I took his place in the Seamen's Chapel. The frigate had the advantage in the arrangement, but I intended to look out for my floating parish. In the afternoon I was, by appointment, in the pulpit of the King's chapel.

"The spacious edifice was crowded. His Majesty, the court, and chiefs, were present, and an auditory of some three thousand. They had assembled under the vague expectation that Commodore Stockton might address them; for a report to that effect, without the Commodore's knowledge, had been circulated through the town. I felt, in common with the missionaries, a desire that they should not be disappointed. But, as the Commodore was wholly unprepared, and averse to any arrangements that might seemingly trench upon proprieties, it was no easy matter to have their wishes realized.

"Backed by the Rev. Mr. Armstrong, I made a bold push, and, having addressed the audience for half an hour, through him as interpreter, on the religious enterprises in our own country, which were throwing their light and influence into other lands, stated that I was aware of their desire that Commodore Stockton should address them, and that I would take the liberty of expressing the hope that he would gratify their wishes. He was sitting at the time by the side of the King; and, while the choir were singing a hymn, Mr. Armstrong descended from the pulpit and urged with him the public expectation. He finally assented, and, taking the platform under the pulpit, commenced a train of pertinent and eloquent remarks."

Mr. Colton, after a brief synopsis of the Commodore's address, proceeds:—

"Such was the tenor of his remarks, which were delivered with as much freedom and force as if they had been well considered and arranged. Their effect was obvious in the eager attention which pervaded the great assemblage. At the conclusion, the King and the chiefs came up, and, with undisguised emotion, thanked the Commodore for his address. The Commodore may win laurels on

---

"Deck and Port," p. 349.

the deck, but none that can bloom more lastingly than these. If there be consolations in death, they flow from efforts made and triumphs won in the cause of humanity and God."

Three days after these ceremonies the Congress sailed for Monterey, and the Commodore never supposed that note or comment would be made of his speech on this occasion. Fortunately, however, it so happened that a native South Sea Island stenographer was present and executed a *verbatim* report of the address in English, which was subsequently forwarded to the United States by the missionaries and republished in 1847 in many religious as well as other papers. It is a remarkable production, and displays in an eminent degree the intellectual vigour of Commodore Stockton's mind as well as the high moral tone of his character. We should be surprised if any one, after a perusal of this discourse, did not admit Commodore Stockton to be the most remarkable sailor on record.

COMMODORE STOCKTON'S ADDRESS BEFORE MR. ARMSTRONG'S CON-
GREGATION ON THE AFTERNOON OF JUNE 21, 1846.

I came up here this afternoon by no means prepared for such an exercise as that requested of me, and, if I consulted my own feelings on being thus suddenly called upon, I should certainly remain in silence. But standing here in the temple of God, and remembering that the opportunity to do good but rarely occurs, while that to do mischief and evil is the event of every day, I cannot refuse. What I do say I will say in the sincerity of my heart; it is the feeling I entertain towards you all, from your king down to his humblest subject, which will not allow me to keep silence.

We are always in the habit of referring to past times, and speaking of ancient nations and their learning and knowledge; but the truth is that in sound philosophy—paradoxical as it may seem—you being the youngest nation are in fact the oldest, and with your position as such you bear a commensurate responsibility. You are responsible for the advantages which surround you. You have been told by your spiritual advisers that our Saviour died for you; his bloody sweat and agonies were for you; his cross and passion were for you; his precious death and burial were for you; the ascension was for you. All the blood and suffering, all the trials and all the deaths which have happened in this world in the cause of civil and religious liberty, were for you. You have all the advantages of the past and all those of the present. But all this experience purchased by others and all these advantages are not given to your king and you for his and your simple benefit; it is a solemn trust from Almighty God, and all of you will be held responsible for the fulfilment of your duties. This is a position you cannot escape; it is written upon every page of the Bible. With that belief, let me ask you whether it is not well to consider what the advantages are of the age in which you live. Is it your belief that those advantages consist in the fact that architecture now raises her stately piles, or that the paintings of our day rival the art of the ancient masters, or that music swells her most delicious strains? No! These are all well. It is well that all the arts and sciences, under divine Providence, are rapidly advancing. But it is in the spread of God's word and the principles of the gospel that your advantage lies. You cannot doubt the advantages of true religious light, or that religion is interwoven with man's nature. The history of the world shows that the earliest nations of the earth, no matter how far separated, no matter that they had never seen each other or heard of each other, all agreed in bowing the knee to the Father of light.

Whence comes this island? How came this island to lift its majestic head above the roaring ocean? How comes this island to be peopled? By the arm of omnipotent power only. Again: how comes it that you are known to other nations of the world? how comes it that I see myself surrounded by persons from different and distant parts of the globe? how comes it that the missionaries, braving every danger, and leaving friends and kindred, live among you, your preceptors in the knowledge of God? How comes it? By the will of God. Was it his will, think you, that you should merely eat, drink, and be clothed? Think you it was God's will that only the animal and physical wants of man should be administered to?

The Almighty Power that first created the world afterwards destroyed man from off the face of that world. He was kind and benevolent, but man was rebellious and wicked. Man became so bad, he turned so constantly from the face of God himself, despised his warning voice heard in the murmuring leaves, defied his power seen in the tempest and felt in the lightning and the earthquake,— in short, he became so bad that the only way to recover the earth that he had polluted was to destroy him from off it. Hence all the world, except one man and his family, were destroyed. Since that era God has constantly been bestowing upon man his kindest blessings, and man has ever since been and still seems to be in rebellion against God. Look at the nations of the earth which have been but are not. We have just heard mention made of Rome and Greece; but go back to the farthest page of history, and see how nation after nation fell. Their laws were not founded in the fear of God, and with them might was right.

But the Bible teaches peace on earth and good-will towards man. Turn over its holy pages, for in them the best lesson in individual and national happiness is to be found; and therefore it is, as I have had occasion to observe in another place, that you have enjoyed so much happiness and arrived at so much prosperity. This comes from your having been taught the word of God.

And now turn over the bloody record of man's doings. Reckless of their own happiness, and in defiance of the word of God, what has become of them? Nation after nation has become mistress of the world; nation after nation has usurped the sovereignty of the sea; and now you can hardly discover where their gorgeous palaces and their imperial thrones were once erected.

What think you, then, in view of these things? Think you this island was brought out of the vasty deep to afford a field for the reception of such dark doings? There has been kindled here on these islands a flame which flourishes and increases, and joins with that other light which our noble missionaries have erected on the coast of Africa,—a beacon by which those who will may guide their course to heaven.

And thus it is that you have the responsibility placed upon you by God to guard this priceless treasure. But when he gives you the Bible, he does not give it you to keep, but to read; on the contrary, he will hold you answerable for a proper use of it. Give me this Bible, and I defy the world in arms. When I rely on it, I appeal not to the power of man, but to the Lord of hosts.

I have said that the decay and fall of other nations is attributable to their disregard of the principles of this holy book. But let me revert for a single moment to one example in the very ocean upon which this island reposes itself. I speak of the Spaniards and Spain. She who in ancient times carried her portly bearing and her chivalry so high,—she who had all nature to cheer her and all art and science to instruct her,—where is she now? The short-sighted politician would tell us she wants resources, physical as well as mental; but can we of the present age be satisfied with such an explanation? It is because the word of God's justice has gone forth. The curse of successful avarice and unbending brutality and unsparing tyranny is upon her. She made for herself a golden calf, and fell down and worshipped it; and now the blood of thousands and tens of thousands of unfortunate victims is smoking to heaven for vengeance; and when God in his mercy shall see fit to remove the curse, and not till then, will that unfortunate country revive again.

From the Bible are to be taken lessons not only for nations to use as charts and principles, but for individuals also. It points the way to happiness in this world and in the next. All philosophers, ancient and modern, from the remotest times down to our own Franklin, have held happiness to be the great object of every man; but so dark have been men's hearts, that the happiness of many has been sought in the destruction of the happiness of others. Envy and malice, contention and strife, war and misery, have been fostered for the gratification of men's pleasures. The dirk of the assassin has been plunged into the heart of many a victim to procure the happiness of men. A man is ruined and his family beggared for the happiness of others. How can it be that in seeking happiness—the great object of all our lives—man involves so many fellow-men in misery? It is because man disregards the whispering of God in his ear, which tells him to consider what happiness consists in.

Let any man or woman who has arrived at the age of maturity ask himself or herself whether, in the pursuit of happiness, that person has not, as far as appears, gone directly in the wrong road.

Man is a much better animal, in my judgment, than is generally supposed. From the time of his first rebellion against God, man has been a sinful creature, and unable to be saved but by the blood of our Saviour; and yet I believe that, when uncontaminated, he is much better than most persons believe. My own experience of mankind has been considerable, and I will venture to say there is not one man in this assembly, no matter what his feelings of bitterness may be against his neighbour, or what he says of his friend behind his back, or what language he uses, but would rather befriend a man and do him good than do him harm.

Let me request of you to examine yourselves upon a question,—and I do not believe there is one individual here but will answer in the affirmative:—that is, whether in your intercourse with others it does not afford you ten thousand times more pleasure to do a good action than it does to do an evil one? Man's kindness to his fellow-man will become the rule when this Bible succeeds in regulating the will and passions of mankind.

All the troubles between man and man, and all the troubles that have arisen in the Christian community, arise in the first place from a disregard of its sacred precepts. Men are very apt also to excuse themselves by referring to the conduct of others, and to comfort themselves by asserting that what others are doing must be right, and they are only doing the same as others. It is very easy, as the English proverb says, for the monkey to use the cat's paws to get the chestnut out of the fire.

I have seen violent men, I have seen men supposed capable of swallowing fire, I have seen men put into heated ovens; but I have never yet seen that man who, if his mind were properly directed, would not rather do a kindness than an injury.

The best man, and the most charitable, and the most generous, is, I will venture to say, the happiest man. What is it that constitutes human happiness, except it be the exercise of benevolence and charity? The reciprocation of good-will between man and man during their short journey to the grave makes up the sum of happiness. I speak as an individual having had some experience.

We see men living in magnificence, surrounded with wealth, and commanding all that can administer to their happiness, and yet they are not so happy as the humblest peasant, who, as he sees a stranger in want passing by his door, gives him assistance out of his too scanty means. Such a one feels happiness indeed. Learned men, and we who pride ourselves upon Christianity, are very angry if told that intellectual enjoyments are not superior to enjoyments of an animal kind; but how many of the learned are there who learn just enough to wish to know more, and who find that learning by itself too often produces nothing but discontent in the human mind?

One word more. My belief is that the most benevolent man is the happiest. Were I to look abroad in the world for an example of happiness, I would search for the most benevolent man. The man that can forgive his enemy, that can conquer the proud feelings of the human heart, that can return good for evil, that is the man I envy.

The man who can go in search of the distressed, of the widow and her desolate children, and, having found them, can relieve them, that is a happy man. He who can go into prison, like Howard, the English philanthropist, and relieve the wants and miseries of the most abject and sinful of his race, must indeed be happy. Oh, compare happiness such as his with that derived from power! Where is there one man in the civilized and Christian world that would not rather wear the humble garment of Howard's happiness than the purple of imperial Rome?

Now, I say that the only hope of happiness, not only for this but for all countries, is that they shall avoid the rock upon which older nations have split.

If I could envy any one, I could envy this gentleman standing by me (the Rev. R. Armstrong) and all his fellow-labourers in the good work. For my own part, I may never see you more, for I am going to return to the far, far distant land from whence I came. My poor name may perish and be lost, but this book (holding up the Bible) will ever remain; and do you remember, as the Almighty destroyed one generation for its perverseness, he may destroy another; therefore, hold fast to this book as the foundation of your prosperity.

In bidding you farewell, I beg of you to search for that which is good, that you may be prosperous, and never to forget the responsibility imposed upon you. In your islands I have beheld the most interesting scene that my eyes have witnessed: it is not merely that you are Christianized, but that in that fact I see the spread of that gospel which shall one day be known wherever the sun rises on this globe.

Once more I tell you that the prosperity of your country and the happiness of every individual in it depends upon your endeavouring to live at peace with God and in good-will towards man.

[The Commodore's remarks were interpreted by the Rev. Mr. Armstrong as he spoke. The natives listened with attention, and it is believed they made a deep impression upon them.]

CHAPTER IX.

UPON his arrival at Monterey, Captain Stockton reported to
Commodore Sloat, his senior officer, then in command of the Pacific
squadron, consisting of the frigate Savannah, sloops-of-war Portsmouth, Cyane, and Warren, and store-ship Erie, to which was now
added the frigate Congress. A few days previous to the arrival of
the Congress, Commodore Sloat had received intelligence of the
commencement of hostilities on the Rio Grande between Mexico
and the United States, and he had landed with a part of his crew,
and raised, without resistance, the flag of the United States at
Monterey. Under his directions it had also been raised at two
other points. It was not, however, within the scope of his plan of
operations to conduct any further military operations on shore.
The Commodore was an old-fashioned sailor, who was content with
the performance of his duty on his own element, and he declined
taking the responsibility of directing a campaign on the land. He
was not disposed to convert his sailors and marines into land-forces.
No such programme was expressed in any orders then received.
He was satisfied with the elevation of the American flag and the
issue of his proclamation declaring that he had taken formal possession of California in the name of the United States. He declined,
therefore, receiving the proffered services of Colonel Fremont and
his men. He doubtless felt embarrassed in his position, particularly after Captain Stockton expressed to him very freely his opinion
that active offensive measures were absolutely indispensable to keep

the flag of the United States flying in California; that the Californians it could not be expected would yield the country without resistance; and that, as soon as time should be afforded them to collect an adequate force, the American flag, unless defended by the most decided movements, would be expelled. Commodore Sloat was a patriotic, gallant officer; and, though he did not perceive how it was possible for the sailors and the marines of the American squadron to carry on successfully a war of conquest on land, he was unwilling to be an obstacle in the way of others who chose to take the responsibility of such a novel procedure. He accordingly informed Captain Stockton that, as his health was not good, and as his instructions authorized him to return to the United States after being relieved, he would relinquish to him the command. On the 23d of July, therefore, Commodore Sloat carried into effect these intentions, and sailed for the United States, leaving Commodore Stockton in command of the squadron.

Before proceeding to narrate the operations of Commodore Stockton in California, a few remarks may properly be here made respecting the condition of that country, and the state of public affairs therein at that time.

California had been neglected by Spain, the mother country, before the Mexican War of Independence. Her inhabitants were left pretty much to themselves and their priests. It is said that the priests, who were aware of the existence of gold in California, concealed its discovery, and in various ways discouraged colonization, lest a knowledge of the abundance of the precious metals might lead to a large emigration, which would interfere with their ascendency in California. The population of California was scattered over an immense surface along the Pacific coast, and engaged principally in agricultural pursuits; but, owing to the proximity of several powerful and warlike nations of Indians, who made frequent hostile inroads, the Californians were not unused to arms. They were expert horsemen, and all their Indian wars were waged with cavalry. The hunting and capture of wild horses and cattle was a favourite amusement with them, and the practice of this sport made them bold and skilful in the saddle. At full gallop they would throw the lasso or hurl the lance with unerring certainty and precision.

California, at this time, had all her military capacities been put in requisition, could bring into the field at least two thousand mounted men, constituting as fine a cavalry force as any country could produce. A more hardy and vigorous race than the Mexicans of the eastern states, the Californians were capable of great endurance; and, under bold and intelligent leaders, would have proved formidable enemies to any invader.

In the fall and winter of 1845–6 a considerable emigration from the western frontier of the United States had marched for California and Oregon. As the emigrants arrived in California, allured by the beauty and fertility of the country, they commenced forming settlements along the Sacramento and San Joaquin Rivers, in conformity with the original invitation which they had received from the authorities.

In January, 1846, Colonel Fremont, of the Topographical Corps, also arrived, on an exploring expedition. The Californian commandant of Monterey, General Castro, at first received Fremont in a friendly and hospitable manner; but, whether prompted by advices from the city of Mexico of the probability of a war, or alarmed at the numbers and bold, independent character of the emigrants, or suspecting the enterprising Anglo-Saxons of some latent ambitious designs, he suddenly changed his deportment towards both Fremont and the emigrants, and manifested a determination to arrest the progress of Fremont and disturb the settlements of the Americans. Several outrages were perpetrated on the latter, and a considerable military force called out to arrest the former. The American emigrants at once united for mutual defence, and called a convention to determine on the best means for protection. The convention assembled at Sonoma, of which they took military possession, and selected for their leader a gentleman of the name of William B. Ide. Colonel Ide, on the 18th of June, 1846, issued his proclamation, denouncing the treachery of the Californians, reciting the oppression and misgovernment of the province, and inviting the people to unite in an effort to secure their independence. On the 4th of July the Americans assembled at Sonoma, declared their independence, and hoisted what was called the Bear flag, and elected Colonel Fremont governor. Colonel Fremont, not altogether satisfied with the propriety of proceeding without the co-operation of the American squadron, then at Monterey, repaired to that place to confer with Commodore Sloat. Though Commodore Sloat declined to co-operate with him, he was informed by Commodore Stockton, soon after his arrival, that he would accept the offer of his services as soon as Commodore Sloat had relinquished the command of the squadron.

Immediately after that event, Commodore Stockton communicated his views fully to Colonel Fremont. He informed him that he should take the chief direction of affairs into his own hands, and at once commence active operations to reduce the whole of California to a state of complete submission to the authority of the United States. He agreed that such men as Colonel Fremont could enlist should be organized into a battalion, and that he would commission Fremont as major and Captain Gillespie as the captain of it. Fremont was instructed to invite the co-operation of the American emigrants who had hoisted the Bear flag. These hardy and adventurous men, true Americans at heart, of course, with Colonel Fremont, preferred fighting under the flag of their own country; and they constituted the principal part of the volunteers who formed the California battalion. The proceedings at Sonoma on the 4th of July and the Bear flag were thus *ignored*, all the parties thereto hastening to take service under Commodore Stockton. Fremont and Gillespie entered into a specific agreement with the Commodore that they would continue to act under him as commissioned while he should require their services. He considered and treated them as part of the naval forces under his command throughout the Californian war.

The bold and decided views taken by Commodore Stockton, at this time, of his duty, and the course he pursued towards the enemy, have been entirely approved by the government and people of the United States, while the complete success which rewarded his operations vindicates the strategetical sagacity which they displayed. But his was a novel and perplexing position,—more so than that in which any military commander of the United States had ever before been placed. He was entirely without instructions adapted to this exigency. He was compelled to rely on his own independent resources. The flag of his country had been raised in California,—a country in possession of a gallant and warlike people. These people had not been informed of the commencement of hostilities on the Rio Grande, when they were exasperated by a handful of straggling strangers and squatters (as they considered them) from the United States, invading their peaceful valleys, taking possession of fertile tracts of country, and immediately assuming a hostile position and declaring their independence. A proclamation had been issued by the military commandant of California, breathing vengeance against all foreigners, but designed to apply altogether to the American emigrants. The raising of the American flag at Monterey was believed to be a fillibuster proceeding, and only excited more vindictively the animosity of the Californian authorities.

The Legislature of the State was in session, and grants of vast

8

tracts of territory were about being made to British agents, which
would have absorbed the most valuable portion of the public lands.
These British agents, better informed than the Californians, foresaw
that, if California should be acquired by the United States, all
real estate would be enhanced in value. Those Californians who
were under the influence of British agents were quite willing, if
there were any probability of the transfer of the country to the
United States, that it should be made as worthless to our government as possible. They were, therefore, well disposed to cede
away every foot of land for which they could find a purchaser.
Commodore Stockton was apprised of their designs, and he saw that
prompt and energetic measures only could defeat them.

Besides, the emigrants now coming into California, unless active
steps were taken to engage all the military strength of the ambitious
chieftains who controlled it, would be at their mercy. They would
have been cut off in detail as they arrived, exhausted by the fatigues
and privations of the overland journey. The only hope of their
salvation, Stockton perceived, was in a campaign which would not
allow the Californians time or opportunity for any hostile expedition against the new-comers.

The population of California, as we have before observed, was
dispersed over a very extensive surface. From Suter's settlement,
one hundred and thirty miles north of San Francisco, to San Diego,
in the southern part of Upper California, it was near eight hundred
miles. The most populous parts of this expanse of territory were
in the vicinity of the *pueblos* or towns dotted at intervals along
the coast or a few miles from it in the interior. The Commodore
knew that it would require some time for the Californian leaders to
draw together the whole strength of the country from these remote
distances; and he perceived, with the intuition of a military eye,
that by a rapid movement he might defeat and disperse the enemy
before they could collect such a superior force as would render any
attempt to encounter them impracticable. The success of such demonstrations would infallibly determine many of the natives to
remain at home and refrain from any participation in the conflict.
It would certainly break up the session of the Legislature, frustrate
the spoliation of the public property, and protect the in-coming
emigration.

Had Commodore Stockton failed to pursue this bold and enterprising plan of military operations, it is hardly probable that California would have been reduced before negotiations for peace were
commenced. The whole military strength of the country would have

been embodied, and perhaps large bodies of Indians would also have been armed to resist the approach of General Kearney. Arriving in an exhausted condition, destitute of supplies, his fate and that of his army might have been still more disastrous than that which befell the small detachment with which he ultimately came.

When we consider the extent of surface in California which was to be made the theatre of war,—the nature of the force opposed to Commodore Stockton, comprising an armed body of the finest cavalry in the world, well acquainted with the country and all its difficult passes, so capable of being defended by the few against the strong,—and when, also, we advert to the nature of his own force, comprising only between three and four hundred sailors and marines, imperfectly armed, unacquainted with the country, unused to service on shore, assisted by one hundred and fifty volunteers under Fremont, equally strangers to the country,—it must be admitted that it required great moral courage to assume the responsibility of the enterprise which Commodore Stockton thought it his duty to undertake. He had no precedent in American history to guide him. He had no instructions which applied to the emergency. And we are informed that he held no council, with whose deliberations he might divide the responsibility of his decisions. His decisions were the result of his own reflections and his own patriotic sense of duty. Indeed, we have been informed that he has said, that from his departure from the United States, in the fall of 1845, to the close of his career in California, he never asked the advice of any one, or took any counsel in relation to any measure of importance.

Few naval officers could have secured the same cheerful performance of extraordinary duties from sailors and marines as Stockton obtained, without effort, from his men. The secret of his ascendency, however, over those commanded by him, is known to all who have served with or under him.

While he treats all alike with that scrupulous courtesy which cherishes self-respect and flatters personal importance, yet he constantly exacts the most implicit obedience; and his men always know that he will permit none of them to encounter any danger which their commander is not willing to be the foremost in sharing. Indeed, while prodigal of his own exposure, he is careful to allow his men to subject themselves to no risks which are not indispensably necessary.

Having determined upon the most decisive measures, Commodore Stockton, assuming the command-in-chief, civil and military, issued his proclamation placing the country under martial law. The proclamation was well conceived for the purpose of exciting the apprehensions of those who were disposed to resist, and of soothing and allaying the fears of those who were willing to remain at home peaceful and neutral. The civil jurisdiction of the magistrates and legal tribunals was not to be disturbed while held in subordination to the authority of the commander-in-chief. But the most vigorous treatment was threatened against all hostile parties.

This proclamation bears date the 23d of July, 1846,—the same day on which Commodore Sloat relinquished and Commodore Stockton assumed command of the squadron, and is as follows:—

PROCLAMATION.

CALIFORNIANS:—The Mexican goverment and their military officers have, without cause, for a year past, been threatening the United States with hostilities.

They have recently, in pursuance of these threats, commenced hostilities by attacking, with 7000 men, a small detachment of 2000 United States troops, by whom they were signally defeated and routed.

General Castro, the commander-in-chief of the military forces of California, has violated every principle of international law and national hospitality, by hunting and pursuing with several hundred soldiers, and with wicked intent, Captain Fremont, of the United States army, who came here to refresh his men, (about forty in number,) after a perilous journey across the mountains on a scientific survey.

For these repeated hostilities and outrages, military possession was ordered to be taken of Monterey and San Francisco until redress could be obtained from the government of Mexico.

No let or hinderance was given or intended to be given to the civil authority of the territory, or to the exercise of its accustomed functions. The officers were invited to remain, and promised protection in the performance of their duties as magistrates. They refused to do so, and departed, leaving the people in a state of anarchy and confusion.

On assuming the command of the forces of the United States on the coast of California, both by sea and land, I find myself in possession of the ports of Monterey and San Francisco, with daily reports from the interior of scenes of rapine, blood, and murder. Three inoffensive American residents of the country have, within a few days, been murdered in the most brutal manner; and there are no Californian officers who will arrest and bring the murderers to justice, although it is well known who they are and where they are.

I must, therefore, and will, as soon as I can, adopt such measures as may seem best calculated to bring these criminals to justice, and to bestow peace and good order on the country.

In the first place, however, I am constrained by every principle of national honour, as well as a due regard for the safety and best interests of the people of California, to put an end at once, and by force, to the lawless depredations daily committed by General Castro's men upon the persons and property of peaceful and unoffending inhabitants.

I cannot, therefore, confine my operations to the quiet and undisturbed possession of the defenceless ports of Monterey and San Francisco, while the people elsewhere are suffering from lawless violence, but will immediately march against these boasting and abusive chiefs, who have not only violated every principle of national hospitality and good faith towards Captain Fremont and his surveying party, but who, unless driven out, will, with the aid of the hostile Indians, keep this beautiful country in a constant state of revolution and blood, as well as against all others who may be found in arms, or aiding or abetting General Castro.

The present general of the forces of California is a usurper, has been guilty of great offences, has impoverished and drained the country of almost its last dollar, and has deserted his post now when most needed.

He has deluded and deceived the inhabitants of California, and they wish his expulsion from the country. He came into power by rebellion and force, and by force he must be expelled. Mexico appears to have been compelled, from time to time, to abandon California to the mercies of any wicked man who could muster one hundred men-in-arms. The distances from the capital are so great that she cannot, even in times of great distress, send timely aid to the inhabitants; and the lawless depredations upon their persons and property go invariably unpunished. She cannot or will not punish or control the chieftains who, one after the other, have defied her power and kept California in a constant state of revolt and misery.

The inhabitants are tired and disgusted with this constant succession of military usurpers and this insecurity of life and property. Therefore, upon them I will not make war. I require, however, all officers, civil and military, and all other persons, to remain quiet at their respective homes and stations, and to obey the orders they may receive from me, and by my authority; and, if they do no injury or violence to my authority, none will be done to them.

But notice is hereby given, that if any of the inhabitants of the country either abandon their dwellings or do any injury to the arms of the United States, or to any person within this territory, they will be treated as enemies and suffer accordingly.

No person whatever is to be troubled in consequence of any part he may heretofore have taken in the politics of the country, or for having been a subject of General Castro. And all persons who may have belonged to the government of Mexico, but who, from this day, acknowledge the authority of the existing laws, are to be treated in the same manner as other citizens of the United States, provided they are obedient to the law and to the orders they shall receive from me or by my authority.

The commander-in-chief does not desire to possess himself of one foot of California for any other reason than as the only means to save from destruction the lives and property of the foreign residents and the citizens of the territory, who have invoked his protection.

As soon, therefore, as the officers of the civil law return to their proper duties, under a regularly-organized government, and give security for life, liberty, and property, alike to all, the forces under my command will be withdrawn, and the people left to manage their own affairs in their own way.

R. F. Stockton,
Commander-in-chief, &c. &c. &c.

It was ascertained at this time that the Californians had collected an army of between one thousand and fifteen hundred men at Ciudad de los Angeles, the seat of government of the State. There the Commodore determined to go at once and commence offensive operations, notwithstanding the disparity of his forces. He hoped to attack and defeat the enemy before he could obtain any certain intelligence of the numbers of the Americans.

In twenty-four hours after assuming the command, the Commodore organized and accepted the services of the California battalion, one hundred and sixty in number, and despatched them on the sloop-of-war Cyane to San Diego, with directions to Major Fremont, after securing a supply of horses and cattle in that neighbourhood, to co-operate with the proposed attack on Ciudad de los Angeles. Delos Angeles is four hundred miles south of Monterey, and San Diego one hundred and fifty miles farther.

On the 1st of August, Commodore Stockton sailed with the Congress to Santa Barbara, whence, after leaving a garrison, he proceeded to San Pedro, on the coast, about thirty miles distant from Ciudad de los Angeles. He landed at once with about three hundred and fifty sailors and marines, (as many as could be spared from the ship,) established them in camp, and commenced drilling them for the service contemplated.

To create an army out of sailors for land-service was a novel experiment. It could have succeeded only with a commander who possessed the confidence and affections of his men, and who could infuse into them the same heroic spirit by which he was himself animated. It was in vain to attempt to subject the sailors to the ordinary drill of soldiers, or to expect from them the sort of discipline which is required in the army. No such attempt was made. They were simply directed to obey a few words of command, such as "halt," "march," "form line," "form square," "charge,"—and *always to keep the same comrade on the left or right.* In executing the necessary evolutions in which they were exercised, though all at first appeared confusion, yet every man soon rapidly took his proper place, and the most perfect order was immediately obtained. With that versatility for which Americans are remarkable, the sailors adapted themselves with the utmost alacrity and cheerfulness to their new vocation, and exhibited entire docility in the performance of their extraordinary duties. They saw their Commodore sharing with them all their hardships, partaking their rations and their toils, marching side by side with them—always going ahead in time of danger,—and they caught with inspiration the ardour which excited him. No insubordination or discontent were exhibited by any of them; but each one vied with the other in the patriotic performance of duty. There were only about ninety muskets in the whole corps. Some were armed with carbines, others had only pistols, swords, or boarding-pikes. They presented a motley and peculiar appearance, with great variety of costume; and, perhaps, no other army similarly armed and equipped was ever before marshalled for field operations either in savage or civilized warfare. Owing to the protracted extension of their absence from home, the supplies of shoes and clothing had fallen short; and the ragged and diversified colours of their garments, as well as the want of uniformity in their arms and accoutrements, made them altogether a spectacle both singular and amusing.

While engaged in exercising his men, and rendering them expert, or at least familiar with the manœuvres necessary to enable them to move with facility and in order, messengers with a flag of truce appeared on one of the distant hills in the direction of De los Angeles. As soon as the Commodore was informed of their approach, he believed that they had come for the purpose of observation as much as for any thing else, and he determined that the knowledge they derived from their visit should contribute to his own benefit. Accordingly, he resolved on such a display as would deceive the enemy with respect to his numbers, and compel the bearers of the flag of truce to return with very exaggerated ideas of the formidable army which they were soon to encounter. He ordered all his men under arms, and directed them to march, three or four abreast, with intervals of considerable space between each squad of three or four, directly in the line of vision of the approaching messengers, to the rear of some buildings on the beach, and thence to return in a circle and continue their march until the strangers had arrived. Part of the circle described in the march was concealed from view, so that to the strangers it would appear that a force ten times greater than the actual number of it was defiling before them.

When the bearers of the flag of truce had arrived, he ordered them led up to him alongside of the artillery, which consisted of several six-pounders and one thirty-two-pound carronade. The guns were all covered with skins in such a manner as to conceal their dimensions, excepting the huge mouth of the thirty-two-pounder at which the Commodore was posted to receive his guests. He supposed that, in all probability, neither of them had ever before seen such an instrument of war, and that the large and gaping aperture of the gun, into the very mouth of which they were compelled to look, would be very likely to disturb their nerves.

As his purpose was that of intimidation, he received them with sternness, calculated to co-operate with the impression to be produced by the artillery. They proved to be bearers of despatches from General Castro. He warned the Commodore to desist from his contemplated expedition, and proposed a truce, by the terms of which each party should maintain its present position, unmolested by the other, until intelligence of a more definite character could be obtained from Mexico and the United States, or until the conclusion of peace. Delay, however, was just exactly the opportunity which the Commodore had not the remotest idea of affording the enemy. He knew that, as soon as the Californian generals should discover his comparative weakness, they would not be likely to observe any truce. The authority of one General to conclude a truce might be disavowed by another. The advantages of a truce would be entirely with the enemy. It would enable them to ascertain their own superiority of numbers, which it only required time to concentrate, when they would inevitably become invincible by any available force within the Commodore's control.

He directed the Californians to return to their master and inform him that the American commander intended to march immediately on Ciudad de los Angeles; that General Castro should prepare to surrender his arms, disperse his forces, and require his men to return to their homes and demean themselves peaceably, under penalty of being dealt with in the most rigorous manner. He ordered them to tell Castro that he would not negotiate with him on any other terms than those of absolute submission to the authority of the United States. Having, through an interpreter, delivered this message in the most fierce and offensive manner and in a tone of voice significant of the most implacable and hostile determination, he waved them from his presence imperiously with the insulting imperative, "Vamose." The Californians made haste to escape from the presence of an enemy apparently so ferocious and formidable, and their ominous retiring glances at the terrific gun showed but too plainly that the work of intimidation was effectual.

The Commodore, after they were beyond hearing, expressed the opinion to his officers that these messengers would carry to Castro's camp such an account of their observations as would supersede the necessity of any very desperate battle.

Two days afterwards, another embassy from Castro arrived. This renewed attempt to negotiate satisfied the Commodore that his treatment of the first messengers had operated well, and he repeated his experiment of intimidation, by refusing again in the most insulting manner any overtures for a suspension of hostilities. The offer to treat at this time was accompanied with sonorous and boastful threats and bombastic defiance. Castro in a letter informed the Commodore of his certain defeat in case he advanced, and that the Californians were determined, to the last man, to perish in defence of their country. The bearer of this last despatch was received and treated with the same uncompromising severity as the first.

The Commodore undoubtedly succeeded in deceiving Castro respecting the numbers and strength of his little army. Otherwise, the Californian general never would have suffered him to penetrate to De los Angeles without more than one effort to impede his progress.

The forces of Castro were treble that of the invaders. He had a fine park of artillery, his men were well mounted and equipped. There were several narrow defiles between San Pedro and Los Angeles, where a few determined men might have maintained their ground against ten times their own numbers. Under a brave and skilful leader, the troops in command of Castro were sufficiently numerous to have driven the sailors to their ships, or to have slaughtered or captured every man of them. But, ignorant of the Commodore's strength, and impressed with the belief that it was far greater than his own, Castro failed to take advantage of the most favourable passes in which to meet his enemy, and, anxious to keep a position where access to the open plains would afford him the facilities for escape, he intrenched himself in the vicinity of Ciudad de los Angeles, and apparently prepared to fight a pitched battle on the plain.

Having made all suitable arrangements, Commodore Stockton, after waiting to hear from Major Fremont as long as he thought it prudent, determined to proceed without him. He, however, despatched a courier to inform the Major of his advance, and on the eleventh of August commenced his march on Ciudad de los Angeles.

The only provisions of the little army were cattle and sheep, which were enclosed in a hollow square, and thus protected both from the marauding attacks of the enemy and from escape. The enemy were often in sight, threatening their flanks or advance-guard, and hovering on the brows of the adjacent hills. The artillery and ammunition-carts were dragged along by the sailors over hills and through tedious valleys of sand, but without complaint or reluctance.

On the twelfth, as they approached within a few miles of Castro's position, another courier from him presented himself. He was commissioned to deliver a pompous message, informing the Commodore "that if he marched upon the town he would find it the grave of his men." "Then," said he, "tell your general to have the bells ready to toll in the morning at eight o'clock, as I shall be there at that time."*

He was there at that time; but the Californian general of couriers and despatches was unwilling to risk a battle. Both he and his troops were evidently panic-stricken. Their fears had been excited by the bold and confident deportment of their adversary,

---

* Colton's Three Years in California.

and they shrunk from conflict with a foe apparently so desperate and daring, who would neither parley nor negotiate, and whose demands were as arrogant as they were uncompromising.

Castro did not wait to receive a charge, but, without firing a gun, and before the Commodore was visible to him, broke up his camp, ordered the bulk of his army to disperse, and, with a small detachment of followers, mounted on their swiftest coursers, fled in the direction of Sonora.

His artillery fell into the hands of the Americans. His principal officers and a portion of his troops surrendered prisoners of war. On the following day, Don Andreas Pico, former governor, and General Jose Maria Flores, also surrendered, and were set at liberty on their parole of honour not to serve against the United States during the war.

Ciudad de los Angeles capitulated without any specification of terms, and, on the 13th of August, Commodore Stockton took possession of the capital of California.

The effect of this successful expedition, though achieved without bloodshed, was equivalent to the most triumphant victory. As a skilful chess-player, who checkmates his opponent without the loss of a man on either side, so the Commodore, by the sagacity and boldness of his demonstrations, gained every thing which could have been obtained by a well-fought and bloody battle.

The flight of Castro, the dispersion of his troops, the capture of Ciudad de los Angeles, the dissolution of the Legislature, and, indeed, of the government, by the surrender of Pico and Flores, and the general submission of all other functionaries, apparently terminated all contest in California.

Those disposed to fight were without leaders in whom confidence could be placed. The spirit of resistance was humbled and subdued. The whole population were impressed with exaggerated opinions of the powers and desperation of the foe. There was no general to whose standard they could rally. All the principal seaports were in the possession of the Americans. The country was, in fact, conquered, and it only remained for the conqueror to establish laws for its civil government in order to complete the work of subjugation. This he proceeded to do without delay.

The territory was divided, for its military government, into three departments, in each of which a military commandant was appointed. Colonel Fremont, who had arrived after the flight of Castro, was appointed military commandant for the whole territory, with a general superintendence over all the departments.

Commodore Stockton was averse to the continuance of martial law after the general submission of the inhabitants. But, as many of the civil officers of the recent government were unwilling to act under the new order of affairs, the Commodore ordered an election to supply their places. The election was held on the 15th of September, and the officers elected were duly commissioned by the Commodore, and entered upon the discharge of their duties. The Commodore likewise prescribed an ad-valorem tariff upon all duties on imports, and appointed appraisers, collectors, and other port-officers, for the collection of the revenue. Thus, in little more than a month after Commodore Stockton landed at San Pedro, the new government, civil and military, was organized and put in operation, with every indication that the people of California would acquiesce in submission to it without further resistance.

Commodore Stockton, immediately after these events, despatched a courier (the celebrated Kit Carson) to Washington, with full intelligence of his proceedings.* He likewise informed the government that, upon returning to his ship and relinquishing the command-in-chief in California, he should appoint Colonel Fremont governor.

The Commodore, while engaged in overrunning and subduing California and performing the duties of a General of land-forces, had not neglected the conduct of hostilities on the ocean and along the coast. The Cyane, under Commander Dupont, and the Warren, under Commander Hull, were ordered to cruise on the Pacific coast, from Mazatlan to the mouth of the Columbia. Thirteen prizes were captured by them; among others, the Malek Adel, of some celebrity. Indeed, they so effectually scoured the coast as to clear it of every hostile vessel.

After making all necessary territorial dispositions, leaving garrisons at San Diego, De los Angeles, San Pedro, and Santa Barbara, and appointing Major Gillespie commandant of the southern military department, the Commodore proceeded north to examine into the state of affairs in that direction. A reported incursion of the Indians brought him to San Francisco. There he learned that the report was unfounded, and, after a satisfactory interview with some of the Indian chiefs, he was assured that no danger was to be apprehended from them. He found the whole North as quiet and as submissive to his authority as the South when he left it. He was received at all the principal towns and settlements which he visited

---

* See Appendix, Official Letter of September 15, 1846, to Secretary of Navy.

with demonstrations of admiration and respect. His arrival at San Francisco was celebrated by a general turn-out of the inhabitants, the formal presentation of a congratulatory address, a procession, and other festivities, concluding with a grand banquet and a ball.

The inhabitants in this part of the territory appeared to rejoice in the change of government, which relieved them from the exactions and oppression exercised by the tyrannical governors and petty military commandants who had so long tyrannized in California. Security of personal property was now perfect under the authority of the officers of the new government, and no outrage could be perpetrated with impunity. The most intelligent among them foresaw that the transfer of the country to the United States would result in greatly augmenting its prosperity, and none, excepting a few lawless and reckless dependants of the deposed Mexican authorities, regretted the success of the American arms.

These feelings of the people were distinctly manifested upon the report that a large Mexican force was collecting in Sonora for the invasion of California and the restoration of Mexican supremacy. They crowded around the Commodore and tendered their services as volunteers, and called upon him to protect them from the invaders. The restoration of Mexican ascendency they seemed to consider the worst calamity which could befall them. The report, however, proved to be unfounded, and the whole surface of the country appeared tranquillized and its subjugation complete.

Commodore Stockton now, (the last of September, 1846,) believing that no further active operations in California required his presence, conceived the design of prosecuting the war in Mexico. He proposed leaving the battalion of volunteers under Major Fremont and Captain Gillespie in charge of California, occupying the principal positions and towns; and, with an additional force of a thousand men, to be raised from among the hardy adventurers and emigrants from the United States now pouring into California, he formed the plan of sailing for Acapulco, on the western coast of Mexico, from whence he designed to strike across the country, with the view of reinforcing and co-operating with General Taylor or General Scott, one of whom he supposed would about this time be on the way towards Mexico City. It certainly would have alarmed the Mexican government, while mustering all its strength to repel an invasion from the North and East, to have heard of the sudden advance of an American army from the West and South,—a direction from which they would least expect an enemy. The conception of such an expedition indicates the bold and enterprising character of Stockton. Had it been put in execution, it would have produced an important diversion in favour of General Scott. This daring and adventurous scheme has never received that attention from the country which it has deserved. Nothing, however, prevented its being carried into effect but the unexpected insurrection in California. As part of the history of Commodore Stockton's campaigns in California, the evidence of the fact that he projected such an enterprise cannot fail to be considered interesting and important:—

(From Senate Document No. 31, Thirtieth Congress, Second Session.)

"UNITED STATES FRIGATE CONGRESS,
HARBOUR OF SAN FRANCISCO, October 1, 1846.

"SIR:—On my arrival here with the Congress and Savannah in pursuit of the Walla-Walla Indians, I was glad to find that their numbers had been greatly exaggerated and that they were friendly-disposed.

"I have a message from the chief stating that he was friendly and would come down to see me. I will send the Savannah on her cruise to-morrow, and the Portsmouth in a few days, and will follow myself in the Congress as soon as I can, (if not sooner superseded by Commodore Biddle,) to carry out my views in regard to Mexico, with which I have not thought it necessary or expedient yet to acquaint the Department.

"Our new government goes on well. I am arranging for a weekly mail from one end of the territory to the other: it will not, I think, cost over three or four thousand dollars per annum, which will be less expensive than the necessary expenses to keep one properly informed in regard to every part of the territory.

"If any chance is given, I have no doubt an effort will be made by the Mexicans to recover the territory. Troops are ready to come from Mexico; but, if they are not seen on their way, I'll make them fight their first battle at Acapulco, or between that and the city of Mexico.

"I have not, it is true, a great force; but their enthusiasm and impetuosity must make up the want of numbers.

"Faithfully, your obedient servant,
"R. F. STOCKTON, *Commodore, &c.*
"To the Hon. GEORGE BANCROFT,
"*Secretary of the Navy, Washington, D.C.*"

(Confidential.)

"UNITED STATES FRIGATE CONGRESS,
BAY OF MONTEREY, September 19, 1846.

"DEAR SIR:—I have sent Major Fremont to the North to see how many men he could recruit, with a view to embark them for Mazatlan or Acapulco, where, if possible, I intend to land and fight our way as far on to the city of Mexico as I can.

"With this object in view, your orders of this date, in relation to having the squadron in such places as may enable me to get them together as soon as possible, are given.

"You will, on your arrival on the coast, get all the information you can in reference to this matter. I would that we might shake hands with General Taylor at the gates of Mexico.

"Faithfully, your obedient servant,

"R. F. STOCKTON, *Commodore, &c.*

"To CAPTAIN WILLIAM MERVINE,

"*United States Frigate Savannah.*"

(Private.)

"UNITED STATES FRIGATE CONGRESS,
HARBOUR OF SAN FRANCISCO, September 28, 1846.

"SIR:—I am here, anxious to know what prospect there is of your being able to recruit my thousand men for a visit to Mexico.

"Let me know as soon as possible. Many serious arrangements will have to be made, all requiring more or less time, which, you know, in war is more precious than 'rubies.'

"Your faithful friend and obedient servant,

"R. F. STOCKTON, *Governor, &c.*

"To MAJOR FREMONT, *Military Commandant*
of the Territory of California."

CHAPTER X.

WHILE Commodore Stockton was preparing for a campaign in
Mexico, in co-operation with the army of General Scott, he received
intelligence which confined his attention to California. No sooner
was it known to Pico and Flores that the Commodore had gone
north, than those treacherous enemies of the United States, regardless of their parole of honour not to serve again during the war,
secretly collected together the remnants of their former army, and
resolved upon another effort to expel the Americans. They were,
doubtless, indignant and ashamed that they had suffered themselves
to be discomfited by a force so inferior to their own. Now that
they knew their own superiority in numbers and equipment, they
felt confident that the same disastrous result would not take place
in case of another rencontre. The season for action was favourable.
The formidable Commodore, who had struck terror to their hearts,
was absent. Ciudad de los Angeles, San Diego, Santa Barbara,
were each of them garrisoned with less than a hundred men. Accordingly, Pico and Flores, with four or five hundred men, suddenly
appeared before Ciudad de los Angeles. Major Gillespie, the commandant of the southern department, considered it vain to attempt
resistance to a force so superior. He accordingly capitulated, and
was allowed to retire to San Pedro. Santa Barbara was likewise
captured, and San Diego closely besieged. Flores and Pico issued
a flaming proclamation, calling upon their countrymen to rise in
defence of California and drive the insolent invaders from their soil.
They pretty generally responded to the call, and an army of about
a thousand mounted men was soon collected.

As soon as the Commodore was informed of their proceedings,

he made arrangements, with his usual promptitude, to quell this insurrection and restore peace to the territory. Captain Mervine, with the frigate Savannah, was ordered to proceed to San Pedro, with directions to hold the enemy in check till he should be reinforced by the Commodore. Colonel Fremont was summoned to San Francisco with his battalion of volunteers. On the 12th of October he arrived with one hundred and twenty men. He was immediately despatched on the Sterling, with one hundred and sixty men, to Santa Barbara; at which place, after procuring horses, he was directed to hold himself in readiness to join the Commodore in his march against the rebels at Ciudad de los Angeles. The Commodore, on the frigate Congress, sailed in company with the Sterling, but ran into Monterey, and, having strengthened the place with fifty men, proceeded to San Pedro.

On his arrival there he found that the enemy were in the neighbourhood, with a force estimated at eight hundred men. Captain Mervine had landed, and with his crew commenced an advance on Ciudad de los Angeles. The enemy attacked him before he had made much progress, and after a short conflict defeated and drove him to his ship, and took possession of San Pedro.*

The morning after his arrival, the Commodore landed, with three hundred men, in the face of the foe, and, after a skirmish, compelled them to retreat. A camp was formed at once, intrenchments thrown up, and preparations made with all haste to receive a renewed attack. But, aware of the presence of the commander-in-chief, the enemy declined a battle, which was repeatedly offered by the Commodore, and contented themselves with harassing and threatening the Americans. When charged, they retreated with their flying artillery, and, taking a new position, continued to pour their fire into the American camp. Having no horses with which to manœuvre his guns or pursue the assailants, there was danger that his men would be worn out with fatigue. Learning also from his scouts the superior strength of the Californians, the Commodore was convinced that more ample preparations were necessary to justify his advance. San Pedro, however, was not the place where supplies could be obtained of cattle and horses. The anchorage was too insecure to risk his ships there at that season for any length of time. San Diego afforded a good and secure harbour, and there he determined to proceed and consummate his preparations for further offensive measures. There, too, he hoped to hear from

---

* See Appendix A, Letter of Commodore Stockton to Secretary of the Navy, November 23, 1846.

Colonel Fremont, and strengthen himself by a junction with the California battalion.

On his way to San Diego, the Malek Adel was spoken, and information received that Colonel Fremont, unable to obtain horses at Santa Barbara, had gone to Monterey for that purpose. Monterey was between five and six hundred miles north of San Diego. And the intelligence that Colonel Fremont had gone there, instead of southward, seemed to afford no flattering prospect of any aid from him in time for an early movement on Ciudad de los Angeles. From the Malek Adel also the Commodore heard that Lieutenant Minor was besieged in San Diego; and on his arrival there he found this to be the case, and the garrison reduced to severe straits. All the male inhabitants had deserted the place, leaving their destitute families dependent for food on Lieutenant Minor. In addition to these unfavourable circumstances, in attempting to enter the harbour of San Diego the Congress grounded and was in danger of tumbling over. While the crew were engaged in staying the ship with spars, the town was vigorously attacked. Notwithstanding the perilous and embarrassing position of his ship, the Commodore, with as many of his men as could be spared, immediately landed, and, after a severe action, repulsed the enemy.

As soon as the Congress was got off and securely anchored, all the marines and sailors of the Congress and Savannah were landed, and preparations commenced for the march on Ciudad de los Angeles. But the country in the neighbourhood had been scoured by the enemy, and every horse and quadruped driven away. The first preparation for an advance, therefore, was the acquisition of a supply of horses, cattle, and sheep. These could not be obtained except from a distance so far south as to be beyond the sweep of the Californian rangers.

Captains Henseley and Gibson were sent with a small detachment, for this purpose, to Lower California; but it was some time in December before they succeeded in collecting a sufficient number of horses and cattle. In the mean time the Commodore was indefatigable in performing all the duties of a provident commander. A portion of the men were employed in constructing a fort for the defence of San Diego. Others were directed to manufacture saddles for the horses, and shoes of canvass and hides, for the sailors were almost destitute of this indispensable article. Gun-carriages for the artillery also had to be made. The sailors were regularly exercised in the peculiar drill prescribed for them.

About the 1st of December, supposing that Colonel Fremont

must have succeeded in mounting his men, and consequently would be on his way down along the shore, the Commodore despatched a gunboat, under Lieutenant Selden, to cover his march at the maritime Pass of Rincon—a narrow pass between the mountains and the sea,—where a small hostile force might otherwise have impeded his advance. No intelligence, however, had been received from Colonel Fremont; nor did the Commodore know what had been his success in mounting his men or obtaining supplies. The extensive region of country between San Diego and Monterey, where Fremont was last known to have gone, was in the hands of the enemy. This would render any communication from Fremont, except by way of the sea, impossible. Nevertheless, the Commodore, having full confidence in the zeal and enterprise of Colonel Fremont, felt assured that he would, by this time, be on his march to Ciudad de los Angeles, and, without hearing from him, he determined on his own advance, as soon as Captains Henseley and Gibson (now expected every day) should arrive from the South with supplies. Scouts were sent off in various directions to reconnoitre the movements, position, and strength of the enemy, and his entire force held in such a state of preparation that on the shortest notice they would be able to proceed on the expedition.

We may well conceive how distasteful to a commander of the Commodore's temperament this delay at San Diego must have been. Though delighting in action, and, when prepared to act, impetuous and rapid in his movements, Commodore Stockton unites caution and prudence with those active qualities which characterize him. He leaves, if possible, nothing to chance. He makes every needful provision for emergencies with the most careful circumspection. He calculates every step before he advances. But, when he determines upon action, he moves swiftly, he tolerates no delay: no obstacle is then deemed unsurmountable, no dangers formidable, no achievement impossible.

While impatiently awaiting the return of Captains Henseley and Gibson, the Commodore was surprised by a messenger from General Kearney, bearing the following letter :—

"HEAD-QUARTERS, ARMY OF THE WEST CAMP AT WARNER'S,
December 2, 1846

"SIR :—I this afternoon reached here, escorted by a party of the first regiment of dragoons. I came by orders of the President of the United States. We left Santa Fe on the 25th September, having taken possession of New Mexico, annexed it to the United

States, established a civil government in that territory, and secured order, peace, and quietness there.

"If you can send a party to open a communication with us on the route to this place, and to inform me of the state of affairs in California, I wish you would do so, and as quickly as possible.

"The fear of this letter falling into Mexican hands prevents me from writing more. Your express by Mr. Carson was met on the Del Norte ; and your mail must have reached Washington at least ten days since.

"You might use the bearer, Mr. Stokes, as a guide to conduct your party to this place.

"Very respectfully, your obedient servant,
"S. W. KEARNEY,
"*Brigadier-General U. S. A.*
"COMMODORE R. F. STOCKTON,
"*United States Navy, commanding
Pacific Squadron, San Diego.*"

To this letter the Commodore, on the evening of its receipt, sent the following prompt reply:—

"HEAD-QUARTERS, SAN DIEGO, December 3, 6½ o'clock P.M.

"SIR:—I have this moment received your note of yesterday by Mr. Stokes, and have ordered Captain Gillespie, with a detachment of mounted riflemen and a field-piece, to proceed to your camp without delay.

"Captain Gillespie is well informed in relation to the present state of things in California, and will give you all needful information. I need not, therefore, detain him by saying any thing on the subject.

"I will merely say that I have this evening received information, by two deserters from the rebel camp, of the arrival of an additional force in this neighbourhood of one hundred men, which, in addition to the force previously here, makes their number about one hundred and fifty.

"I send with Captain Gillespie, as a guide, one of the deserters, that you may make inquiries of him, and, if you see fit, endeavour to surprise them.

"Faithfully, your obedient servant,
"R. F. STOCKTON, *Commander-in-chief
and Governor of the Territory of California.*
"To BRIGADIER-GENERAL KEARNEY,
"*United States Army.*"

The letter of General Kearney did not inform the Commodore that the General was in any danger; and his messenger represented him to have a force of three hundred and fifty men. On the evening on which the General's letter was received, the Commodore ordered Lieutenant Beale and Major Gillespie, with thirty-five men, to proceed as an escort to meet and welcome the General. A day or two after Lieutenant Beale and Major Gillespie had left, a messenger arrived from General Kearney with official information that the General had been attacked by a superior force and defeated, with the loss of eighteen men killed and many wounded, including the General himself, and the loss of part of his artillery.

The messenger delivered the following despatch from General Kearney's camp:—

"HEAD-QUARTERS, CAMP NEAR SAN PASQUAL,
December 6, 1846.

"SIR:—I have the honour to report to you that at early dawn this morning, General Kearney, with a detachment of United States dragoons, and Captain Gillespie's company of mounted riflemen, had an engagement with a very considerable Mexican force near this camp.

"We have eighteen killed and fourteen or fifteen wounded—several so severely that it may be impracticable to move them for several days. I have to suggest to you the propriety of despatching, without delay, a considerable force, to meet us on the route to San Diego, via the Lolidad and San Bernardo, or to find us at this place; also, that you will send up carts, or some other means of transporting our wounded to San Diego. We are without provisions, and in our present situation may find it impracticable to obtain cattle from the ranchos in the vicinity.

"General Kearney is among the wounded, but, it is hoped, not dangerously; Captains Moore and Johnston, 1st dragoons, killed; Captain Gillespie, badly, but not dangerously, wounded; Lieutenant Hammond, 1st dragoons, dangerously wounded.

"I am, sir, very respectfully, your obedient servant,
"H. S. TURNER,
"*Captain United States Army, Commanding.*"*

Immediately on the receipt of this letter the Commodore prepared to march at the head of all his little army to the relief of the General.

---

* This letter, and the two which precede it in this chapter, are part of the report of the Secretary of the Navy, Feb. 14, 1849. Having inserted them *here*, they are omitted in Appendix A.

But, before he could carry this intention into execution, Lieutenant Beale came in and furnished the first reliable account of the enemy's strength. They did not amount to more than a hundred and twenty-five men. A detachment, under Lieutenant Gray, of two hundred and fifteen men, were then immediately sent to the General's camp. They found him besieged on the hill of San Bernardo, without water, provisions, or horses, and his men worn out with fatigue. Upon the approach of Lieutenant Gray the enemy withdrew, and the General and his dragoons were safely escorted to San Diego.

General Kearney, in the spring of 1846, having overrun New Mexico and suppressed whatever of hostile resistance to the United States was exhibited there, was directed, by instructions from the War Department bearing date the 3d and 18th of June, to raise one thousand men, and proceed with them across the country to California, and, "should" he "conquer and take possession" of the country, "to establish a temporary civil government therein."* July 12, similar orders were issued to the naval commander in California.

When only four days' march from Santa Fe, the general met Kit Carson, the express of Commodore Stockton, *en route* for Washington, bearing despatches to the government, with the information that California had been conquered, and a civil government organized which was peaceably acquiesced in by the inhabitants. Carson communicated the substance of this information to the General. The General, with no great courtesy to the Commodore, compelled Carson to return with him,† forwarding his despatches by a messenger of his own selection.‡

General Kearney, having thus learned that the objects of his expedition had been anticipated and the orders of the government addressed to him already executed, might with propriety have turned back himself. He did dismiss the greater part of his men, and sent them back to New Mexico, but proceeded with about eighty dragoons on his way to California. He should either have carried into effect strictly the *whole* of his orders and gone to California with the 1000 men he was directed to raise for that purpose, and with whom he had started, or, upon being informed that the special duty which he was instructed to perform was already successfully

---

* See despatch of 3d June, in Appendix B.

† See Carson's statement from Mr. Benton's speech, in Appendix C.

‡ Mr. Benton, commenting on this interference by General Kearney with the express of Commodore Stockton, says, that if Carson had been permitted to proceed, he would have returned from Washington in time to have prevented all collision between the Commodore and the General.

accomplished by others, he should have abstained altogether from going. It by no means should have been taken for granted by him that the services of all his troops would not be needed in California, although it had been already conquered.

From subsequent events it may be inferred that the chief object of General Kearney in proceeding to California with his slender escort, after he had heard of its conquest by Commodore Stockton, was to assume and exercise the functions of governor. This mistake of the General, no matter to what motives attributed, produced the subsequent conflict of authority between Commodore Stockton and himself.

The facts in relation to this conflict constitute part of the history of Commodore Stockton's proceedings in California, and an authentic narrative of them is necessary to a complete understanding of those proceedings. Justice to the living requires that the whole truth should be told, whoever may suffer by the revelation.

After being reinforced by Lieutenant Beale and Major Gillespie, the General found his progress impeded by the enemy, and on the 6th of December attempted to surprise them at San Pasqual. The accounts we have received from officers who were present and engaged in the action, as well as from official documents, vary ma-terially from General Kearney's official report. Doubtless the General supposed that the Californians were as feeble and cowardly a race as the New Mexicans, whom he had vanquished so easily. Whether such was the case or not, it turned out that he was himself surprised.

The Californians feigned a flight, drew his best-mounted dragoons into the open plain, (thus separating them from the remainder who were more imperfectly mounted,) and then, suddenly wheeling upon those in the advance, dashed with the speed of Arabian coursers into their ranks, disordered by this unexpected charge, lancing and shooting his men, and compelling the survivors to save themselves by flight. Eighteen men were killed and fifteen wounded. Captains More and Johnston, of the dragoons, were among the killed. General Kearney and Lieutenant Beale and Captain Gillespie were among the wounded. After lancing the artillery-men, the enemy succeeded in capturing and driving off the mules hitched to one of the howitzers. Satisfied with their success, the Californians abstained from any further attack, and contented themselves with holding him in check. The General took refuge on the hill of San Bernardo, where they surrounded and besieged him. He was without water, supplies, or ammunition. Major Emory, one of his officers, in his

"Notes of a Military Recognisance through New Mexico to California," published by order of Congress, thus states the condition of General Kearney at San Bernardo :—"Our provisions were exhausted, our horses dead, and our men, now reduced to one-third their number, were ragged, worn down by fatigue, and emaciated."

While thus besieged, with the prospect of being compelled to capitulate or else to attempt cutting his way through at all hazards, Lieutenant Beale, Mr. Godey, and an Indian, on the night of the 7th succeeded in eluding the vigilance of the foe and escaped. After great privations, they reached San Diego by different routes, and gave the Commodore precise intelligence of the General's critical condition, from which he was relieved by Lietenant Gray and his detachment, sent, as we have stated, by Stockton.

General Kearney was received by the Commodore with the utmost cordiality and kindness. He surrendered to him his own quarters, and treated him with the most delicate attentions and chivalric courtesy. Every reasonable effort was made to supply all his necessary wants and to minister to his comfort. He was immediately put in possession of the Commodore's plans,—his intended expedition to Ciudad de los Angeles and the expected co-operation of Fremont,—and furnished with all the information necessary to a complete understanding of the posture of affairs.

Though it was quite natural that, after making the needful preparation for the march on Ciudad de los Angeles, the Commodore should feel desirous to conduct it himself and reap the honours which might accrue from success, yet, nevertheless, appreciating and conceding the qualifications of General Kearney to command a land-force, and more anxious that the enterprise should succeed than that he should himself enjoy the glory of success, he magnanimously tendered the command-in-chief to General Kearney, and offered to accompany him as his *aid-de-camp.* This generous offer was peremptorily declined. Whether the General supposed the Commodore better qualified to command the army consisting principally of seamen, or whether ashamed to supersede his benefactor, or, perhaps, shrinking from the responsibility of conducting so important an expedition with *such an army*, ludicrously armed and equipped, he thrice declined the offers of the Commodore to devolve on him the command-in-chief,* and offered to go as his aid. But, though unwilling to assume the command-in-chief, the General, after

---

* See, in Appendix A, Commodore Stockton's Official Letters ; also, Appendix B, extracts from Proceedings of Court-martial on Fremont.

exhibiting his orders from the Secretary of War of June 3 and 18, 1846, intimated his expectation that he would be permitted to exercise the functions of civil governor.

The Commodore, having furnished copies of his own correspondence with the government for the General's information, in which all his proceedings in California were detailed and his intention to appoint Colonel Fremont civil governor distinctly expressed, courteously but explicitly informed the General that his orders, even if they had not been superseded by those of a later date, had nevertheless been anticipated and executed previously to his arrival. General Kearney's orders made his assumption of the civil government of California contingent upon his own conquest of the country. That contingency could never take place. Commodore Stockton's official information of these facts was before the government, and, until its pleasure, as enlightened by these facts, had been communicated to him, he would not alter or modify his intentions or arrangements.*

Nothing more was said at this time by General Kearney on the subject of his claim to the civil governorship of California. He apparently acquiesced in the decision of the Commodore, who really supposed that General Kearney, upon further reflection, coincided with the views which had been presented to him. The Commodore believed that General Kearney, agreeably to his offer, would accompany him as his aid on the expedition to Ciudad de los Angeles.

It must be apparent, from the previous narrative, that General Kearney was well informed of the proposed advance on Ciudad de los Angeles, for it was in reference to that advance that he had offered to act as aid to the Commodore. He was cognizant of the preparations made for it, and knew that the Commodore was only awaiting the return of Captains Henseley and Gibson with a supply of horses and cattle. With this knowledge, on the 22d of December he addressed the Commodore the following extraordinary letter :—

" SAN DIEGO, December 22, 1846.

"DEAR COMMODORE :—If you can take from here a sufficient force to oppose the Californians, now supposed to be near the Pueblos and waiting for the approach of Lieutenant-Colonel Fremont, *I advise that you do so,* and that you march with that force as early as possible in the direction of the Pueblos, by which you will be able to form a junction with Lieutenant-Colonel Fremont, or make a

---

* See Appendix B.

diversion very much in his favour. I do not think that Lieutenant-Colonel Fremont should be left unsupported to fight a battle upon which the fate of California may for a long time depend, if there are troops here to act in concert with him. Your force as it advances might surprise the enemy at the San Luis mission, and make prisoners of them. I shall be happy in such an expedition to accompany and to give you any aid either of head or hand of which I may be capable.   "Yours truly,

                    "S. W. KEARNEY, *Brig.-General.*
"COMMODORE R. F. STOCKTON,
     "*Commanding U. S. Forces, San Diego.*"*

There could be no possible motive for writing such a letter except, first, to found on it a claim to the credit of having suggested the expedition to Los Angeles; and, second, to use it with Fremont as a claim to his support against Stockton. Accordingly, we find, in his testimony on the court-martial of Colonel Fremont, that General Kearney *actually did make this use of it.* On page 47 of those proceedings, General Kearney testifies:—"In the latter end of December an expedition was organized at San Diego, to march to Los Angeles to assist Lieutenant Fremont, *and was organized in consequence, as I believe,* of a paper which I addressed to Commodore Stockton."

Commodore Stockton at once saw through the purposes of the General. Having only the previous morning informed him of his intention to move onward, he must very naturally have considered the General's volunteer advice to do that which the General well knew he intended to do, as insulting and prompted by some sinister motive. It was an attempt on the part of the General to make out a paper-claim to the paternity of a movement for which the Commodore had been preparing more than two months. It is quite probable that Stockton was aware, from various little indications, that Kearney was jealous of his exercise of authority, and mortified at his refusal to surrender it to him, and that a breach with him, sooner or later, was inevitable. Kearney had been heard to speak contemptuously of the sailors as land-forces, and to doubt their ability to cope with the mounted Californians. The Commodore, therefore, whose nature it is to meet an enemy more than half way, replied to the General in such a manner that, if he were disposed to take offence, he would not fail to do so for want of an opportunity.

---

* Proceedings of Court-martial of Colonel Fremont, p. 47.

The insult conveyed by the General's letter was ambiguous on the face of it. But, whether written merely to support his claim to having originated the expedition, or whether designed to convince Fremont that he was a better friend of his than Stockton, it was equally offensive. But there was no ambiguity in the reply of the Commodore. The turpitude of the imputation was as plain as language could make it, and must have required all the General's philosophy to digest. The reply was as follows:—

"HEAD-QUARTERS, SAN DIEGO, December 23, 1846.

"DEAR GENERAL:—Your note of yesterday was handed to me last night by Captain Turner, of the dragoons.

"In reply to that note, permit me to refer you to the conversation held with you yesterday morning at your quarters. I stated to you that I intended to march upon San Luis Rey as soon as possible with a part of the forces under my command; that I was very desirous to march on to the Pueblo to co-operate with Lieutenant-Colonel Fremont, but my movements, after taking San Luis Rey, would depend entirely on the information that I might receive as to the movements of Colonel Fremont and the enemy. It might be necessary for me to stop the pass at San Filippe, or march back to San Diego.

"*Now, my dear General, if the object of your note is to advise me to do any thing which would enable a larger force of the enemy to get in my rear, and cut off my communications with San Diego, and hazard the safety of the garrison and the ships in the harbour, you will excuse me for saying I cannot follow any such advice.*

"My purpose still is to march for San Luis Rey as soon as I can get the dragoons and riflemen mounted, which I hope to do in two days. Faithfully, your obedient servant,

"R. F. STOCKTON, *Commander-in-chief, &c.,*

"*Governor of the Territory of California.*

"To BRIGADIER-GENERAL S. W. KEARNEY,

"*U. S. Army.*"*

To this suggestive epistle the General replied in the following deprecatory and apologetic terms:—

"SAN DIEGO, December 23, 1846.

"DEAR COMMODORE:—I have received yours of this date, repeating, as you say, what you stated to me yesterday; and, in reply, I

---

* Proceedings of Court-martial on Fremont, p. 111.

have only to remark that, if I had so understood you, I certainly would not have written my letter to you of last evening.

"You certainly could not for a moment suppose that I would advise or suggest to you any movement which might endanger the safety of the garrison and the ships in this harbour.

"My letter of yesterday's date stated that 'If you can take from here,' &c., of which you were the judge, and of which I knew nothing.   Yours truly,

          "S. W. KEARNEY, *Brigadier-General.*
"COMMODORE R. F. STOCKTON,
  "*Commanding U. S. Navy, &c. &c., San Diego.*"*

On the 29th of December, having received his supplies and made every needful arrangement in his power, the whole force was paraded for the advance on Ciudad de los Angeles.†

Each officer had his appropriate duty assigned him. Captain Turner's company of dismounted dragoons preferred marching on foot,‡ declining the horses tendered them by the Commodore as unfit for duty. They, aided by Lieutenant Davidson, Lieutenant Tilghman with six pieces of artillery, Midshipman W. W. A. Thomson, and Captain Gillespie's mounted riflemen, acted as the advance, the rear, and vanguard. The marines of the Congress and Portsmouth were commanded by Captain Zeilen, who also acted as adjutant of the battalion. The musketeers of the Congress, Savannah, Cyane, and Portsmouth, were officered by Lieutenants Renshaw, Hunter, and Higgins, Midshipmen George Morgan, Philip, Lee, Allmand, Wells, Grafton, Duvall, Haywood, and Commodore's Clerk Mr. Simmons. The carbineers of the Congress were under Midshipmen Duncan and Stenson and Sailmaker Reed, aided by Midshipmen Parish and Shepherd,—in all, about six hundred men. Purser Speiden performed the duties of commissary; Lieutenant Minor, of the Savannah, acted as quarter-master; Mr. Southwick, carpenter of the Congress, was chief engineer, and Captain Emory adjutant-general. Lieutenant Rowan was to act as commander of the division. Lieutenant A. F. V. Gray and Captain Miguel Pedrovena were appointed aids to the commander-in-chief; which position, also, the Commodore, up to this time, supposed General Kearney was to occupy, agreeably to his previous offer. He had heard, pre-

---

* See proceedings of Court-martial, p. 112.
  † For the order of the march see Commodore Stockton's Letter, February 5, 1847, Appendix A.
  ‡ See Captain Turner's Letter, Appendix B.

vious to that moment, when the advance was commencing, no intimation that the General desired any other post.

It is possible that he had not till then decided whether or not he
would accompany the expedition.   But, just before the march commenced, he approached the Commodore and inquired who was to have
command of the troops.   The Commodore informed him that Lieutenant Rowan had been designated for that duty.   Kearney then
expressed a wish to take charge of them; when the Commodore,
with that courtesy which marked his personal intercourse with the
General, immediately called up several officers, including Lieutenant
Rowan, and informed them of the General's wish.   Lieutenant
Rowan cheerfully gave way to the General; and the Commodore
informed them that General Kearney would take the place of Lieutenant Rowan, while he would himself act as Commander-in-Chief.*

---

* See Appendix D,

CHAPTER XI.

MARCH ON CIUDAD DE LOS ANGELES—COMMISSIONER FROM FLORES—THE COMMODORE'S
TREATMENT OF HIM—LETTER TO COLONEL FREMONT—BATTLES OF SAN GABRIEL AND
THE MESA—DISPERSION OF THE ENEMY—COMMODORE STOCKTON RE-ENTERS CIUDAD
DE LOS ANGELES—TREATY OF COENGO—COLONEL FREMONT APPOINTED CIVIL GOVER-
NOR—GENERAL KEARNEY'S PRETENSIONS—DISMISSED FROM HIS COMMAND OF THE
TROOPS—GENERAL PACIFICATION OF CALIFORNIA—COMMODORE STOCKTON RETURNS
TO HIS SHIPS—KEARNEY AND FREMONT—ENTIRE APPROVAL OF STOCKTON'S PRO-
CEEDINGS BY GOVERNMENT — PRESIDENT'S MESSAGE — REPORTS OF SECRETARIES
OF NAVY AND WAR.

CIUDAD DE LOS ANGELES is distant about one hundred and fifty
miles from San Diego. The route is intersected with abrupt
mountains, deep ravines, and plains of sand. It afforded the most
favourable facilities for defence by the enemy, had they possessed
the sagacity or enterprise to profit by them.

The troops under Commodore Stockton in this expedition consisted of between five and six hundred sailors and marines, and
General Kearney's sixty dismounted dragoons. There were six
guns, principally six-pounders, and a howitzer brought by General
Kearney. There were but about two hundred muskets in the whole
army. The sailors were armed principally with carbines and boarding-pikes. The horses procured by Captains Gibson and Henseley
were rejected by General Kearney as unfit for use, and those which
were employed for the transportation of the artillery, ammunition,
and baggage, were so emaciated and feeble that the sailors had to
perform the chief part of their labour.

The army depended for provisions almost exclusively on the cattle
and sheep procured by Captains Gibson and Henseley. They
were herded together and enclosed· in a hollow square, and thus
guarded both from the depredations of the enemy and from the
danger of escape.

In crossing the dry sandy bed of the San Diego three hours
were consumed. This unpromising commencement of the march
induced many to express the opinion that it was impossible to
proceed. The Commodore inquired of the guides if there was water
to be obtained on the route. They said, " No, no; not until they
arrived at the Solidad,"—the end of the proposed march for the

first day. "Then," said the Commodore, "there we must go, cost what it may." And there they did go, though the carts and guns had to be drawn by hand two-thirds of the way. On the next morning the men came in squads and asked the Commodore for twenty-four hours' rest. This request at first was granted, and orders to that effect issued. But, after a few hours, his restless perseverance induced him to resume the march, and they proceeded eight miles to the next watering-place. During the march, his men, on frequent occasions, preferred similar demands for rest, but without obtaining the wished-for respite.

It was owing to this rapid advance of the Commodore that the enemy were compelled to abandon a plan they had formed to attack and intercept Colonel Fremont. They were afraid to leave the city of Los Angeles lest it should be captured by the Commodore. Nor, with the exception of a few skirmishers, who hovered on his advance, did they attempt any offensive operations until he had approached within two days' march of Ciudad de los Angeles.

A few days after leaving San Diego, commissioners, bearing a communication to the Commander-in-Chief, made their appearance, and, having been first met by General Kearney, were referred to the Commodore. They were bearers of a letter from General Flores, the Californian commander. The Commodore refused to receive any communication from him, he having broken his parole of honour. He rejected the letter without reading it, and directed the commissioners to inform General Flores that if he should be captured again he would be shot; that he was not an honourable man, and that no negotiations could be held with him.

San Luis Rey was reached on the 2d of January. On the 3d, Commodore Stockton despatched a courier, Mr. Hanly, to find Fremont, with a letter, which, as it is quite characteristic, we shall transfer to our narrative.

"CAMP AT SAN LUIS REY, January 3, 1847.

"MY DEAR COLONEL:—We arrived here last night from San Diego, and leave to-day on our march for the City of the Angels, where I hope to be in five or six days. I learn this morning that you are at Santa Barbara, and send this despatch by the way of San Diego, in the hope that it may reach you in time. If there is one single chance for you, you had better not fight the rebels until I get up to aid you, or you can join me on the road to the Pueblo.

"These fellows are well prepared, and Mervine and Kearney's defeat has *given them a deal more confidence and courage.* If you do fight before I see you, keep your forces in close order. Do not allow them to be separated or unnecessarily extended. They will probably try to deceive you by a sudden retreat or pretended runaway, and then unexpectedly return to the charge after your men get in disorder in the chase. My advice to you is to allow them to do all the charging and running, and let your rifles do the rest.

"In the art of horsemanship, of dodging and running, it is in vain to compete with them.

"In haste, very truly, your friend and obedient servant,

"R. F. STOCKTON.

"To LIEUTENANT-COLONEL FREMONT, &c."*

On the evening of the 7th of January, being satisfied that the enemy could not be far distant, the Commodore ordered some of the scouts, under cover of night, to proceed in advance and ascertain their position. At ten o'clock P. M. the scouts returned with the information that the enemy were encamped on the river San Gabriel, but a few miles off. He was of opinion that they intended to offer battle on the next day. "The day suited" him, as he said in his despatch to the Secretary of the Navy of the 5th of February, 1847.

On the morning of the 8th, as the Commodore sprang from his pallet before day, he said to his aid, Lieutenant Gray, "If I live, and the enemy will fight, I will give the San Gabriel a name in history along with that of the Bridge of Lodi."

. At nine o'clock, as they came out on the plain, he marshalled his little army in square, with the cattle, ammunition, and baggage-carts in the centre, and thus advanced until they came in sight of the opposing force. He found them advantageously posted on a bluff or range of low hills on the other side of the river, about six hundred yards from it. Their artillery was so placed as to command the ford, and strongly supported on each side with detachments of cavalry. The position of the enemy was well chosen, and their numbers about the same as that of the Americans. Before the latter had reached the river, about one hundred and fifty Californians crossed, but, without attempting a charge, soon retraced their steps, being driven by Captain Henseley's dismounted skirmishers. The Commodore now disposed his force for an assault on the enemy's position, and, passing through the ranks of his men, reminded them that it was the 8th of January, and that he expected

---

* See proceedings of Court-martial on Colonel Fremont, page 272.

their conduct would add new lustre to the day. As his men advanced in broken files to the ford, the enemy opened a galling fire of round and grape shot. On the brink of the river, the column was halted, the · guns unlimbered, by order of General Kearney, to return the fire of the enemy. Commodore Stockton, as soon as he perceived this, ordered the guns limbered up, and that not a shot should be fired until they had reached the opposite bank.*

In the face of the incessant fire of the foe, the whole force moved forward. General Kearney proceeded to try the ford, and, when about midway over, sent a message to the Commodore that it would be impossible to pass over the guns, as the bed of the river was a quicksand. On receiving this message the Commodore sprang from his horse into the river, and, taking hold of the ropes, said, "Quicksand or no quicksand, the guns shall pass over!" The men, cheered by his example, seized the ropes also, and soon landed the guns, with three cheers, on the other bank.

The enemy stood their ground bravely, and continued an incessant fire. One man was killed alongside the Commodore. But their shots mostly passed over the heads of the assailants.

The whole force was now disposed for a charge up the bluff. The artillery in the centre, before the charge was ordered, under the immediate direction of the Commodore, opened a fire on the position of the enemy. He levelled and aimed the guns himself, and such was the precision of his shots, that at the second or third round he disabled one of the enemy's guns and silenced their battery. They retreated from their guns several times, but soon returned, and finally withdrew them to their rear. General Kearney, on the right, was now ordered to form a square to support the left flank, which was threatened by a charge from the enemy's right. The charge was made and gallantly repulsed. The Commodore then sent his aid, Lieutenant Gray, to General Kearney, with orders to charge up the hill with his square,† while he advanced with the

---

* See Proceedings of Court-martial, Appendix, Purser Speiden's Letter.

† As General Kearney in some of his despatches claims to have commanded in this battle as well as during the whole expedition, we insert here the testimony of Lieutenant Gray on this point, given on the trial of Colonel Fremont. See also Appendix for further information on this subject.

Extract from Proceedings of Court-martial of Colonel Fremont, p. 210.

"Andrew F. Gray, a lieutenant in the navy, a witness on the part of the defence, being duly sworn by the judge-advocate, according to law, testified as follows:—

"*Question.*—State the position you held under Commodore Stockton at San Diego.

"*Answer.*—I was his aid, and one of the lieutenants of the Congress.

10

centre and the artillery in battery. The enemy defended their position but a few moments, and then broke and retreated, their main body taking a position, flanked by a ravine, a half mile from the bluff. Their right wing, making a circuit, attacked the American rear under Captain Gillespie, who, though encumbered with the baggage and cattle, gave them such a reception that they fled across the river.

The left wing of the enemy and their centre from the ravine now opened with their artillery on the Americans. The Commodore, with his usual care of his men, made them lie down to avoid the shot, and took charge of his guns in front, aiming and firing them himself, until the foe were driven from their batteries. As soon as

---

" *Question.*—Did you hear Commodore Stockton offer to go as General Kearney's aid? And did you hear General Kearney offer to go as Commodore Stockton's aid?

"*Answer.*—I did.

" *Question.*—Did you hear the address of Commodore Stockton to his officers at the time when the position which had been assigned to Lieutenant Rowan was given to General Kearney? and if so, will you state what passed on that occasion?

"*Answer.*—I was present on the occasion referred to. I heard Commodore Stockton confer the command of the forces on General Kearney, reserving to himself the office of commander-in-chief.

" The words were, ' Gentlemen, General Kearney has kindly offered to go with us. Public duty requires that I should appoint him to the command of the forces. You will obey him accordingly, reserving to myself the office of commander-in-chief.' Those are the words, as nearly as I can recollect them.

" *Question.*—Did you bear an order from Commodore Stockton on the 8th of January, 1847, on the field of battle? If so, state the order and the circumstances.

"*Answer.*—I did bear such an order on the 8th of January to General Kearney on the field of battle. The enemy had been observed to withdraw their guns from the height. The Commodore directed me to go to General Kearney and say to him to send a square and a field-piece immediately upon the height to prevent the enemy returning with their guns. I went and gave him the order, and, on my returning to Commodore Stockton, observed the division or square near General Kearney moving towards the hill.

" *Question.*—Did you bear that order in your character of aid-de-camp to Governor Stockton?

"*Answer.*—Yes.

" Cross-examined by Judge-Advocate.

" *Question.*—Do you recollect the words and manner in which you delivered that order? Did you deliver it so that General Kearney must have received it as a peremptory order or as a suggestion?

"*Answer.*—I carried it as an order in the usual respectful way. How General Kearney received it, of course I cannot say. He did not show by his manner that it was disagreeable, according to the best of my recollection."

See also Appendix B.

he perceived them waver, he ordered an advance of his whole force, when the enemy left their guns and fled in confusion. Having no cavalry, it was impossible to follow them.

The American loss was only two killed and nine wounded. The loss of the enemy, as afterwards ascertained, was over seventy killed and one hundred and fifty wounded.

The Americans encamped on the field of battle near the river San Gabriel.

On the morning of the 9th they pursued the track of the retreating foe in the direction of Ciudad de los Angeles. After proceeding about six miles across the plains of the Mesa, the Californians appeared in battle-array in a position well chosen, flanked by a ravine, on the brink of which their artillery was fixed. As soon as the Americans approached near enough to be reached by it, their artillery began to play. The Commodore again took charge of the American guns, directing his men to lie flat on the ground; he alone stood up with the men who worked the guns, and he ordered them, too, to fall as soon as they saw the flash of the enemy's guns. In a short time he made the enemy's position so dangerous that they prepared to charge. The Americans were then formed into a square, with their baggage, cattle, and mules in the centre of it, the Commodore, with the artillery, occupying a position on the side of the square opposite to the enemy. As they approached, their force divided for the purpose of attacking, simultaneously, three sides of the square. The Commodore ordered his men to reserve their fire until they could see the faces of their foes distinctly, and till they should hear the report of his rifle.

The appearance which the Californians made on this occasion, mounted on fine horses, gaily caparisoned with ribbons and pennons streaming to the breeze, was brilliant and exciting. On they came at full gallop, the earth quivering beneath their hoofs, their bright weapons flashing in the rays of the sun,—apparently, with desperate valour, bent on hurling themselves upon the small, compact, and silent mass which awaited their charge. But, when they had approached as near as the Commodore thought proper, he gave the signal, and a deadly fire from the Americans emptied many a saddle and checked their gallant advance. Retiring a little, they rallied their disordered ranks, and again charged. Three times this charge was bravely made and as bravely repulsed, when, in despair, and finding the American square impenetrable and unterrified, the Californians abandoned the field and fled, dispersing in different directions. Having no cavalry of importance, it was impossible for the Americans to pursue them. The enemy's loss was considerable, though it could not be ascertained, because they carried off in their flight both their dead and wounded.

The Commodore continued his march on the 9th, and arrived in the neighbourhood of Ciudad de los Angeles in the evening. On the following day, at the head of his army, he marched into the city and again took possession of it. The same American flag which Major Gillespie had been compelled to strike, the Commodore ordered to be again raised.

The battles of San Gabriel and the Mesa, on the 8th and 9th of January, decided the fate of California. They broke effectually the spirit of resistance to American authority. The Californians made a gallant and brave stand to uphold the supremacy of Mexico. Under abler and more experienced commanders it would have been impossible to have conquered California unless with an army far superior in numbers and training to that led by Commodore Stockton. It may well be doubted, however, without any disparagement to others, whether any other commander than Stockton, with such a force, so heterogeneous and extraordinary, could have accomplished similar results.

The scattered remnants of the Californian army, under Flores and Pico, a few days after the Commodore took possession of Ciudad de los Angeles, hearing of the approach of Colonel Fremont, threw themselves in his way and made overtures of peace. Having already been repulsed by Stockton in their attempts to negotiate, because they had broken their parole of honour, they now addressed themselves to Colonel Fremont; he granted them an armistice, and opened negotiations for a final pacification. On the 13th he concluded a formal treaty with them, by which they agreed to cease all hostilities and to acknowledge the authority of the United States. His treaty of capitulation he despatched by the hands of Colonel W. H. Russell to Ciudad de los Angeles, with directions to submit it to Commodore Stockton or General Kearney, whichever was acting as commander-in-chief.

Colonel Russell, upon his arrival at Ciudad de los Angeles, waited upon General Kearney first, but was directed by him to submit it to Commodore Stockton as the commander-in-chief.* He finally,

---

* *Extract from Proceedings of Court-martial,* p. 321.

"Mr. H. RUSSELL—*a witness.*

"*Answer.*—As before stated in my chief examination, I was despatched by Lieutenant-Colonel Fremont, on the evening of the capitulation of General Andreas Pico,

though not without hesitation, approved the articles of capitulation. Courtesy and kind feelings towards Fremont made him disposed to ratify a treaty which afforded him some claim to have participated in the important events which terminated in the acquisition of the country. Clemency after victory likewise he thought to be sound policy. The subsequent tranquillity of the country justified this conclusion. The inhabitants thenceforward peacefully submitted to the authority of the United States.

However meritorious the conduct of Colonel Fremont in co-operating with Stockton and sustaining his authority by the levy of troops and obedience to his orders, nevertheless he was not so fortunate as to participate in any of the conflicts which decided the fate of California. Castro was driven out of the country without his direct aid. He was too late to take part in the decisive actions of the 8th and 9th of January. Indeed, from the time the Commodore left San Diego until his second occupation of Ciudad de los Angeles, he had heard nothing from Fremont and knew nothing of his movements. Undoubtedly the force which Colonel Fremont had levied and was marching forward to co-operate with Stockton exercised a salutary influence on the minds of the Californians. The ready obedience of Fremont to the directions of his commander-in-chief, his industry and perseverance, and the fortitude with which he contended against great obstacles, entitle him to high praise as well as the grateful consideration of his country. The general plans of both the campaigns, however, by which California was conquered and reconquered, were conceived, directed, and executed by Commodore Stockton. This was abundantly shown by Colonel Fremont in his defence when on trial before the court-martial at Washington in November and December, 1847. A large number of witnesses who were present in California during the whole war were examined on that trial, and their testimony can justify no other conclusion.

---

commander-in-chief of the Californians, to Los Angeles, where both Commodore Stockton and General Kearney were, and specially instructed by him (Colonel Fremont) to ascertain by all means possible who *was in chief command,* and to make a report accordingly of the capitulation of that day. I called first on General Kearney, and delivered to him a note or letter addressed to him by Colonel Fremont in acknowledgment of one that he (Colonel Fremont) had received from General Kearney on the march. I told General Kearney my business, and was directed by him to make my report to Commodore Stockton, *whom he acknowledged as being in chief command,* and admitted to me that he had served under him, *as such,* from San Diego to Los Angeles. I accordingly made the report to the Commodore."

From the day when the Commodore commenced his march from San Diego to his triumphant entry into Ciudad de los Angeles, General Kearney, as well as all others under him, acted in entire subordination to his authority. The Commodore was the commander-in-chief, as such was addressed in all the letters and notes he received from Kearney. He ordered when the army should move and when it should halt and where it should encamp. He received and rejected contemptuously the message from Flores. To him the Adjutant-General Emory, the particular friend of Kearney, reported the list of killed and wounded after the actions of the 8th and 9th.*

Colonel Fremont arrived in Ciudad de los Angeles on the 15th day of January. Having inadvertently suffered himself to be drawn into correspondence by General Kearney, the General assumed to find in one of his letters a recognition of his authority from seniority of rank. Fremont, however, throughout the California war, was strictly and technically in the naval service under Commodore Stockton. He had taken service under him with an express agreement that he would continue subject to his orders as long as he continued in command in California. This engagement both he and Captain Gillespie had entered into from patriotic motives and to render the most efficient service to the country.

He visited California originally upon topographical, and not on military duty. His volunteering under Stockton on special service was a patriotic impulse, in complying with which the government were in honour bound to sustain him. He, therefore, very properly refused to violate his agreement with Stockton and unite with Kearney against him.

Having failed to compel Fremont to acknowledge his authority, the General addressed himself to the Commodore and demanded that he should abdicate the command-in-chief.

The Commodore, considering the subjugation of California complete, and that no further hostilities were likely to take place, was of opinion that he might now relinquish his governorship and command-in-chief and return to his ships. But, having informed the Government that upon that event he intended to appoint Colonel Fremont governor, he now proceeded to carry that design into execution. General Kearney, learning this to be the purpose of the Commodore, and desirous of exercising the functions of governor himself, addressed to him the following letter, which, with the en-

---

* See Appendix A, B, D.

suing correspondence, will apprise the reader of the true relations of the parties better than we could state them.

> " HEAD-QUARTERS, ARMY OF THE WEST,
> CIUDAD DE LOS ANGELES, January 16, 1847.

" SIR :—I am informed that you are now engaged in organizing a civil government and appointing officers for it in this territory. As this duty has been specially assigned to myself, by orders of the President of the United States, conveyed in letters to me from the Secretary of War, of June 3, 8, and 18, 1846, the original of which I gave to you on the 12th, and which you returned to me on the 13th, and copies of which I furnished you with on the 26th December, I have to ask if you have any authority from the President, from the Secretary of the Navy, or from any other channel of the President, to form such government and make such appointments.

" If you have such authority, and will show it to me or furnish me with a certified copy of it, I will cheerfully acquiesce in what you are doing. If you have not such authority, I then demand that you cease all further proceedings relating to the formation of a civil government for this territory, as I cannot recognise in you any right in assuming to perform duties confided to me by the President.

> " Very respectfully, your obedient servant,
> " S. W. KEARNEY,
> " *Brigadier-General United States Army.*

" COMMODORE R. F. STOCKTON,
" *Acting Governor of California.*"

> " HEAD-QUARTERS, CIUDAD DE LOS ANGELES,
> January 16, 1847.

" SIR :—In answer to your note received this afternoon, I need say but little more than that which I communicated to you in a conversation at San Diego :—that California was conquered, and a civil government put into successful operation; that a copy of the laws made by me for the government of the territory, and the names of the officers selected to see them faithfully executed, were transmitted to the President of the United States before you arrived in the territory.

" I will only add, that I cannot do any thing nor desist from doing any thing on your demand, which I will submit to the President and ask for your recall. In the mean time you will consider yourself suspended from the command of the United States forces in this place.

> " Faithfully, your obedient servant,
> ' R. F. STOCKTON,
> " *Commander-in-Chief.*
" To BREVET BRIGADIER-GENERAL, S. W. KEARNEY."

> " HEAD-QUARTERS, ARMY OF THE WEST,
> CIUDAD DE LOS ANGELES, January 17, 1847.

" SIR :—In my communication to you of yesterday's date I stated that I had learned that you were engaged in organizing a civil government for California. I referred you to the President's instructions to me (the original of which you have seen, and copies of which I furnished you) to perform that duty, and I added that if you had any authority from the President, or any of his organs, for what you were doing, I would cheerfully acquiesce, and, if you had not such authority, I demanded that you would cease further proceedings in the matter.

" Your reply of the same date refers me to a conversation held at San Diego, and adds that you ' cannot do any thing or desist from doing any thing or alter any thing on your (my) demand.' As, in consequence of the defeat of the enemy on the 8th and 9th instants, by the troops under *my command,** and the capitulation entered into on the 13th instant by Lieutenant-Colonel Fremont with the leaders of the Californians, in which the people under arms and in the field agree to disperse and remain quiet and peaceable, the country may now, for the first time, be considered as conquered and taken possession of by us ; and, as I am prepared to carry out the President's instructions to me, which you oppose, I must, for the purpose of preventing a collision between us and possibly a civil war in consequence of it, remain silent for the present, leaving with you the great responsibility of doing that for which you have no authority, and preventing me from complying with the President's orders.

> " Very respectfully, your obedient servant,
> " S. W. KEARNEY,
> " *Brigadier-General U. S. A.*
" COMMODORE R. F. STOCKTON, *U. S. N.,*
> "*Acting Governor of California.*"

---

* See Appendix D.

"HEAD-QUARTERS, ARMY OF THE WEST,
CIUDAD DE LOS ANGELES, January 17, 1847.

" SIR :—I have to inform you that I intend to withdraw to-morrow from this place, with the small party which escorted me to this country.

" Very respectfully, your obedient servant,

" S. W. KEARNEY,
" Brigadier-General.

" COMMODORE R. F. STOCKTON, U. S. N.,
" Acting Governor of California."

"CIUDAD DE LOS ANGELES, January 17, 1847.

" SIR :—I have the honour to be in receipt of your favour of last night, in which I am directed to suspend the execution of orders which, in my capacity of military commandant of this territory, I had received from Commodore Stockton, Governor and Commander-in-chief in California. I avail myself of an early hour this morning to make such a reply as the brief time allowed for reflection will enable me.

" I found Commodore Stockton in possession of the country, exercising the functions of military commandant and civil governor, as early as July of last year; and shortly thereafter I received from him the commission of military commandant, the duties of which I immediately entered upon and have continued to exercise to the present moment.

" I found, also, on my arrival at this place some three or four days since, Commodore Stockton still exercising the functions of civil and military governor, with the same apparent deference to his rank on the part of all officers (including yourself) as he maintained and required when he assumed them in July last.

" I learned, also, in conversation with you, that on the march from San Diego, recently, to this place, you entered upon and discharged duties implying an acknowledgment, on your part, of supremacy to Commodore Stockton.

" I feel, therefore, with great deference to your professional and personal character, constrained to say that, until you and Commodore Stockton adjust, between yourselves, the question of rank, where I respectfully think the difficulty belongs, I shall have to report and receive orders, as heretofore, from the Commodore.

" With considerations of high regard, I am, sir, your obedient servant,

" J. C. FREMONT, Lieutenant-Colonel U. S. Army, and
Military Commandant of the Territory of California.

" BRIGADIER-GENERAL S. W. KEARNEY, U. S. Army."

In pursuance of his original intentions as communicated to the Government in August, 1846, Commodore Stockton now appointed Colonel Fremont Civil Governor of California, and Colonel William H. Russell, Secretary. Governor Fremont immediately entered on the duties of his office, and the people acquiesced in his exercise of authority.

The Commodore and his maritime army returned to the squadron.

The performance of his duties as Governor of California by Colonel Fremont were incompatible with the authority which General Kearney attempted to exercise over him by virtue of seniority of rank. Notwithstanding the President and Secretary of War both justified the appointment of Colonel Fremont by Commodore Stockton as Civil Governor of California, yet, nevertheless, he was permitted to be brought to trial on charges of disobedience preferred by General Kearney. He was found guilty on several charges and specifications by a court evidently disposed to favour General Kearney. The finding of the court was approved in part by the President, but the sentence remitted.

Indignant with the injustice and inconsistency manifested by the Government, Colonel Fremont promptly resigned his commission in the army.

Towards the close of the Mexican war, the army was powerful and popular at Washington. The *esprit de corps* of military gentlemen was piqued and offended with Fremont's deference to a naval commander, and his sacrifice was demanded. The President and Secretary of War had not the moral courage and firmness which the occasion required, and Colonel Fremont was driven from the army.

The Government received intelligence of the success of Commodore Stockton in California in October, 1846, and were well pleased with the prospect of the realization of their views respecting that country.

The President, in his annual message of December, 1846, approved and justified the proceedings of the Commodore in the most comprehensive terms. He says:—

"Our squadron in the Pacific, with the co-operation of a gallant officer of the army and a small force hastily collected in that distant country, have acquired bloodless possession of the Californias, and the American flag has been raised at every important point in that province. I congratulate you on the success which has thus attended our military and naval operations.

"By the laws of nations, a conquered territory is subject to be governed by the conqueror during his military possession and until there is either a treaty of peace or he shall voluntarily withdraw from it. The old civil government being necessarily superseded, it is the right and duty of the conqueror to secure his conquest and to provide for the maintenance of civil order and the rights of the inhabitants. This right has been exercised and this duty performed by the establishment of temporary governments in some of the conquered provinces of Mexico, assimilating them, as far as practicable, to the free institutions of our own country."

The Secretary of War, in his annual report of the same year, (1846,) thus speaks of the events in California:—

"Commodore Stockton took possession of the whole country as a conquest of the United States, and appointed Colonel Fremont governor, *under the law of nations*, to assume the functions of that office when he should return to the squadron."

Extract from a letter of the Secretary of the Navy to Commodore R. F. Stockton, dated November 5, 1846. *

"The difficulties and embarrassments of the command, without a knowledge of the proceedings of Congress on the subject of the war with Mexico, and in the absence of the instructions of the department which followed those proceedings, are justly appreciated, and it is highly gratifying that so much has been done in anticipation of the orders which have been transmitted."

Extract from a letter of the Secretary of the Navy to the commanding officer of the Pacific squadron, June 14, 1847.

"At the commencement of the war with Mexico, the United States had no military force in California of any description whatever, and the conquest of that country was, from necessity, therefore devolved exclusively upon the navy."†

Extract from Annual Report of 1848 of the Secretary of the Navy, in Ex. Doc. No. 1.

"In the Pacific, our squadron, with means not fitted for inland operations, acting independently and in co-operation with a small

---

* Proceedings of Court-martial, p. 51.
† Proceedings of Court-martial, p. 367.

portion of our gallant army, effected the conquest of California. In supplying the deficiency of his means, and in preparing for and executing an inland campaign with the crews of his ships, Commodore Stockton displayed the highest military resource and the greatest energy. Since his memorable march from San·Diego to the Ciudad de los Angeles, and the battles of the 8th and 9th of January, 1847, that country has been tranquil, our possession undisputed, and its inhabitants have hailed the cession of California to the United States with grateful satisfaction.''

An unofficial letter from the Secretary of the Navy to Commodore R. F. Stockton.

"[UNOFFICIAL.]   WASHINGTON, March 7, 1849.

"MY DEAR SIR:—I enclose you a copy of a general order announcing to the navy the thanks of Congress for the zeal and ability with which its duty was performed during the late war with Mexico.

"My connection with the Navy Department for all exercise of official power has ceased, and I may gratify my own personal feelings by renewing to you in this note what I have said and intended to convey in my official reports,—my high estimate of your zeal, energy, and gallantry, in the performance of your duties in the great service which resulted in the acquisition of California. Your energy and military resource in supplying your deficiency of means, the courage and skill with which you conducted your well-planned operations, the success with which you imparted your own enthusiasm to those whom you commanded, entitle you to the highest praise; and the results of your brilliant achievements have added largely to the national strength and to the national honour.

"With such convictions on my mind, I cannot take leave of you without saying thus much, and to express the hope that I shall ever have the happiness of cultivating with you personally the relations of friendship.

"With the highest esteem,
"I am very truly yours,
"J. Y. MASON.
"COMMODORE R. F. STOCKTON, *U. S. Navy.*"*

---

* See Extract from Cooper's Naval History, in the Appendix; also Commodore Stockton's Official Correspondence, Appendix A. See also Proceedings of Court-martial on Colonel Fremont, and Senator Benton's speech, July, 1848, Congressional Globe, Appendix, 1848.

CHAPTER XII.

COMMODORE STOCKTON'S ABSTINENCE FROM SPECULATION WHILE IN CALIFORNIA —
ESTABLISHES THE FIRST PRINTING-PRESS AND THE FIRST FREE-SCHOOL IN CALI-
FORNIA—REV. WALTER COLTON'S LETTER—DRAWS ON WASHINGTON ON HIS OWN
RESPONSIBILITY FOR FUNDS TO PAY EXPENSES OF THE WAR—PREPARES FOR
OVERLAND JOURNEY — DESCRIPTION OF HIS PARTY — ATTACKED BY INDIANS —
WOUNDED — PUNISHMENT OF THE ENEMY — EXTRICATES HIS MEN FROM AMBUS-
CADE — BUFFALO HUNT — ARRIVES AT ST. JOSEPH — RECEPTION — PARTING WITH
HIS MEN—ARRIVES AT WASHINGTON.

FROM the abdication by Commodore Stockton of the supreme
command to the period at which the war was closed by the treaty of
Guadaloupe Hidalgo, no further resistance was offered on the part
of the inhabitants of California to the authority of the United
States.

It is well known that, immediately subsequent to this event,
extensive speculations in lands were made by many Americans,
which subsequently proved of immense value. Commodore Stockton saw and appreciated as well as others the certain improvement
in value of property in California, and particularly at San Francisco.
Opportunities were offered him of investments in property there
which would have made him, had he embraced them, the most opulent man on the continent. But, occupying a public position which
gave him the greatest facilities for speculation, ho considered it his
duty to abstain from all complicity in such pecuniary operations.
It was his ambition rather to bestow benefits on California than to
receive them from her.

A printing-press having been procured at San Francisco, Commodore Stockton, from his own purse, provided the means for
establishing a newspaper there, which he gave in charge of the Rev.
Walter Colton, chaplain of the Congress. The following letter of
Mr. Colton, which appeared in a contemporary paper, in relation to
this subject, is too interesting to be omitted here.

"MAGISTRATE'S OFFICE, MONTEREY, June 4, 1847.

"DEAR SIR:—The generous policy which you have pursued towards this office makes me regret that I have put you to the trouble

to send the chairs from the ship, and am grateful for them, but did not consider that we had any claim, considering how much you have done.

"*To you California is indebted for her first press and her first school-house.* This may not be known generally now, but it will if I live. It is something to conquer a country; it is also something to provide for the progressive intelligence of its inhabitants; but it is rarely that, as in the present instance, the honour of both appertains to the same individual.

"These facts may seem shaded to some, but truth will vindicate itself, and every thing will stand out in its own distinct, impressive light.

"I have taken notes of all that has occurred in California since our arrival here. I commenced with your repudiation of the Bear flag, and have continued the history of events up to your second capture of the Pueblo; and now I will state what no one knows but myself,—that the facts contained in Mr. Speiden's graphic description of the march from San Diego* and the battles of the 8th and 9th are in my journal just as I recorded them the day after the letter was received. I mention this merely to vindicate my feelings on the occasion, and these are feelings which remain unchanged.

"I am, dear sir, very faithfully yours,
"WALTER COLTON.
"COMMODORE R. F. STOCKTON,
"*United States Frigate Congress.*"

Upon the first organization of a civil government in California, Commodore Stockton ordained that the proceeds of the confiscation of enemy's property, or of property which escheated to the existing government for the want of an owner, should be appropriated to the construction of school-houses and for the employment of teachers and the support of a free school. The first school-house was built at San Francisco, and the first free-school organized and put in operation by the funds thus appropriated by Stockton.

In the latter part of January, Commodore Shubrick arrived, and, soon after, Commodore Biddle, both of whom being seniors to Commodore Stockton, superseded him in command of the squadron.

In May the Commodore formed the determination of returning home across the Rocky Mountains. He was delayed somewhat by the detention of Major Gillespie, upon whose co-operation in making

---

* See Appendix D.

the necessary preparations for the overland journey he had relied.*

Before leaving, Stockton determined that all the debts which he had contracted for the purchase of horses, or by the appropriation of other property of the emigrants and settlers, on account of government, should be liquidated. He applied to Commodore Biddle to approve his drafts on the government for that purpose; but Biddle declined to take the responsibility. Commodore Stockton, on his own authority, drew on the proper offices at Washington drafts sufficient in amount to pay all those demands which he felt bound in honour to satisfy. The drafts were all duly honoured.

Having collected the required number of mules and horses, and his men having made their saddles, his returning band, numbering forty-nine, commenced their journey June 20, 1847.

His men were a heterogeneous collection of all nations almost, and professions and pursuits: some were Canadians; some Rocky Mountain trappers and hunters; some sailors; some Spaniards; some Irishmen; some French. Many of them were men of the most desperate and lawless character, and noted for their sanguinary and ferocious habits and actions. Among them, however, he was so fortunate as to secure the services of three men as guides, who had passed the greater part of their lives as hunters among the Rocky Mountain Indians, and were acquainted with their dialects, and therefore qualified to act as interpreters.

Stockton immediately appreciated the necessity of holding such men in the most rigorous subordination. On the outset of their journey, therefore, he informed them that, considering the safety of the whole party as at stake upon the implicit obedience of each one, the death-penalty would be the award of any act of mutiny or any refusal to obey his orders; that the exhibition of cowardice in presence of the enemy, whom they would be sure to meet on their way, would likewise be punished with death; that he would ask no one to encounter any danger which he was not himself the first and foremost to brave.

After some days' progress, they began to perceive evidence of their being watched and dogged by Indians; and, upon his men attempting to camp for the night among the bushes and trees, he compelled them, very much against their inclination, to sleep in the open plain, where the guard could see the approach of an enemy before he could come in contact with them. He, however, particu-

---

* See Proceedings of Court-martial, Gillespie's testimony.

larly cautioned his men that on no account should they shoot an Indian. The old Indian-fighters and mountaineers opened their eyes with incredulous astonishment at such instructions, and endeavoured to reason with the Commodore on the absolute necessity of shooting Indians in order to prevent being shot themselves; but he was inflexible. He said human nature was the same among all nations and races; that, if the Indians were treated well, they would appreciate kindness and abstain from hostilities; that they were a poor, abused race, who had been driven to outrage and revenge by innumerable injuries; and that for his part he would not, except in self-defence, consent to take an Indian's life. The old trappers and hunters told him that he did not know the Indians. They subsisted by plunder and murder, and nothing but fear would restrain them. Those of the party most familiar with the habits of the Indians who roved along the route which the travellers pursued, consoled themselves with the expression of the opinion that, whatever the Commodore's views respecting the Indians might then be, he would soon, from necessity, be compelled to change them.

It sometimes happens to parties taking the overland route to or from California that they meet no Indians; others meet occasionally small straggling companies of them; while others, still, meet numerous bands, and are compelled to fight almost their whole journey through.

General Kearney and his party, though travelling nearly on the line of Stockton's return-route, met scarcely any Indians; while, during the whole journey of the Commodore, his party were almost constantly in the presence of Indians more or less numerous. One of the oldest among the Rocky Mountain hunters in the party said that, as often as he had travelled the route, he had never before seen so many Indians or found them so troublesome and dangerous.

The party were frequently surrounded by bands of Indians immensely superior, and often placed in the utmost jeopardy. From this peril they were several times rescued by the presence of mind, courage, and sagacity, of Stockton.

They had advanced but a few days' journey when the Indians began to appear, dogging their progress and hovering in the vicinity to cut off stragglers or seize upon some property belonging to the party,—a stray horse or mule, or something of the sort. As the day wore away, the Indians were observed to become more numerous. The larger part of the company had preceded, on this occasion, the Commodore; and as he overtook them near night, he found them encamped by the side of a river in a valley, instead of pitching their tents on an eminence, as he generally directed. He would have made them remove their camp, had it not been that one of the men had been suddenly taken sick and was too ill to be removed. He told them, however, that they must be vigilant, as they would probably be attacked that night as soon as the moon rose.

It turned out as he had predicted. As soon as the moon poured her light upon their camp, a volley of arrows informed them of the presence of a pretty large party of Indians. He made his men shoot over the heads of the Indians, and enjoined them not to kill them, saying that in the morning he would endeavour to treat with them.

In the morning, however, as they were just sitting down to breakfast, another flight of arrows poured into the camp, one of which struck the Commodore, passing through the fleshy part of one thigh and nearly through the other. Immediately as he was struck he broke the arrow in two and pulled both pieces out. Having been informed that these Indians frequently poisoned their arrows, he sent for one of the old trappers, a man who had lived twenty years among the Indians and had a Crow squaw for his wife, and asked him if he supposed the arrow to be poisoned, the pieces of which he showed him. The old trapper, looking him fiercely in the eye, said, "Yes! by G—d! and you have not half an hour to live!" The Commodore, who well knew that the only way to retain his command over his men was by the exhibition of the most desperate fearlessness and rigour, supposing that the lawless and reckless old fellow wanted to frighten him, said instantly, "You old liar! do you suppose you can frighten me? If you had said I might die in a few days or a week, I might have thought you believed what you said. Begone out of my sight, before I blow out your brains!" And off he went, as fast as he could run.

If the arrow was poisoned, its immediate extraction and the consequent flow of blood, doubtless, prevented the poisonous matter from being dissolved and absorbed, or perhaps washed it out. No serious injury followed, and the wound soon healed, without interrupting the progress of the party.

But the wound dissipated the Commodore's sublimated feelings of forbearance towards the Indians. He became a convert to tho lessons taught by the experience of his hunters and trappers, and at once took steps to chastise the foe. Being detained by the sick man, he felt assured that they would be attacked the following

11

night by an increased force; he determined to have the first shot, and to inflict such a punishment on the enemy as would be remembered by them.

The Indians, he had observed, retreated across the river, and would have to recross it to renew their attack. He discovered the ford at which they passed the river about half a mile from the camp. There he repaired just before the moon rose, and placed his men in the bushes, with directions not to fire without good aim and not until the Indians were crossing the ford. As soon as the moon showed herself over the hills, the stealthy pace of the Indians was heard along the shore. They stepped into the river in single file, and when about fifty of them were half-way over, the simultaneous crack of a score of rifles stopped their progress. They raised a fearful yell, and fled, scattering in every direction. How many were killed could not be ascertained; but this chastisement prevented their renewing their attack on the following day, and the travellers were not again seriously threatened by the same Indians.

On another occasion, having been without water for some time, and suffering for the want of it, they fell in with some Indians who engaged to conduct them to a stream. As they advanced, the Indians appeared in greater numbers; but, as they were friendly and seemed to be acting in good faith, the Commodore intrusted himself to their guidance, until his suspicions were excited by their leading him off the open plain into a dense thicket of underwood. Observing their movements, he at last became satisfied that they were leading him into an ambush.

As soon as he was convinced of this, he suddenly halted; and, through an interpreter, told them he had an important communication to their chiefs and head-men, and desired to have a talk with them. The chiefs, to the number of fifteen or twenty, soon came forward. He made them sit down, and then surrounded them with his men, so as to keep the crowd of Indians from pressing upon them. He then told the chiefs that his party was a war-party returning after a great fight in California, where they had killed many, and achieved the most terrible exploits; that he was afraid the presence of the young warriors might excite their love of blood, and induce them to kill the Indians; and that, therefore, he wished the young warriors to keep away, and not come in contact with the war-party of white men; and, if the chiefs would so advise their young warriors, he would give them plenty of tobacco, and a horse upon which they might feast. The chiefs readily assented to the proposition. But before making the presents the Commodore required the chiefs to,conduct him out on the open plain.   He then ordered each chief to take a horse, on which one of the party was mounted, by the bridle, and lead him out.   He ordered also two men to keep watch with their drawn pistols on each chief, and to shoot the first one who should attempt to break away.   Thus marshalled, they were conducted safely out of the dangerous trap into which they had been led, upon the open plain.   After they had reached the plain, the Commodore selected a horse for the feast, and gave it to the outside Indians, who were now crowding around him in numbers four or five times greater than his band, and told them to take it off and slaughter it for themselves and the chiefs who would soon follow them.   They took the horse and soon disappeared with him over the undulations of the plain.

As soon as they were out of sight, the Commodore ordered the chiefs to take hold of the horses' heads again, and, giving his men the same charge as in the first instance, he started off on a trot in an opposite direction to that in which the rest of the Indians had gone. It was now late in the afternoon.   He kept up the trot, with the chiefs at the horses' heads, for several miles, till he was satisfied that it would be impossible that the Indians whom they had left could overtake them.   He then dismissed the chiefs, who were glad to be relieved from their arduous duties, and at once hastened off at a full run to rejoin their people before the feast was over.   It is obvious that the whole party were saved from massacre by the presence of mind and sagacity of their leader.   The fertility of his mind in resources to meet all difficulties, however novel or sudden, is indicated by this incident.

The Commodore acted as commissary as well as commander of the party, and throughout the whole journey kept them supplied with an abundance of game.   Though he had never before seen a buffalo on his native plains, he proved himself as expert in the chase of that formidable animal as the oldest hunter, if, indeed, he did not excel him; for several said they never had seen any bolder or more successful sportsman in pursuit of buffalo.   He killed forty-five with his own hand during the journey.

Before they had come to the buffalo country, several of the party, who considered themselves hunters of unrivalled merit, frequently descanted upon the pleasures of chasing buffalo, and promised the Commodore to initiate him in the science of the sport. He admitted his ignorance, and signified his willingness to be taught.

It was a bright and cloudless morning, when, on rising from their blankets one day, they saw, far as the scope of vision extended, in every direction, the whole surface of the earth — to the distant horizon—covered with countless thousands of buffalo. Soon the hunters were mounted on their best horses and prepared for the exciting pursuit. The first business was to make a circuit, and get to leeward of the animals, so that they could not scent the approach of the party. Having done this, they then proposed dismounting and crawling near enough to obtain a deadly shot with their rifles. The Commodore, however, demurred to this ignoble way of approaching such game. He ordered them to dismount and tighten the girths of their saddles, and then told them that he might be depended upon for two buffalo cows, and charged each of the party to secure at least one. Then, putting spurs to his horse, (the same which he rode through the whole of his California campaign,) he charged the herd at full gallop.

The chase of the buffalo pursued in this way is, perhaps, the most exciting and dangerous of all field-sports, not, perhaps, excepting that of lions or tigers in India and Africa. The horse rushes into the drove, and soon partakes of the alarm and terror with which he inspires the buffalo. A cloud of dust rises, obscuring all objects except those close at hand. The buffalo bulls roar; the earth trembles sensibly beneath the hoofs of the multitudinous animals as they rush headlong onwards. The rider's whole strength is required to hold and guide his horse and keep the saddle,—standing erect in his stirrups,—the horse springing from one side to the other to avoid contact with the buffalo, and, snorting and plunging, requires a skilful and powerful hand to direct him. Thus, bounding on, the hunter singles out the animal which he prefers, and rides with it side-by-side till a favourable opportunity occurs for a successful shot. As soon as this is had, his next effort is to extricate himself from the herd. This he does by gradually dropping in the rear, and, when a favourable opening is observed through the drove to the right or left, guiding his horse out of the line of direction in which the buffalo are travelling. But, should the hunter unfortunately be thrown from his horse, the danger is imminent that the buffalo will trample him down.

The hunt which we have described was the first buffalo hunt in which the Commodore engaged. He soon killed his two cows, and, after getting out of the drove, ascended a hill and blew his horn. But it was long before any of the party were visible. After a while they all came in, and all claimed to have shot a buffalo; but no buffalo could be found but the two killed by the Commodore with his pistols. The old hunters told him that it was not necessary for them to give him any more instructions.

The buffalo are not generally dangerous, unless the hunter falls or loses his horse in the drove, or unless, when wounded, the beast stands at bay. In the latter case the animal becomes furious and rushes on his enemy. Then wo to the daring hunter whose rifle is unloaded or whose horse fails him! He is tossed on the horns of his foe and trampled to death.

On one occasion the Commodore had singled out a powerful bull which he had determined to kill, if possible, for the sake of his hide. He had discharged his rifle at him without fatal effect. The bull took refuge in a grove or thicket, and the Commodore dashed into the grove close upon his heels. But suddenly, as soon as he entered the grove, the buffalo wheeled and stood at bay, with his tail coiled over his back, pawing the ground, bellowing, and his eyes like balls of fire, his head lowered, prepared to rush forward upon his enemy. The horse directly, as he saw the buffalo, sprang aside. The Commodore remembered to have heard the hunters say that it was vain to shoot at a buffalo bull's forehead, as the ball could not penetrate his skull. But he determined to make the experiment, and, levelling his pistol, fired. The horse bounded past the buffalo, and, as the Commodore reined him up to return and see the result of his experiment, he felt his face wet, and, wiping it with his hand, found the moisture to be blood. At first he thought the ball had rebounded and wounded him; but after a while he discovered that, in shooting, his ball had passed through the ear of his horse, who, tossing and shaking his head, flung the blood in the Commodore's face. On coming up to the buffalo, he was found dead, the ball having entered his forehead, killing him instantly. Many other anecdotes are related by the companions of the Commodore on this expedition, illustrating his boldness as a hunter and the keen relish with which he enjoyed the sport of pursuing buffalo.

They say that he was often heard to remark that he never knew what was the true luxury of a repast until he sat by his camp-fire, after a hard day's ride, gnawing the rib of a buffalo.

So captivated was he with the bold and romantic adventures afforded by this trip across the Rocky Mountains, that he was often heard to say, after his arrival at St. Joseph's, that, if he had no ties or duties to draw him homeward, nothing would afford him greater satisfaction than to turn back and make the trip over again.

The whole party arrived in safety, early in November, at St. Joseph's, having performed the journey in a little more than four months.

The people of St. Joseph's came across the river in crowds to greet the Commodore. He was invited to a public dinner by the authorities of the place, which being compelled to decline, a public reception was given him and a complimentary address made to him.

Here he was obliged to take leave of the greater part of his band. Their parting showed with how strong and sincere an attachment he had inspired the rough and unsophisticated hearts of his men. Tears coursed down the weather-worn cheeks of the bold and hardy mountaineers, when they took the last friendly grip of the Commodore's hand. They implored him, if he ever made another overland journey to or from California, to send for them; and, no matter where they might be or how engaged, they would come at his bidding. Lawless, reckless, desperate, wicked, and callous, as many of them were, Stockton had found the tender spot in each man's heart and made a lodgment there.

But their case was not singular. Whether on sea or shore, few men were ever commanded by Commodore Stockton who did not become enthusiastically devoted to him. Yet no commander ever exacted more complete submission to his authority.

The Commodore on his way east through St. Louis, Louisville, Cincinnati, and other cities of the Great Valley, was urgently invited to remain long enough to receive some demonstrations of municipal hospitality in those cities. But the necessity for his rapid movement, in order to be present and testify at the court-martial then sitting at Washington, prevented his acceding to any of these friendly overtures. He proceeded with all the despatch of which steamboats and railroads would admit, and arrived at Washington about the 1st of December, 1847.

His testimony on the trial of Fremont was sustained and corroborated generally, and in every particular, by every witness called on that trial. By the publication of the proceedings of that trial, the false statements* in relation to the California campaigns, which had appeared in the papers and in various other quarters, (the authors of which were screened from exposure by the court-martial which so unjustly convicted Colonel Fremont of insubordination,) were entirely exploded and discredited.† The chief merit of the con-

---

* Proceedings of Court-martial, pp. 129–133.

† See the speech of Senator Benton, (in *Appendix to Congressional Globe*, 1848,) on the brevet-nomination of General Kearney. Of all the senatorial efforts of this distinguished statesman, none equal this speech. Indeed, for severe analysis, keen logic, powerful argument, and commanding eloquence, there is no specimen of forensic or parliamentary eloquence in the English language which surpasses it.

quest of California is now universally conceded to belong to Stockton. History will forever bear record that its acquisition by the United States was the result of his masterly proceedings.

Had California been wrested from us after the American flag had been first raised there by Commodore Sloat,—as she would have been but for Stockton,—Mexico would hardly have been willing to relinquish her at the Treaty of Guadaloupe Hidalgo. A treaty might have been made without the cession of California; or, if our Government would not have made peace without such a cession, the war might have been prolonged till the discovery of the gold-placers, when Mexico would have sold California to Great Britain rather than have ceded her to the United States. The quiet and undisturbed possession of California which Stockton acquired and secured for the United States, until negotiations for peace commenced, must have afforded a powerful motive for our negotiators to demand the cession, while it gave to Mexico an excuse for the surrender of that valuable country.

It is hardly within the scope of our object to enlarge upon the value and importance of the acquisition of California to the United States. But we cannot forbear expressing the opinion that, in the history of this republic, it will be considered secondary only to the acquisition of Louisiana in its influence upon the prosperity, grandeur, and power of the republic. It will probably accelerate, by at least a quarter of a century, the period when the United States will become, in all the elements of national greatness, the commanding power of the globe. It must hasten the day when all of North America will be covered by that conquering race of Anglo-Saxon origin, in conflict with which every other race is compelled to succumb. It is a little remarkable that the national gratitude has never been excited even to the just recognition of the services of the Conqueror of such an invaluable addition to the territory of the United States.

There is hardly a county or a village in the United States whose citizens have not gone forth to the new El Dorado on the Pacific, and returned laden with its treasures. There is not a city on the coast, nor in the interior, whose commerce has not felt the stimulus afforded by the trade of California. There has not been a year

---

Mr. Benton traces home to their origin all the base attempts to detract from the merit of Commodore Stockton's proceedings in California. He literally overwhelms, with demonstration on demonstration in his favour, every question which has ever been raised in relation to his California services. His speech on this occasion is an unanswerable and triumphant vindication of the truth of history.

since 1850 in which California gold has not protected the country from the most wide-spread and calamitous revulsion. But, notwithstanding all these results of the acquisition of California, there is hardly one citizen in a hundred who has that knowledge of the conquest of California which would enable him to do justice to Stockton and his sailors.

We have endeavoured to supply that deficiency of information which prevails in relation to this subject. We have done so from the most authentic sources; and, the more completely and thoroughly investigation may be prosecuted into those sources, the more will the correctness and truth of this narrative be vindicated.

CHAPTER XIII.

RECEPTION OF COMMODORE STOCKTON BY HIS FRIENDS—COMPLIMENTARY DINNER AT
PHILADELPHIA—RECEPTION BY THE LEGISLATURE OF NEW JERSEY—RESIGNATION
OF COMMISSION—STATE OF PARTIES IN THE UNITED STATES—LETTER TO MR.
WEBSTER ON SLAVERY—DECLINES AN ELECTION TO THE SENATE OF THE UNITED
STATES—HIS ELECTION.

THE reception of Commodore Stockton by his friends in New
Jersey was cordial, and manifested by various demonstrations. The
fame of his exploits had preceded him, and excited the utmost
curiosity for an account of the particulars of his extraordinary
career in California.

The people of his native village, Princeton, assembled in public
meeting and adopted a series of resolutions expressive of their admiration of his patriotic services, awarding him the tribute of their
thanks for the honour which his achievements reflected on his native
State. His friends, from various parts of the State, crowded round
him to express their gratification at his safe return and welcome
him home.

Soon after his arrival at Philadelphia a public meeting was called,
and the Commodore was invited to a banquet given in testimony of
the estimation in which his services were held by his fellow-citizens.
The call was subscribed by the principal merchants and professional
gentlemen of the city.

We insert from the North American Gazette a full report of the
proceedings of this festival, which took place December 31, 1847 :—

From the North American Gazette.

Some six or seven hundred gentlemen assembled yesterday evening
at the Musical Fund Hall around a board occupying the whole of
that large saloon and furnished with all the luxuriousness, elegance,
and taste for which Messrs. Bagley, McKenzie & Co. of the Columbia House have made themselves so celebrated. We have never
seen so large a company seated in such admirable order and with
so little confusion and noise.

The organization took place by the appointment of Hon. John

Swift as chairman, assisted by Vice-Presidents Henry D. Gilpin, Josiah Randall, John M. Read, Henry L. Benner, Mayor Belsterling, and William G. Alexander. Among the distinguished gentlemen present as guests, we noticed Senators Downs, of Louisiana, Hon. D. D. Thurston, of Rhode Island, Hon. R. J. Thomas, of Tennessee, Hon. Mr. Morse and Hon. Mr. Gibson, of Louisiana, Judges Burnside and Bell, V. S. Macauley, United States Consul to Tripoli, Hon. L. C. Levin, Hon. M. Hampton, Hon. L. B. Chase, &c. &c.

After due honour had been done to the good things so bountifully provided, the chairman rose and announced the regular toasts, as follows :—

1. The President of the United States.
2. The Vice-President of the United States.
3. The Governor of the State of Pennsylvania.
4. Our country—may she ever be right! but, right or wrong, our country.

The chairman then said—"Fellow-citizens, preparatory to offering you the next toast in succession, I will take leave to address a few remarks to this assemblage, and I know in no better way how to begin than in referring to the antecedent toast—'Our country, right or wrong.' (Great applause.) We are involved in a foreign war. There are differences of opinion among us in relation to the causes of the war ; but God forbid that there should be any difference as to the mode in which the war should be carried on. (Great applause.) There is a great consolation growing out of the prospect for this country—growing out of the war,—the moral effect that will be produced by our many victories, not over unfortunate, miserable Mexico, but the whole world, (applause,) from the Autocrat of all the Russias to the lowest duke on the Rhine. They will hereafter ponder well all matters that might have any tendency to open controversy with the United States. (Loud applause.) We have shown that we are a nation prepared not only to meet, but to conquer, every foe. They will hereafter look, as they look now, at Palo Alto ; at Resaca de la Palma ; at Matamoras ; at Monterey ; at Buena Vista ! (Tremendous applause.) Then they will look at Vera Cruz, at Cerro Gordo, at Puebla, at Churubusco, at Chapultepec, and at Mexico itself. (Renewed applause.) And then they will go to the Pacific. (Tremendous cheering.) They will find recorded upon the pages of history, at the first-mentioned places, the names of Taylor and of Worth. And then, as they go towards Vera Cruz, they find a Scott, a Shields, a Quitman, a Smith, a Cadwallader, and other worthies that I cannot now take time to enumerate.

Next they will go to California, and at Los Angeles they will find a Stockton! (Enthusiastic and long-continued cheering.)

"Were it now my task to eulogize the memory of some distinguished man, I might narrate his bright achievements—I might dwell upon the story of his fair renown—I might enter into details and refresh the recollections of those who were his compatriots, and the narrative of his deeds and his prowess—I might enchain the attention of ingenuous youth by relating those deeds of chivalry and prowess, holding up to them the example as a fit model of their imitation. But I am now speaking of one who, thank God, is now in the midst of us, blessed with health and strength. I have known him for my whole life, and could readily narrate instances of his prowess, his chivalry, and his valour, but I will not. I cannot offend the modest ears of one so good and brave. (Great cheering.) His reputation and character and deeds belong to his country. History will record them, and posterity will recognise in him the genuine American patriot. They will bless God that theirs is the privilege and the honour of owning the same land that gave him birth as the place of their nativity. (Great cheering.)

"Mr. Vice-President, I give you ' COMMODORE R. F. STOCKTON, as distinguished for his civil acquirements as he is for his military renown; equally at home, whether on land or sea, when called upon to meet the enemies of his country, the soldier and the sailor; a man who never turned his back on friend or foe.' "

This toast was received with indescribable enthusiasm. The whole of the vast assemblage started simultaneously to their feet and burst into deafening and long-continued cheering.

When the applause had at last subsided, Commodore Stockton rose to make his acknowledgments. He was greeted with long-continued applause. He said,—

" GENTLEMEN—FRIENDS :—How can I have deserved, how can I return, such kindness? How can I suitably express my sense of the honour which has this day been conferred upon me? In what fitting phrase or figure of speech shall I give expression to the feelings with which I am now oppressed? Words seem so feeble when summoned to express the emotions of the human heart excited by a deep sense of gratitude, that I can hardly make the effort to convey to you my sense of the kindness of this reception. (Renewed applause.)

"Returning, after a lengthened absence from this country, I might, perhaps, without presumption, have expected that my personal friends, to whom I was best known, would appreciate my poor, but at all events well-intentioned, efforts in the cause of my country; and that here and there I might have met a friendly greeting, with instances of personal friendship and hospitality. But when I look around me now,—when I see the old and the young, the citizen and the soldier, the patriot and the scholar, assembled here to do me honour,—my heart fairly sinks within me, under the consciousness that this reception as far transcends any merit of mine as it is wholly unexpected. I am left, indeed, without any thing to say in this wide world save the altogether-inadequate and commonplace expression that I return to you my most cordial, my most sincere, thanks. (Enthusiastic applause.)

"Attributing, as I will, your congratulations to-day to the general result of things in California, without reference to the causes or agents by which it was produced, and applying to myself but a small portion of your approbation, I may be permitted to mingle, without stint, my congratulations with yours that California is now under the protection of the United States. (Great cheering.) California is, in my judgment, a valuable country. Her agricultural, her horticultural, her mineral resources are abundant. She has beautiful skies and verdant fields; her population consists of a fine-looking race of men and women; they are kind, hospitable, and valiant.

"Annexation—nay, acquisition—is not a necessary consequence of conquest, and, therefore, it is not on that account that I would offer my congratulations here to-day. Oh, no!

"I care not for the beautiful fields and healthful skies of California; I care not for her leagues of land and her mines of silver. The glory of the achievements there, if any glory there be, is in the establishment of the first free press in California; (tremendous applause;) in having built the first school-house in California; (renewed applause;) in having lighted up the torch of religious toleration, as well as of civil liberty, in California. (Tremendous applause.) May the torch grow brighter and brighter, until, from Cape Mendocino to Cape St. Lucas, it illumines the dark path of the victim of religious intolerance and political despotism! (Thunders of applause.)

"The inhabitants of California number, I believe, about twelve or fifteen thousand. A large portion of them, if not all of them, prefer the institutions of the United States; and it is much to be hoped—may I not say fervently, devoutly to be prayed for?—that they shall in some way or other be secured in the permanent enjoyment of civil and religious liberty, (great applause,) and that our friends there may not pay the dreadful penalty the Mexican always demands,—his life for his fidelity to us! (Great applause.) Well, however this may turn out, if it should be otherwise, if these pleasing anticipations should not be realized, other hands must muzzle the free press; other hands must tear down the school-houses; other hands must put out the light of liberty! (Great cheers.) For me and mine, before God, we'll take no part in such a business! (Enthusiastic applause.)

" California has within herself the elements of wealth and power; and when art and science and religion, when all the genial influences of civilization, which in our day is advancing with such marvellous rapidity, are brought to bear upon her, may we not reasonably assert that the years will be but few before we behold her standing erect in the attitude of a free and independent nation? (Great applause.)

" The investigations going on at Washington will prevent me, or rather will not permit me, with propriety, to say much in relation to the military operations in California. I cannot in these circumstances say all that I might otherwise feel disposed to offer. I shall say very little, therefore, of myself. But it is known to you all that —whether from bad motives or from good motives, whether intentionally or unintentionally, the truth is known—a shadow was thrown across my path, which, for a season, so obscured my conduct as to make some of my fellow-citizens hesitate in their judgment with regard to my conduct in California. I state the fact not by way of complaint; I never have complained; I will not complain; I do not complain. Conscious of having exerted my humble abilities to the best of my power in the cause of my country, and choosing rather to be regarded as a fool than a knave, I shall rely upon faithful history for my vindication, if vindication be necessary. (Long-continued cheering.)

" I have alluded to these matters only to excuse the little that I deem it necessary to say on account of myself. I was Commander of the squadron in the Pacific Ocean as well as Commander-in-chief of the land-forces from the time Commodore Sloat left until a superior officer arrived.

" I was Governor of the Territory as well as Commander-in-chief from the time of the conquest until I gave the supreme authority into other hands. We were at a great distance from home; we were out of the reach of instructions from the Navy Department; our resources were limited; we had no navy-yards nor arsenals to which to resort; we were obliged to mount our own guns, to make our own harness, to supply ourselves with other necessaries in the best manner we could. In the midst of these embarrassing circumstances we thought that, as sailors, we had done very well. (Laughter and enthusiastic cheering.) But we urge no claim to any thing due to us save the acknowledgment that we unsparingly devoted our faculties, all our energies, to the service of our country. (Great applause.)

"Having said thus much, what seemed to me to be proper for me to say in regard to California, permit me now to say a word or two in reference to the present position of the United States and Mexico.

"No thoughtful observer of the progress of the United States can fail to be impressed with the conviction that we enjoy a degree of happiness and prosperity never heretofore vouchsafed to the nations of mankind. With an unexampled measure of political liberty, unbroken social order, extraordinary growth of the arts and sciences, philanthropic and benevolent institutions—the fair offspring of the Christian faith, extending their blessed agency in all directions,—unbounded religious toleration, heaven's best gift, for which our fathers risked and suffered most,—with all these rich endowments, do we not, indeed, present an example of the beneficent care of Providence for which we can find no parallel in the history of man? And now, when engaged in war, we find ourselves followed by the same blessed influences. Wherever our soldiers have carried our arms victory has awaited them. We see them rushing against walls bristling with bayonets and artillery and lined with legions of armed men; we see our youthful heroes precipitating themselves from parapet to parapet, and charging from bastion to bastion; we hear the crash of grape and canister, and, amid the smoke and thunder of the battle, we behold the flag of our country waving—(the remainder of the sentence was lost in the tremendous cheering which here burst forth from the assemblage.) We behold the flag of civil and religious freedom waving over what had been regarded as impregnable fortresses, and the remains of armies fleeing to the mountains.

"Gentlemen, how has all this been accomplished? Whence those achievements? I speak to intellectual men. All in the hearing of my voice entertain, I doubt not, a just and abiding sense of their deep responsibility not only on this earth, but in time hereafter. I ask you, then, how has all this happened? Is it to be attributed exclusively to the wisdom of our cabinet and the prowess of our armies? These are all well, admirably well. But our successes have overleaped the bounds of all human calculation and the most sanguine hope. Therefore we must look beyond all this for the

secret of our successes and the source of our remarkable prosperity.
It is because the spirit of our pilgrim fathers is with us; it is because the God of armies and the Lord of hosts is with us. (Tremendous applause.) And how is it with poor, unfortunate, wretched
Mexico? Ever since the days of the last of the Montezumas, intestine broils have disturbed her peace. Her whole territory has been
drenched with the blood of her own children. Within the last
quarter of a century, revolution has succeeded revolution. Now,
in the encounter with us she has been beaten in every field. She
has been driven from fortress to fortress, from town to town, until
the scattered remnants of her broken armies are fleeing to the
mountains and calling upon the rocks to hide them. (Applause.)
Is it not, therefore, in this disposition of public affairs, proper to
rise superior to the considerations of party influences, and in the
true philosophical spirit and patriotic fidelity take an honest view
of our condition in the sight of God and beneath the scrutiny of
the Christian and civilized world?

"What you may think of it, I know not, and, you must permit
me to add, I care not; but for myself I speak to you not as a party
man. Remember, gentlemen, that I go for my country. I cannot
be bound; I cannot be kept within the restraints of party discipline
when my country calls me forth. (Tremendous cheering, which
lasted several minutes.) I go for my country, my whole country,
and nothing but my country. I desire to address you now in the
spirit of the father of a large family, desirous to transmit to his
latest posterity the blessings of civil and religious liberty. I speak
to you as a Christian man—as a son, perhaps an unworthy son, of
this great republic, but one whose heart burns with an ardent desire
to transmit not only to his own immediate descendants the blessings
of which I speak, but to extend them to our neighbours on this continent. (Great applause.)

"But do not mistake me; do not misunderstand me. I am no
propagandist, in the common acceptation of the term. In my judgment, principles depend much upon relations and circumstances,
and that which in the abstract may be well enough often wastes
itself in fanaticism. All things must bide their time.

"I have no respect for the man or set of men who will recklessly
disturb the social order of any community and produce civil war
for the purpose of hastening such a result, no matter how beneficial
in the abstract it may seem to be. (Cheers.) And I am bound to
say further, that I have quite as little respect for the man or set
of men who have, in the providence of God, been placed in sta-

tions, when the great questions of civil and religious liberty are to be determined, who will shrink from the responsibilities of that station. (Cheers.) In the application of these principles to the future policy of this country, let it not be supposed for a moment that I would presume to censure the great men of this nation. Nor would I attempt to instruct the most humble of my countrymen. I present these views merely for the purpose of rendering more distinct and clear the remarks which I have offered, and which I may not have stated with sufficient explicitness

"I suppose the war with Mexico was caused by the repeated insults which time after time she had offered this nation. (Great applause.) I regard this much talked-of indemnity as merely collateral or incidental, arising out of the circumstances of the war. In my opinion, that question will be set aside, if not wholly lost sight of, in the pressure of the great considerations which are to grow out of the high responsibilities and delicate duties crowding upon us, and the unexampled victories which have attended our arms. (Cheers.) In pursuing a legitimate object of war, in the providence of God we are placed, or are likely soon to be placed, in a position where, by a fair and legitimate construction of the law of nations, the fate of Mexico and the peace of this continent, to a greater or less extent, will devolve upon the virtue, the wisdom, and the humanity of our rulers. (Applause.) In these rulers I have the greatest confidence, and for them I entertain the most profound respect. (Applause.)

"I tell you again, gentlemen, this matter of indemnity, in money or any thing else, will be secondary, altogether secondary, in comparison with the considerations which I have no doubt will be presented to this nation in the further prosecution of this war. The insults have been resented—nobly resented; they have been wiped out; they have been washed out with blood. (Enthusiastic applause.) If, then, indemnity mean money, any financier will tell you that, if *that* is what you seek as the only object of the war, you had better withdraw your troops as soon as possible, and you will *save* money. (A laugh.)

"But the indemnity is not the object of the war. No man here or elsewhere will consent to weigh blood against money. (Great applause.) I do not care who presents the proposition, when it is presented, or to whom it is presented, Whig or Democrat, no man will weigh blood for money. (Renewed applause.) But this is not, I repeat, our condition. Higher and nobler objects present themselves, for the attainment of which you must increase your armies in Mexico, *cost* what it may. (Great applause.) Fifty thousand men must go to Mexico. (Renewed applause.) Let me then state the objects for the attainment of which, in my judgment, this augmentation of our force in Mexico, is required.

"Mexico is poor and wretched. Why? Misgovernment, insatiable avarice, unintermitted wrong, unsparing cruelty, and unbending insolence,—these have inflicted their curse on the unhappy country and made her what she is. But as the darkest hour is that which just precedes the advent of the morning sun, so let us hope that a better and happier day is now about to dawn upon unfortunate Mexico. Be it ours now to forgive her all her trespasses, and, returning good for evil, make her free and happy! (Enthusiastic applause, which lasted several minutes.)

"If I were now the sovereign authority, as I was once the viceroy, (laughter,) I would prosecute this war for the express purpose of redeeming Mexico from misrule and civil strife. If, however, such a treaty were offered me as that offered to the Government of the United States, before God, I would consider it my bounden duty to reject it. (Loud applause.) I would say to them, ʻ We can pay the indemnity ourselves. But we have a duty before God which we cannot—we must not—evade. The priceless boon of civil and religious liberty has been confided to us as trustees.ʼ (Cheers.) I would insist, if the war were to be prolonged for fifty years, and cost money enough to demand from us each year the half of all that we possess, I would still insist that the inestimable blessings of civil and religious liberty should be guaranteed to Mexico. We must not shrink from this solemn duty. We dare not shrink from it. We cannot lose sight of the great truth that nations are accountable as well as individuals, and that they too must meet the stern responsibilities of their moral character; they too must encounter the penalty of violated law in the more extended sphere adapted to their physical condition.

"Let the solemn question come home to the bosom and business of every citizen of this great republic—ʻWhat have I done—what has this generation done—for the advancement of civil and religious liberty?ʼ (Applause.)

"It is in view of this responsibility, of our obligations to the infinite Source of all our peace, prosperity, and happiness, of our duty to fulfil the great mission of liberty committed to our hands, that I would insist, cost what it may, on the establishment of a permanent, independent republic in Mexico. (Cheers.) I would insist that the great principle of religious toleration should be

12

secured to all; that the Protestant in Mexico should be guaranteed the enjoyment of all the immunities and privileges enjoyed by Mexicans in the United States. (Loud cheers.) These great and benevolent objects I would accomplish by sending into Mexico a force adequate to maintain all the posts which we now occupy, to defend them against any assaults that might be made against them, and to keep open our communications. I would seize upon Paredes, Arista, and other military chieftains, and send them to St. Helena, if you please. (Laughter and applause.) I would declare an armistice; and the Executive should be called upon to issue a proclamation, and send six or more commissioners to meet Mexico in a liberal and generous spirit.

"We have vanquished Mexico. She is prostrate at our feet; we can afford to be magnanimous. Let us act so that we need not fear the strictest scrutiny of the Christian and civilized world. I would, with a magnanimous and kindly hand, gather these wretched people within the fold of republicanism. (Loud applause.) This I would accomplish at any cost. 'Oh!' but, it is said, 'this will bring us to direct taxation.' Well, let it come. We must not shrink from our responsibility. We have ample means. Throwing aside long financial reports which nobody understands, (laughter,) let us in a manly, upright, and philanthropic spirit, meet every emergency which we may be called upon to encounter in the discharge of duty. (Applause.)

"But I have already detained you too long. Let me conclude, and, again returning my heartfelt thanks for your kindness, offer you the following sentiment:—

"'Philadelphia—Renowned for her encouragement of the fine arts; with one moiety of the public patronage bestowed elsewhere, she would stand as unrivalled in the mechanic arts as the State of Pennsylvania now does in her agricultural and mineral resources.'"

This toast was received with great enthusiasm, and the distinguished guest resumed his seat amid long-continued cheering.

It will be perceived, from the date when this speech was delivered, that peace with Mexico had not then been concluded. It may be inferred, from the sentiments expressed by Commodore Stockton on this occasion, that he could not have approved entirely the Treaty of Guadaloupe Hidalgo. He seems to have been of opinion that the United States should have retained some sort of a protectorate over Mexico until she should become capable of self-government. However startling such a proposition may seem, it may well be doubted whether such a policy would not have conferred on Mexico blessings of inestimable value. Political sagacity may yet be baffled to discover any other method, by means of which that beautiful country can be restored to a state of progressive civilization, or its relapse into degraded barbarism averted.

The expression of such an opinion at that time was certainly in advance of the age, if it be not so now, even after the lamentable events in Mexican history during the last eight years. But the attentive observer of the career of Commodore Stockton will perceive that it is characteristic of his mind to be in the advance of his day and generation. This is indicated by his early attention to the internal improvement of New Jersey, by his construction of the steamer Princeton, his general views on naval defences, his repudiation of Van Buren, his Kossuth speech, his advocacy of the abolition of flogging, and by his adoption of the American doctrines at the Philadelphia banquet. Though at that time the Americans, as a party, were of insignificant strength, we find in this speech intrinsic evidence that he then entertained the leading doctrines by which recently they have become so well known. He distinctly avows the principle that it is the duty of the United States to exact from foreign governments, in favour of American residents, the same freedom of religious worship that the United States concedes to foreigners residing in this country.

The speech is evidently incompletely reported; but there is enough of it preserved to indicate the boldness and the originality of the views of Commodore Stockton with respect to our relations with Mexico, as well as to other subjects.

The Commodore, it is known, never approved of the boundary-line fixed by the treaty of Guadaloupe Hidalgo. He had, in his first despatches to the Navy Department from California, urged upon the Government the expediency of obtaining Lower as well as Upper California.* In his letter of the 18th September, 1846, addressed to Mr. Bancroft, Secretary of the Navy, he says:—

"We must, therefore, hold the country along the sea-coast as far south as St. Lucas, and make the river Gila, and a line drawn from that river across to the Del Norte, the southern boundary; all of which is now in our possession. It is not my business, perhaps, to say more on the subject. I will send you, however, a map which I have made, and on which I have traced with red ink the boundary-line above suggested." That map was sent, and is now on file at Washington in the proper Department.

---

* See Letter, in Appendix.

Among the honours conferred on the Commodore soon after his return was a formal reception by the Legislature of his native State.

The following joint resolutions of the Legislature of New Jersey were submitted in the House of Assembly on the 6th of February, 1848, and were unanimously adopted by both Houses:—

"WHEREAS, Commodore Robert F. Stockton has, at all times, promptly and efficiently responded to the call of his country, and in the exciting war with Mexico has signally maintained the honour and gallantry of his native State—therefore,

"*Resolved*, That the thanks of the Legislature of New Jersey be tendered to Commodore Robert F. Stockton for the distinguished alacrity, courage, and ability, with which he has discharged the arduous and multiplied duties assigned him in California.

"*Resolved*, That a joint committee of the Senate and General Assembly be appointed to carry into effect the foregoing resolutions."

We take the following proceedings of his reception by the Legisture from the "Trenton State Gazette" of March 3, 1848:—

COMMODORE STOCKTON AND THE LEGISLATURE.

Yesterday, in accordance with the previous arrangements, the resolutions of the Legislature, testifying their high sense of his recent services in California, were presented to Commodore Stockton in the Assembly-room, by the two Houses of the Legislature, through Mr. Goble, the chairman of the committee. Soon after 12 o'clock, Commodore Stockton was waited upon at Snowden's, by the committee of the Legislature, and was escorted thence, by them and a number of citizens, to the Assembly-room. The Commodore was in the uniform of his rank. The hall of the Assembly was occupied by the Senators and Assemblymen. The lobbies and the aisles were crowded with spectators. The galleries, having been reserved for their use, were filled with ladies. Commodore Stockton was escorted by the committee to the left of the Speaker's chair, the members of both houses rising to receive him. The Speaker then called the house to order, and Mr. Goble addressed Commodore Stockton as follows:—

"COMMODORE STOCKTON:—On behalf of the joint committee appointed for that purpose, I present to you the resolutions of thanks passed unanimously by the Legislature of the State of New Jersey for your public services in Mexico. In a remote clime you have nobly sustained the American flag, and have advanced the reputation of the American navy. Your gallant achievements in California and on the Pacific coast have endeared your name to the people of your native State, and have rendered this expression of approbation from its constituted authorities as becoming to them as it has been deserved by you. Nor have we forgotten, in the brilliancy of your naval and military career, the important services you have performed on a less dazzling but no less meritorious field of action. The cause of internal improvements in the State of New Jersey has been greatly promoted by your active and strenuous exertions. As a token, therefore, of the respect and admiration you have justly inspired, I tender you a copy of the resolutions recently adopted by the Legislature."

Mr. Goble then presented to Commodore Stockton a parchment copy of the resolutions of the Legislature.

Commodore Stockton then replied as follows:—

"GENTLEMEN OF THE SENATE AND HOUSE OF ASSEMBLY:—Nobleness of sentiment, correctness of conduct, and the love of liberty, have ever characterized our citizens wherever they have carried our victorious arms. Actuated by a desire of fame or an ardent affection for their country, our heroes have conquered and our patriots have bled. Sacrifices of the most heroic kind have been made, and actions have been performed which almost exceed our belief of human power and endurance. That, amid such scenes of glory and congratulation, I should have been thought of at all, and especially that I should have been so kindly and so honourably remembered by the representatives of the State of New Jersey, in General Assembly convened, is, and must always be to me, a source of unfeigned, unmixed, pride and satisfaction. There is—undoubtedly there is—a desire for praise and fame which encourages a weak and ignoble pride; but there is also a noble, generous, manly, and moral regard for the good opinion of our fellow-citizens which elevates the mind and improves the heart. The age in which we live, and our own country particularly, is remarkable for the manner in which those who serve the public are commended and rewarded. The gorgeous equipage, the triumphal arch, the imperial purple, the crowns and tablets of gold and silver, give way to the more simple, eloquent, touching, and godlike commendation of "Well-done, good and faithful servant." For, whatever of commendation and honour may have elsewhere been bestowed upon me, I hope that I have a full

and abiding sense of gratitude; but this is my native State, here I
was born, here I have lived, and here I hope to die. This is my
home; and the thanks of the representatives of my fellow-citizens,
who have known me in private as well as in public life, is the most
heartfelt and the greatest reward that can be given for my poor
but well-intended efforts in the service of my country. Oh! yes!
this is my native land.

> " 'Lives there a man with soul so dead,
> Who never to himself hath said
> This is my own, my native land?'

At this time, and under the interesting circumstances of this occasion, I cannot, I do not, wish to say one word about myself, or of
the deeds that I have done. They are, indeed, so poor in comparison with the honour which you have this day conferred upon
me, that I dare not, by their recital, run the risk of dissolving the
charm which your thanks have thrown around my heart. I would
not for the world's extent say any thing or do any thing that would
loosen or in any degree weaken the bonds of reciprocal regard and
confidence which this day binds us together. I would leave the
matter with you, just as it is. I would not add or take from it one
jot or tittle. Let it be just so. You have given to me your thanks;
and I here renew to you my fidelity to my native State and my
country.

"A few words as to Mexico, and I have done. The causes of the
war and the circumstances attending its prosecution are as well
known to you as to myself. It does not become me to say any
thing upon that topic. It is understood, however, that a treaty of
peace between the United States and Mexico has been received by
the President and sent to the Senate of the United States, and it
may not be inappropriate or unacceptable to say a word or two upon
that subject.

"In my judgment, there are two views which may be taken of this
matter.

"The first is the Christian, philanthropic, statesmanlike view,
which will prevent our giving up Mexico and withdrawing our troops,
until a free, independent, republican Government shall be there established, and until we shall have made with such a government a
treaty securing to the Protestant of these United States the same
privileges which, by our Constitution, are secured to the Roman .
Catholic, and thereby remove all pretence for European interference
in the affairs of Mexico.

" The other view of the subject embraces the idea that we are to entertain no sympathy for any but ourselves; that we have no concern in any portion of this continent but our own; that it is a matter of no consequence to us whether we leave Mexico in a state of revolution and blood, or whether a monarchical or republican government should be established there; that all we want is peace, and peace we must have, cost what it may.

" If this last view obtains, I would recommend to its advocates to get as many of the dirty acres as they can, ratify the treaty, and close the war as soon as possible.

" Mr. Chairman and Gentlemen of the Committee:—I hardly know how properly to return my acknowledgments to you for this kind reception and for your eloquent and generous address to me. While I am free to admit 'they greatly exceed my poor deserts, still it would be to indulge a puerile and unworthy affectation were I to hesitate to say that they have given me the most unbounded pleasure. For the part which you have taken in these ceremonies, so kind and honourable to myself, permit me to return to you my best, kindest, humblest, thanks.''

In 1849, Commodore Stockton resigned his commission in the navy. Peace had been restored between Mexico and the United States in 1848. His father-in-law, John Potter, Esq., having died, also in this year, devolving upon him, in the settlement of a large estate, duties and responsibilities additional to those which a numerous family of his own and his connection with the public works of New Jersey already imposed, he thought that the time had arrived when his age, his past public services, and the condition of the country, would justify his retirement. He was, however, devotedly attached to the navy; and, notwithstanding the imperative nature of his private interests requiring for a while his entire attention, he would not, even at this time, have surrendered his position in the navy had he not felt the injustice of remaining in the service while he was conscious that he would not be able for a long time to perform the duties which might be required of him.

During the whole course of his service, from 1811 to 1849, he had never asked a furlough or even leave of absence. And, no matter how urgent and critical were his own private affairs, in every instance he promptly obeyed every order which he received.

The country was in the enjoyment of profound peace, and no cloud of war was visible on the horizon of the distant.

future. He, therefore, determined no longer to remain callous to the entreaties of his family, who had for many years solicited his retirement from the navy. He had reached the highest grade in the service; he had won laurels quite enough to gratify his ambition; he had conferred on his country an ample return for the confidence she had bestowed on him; he had served her faithfully and given her the prime years of his manhood; and he felt that neither honour nor duty required that he should any longer continue insensible to the demands of affection and of his domestic duties.

In 1850, the organization of the new territories, and the question respecting the application of the Wilmot proviso, excluding slavery from them, became subjects of absorbing interest. The whole country was agitated by the discussion, and, indeed, still continues more or less distracted in relation to the subject.

March 7, 1850, Mr. Webster delivered his great speech in the Senate in favour of compromise. Having been for many years on terms of great personal intimacy with Commodore Stockton, he sent him a copy of this speech, and solicited his views on the subject in the following letter:—

MR. WEBSTER TO COMMODORE STOCKTON.

"WASHINGTON, March 22, 1850.

"My dear Sir:—I send to you, as an old friend, a copy of my late speech in the Senate. It relates to a subject quite interesting to the country, as connected with the question of proper governments for those new territories which you had an important agency in bringing under the power of the United States.

"I would hardly ask your opinion of the general sentiments of the speech, although I know you are a very competent judge, but that, being out of the strife of politics, your judgment is not likely to be biassed, and that you have as great a stake as any man in the preservation of the Union and the maintenance of the Government on its true principles.

"I am, dear sir,
"With great respect, yours,
"DANIEL WEBSTER.

"COMMODORE STOCKTON."

Commodore Stockton responded to this invitation in his celebrated letter on the subject of slavery. It is, perhaps, the most masterly, statesmanlike, national, and comprehensive view of the subject which has ever been taken by any public man. It exercised a powerful influence on the public at that time, and is destined still to exert a most salutary influence wherever it is read by those who can appreciate the importance and value of the Union and an implicit observance of the obligations of the Constitution.*

In the election of 1850, in November, the Democratic party in New Jersey succeeded in obtaining a majority in the Legislature. So soon as this result was known, Commodore Stockton was placed in nomination in various parts of the State as a candidate for the place of Senator, as successor to the Hon. Wm. L. Dayton, whose term expired on the 4th of March, 1852.

The Commodore was by no means ambitious of filling this honourable position. Having resigned his commission for the purpose of attending to his private affairs, he was reluctant to enter a sphere the duties of which would necessarily engross his time and attention for the greater part of the year. With these feelings, before the Legislature met, he published the following letter:—

"PRINCETON, November 19, 1850.

"TO THE EDITOR OF THE 'TRUE AMERICAN':—

"I notice in the papers of the day, have learned from letters, and heard in private circles, that my name is spoken of in connection with the office of United States Senator for New Jersey.

"With gratitude to those of my fellow-citizens who have named me for that high office, I must nevertheless say, frankly and at once, that I decline it.

"*However averse I may be to enter into questions of party politics,* still, permit me to express the hope that the appointment of Senator may be conferred on some one whose heart and hand and voice is pledged to the Union of the States at all hazards, and to the support of the compromises of the Constitution and the execution of the laws with unfaltering fidelity.

"Survive who may, perish who will, the Union must be preserved. To this sentiment, for one, I set my hand and heart, and on its maintenance I am now, as I ever have been, ready to pledge my life, my fortune, and my honour. The people of New Jersey have, at the late election, adopted it and made it theirs, and every citizen everywhere, who loves his country and his race, will respond to it with enthusiasm. R. F. STOCKTON."

The reader will observe the Commodore's remark in this letter

---

* This Letter will be found in the sequel to these pages.

respecting his aversion to party politics. The history of American politics affords few instances of politicians scouting party politics at the very time when they were set up as the candidates of a party. But the Commodore, though in principle he was allied with the Democratic party, and for the most part had acted with them, desired his party friends to understand that he was not that sort of party man who considers *the party* the *alpha* and *omega* of his political creed; that, though in principle with the Democratic party, he did not intend to lose sight of the country, its honour, and interests.

No man has perceived more closely and with more disgust than he the perversion of party to the purposes of the selfish ambition of aspiring men. His own self-respect, therefore, induces him to revolt from the tyranny of party when, under the pretext of principle, it becomes the ancillary of personal ambition. He will go with it while the honour, interests, and welfare of the country are its real objects; but, when they are not absolutely involved, he feels at liberty to exercise the independence of a free man. Of course, entertaining such sentiments, venal, dissolute, and ambitious politicians are not political friends of Stockton. He knows it, and nothing is more gratifying to him than their aversion, except the approbation of the just and good.

Notwithstanding the decided terms in which Commodore Stockton declined the honour of a seat in the Senate of the United States, he was elected at the ensuing session of the Legislature, after a contest which, however acrimonious at the time, has nevertheless left no immedicable wounds. The distinguished gentleman whom he succeeded (the Hon. Wm. L. Dayton) had the magnanimity, only two years after, in a speech at Trenton, before the people, to speak of the Commodore in the following terms :—

"They say Mr. Pierce is a good Democrat, but at the same time they tell us he is opposed to a tariff, and opposed to internal improvement, and the only thing he is in favour of is free trade. He is against every thing that we go for, and, therefore, he is not the man to get our votes. Why, I could have chosen for them a better man to run, from our own neighbourhood—a man whose name *is* known to the country—who has been heard of in Africa, in California, and at San Gabriel—a *real* hero. Everybody knows I am under no obligations to that gentleman; but if the opposite party had taken up Commodore Stockton, I believe they would have had a much stronger candidate; and then we should have had a real Jersey race on both sides."

CHAPTER XIV.

COMMODORE STOCKTON TAKES HIS SEAT IN THE SENATE — KOSSUTH EXCITEMENT — RESOLUTIONS OF LEGISLATURE OF NEW JERSEY—COMMODORE STOCKTON THE FIRST TO GRASP THE PRACTICAL QUESTION PRESENTED BY KOSSUTH— SPEECHES IN THE SENATE ON FLOGGING IN THE NAVY—WASHINGTON'S BIRTHDAY BANQUET—BALTIMORE NATIONAL DEMOCRATIC CONVENTION — THE PRESIDENTIAL NOMINATION — GENERAL EXPECTATION THAT COMMODORE STOCKTON WOULD BE TENDERED THE NAVY DEPARTMENT—RESIGNATION OF SEAT IN SENATE.

THE election of Commodore Stockton to the Senate of the United States was the first instance of the election to that body of a member whose previous life had been passed on the quarter-deck. Instances there had been of the election of senators who, in early life, had belonged to the navy. Mr. Louis McLane, of Delaware, had been a Lieutenant in the navy, but left it when young to pursue the profession of law. Commodore Stockton, however, had never followed any other than the nautical profession, and, having risen to distinction, had but recently resigned his commission as a naval officer. Generals without number, both of the regular army and of the militia, have figured in the Senate as well as in the House of Representatives of Congress. But they have generally, at some period or other, belonged to one of the learned professions, or have enjoyed the advantages of some parliamentary experience in the legislatures of their respective States.

Commodore Stockton entered the Senate without any such preparatory experience. Many, therefore, without any knowledge of his previous history, ignorant of the important part which he had for many years taken in the civil and political affairs of New Jersey, were disposed to sneer at the election of a sailor to the Senate of the United States. They did not believe that the commander of a man-of-war could possess the qualifications for shining in the first deliberative body of the world, where the highest intellectual efforts of the master minds of America were put forth. Of course, no one (except those who knew him well) was prepared to believe that he would add any new lustre to his name by adventure in such a field.

Commodore Stockton took his seat in the Senate about the middle of December, 1851.

It will be remembered that at this time Kossuth was in the zenith of that wonderful popularity which his genius, eloquence, and cause had inspired. He had passed through the country and electrified all classes. The whole nation, with an apparently overwhelming majority, responded to his invocations, and seemed disposed to accede to his invitations and adopt the policy which he advocated. The public ear received coldly and unwillingly any remonstrance adverse to the wishes of Kossuth. The popular feelings were captivated and spell-bound by the Hungarian magician. Presidential aspirants and their friends vied in subserviency to the eloquent foreigner. Under the impulse of the popular ebullition, there was danger that the peace of the country would be compromised, and that we should become entangled in the strife which disturbed Europe.

In this condition of the public mind, the question was presented to the Senate whether they would give Kossuth a public reception or not, and whether they would sanction the doctrines which he had been inculcating?

It was held by some that the Senate were committed to his reception by having invited him to America. Some senators were disposed to refuse any further recognition of the distinguished Hungarian, lest the country might be committed by such action of the Senate. Others were anxious for such recognition for the purpose of gradually leading the United States into some measure of intervention for the benefit of the European republicans. Politicians perceptibly quailed before the influence of the foreign-born population, which was unanimously in favour of Kossuth's policy.

The Senate was visibly perplexed as to the proper course to be taken. Confused notions seemed to be entertained by senators as to the true policy of the United States with reference to the revolutionists of Europe. The oldest senators failed to grapple with the real points at issue, or to present them distinctly to the popular mind. The policy of intervention or non-intervention was rendered more obscure the longer the discussion lasted. Two months of the session had elapsed, and the Senate were apparently as far from a decision as when it commenced.

On the 2d of February, 1852, Commodore Stockton expressed his opinions on the subject. The occasion afforded him for that purpose was the presentation of the resolutions of the Legislature of New Jersey upon intervention and non-intervention.

These resolutions affirmed very broadly that non-intervention was the true doctrine which the United States should maintain. The Commodore, in the most respectful but decided manner, expressed his dissent from this principle asserted by the resolutions. He contended that the non-intervention doctrine, if established as the law of nations, would be fatal to the cause of liberty. He thought the Senate could not hesitate about giving Kossuth a public reception, because they were committed by their previous action. But, to adopt the doctrine of non-intervention, would be to act in accordance with the wishes of the most despotic governments. They had intervened for four thousand years against liberty ; and now that the time was approaching when the United States would soon be able to cope with the world in arms, to say that in no case should we intervene would be to assert the doctrine which tyranny would approve and liberty deplore. And then, grasping the practical question involved in the discussion, and from which all others seemed to shrink with apprehension, he declared that it was *not* expedient for the United States to intervene in behalf of Hungary and against Russia ; that such intervention was a utopian idea, and utterly visionary and impracticable. He was the first public man of any prominence who had the moral courage to avow these opinions. Their practical common sense was apparent to all as soon as they were avowed by him.

General Cass, Senator Douglas, and other leading senators, adopted the views of Commodore Stockton substantially, and vindicated elaborately their soundness.

From that day the sympathizers and non-interventionists began to lose ground, and the whole country awakened from the delusion with which it had been beguiled by the oratory of Kossuth.

The speech of Commodore Stockton on the New Jersey nonintervention resolutions breathes a high-toned devotion to the cause of human liberty. It displays also enlarged statesmanlike views of the true national policy of the United States, with hopeful and generous predictions of the future. It may well be studied for the sound comprehensive principles which it maintains. Though brief and terse, like most of the Commodore's senatorial speeches, it covers a large expanse of controversy and enunciates noble and liberal sentiments with boldness, vigour, and eloquence.

During his short senatorial career, though the Commodore did not speak often, yet he spoke often enough to make a powerful impression on the public mind; no senator was heard with more attention or commanded more respect, and no senator attracted a more numerous audience. When it was anticipated that he would speak the galleries of the Senate were always crowded to overflow.

His speeches on harbour defences and the efficiency of the navy fearlessly proclaimed the imbecility of the bureaux in promoting the development of the navy. They present the practical results of his naval experience, and are replete with valuable suggestions and patriotic advice to prepare in peace for a state of war.

His speech on flogging in the navy was, perhaps, his most elaborate effort while in the Senate. He therein vindicated the opinions on that subject which he was known to have long held. That speech absolutely terminated all controversy on the subject. No one, since the delivery of that speech, has attempted to vindicate the revival of that exploded and barbarous practice. The abolition of flogging in the navy had other able champions; but the testimony of Commodore Stockton in favour of the abandonment of the practice settled the question. Few speeches in Congress have obtained a more extensive circulation or produced a more profound sensation. Among the maritime classes, especially in New England, it has given him a popularity universal and enduring. It is an effort creditable alike to his humanity, the soundness of his judgment, and his patriotism.

Few senators ever acquired the same degree of power and influence as Commodore Stockton exerted in the Senate in so short a time. He never made any serious effort to carry a bill or measure while in the Senate without succeeding.

The day after his bill for reform in the navy passed the Senate, a distinguished senator, opposed to it, riding up with a friend, being asked the fate of that bill, replied, " Oh, it passed; the Commodore is irresistible; to contend with him is certain defeat."

During the prevalence of the Kossuth excitement, a number of members of Congress, who were anxious to check the foreign influence which was evidently seeking to plunge the country into the vortex of European politics, proposed such a celebration of Washington's birthday as would have a tendency to revive the recollection of Washington's policy towards foreigners and foreign nations. Accordingly a very large subscription-banquet was arranged. It was attended by almost all those distinguished members of both houses who were indisposed to submit to the dictation of the distinguished exile.

The committee of arrangements consisted of the Hon. A. H. Stephens, Georgia; Hon. T. H. Bayly, Virginia; Hon. Edward Stanley, North Carolina; Hon. C. L. Dunham, Indiana; Hon.

William Appleton, Massachusetts; Hon. W. L. Polk, Tennessee; Hon. A. L. Miner, Vermont.

The banquet took place at Willard's Hotel, on the evening of Saturday, the 21st of February.

The Hon. R. F. Stockton presided; and the Hon. W. R. King, President of the Senate, G. W. P. Custis, Esq., Judge Wayne of the Supreme Court of the United States, and General Winfield Scott, the Hon. Abraham Venable, and the Hon. John L. Taylor, acted as Vice-Presidents.

The Rev. C. M. Butler, Chaplain of the Senate, returned thanks, when the cloth was removed; when Commodore Stockton rose and delivered in the most solemn and impressive manner the following address:—

"FRIENDS AND AMERICANS:—In calling me to preside over this festive commemoration of the birthday of Washington, a great honour has been conferred on me, for which my best thanks are due.

"As our Republic grows, as she enlarges her sphere, as the multiplying millions diffuse themselves over this vast continent, our federal relations will probably become more complicated and diversified, and the Constitution and the Union may be more severely tried by mistaken construction, reckless violation, or insidious corruption.

"The remembrance of the past, the momentous questions of the present day, and the solemn mysteries of the future, should teach us to appreciate the inestimable treasure that is concentrated in the pure character and holy patriotism of him who was 'first in war, first in peace, and first in the hearts of his countrymen,' (cheers,) and to admonish us of the importance of our keeping fresh in the minds of all this mighty people the memory of our beloved Washington. (Renewed cheers.) That is a talisman whose virtue is more precious than oceans of liquid gold or solid mountains of silver.

"Nobleness of sentiment, heroism of conduct, and love of liberty, have astonished and delighted mankind in every country and in every age; costly sacrifices have been made by patriots, and actions of almost incredible prowess have been performed by mighty men of old. But in those exhibitions of valour and greatness there has almost always been more or less of personal ambition or criminal atrocity. It was left for the age of our Revolution to produce a true hero and patriot—a man whose fame is obnoxious to no such reproach. A Christian hero, he was indeed a stern soldier and conqueror, but without a crime. His eyes glistened with the dew-drops of pity, even when the unsheathed sword reeked with the blood of the

fallen foe.   A statesman and a legislator, neither intrigue, dissimu-
lation, nor injustice, marred his character.   The first man of the
age, his great desire was to occupy a private station.   In every
vocation in which he was called to act, he excelled the most illustrious of all preceding ages, and he differed from the greatest among
them by being untarnished by those imperfections which they exhibited.

"But I will not attempt the vain effort of magnifying his fame
His virtues are the legacy of the greatest value which he has bequeathed.   We have assembled to renew our remembrance of those
virtues, and not to offer incense of praise to his great name.   This
being our *only* object on this occasion, I say, in the language of
Holy Writ, 'It is good for us to be here.'   Let us erect a taber-
nacle in every heart and dedicate it to Washington and the Constitution.   (Applause.)

"Gentlemen, we shall be true to our country—the American
people will be true to their country and to its Constitution—just so
long as we are all true to the memory of Washington.   Through
all time the virtue of our people will be gauged by the intensity of
their veneration for his precepts of wisdom, by the vigour of their
appreciation for his character, and by the respect which they cherish and manifest for his virtues.

"If the time shall come when unholy ambition, the lust for
power, and foreign conquest or the glory of expensive war, shall
animate our public men, and their fierce passions and dangerous
designs cannot be checked by the remembrance of the probity of
Washington and his policy, then, indeed, the golden age of this
Republic will be forgotten.   (Applause.)

"If sectional injustice and animosities almost kindle the fires of
civil war—if illegal power, regardless of the reserved rights of the
States and the people, shall trample, under the victorious march of
party spirit, the Constitution,—then, if an appeal to the memory of
the grave and fastidious caution with which Washington interpreted
that sacred instrument shall be in vain, then, indeed, small hope
will remain to invigorate the efforts of the patriots to bring back
the Government to the purity of that of Washington and Jefferson.

"If the time shall come when, under the influence of generous,
hospitable emotions or ill-considered partiality, our people shall
rashly seek to involve the Republic in the stormy and wretched vortex
of European politics, and, abandoning the ground of Washington,
seek to place themselves on that of foreign powers, forgetful that
their first and chief duty is to take care of their own country, *then*,
if the farewell warnings of the Father of his Country cannot recall

them to a true perception of the duties of patriotism, nothing but those calamities which entangling alliances, and the long and fearful train of evils which float in the wake of pernicious war, will reveal the delusion, the folly and the errors of their degenerate age. (Great and prolonged applause.)

"If the time shall ever come when corruption shall invade the walls of our proud capital and venal crime shall stalk unblushing through its precincts, and profligate extravagance and perfidious peculation abound at the other end of the avenue, *then*, if the remembrance of the frugality, the purity, the simplicity of Washington's administration cannot save us, we shall have foundered upon those rocks on which all other republics have broken to pieces. (Applause.) When corruption reigns here, Washington will be forgotten. (Great applause.)

"Friends and fellow-citizens! following in the footsteps of the immortal Washington, let us cherish his memory and profit by his precepts and his wisdom.

"Members of both houses of Congress! let us keep this Government within its prescribed, constitutional limits; (applause;) preserve it a frugal and economical government, (renewed applause,) drawing from the people no more than is absolutely necessary for the purposes of an honest administration of the Constitution. (Applause.) Let no temptation, however urgent or magnificent, induce us to violate its spirit or its letter. Let forbearance and conciliation towards all the different sections of our country and their diverse interests distinguish our councils; cherish peace; avoid war when not essential for practicable purposes or for the defence of national interests and national honour. Then we shall bid defiance to the remorseless appetite for power; we shall erect an invincible barrier to corruption; we shall thus baffle demagogues at home and check eventually the march of despotism abroad. (Loud applause.)

"By disregarding the maxims and forgetting the virtues of Washington, we might sooner, perhaps, reach the pinnacle of greatness, but it would be at the expense of the longevity of the Republic. Let us adhere to them, for they will conduct us quite soon enough to the topmost round of the ladder of national aspiration; and, while thus adhering to his example and emulating his patriotic devotion to the Constitution, let us look high enough to see and open our hearts wide enough to embrace all the varied interests of this widely-extended country.

"If we have patriotism enough to stand up at all times and under all emergencies for our country, our whole country, and nothing but our country, we may some of us be victims to the little arts of little politicians; but even in death our country—great, glorious, united, and prosperous—will be our monument, attesting our fidelity and honouring our memories. (Great and prolonged cheering.)

"Fellow-citizens, I have the honour to announce the first regular toast:—

"'*The day we celebrate.*—Auspicious to the cause of rational freedom. It gave to liberty its ablest defender, and to republican institutions their truest expounder.'"

In all his speeches the reader will perceive the characteristics of a bold, frank, and honourable man. Fearless and independent in the assertion of principles which he approved, regardless of party ties when they appeared to conflict with his duty, antiquated prejudices found in him a determined foe, and official incapacity stood aghast at the freedom of his denunciations. His speeches show that he is evidently a man of strong and original powers, self-reliant, abundant in resource, and possessed of that intrepid moral courage which never shrinks from the performance of duty nor refrains from doing what is right. He fears no one, nor the opinions of any one. The coolness and self-possession for which he is so remarkable in action never fail him in the deliberations of the council-chamber.

After the election of Commodore Stockton to the Senate, his name was frequently mentioned in prominent papers among those of the candidates for the Presidency. Many of his friends felt confident that he would be nominated by the Democratic Convention of 1852. Nothing which fell from him, however, indicated any such aspirations. No efforts were made by him to secure a delegation from New Jersey to the Baltimore Convention favourable to that object. That would have required no serious exertions to accomplish had he really evinced any desire to become a candidate. His experience of public life at Washington inspired him with no ambition for the Presidency. The delegation from New Jersey was composed of five delegates friendly to his nomination, and two opponents. The vote of the State could, therefore, have been given to him if he would have consented to be a candidate. A majority of the delegates called upon him previous to the meeting of the Convention, and tendered their support. But, so far from consenting to the introduction of his name, he extracted from them a promise not to name him for the Presidency in any event. The Democratic members of the Legislature of New Jersey had subscribed a paper avowing their preference for him as a Presidential candidate. This paper, in conformity with his wishes, was never published.   There are many good reasons to believe that had he been brought forward at that Convention as a candidate he would have received the nomination.   On the day before the nomination of General Pierce, a committee of his friends waited on him and urgently solicited his consent to have his name presented by the New Jersey delegation. They expressed the utmost confidence in his nomination, even at that late hour, were it known that he was a candidate.   He, however, peremptorily refused to sanction any such course.

During the spring of 1852 he was indirectly approached by various parties to ascertain what would be his probable course if elected President.   To all such parties his invariable response was, that he did not want to be President, that the office was neither consistent with his happiness or his interests, but that if, notwithstanding he declined to be a candidate, it should so happen that he were nominated and elected, he intended to go into the office unpledged, uncompromised, and entirely independent.   Doubtless, the declaration of such manly and patriotic sentiments repelled from his support those whose chief object in the selection of a candidate was to find a man who would use the public patronage for the advancement of their interests.

That the Commodore refused to permit his friends to submit his name to the Convention may also be ascribed to another reason. He is said to be of the opinion that these National Conventions which, of late years, have dictated to the people the candidates for whom alone practically they could vote, are usurpations of the popular prerogative ; that they are the machinery of a mere aristocracy of political leaders, constituted for the purpose of controlling and subjecting the popular will instead of truly and honestly reflecting and obeying it. The delegations from some of the States often necessarily represent but a minority of the people ; yet such delegations are permitted to enjoy an equal vote with the delegations of other States which represent actual and often large majorities.   The fundamental principles of republican equality are, therefore, violated in all such conventions.   The people only are the rightful sources of authority and power, and from the people only should emanate the controlling voice which should determine the election of the chief magistrate of the Republic. The present system of National Conventions has become (as the old Congressional Presidential caucus was before it) a mere instrument of cliques of politicians, to control and use the patronage and offices of the Government.   The abolition of the system is only a question of time.   It will be abolished as soon as the people discover the imposition by which they are at present subjugated to work out the will and pleasure of a few men of corrupt and grasping ambition. The people only submit to it because, with good-natured credulity, they have believed that Conventions were what they profess to be—their humble servants.

Whatever may have been the cause, there is no doubt of the fact that the Commodore did, in the most peremptory terms, refuse to permit the New Jersey delegation to submit his name as a candidate to the Convention.*

Whether the proper inference from this reluctance on his part, in 1852, to be made a candidate is, that he has no ambition for the Presidency, we know not. But we do know that on various occasions, for several years, he has suppressed, rather than encouraged, the efforts of his friends to make him a candidate for the Presidency.

He has been heard frequently to say that the responsibilities of a President are of such magnitude that no man ought to seek them; that the office could add nothing to his happiness or that of his family; that it is a position in which the performance of duty might require a man to offend his friends and do violence to his own feelings of clemency and generosity; that it is hardly possible for a President to do justice to the people and the country and not offend the politicians, or to obtain the support of the latter and faithfully perform his duties to the former; and that no man is fit for the office who is not willing to brave every danger, encounter all injustice, and incur every aspersion fearlessly in doing what is right; that, entertaining these opinions, he does not consider the office of President a position to be coveted by any man, while it is the duty of most men who are incompetent to fill it properly, promptly to decline it when its acceptance must prove detrimental to themselves as well as their country.

It will be perceived, from these opinions, that he does not agree with Mr. Lowndes and General Jackson in the sentiment originally uttered by the former:—" that the Presidency should neither be *sought* nor *declined*." He is of opinion that it is the duty of every true patriot and honest man to decline that position if he does not believe himself to be capable of discharging its duties honourably to himself and justly and faithfully to the country

Whatever may be his own views respecting his qualifications for

---

* We have collected several extracts from the papers of 1852, indicative of the general desire in many quarters for the nomination of Commodore Stockton. See Appendix, page 50.

the office of President, it is not to be questioned that numbers in all sections of the country believe him to be eminently qualified for that position.   That he possesses administrative as well as executive talents of a high order cannot be doubted; and that his moral integrity is of that lofty standard which distinguished the era of Washington, must be felt and confessed by all who know the man.

The future historian of this age of the Republic, should he fail to find the name of Stockton on the roll of Presidents, will not ascribe its absence there to his deficiency in the highest qualifications; he will rather ascribe it to the demoralizing influence of faction, which seeks its own gratification at the expense of the public welfare, and recoils with instinctive aversion from the patriot who would make virtue and honour and talents the criteria of promotion to office.

Near the close of the second session of Congress after his election, Commodore Stockton, notwithstanding the most earnest remonstrances of his friends, resigned his seat in the Senate. He had been sufficiently long at Washington to ascertain that the turmoil of political life there had no charms for him, compared with those of private life.

His retirement was universally regretted by the members of the distinguished body in which, during his short term of service, he had occupied so distinguished a position.   During that term he certainly surpassed the expectations of his most sanguine friends.   He acquired a reputation as a statesman and a senator commensurate with his fame as a naval commander.

His resignation was imputed by some to an expectation of receiving an invitation to enter the Cabinet of Mr. Pierce.   There were never any grounds for such an imputation.   Public opinion did indeed manifest itself very distinctly in favour of his being assigned the post of Secretary of the Navy.* But, disapproving, as it is well known he did, the principles indicated by the formation of the administration, it is not likely that he would have been willing to accept any such appointment.   Certainly, if he had entered the Cabinet of Mr. Pierce, its course, both with respect to foreign and domestic affairs, would have been different from the policy pursued, or else the Commodore would soon have abandoned it.

---

* See Appendix.

CHAPTER XV.

SINCE the resignation of his seat in the Senate of the United States, Commodore Stockton has not taken any active part in political affairs.

As an original advocate of the Compromise measures of 1850, however, it has been known that he disapproved the manner in which the friends of those measures have been treated by the administration.

The maintenance and advocacy of those measures, as a final settlement of the sectional question which has so long agitated the country, brought General Pierce into power. It was hoped and believed that his administration would be national; but, from its inception, sectional partisans were particularly the objects of Presidential favour. The peculiar friends of Mr. Van Buren at the North and the most strenuous champions of secession at the South were admitted to his confidence.

The President discovered, in 1854, that he had alienated and disgusted the greater part of those to whose support he was indebted for his election. He perceived that he had lost the South, and that the entire party which had elected him was in imminent danger of dissolution.

The Whig party, it was pretty generally understood, was broken up. It had, therefore, ceased, by its antagonism, to operate on the cohesion of the Democratic party. As in 1824, after the Federal party became extinct, the Democratic party separated into hostile fragments; so in 1854, for the want of a national opponent, its disorganization seemed inevitable.

The political managers, whose secret intrigues had procured the nomination of President Pierce in 1852, became alarmed with the prospect of a change of administration in 1856. Aspirants for the Presidency also (including the present incumbent) foresaw in the dissolution of parties, helped on by the unpopularity of the administration, their probable inability to control the people in the choice of a President in 1856.

The American sentiment of the country had been outraged by the marked distinction with which citizens of foreign birth had been preferred by the President; and a great American party had arisen which threatened to absorb all other party organizations.

To check the growth of this new party, and to consolidate the South in support of the President, or some nominee of his party, a scheme was formed to revive the anti-slavery agitation.

The REPEAL of the MISSOURI RESTRICTION it was thought would accomplish these objects. The scheme was bold and ingenious; and, though its injustice and immorality cannot be palliated or denied, it must be pronounced one of the most dexterous political movements ever made in the history of American parties. It was calculated that the South would be unable to resist so seductive an offer. It was supposed, too, that the national men in the free States, who were committed in favour of popular sovereignty in the territories, might be induced to approve the repeal, while large masses of others would be controlled by party discipline.

The Missouri restriction was repealed upon the ground that it was an unconstitutional exercise of power by Congress.

Though originally a Southern measure, by means of which the admission of Missouri as a State of the Union had been secured, yet the prevailing opinion at the South was, that the Missouri Compromise was unconstitutional.

The issue, therefore, tendered, was, Should an unconstitutional law be sustained?

The free States, however, have, for the most part, declined the issue so adroitly presented. The novelty of deciding the constitutionality of a law by a Presidential election has had few advocates in those States.

If the restriction were unconstitutional, it constituted no impediment to the extension of slavery. It was obviously the province of those who held that doctrine to test its soundness by a case in the courts.

But it is well understood that the Missouri Compromise was a bargain for the sake of peace, without any reference to the question of its constitutionality.

The calculations of the President and his friends respecting the effect of the repeal upon the South do not appear to have been erroneous. But they did not estimate so nicely its effect in the free States. *There* it has been almost universally considered as a gross breach of faith.

Whatever may be the course of professional politicians in those States, the people generally cannot be persuaded to approve a measure which they look upon as an indignity offered to them for the purpose of securing a sectional triumph.

Commodore Stockton has not been called upon to express his opinions on this subject; but it is known in New Jersey and Philadelphia that, from the beginning, he considered it as an insult to the free States, as well as a violation of a compact founded on honour and good faith. The Missouri Compromise he viewed as an honourable adjustment of a dangerous question. There were no reasons for its abrogation, which were not known when it was established. The pro-slavery and the anti-slavery sections were equally bound in honour to adhere to that settlement. The South had received and were in the enjoyment of the consideration of the bargain. Its obligation, resting in honour, good faith, and political comity, was not to be impeached by questioning its conformity to the Constitution. If unconstitutional, it was no restriction in conflict with the rights of any section. Its unconstitutionality might at any time be tested in the Supreme Court. It was a treaty of peace between the two great sections of the Republic, which could not, without the violation of plighted faith, be disturbed, unless with the universal consent of the country.

The abstract doctrine of non-intervention, which he so ably vindicates in his letter to Mr. Webster, has therefore nothing to do with, and is not in any degree involved in, the question as to the justice and expediency of the repeal of the Missouri Compromise. We have no authority for defining the position of Commodore Stockton on this or any other subject; and, in what we have said in relation to his opinions on the Missouri Compromise, we have only stated what are the views imputed to him by those leading gentlemen among his friends in New Jersey, who, from their connection with him, are likely to possess a correct knowledge of his sentiments.

After perusing the speeches and letters which will be found in the sequel to these pages, the reader will know pretty accurately what are the opinions of Commodore Stockton on most questions of national importance. He has never been very scrupulous about saying what he thought on all subjects which he has at any time discussed.

Even when the sycophants of extreme opinions were proclaiming *free trade* to be the only standard of Democratic orthodoxy with regard to the tariff, he freely avowed those liberal and national doctrines on that subject which were held by the Democratic party in 1828–29 upon the advent to power of General Jackson. Stockton has always held that the true national policy consisted in rendering the United States entirely independent of other countries for all those products and manufactures which were necessary or useful for purposes of naval or military defence. He has on this account always advocated ample protection to the production and fabrications of iron.*

He has also maintained that of all other interests those of American labour were those which had the best right to national encouragement, on account not only of their superior magnitude and importance, but because of the obligation resting on the Government to foster and protect them as the only true foundation of national wealth and prosperity.

On the subject of encouraging internal improvements by the Federal Government, he likewise occupies the Jacksonian ground. Works of a national character, such as the improvement of the Mississippi and Ohio, and the Atlantic rivers as high as tide-water ebbs and flows, he believes entitled to national assistance.

Upon the question of preserving intact and unimpaired the reserved rights of the States and of the people, his opinions are on record in the most explicit form. Indeed, the preservation of the Union he considers dependent on the undiminished plenitude of State and popular rights, as they were left or adjusted by the Constitution when it came fresh from the hands of the patriots who formed it. The disregard of reserved rights by the National Government—any attempt on its part to assume powers not granted, if acquiesced in—would unquestionably lead to oppression and injustice by tyrannical majorities, resistance to which would involve civil war and disruption of the confederacy.

In the spring of 1852, Mr. Webster, being in Trenton during the session of the Legislature, was invited by a joint resolution of both houses of that body to a formal reception. It was at a time when Mr. Webster was the object of severe denunciation by the opponents of the Compromise measures, and the Legislature of New Jersey, then composed of a large majority of Democrats, embraced that opportunity to honour him for his national course with respect to those measures.

---

* See Speech on Tariff.

Commodore Stockton, having arrived in Trenton the evening before the reception-day, was waited on by the Governor and the Legislative committee, and invited to attend and witness the ceremony. He was present, therefore, on the occasion as an invited guest.

When the reception had taken place and Mr. Webster had concluded his remarks in reply to the address of the president of the Senate, the Commodore left the House of the Assembly in company with Mr. Webster, though called upon importunately for a speech. But, before he had escaped from the State Capitol, several of his personal friends took him by the arm and insisted that he should return and address the audience, who were extremely desirous to hear him.

He accordingly returned and spoke for a few minutes in his usual frank and unaffected manner. His remarks were reported by a political opponent, who strangely tortured his language, or rather caricatured it, so as to make it as offensive as possible to his political friends. As the Commodore was at this time considered more likely than any prominent man not an avowed candidate to be the choice of the National Democratic Convention, any political speech of his was, of course, seized with avidity by the press and circulated without limit. The first report, therefore, got the start of the genuine article, and those who secretly desired the nomination of General Cass, Mr. Buchanan, or Mr. Douglas, or others, all affected surprise and astonishment and regret that Commodore Stockton should have blasted his own Presidential prospects.

The Commodore took the matter quite coolly, however. He had no Presidential aspirations which could prevent him from expressing with the most unbounded freedom the sentiments of his heart and the conclusions of his understanding. When analyzed, the objections to this speech amount to nothing more than objections to his eulogium on Mr. Webster, to his expression of the sentiment "that when the honour, welfare, and happiness of his country were at issue his party robes hung loosely on his shoulders," and to his avowal that American labour was entitled to protection.

In the appendix to these pages will be found his remarks on the death of Mr. Webster in the Senate, in the course of which he reminded senators (some of whom, doubtless, had lifted up their eyes in serious horror at the Trenton speech) that he *dared* to say of Mr. Webster when alive what so many senators were now anxious to say when he was dead. It was a rebuke which was felt and

* See Appendix E.

appreciated by all who heard this last tribute of Stockton to his departed friend.

Mr. Webster had been the friend of the Commodore's father for twenty years; he had been *his* friend also for near forty years; he had been his counsel in important suits, involving his conduct as an officer as well as his fortune; their social intercourse, frequent and cordial, had never suffered any interruption, though their political associations had, for the most part, been adverse. Under these circumstances, had the Presidency, during life, depended on his abstaining from rendering to Mr. Webster the homage of his heart whenever he spoke of him, Stockton would have spoken all the generous feelings which he cherished towards him with the same unrestrained freedom that he spoke at Trenton.

The sentiments which Stockton expressed with regard to Webster are the sentiments of the nation; of every honest man and patriot who loves the Constitution, (of which Webster earned the title of DEFENDER;) of every friend of the Union, of which Mr. Webster was the champion in its hours of greatest peril. No man, Whig or Democrat, can be a sincere friend to the Constitution and the Union and not feel grateful to Mr. Webster for the courage and ability which he always manifested in their defence. Ignoble, narrow-minded, and mole-eyed political opponents may delight to dwell on Mr. Webster's points of difference with the Democratic party, and may still cherish some of those feelings of animosity towards him which they felt in former days of partisan controversy; but the generous, high-minded American, to whatever party he may belong, proud that his country produced an intellectual giant of Mr. Webster's mental power, would much prefer to remember his achievements "for the country and the whole country," when he stood up the champion of the Union against nullification; when, in that conflict, he stood side by side with Andrew Jackson "and felt his own great arm lean on him for support;"* when he negotiated the Ashburton Treaty; when he forever crushed and annihilated the British pretension of search on American ships; and when, hoary with age and crowned with honours, tottering on the brink of eternity, on the 7th of March, 1850, he sacrificed himself in the service of his country to the remorseless Moloch of sectional faction which, with relentless ferocity, "tracked his steps of glory to the grave."

As to the sentiment that, when the honour and welfare of the

---

* Webster's Speech in the Senate, Jan. 26, 1830.

country are concerned, his party robes hang loosely, no man who can understand his meaning will controvert the justice and propriety of the declaration. No good citizen will deny that, where his duty to the country comes in conflict with partisan opinions or measures, the obligations of duty are paramount; nay, the most rancorous and pharisaical devotee of party politics will not dare to say that party allegiance is superior to the allegiance of the citizen to the country.* But nevertheless, not withstanding the soundness of the principle, political empirics affected to be shocked with the declaration of the principle at the time. And this well illustrates the difference between Commodore Stockton and ordinary politicians.

They would often suppress their acknowledgment of a correct principle for fear that it might prove injurious to their prospects. Stockton will not shrink from the avowal of such a principle on the proper occasion, no matter what may be the consequences to himself personally.

Courage—undaunted intrepidity, which is incapable of any thing like fear—is, perhaps, the most distinguishing trait of Commodore Stockton. This defiant courage makes him, in relation to his political course, as daring and as chivalrous as he is in the field. In relation to action in the field, whether with the enemy of his country or his own personal foe, the reader will perceive in this narrative of his career that wherever danger was visible, Stockton advanced to meet it. He never waits passively to be placed on his defence, but is always the assailant. He approaches danger; he does not wait to be approached by it. He prefers storming his adversary's position to being besieged behind his own ramparts.

When, therefore, in the course of his political life, he has meditated a movement which he was convinced was right, but which others would naturally pronounce fatal to his imputed political aspirations, we do not doubt that, independently of the gratification of doing what he considered right, the risk to be encountered rather increased the charm with which duty irresistibly drew him on in the path to which she pointed.

From this it appears that, although he loves glory, yet the glory which he worships is the glory of doing right—the glory of performing his duty and his whole duty. He did not, therefore, when he gave aid and comfort to the Native Americans of Philadelphia in 1845, do so for popularity or political effect. He espoused their cause because he thought it right; and he never

---

* See Speech in Appendix.

shrunk, under any circumstances, from avowing his concord with them. In his speech of December 31, 1847, before a promiscuous assembly of men of all parties, we find him boldly proclaiming the tenets of the Americans, and challenging for them the assent of all present. He avowed them then because he believed them to be right—not because they were the creed of a party.

In 1854, when the probability of his being the Democratic nominee of the Cincinnati National Convention to assemble in June, 1856, was quite as great as that any one else would be nominated, we find him again, as soon as he was interrogated, fearlessly declaring his assent to the principles which he had before approved. In doing this he disavows no opinions or principles which he has heretofore advocated. When these opinions were thus reiterated by him, it was, indeed, indicated by the general sentiment developed throughout the country that the Democratic party would feel constrained to adopt them.

Sympathizing, as that party generally does, with the highest-toned and most radically patriotic emotions, and generally conforming to the will of the masses, the politicians found it necessary to make great efforts to prevent its becoming Americanized.

The administration came to their aid by the repeal of the Missouri Restitution.

As one irritant is applied by physicians to correct another, so the excitement produced by the abrogation of the Missouri Compromise checked and superseded the excitement produced by the first demonstrations of the American party.

The opponents of the repeal, the remnants of the Whig party and other sectional organizations in New England, rushed impetuously into the American lodges and took possession of them. They sought to make the American party auxiliary to the sectional controversy now revived. These circumstances, together with the preponderance of the foreign element in the Democratic party, effectually arrested any further open demonstrations in its ranks in favour of the American movement.

It is not improbable that if it had not been for these extraordinary causes the Democratic party could not have been forced by its leaders to commit itself so precipitately against the Americans. It might have been persuaded temperately and judiciously to have consented to the reform or modification of some of those laws of which the Americans complain, and, under happier auspices, an adjustment of the great national questions which the American party have raised might have been effected without the struggle which it must now cost.

It remains to be seen whether the leaders and tacticians of the Democratic party have not merely postponed, instead of having defeated, the success of the Americans. It may well be doubted whether those politicians have not miscalculated the strength of party drill and cohesion, and whether they can prevent the great body of the Democratic masses from falling into the American ranks under a suitable leader.

Whatever may be the present aspect of the American party, its ultimate success admits of no doubt. It is absurd to suppose that the people of the United States will much longer tolerate the participation of their sovereignty with those hordes of incompetent aliens annually swarming to our shores. Human nature is incapable of persistence in such folly. It is inconsistent with the principle of self-preservation—the highest of all laws.

Commodore Stockton, when he avowed his American opinions, neither knew (nor, we suppose, did he care) whether the Whig, Democratic, or any other party, concurred with him. He avowed them because he entertained them, and because he believed them to be right. In doing this he probably never calculated the consequences to himself, and, if he did, it was to disregard them. He acted with the same boldness as when in the Senate, the youngest member of that body, he stood up first and declared—what no senator before him had the courage to do, (in relation to the Kossuth excitement,) —that war with Russia, on account of Hungary, was a utopian idea; that it was utterly impracticable. This declaration, though it startled his auditors, found an echo in the common sense of every senator. And so, likewise, whatever professional party men may now say, the American sentiments, and the high patriotic tone of the following letter, addressed to a committee of Americans, will find an echo in all true American hearts; and they will honour and respect the author, *however circumstances may render it expedient that they should now appear to differ with him* :—

LETTER OF COMMODORE STOCKTON TO THE AMERICANS OF TRENTON.

"TRENTON, November 13, 1855.

"HON. R. F. STOCKTON, Princeton:

"DEAR SIR :—The Americans of Trenton intend to hold a meeting on Friday evening, the 16th inst., to celebrate the recent victories of the American party in California, New York, Massachusetts, and Maryland, and to commemorate the principles of the American party.

"It is well known that you have for years approved these principles; therefore, you are earnestly invited to be present and to address your fellow-citizens on that occasion.

" With great respect, your obedient servants,

" E. H. GRANDIN,
" RICHD. BRANDT,
" HENRY C. FURMAN,
" CHAS. M. WHITTAKER,
" J. C. LANGSTINE,
" WM. R. BURNS,
"*Committee of Invitation.*"

'PRINCETON, November 14, 1855.

" TO MESSRS. E. H. GRANDIN, RICHARD BRANDT, HENRY C. FURMAN, CHARLES M. WHITTAKER, J. C. LANGSTINE, WILLIAM R. BURNS, *Committee of Invitation:*—

" GENTLEMEN :—I am informed by your letter of yesterday, that a meeting is to be held at Trenton on Friday, the 16th instant, commemorative of the principles of the American party. You also say ' that it is well known that you have for several years approved those principles, therefore you are earnestly invited to be present and to address your fellow-citizens on that occasion.' I thank you for the invitation, although previous engagements will prevent my being present.

" I am unwilling, however, to permit the occasion to pass without expressing my entire concurrence in the patriotic principles of the American party, which have had for so many years the approval of my head and heart. They are

"*First.* The Constitution with its Compromises.

"*Second.* The preservation of the Union at all hazards.

"*Third.* The naturalization laws should be abolished or essentially modified.

"*Fourth.* Americans alone should rule America. They only should be appointed to the high and responsible executive offices under our Government.

" The men of the Revolution, notwithstanding they gratefully acknowledged the aid derived from France, were fully sensible of the dangers of foreign influence. They incorporated in both the Federal and State Constitutions provisions carefully designed as barriers against the influence of any foreign ingredient in the population. The protracted war which succeeded the French Revolution powerfully affected the public mind in the United States, and political parties were more or less biassed in favour of one or the other belligerent. It required the whole weight of the great Washington's character to prevent the young republic from being entangled in the meshes of European politics. His wisdom enabled him justly to appreciate the desire which has always characterized republican governments to become more or less subject, in one way or another, to foreign influence. The events of his age, however, directed his attention to the counteraction of that influence, exerted in a different manner from that in which it now threatens our safety. The foreign influence which justly alarmed him arose from the sympathy of our people with one or the other of the mighty powers who were contending, as both claimed to be, for liberty and for political predominance in Europe.

"Washington did not anticipate that, in half a century from his age, Europe would be brought within ten days' sail of America, or that within that period half a million of foreigners annually would come to exercise the prerogatives of American sovereigns. Had such a state of things been presented to him, his warning voice would have been heard on the subject, and would have inspired our statesmen with the wisdom and the courage to avert the danger which he would have foreseen. Such was the jealous virtue and patriotism which distinguished the Washington era, that, had the immigration of that period been one-tenth of what it has now become, it is more than probable that no power would have been granted by the people to the Federal Government to enact any laws of naturalization.

"The evil is upon us which Washington deprecated. The evil is radical, and the correction must be equally radical. We must awaken in the public mind that sensitive regard for the preservation of the Constitution and American liberty which inspired the souls of those patriots who were the counsellors and supporters of Washington and the fathers of the country. *The safety and prosperity of our institutions* must be made the cardinal objects of attainment. The spoils of office, the love of power, the subjection to the iron tyranny of a few political oligarchs, must be held in contempt in comparison with the importance of securing these great ends. The crafty engineers of political speculation see no danger, and never will see any, which does not threaten to arrest their profitable control of parties. The doctrine that *Americans alone should rule America,'* designed to restore the government, as it was in the days of Washington, to the hands of 'Americans alone,' is stigmatized by the organized cabal of politicians who wield the machinery for manufacturing the incumbents of office, from that of the Presidency downwards, as a pestilent heresy, and those who hold to this ancient American doctrine are denounced as traitors.

"The progress of events is rapidly bringing the country to the condition when but two parties will contend with each other— the one the *American party*, the other the *Foreign party*. The *American party* will seek the restoration of the Government to American control, such as it was when it came fresh from the American people. The *Foreign party* will seek to propitiate the *foreign element*, pander to its insolent ambition and aspiring predominance, contend for the continuance and extension of its privileges, cringe with servility to its dictates, and offer new bribes for its friendship. The simple fact that the next election of a President of the United States may turn upon the assertion or the renunciation by the American people of the doctrine that 'Americans alone should rule America,' should be sufficient to astonish and alarm us. If the doctrine be renounced, it will be owing to the overpowering force of the foreign element in our population. The mighty power of that element has been gauged by the astute politicians who are allied to it. They have measured its length and breadth, its height and its depth, and they are willing to stake their destinies on its omnipotence. It was the Pretorian guards, composed of foreign mercenaries, who put up for sale the imperial purple at Rome; and it is the foreign mercenaries among us who now offer to the politicians who hold the reins of party sway the next Presidency, as the price of favours to be conferred on them and privileges perpetuated hereafter. There is no country—there never has been any country—where such an issue, if squarely, fairly, and distinctly presented to the people, could be decided any other than one way, and that in favour of the *'country-born.'* Will the people of the United States repudiate a sentiment of this sort? They will do no such thing. Already they have arisen spontaneously and rushed to the standard inscribed with the words, 'The Americans shall rule America.' It is vain for politicians to attempt to arrest the progress of the American party by efforts to compel it to adopt portions of the creeds which distinguish other parties.

14

"It will not thus be induced to endanger the cause in which it is engaged. The safety of the people is the supreme law, and, while that safety is endangered, every thing else is of subordinate interest. 'Place none but Americans on guard' was the order of Washington at a crisis of imminent danger.

"With assurances of high regard,

"I am your friend and obedient servant,

"R. F. STOCKTON."

APPENDIX A.

Parts of the Report of the Secretary of the Navy, communicating copies of Commodore Stockton's despatches relating to the military and naval operations in California.

NAVY DEPARTMENT, February 14, 1849.

SIR:—In compliance with a resolution of the Senate of the 8th instant, I have the honour to communicate herewith "a copy of the despatch of the 5th of February, 1847, of Commodore Robert F. Stockton, commanding the forces of the United States in California," together with copies of "such other despatches of Commodore Stockton relating to the naval and military operations in that country as have not heretofore been communicated to Congress and published."

I have the honor to be, very respectfully, your obedient servant,

J. Y. MASON.

Hon. GEORGE M. DALLAS,
    Vice-President of the United States
        and President of the Senate.

UNITED STATES FRIGATE CONGRESS,
BAY OF MONTEREY, September 18, 1846.

SIR:—I have the honour to acknowledge the receipt of your despatches of the 15th of May, addressed to my predecessor, and sent by Passed Midshipman McRae, who delivered them to me on board of this ship on the night of the 7th of September, soon after we came to anchor in the bay of "Santa Barbara," where I stopped on my way to this place to take on board a detachment of men which I left for the defence of that place, after we had taken it on our way to San Pedro.

I am happy to say, in answer to that despatch, that all your instructions contained therein had been anticipated and executed, and my proceedings forwarded to you by different routes two weeks before the arrival of Mr. McRae—even that part of them suggesting that a messenger be sent across the mountains to Washington; which messenger I hope you will have seen and sent back to me before this can reach you.

I send enclosed the correspondence between General Castro and myself. I did not answer his last letter, but by a verbal message, which does not properly belong to history. We found in and near his camp ten pieces of artillery—six in good order, and four spiked.

The elections as far as heard from have been regularly held, and the proper officers elected. The people are getting over their first alarm, and our friends are not now afraid to avow themselves.

General Castro and the governor having collected at one time so large a force together, and our remaining inactive at Monterey, induced the belief that we were not willing to run the hazard of a fight, and that if we did we must be beaten. No one, foreigner or native, dared aid us even with advice or information.

1

But, since Castro and the governor have been driven out of the country, the aspect of things is changed, and all is going on as well as we ought to desire.

By an intercepted correspondence between the military commandant at Mazatlan and General Castro, it appears that arrangements were making to send troops into California, and General Castro is strongly urged to destroy the "nefarious enemy." But it is too late.

I take the opportunity of this communication to remind you of two things that may be of some importance to be remembered.

1. That neither San Francisco or Monterey are susceptible, within any reasonable expense, of being defended from an attack made from the interior; every commanding position within reach of a cannon-ball from the water is overlooked by adjacent hills, within gunshot. We must, therefore, hold the country along the sea-coast as far south as St. Lucas, and make the river Gila and a line drawn from that river across to the Del Norte the southern boundary, all of which is now in our possession. It is not my business, perhaps, to say more on the subject. I will send you, however, a map which I have made, and on which I have traced with red ink the boundary line above suggested.

2. That this territory within the lines marked by me should be retained by the United States, as indispensable to preserve the lives and property of our fellow-citizens residing here, as well as to secure any thing like permanent peace.

I have put some guns on board the store-ship "Erie," and made a cruiser of her. She will sail on a cruise immediately, to circulate the enclosed notice and to look out for privateers, and will touch at Panama to deliver and receive despatches.

As soon as the schooner Shark returns from the Columbia River, I will send her on a cruise for the protection of our whale-ships.

The Savannah, Portsmouth, and Cyane will continue the blockade of the coast of Mexico, while I will in the Congress go up the Gulf of California and pay my respects to San Jose, La Paz, Loreto, and Guaymas, thence along the Mexican coast, thence to the Sandwich Islands, thence to San Francisco.

The Warren will be obliged to lay by for extensive repairs.

By which disposition of the squadron I hope to meet your approbation, as well as the views of Mr. Webster and his friends, who signed the letter to the President which I found among your last despatches. Besides, I will order the ships of the blockading squadron occasionally to change their ground and take a cruise, one after the other, for the protection of the whalers. By these courses we will cross each other's track, and so traverse the ocean as to render it somewhat hazardous for a privateer to be dodging about within our circle.

Faithfully, your obedient servant,

R. F. Stockton, Commodore, &c.

Your letter to Commodore Biddle will be sent to the Sandwich Islands by the American ship Brooklyn, which leaves this place in a day or two for Honolulu.

Hon. George Bancroft,
    Secretary of the Navy, Washington, D. C.

Ciudad de los Angeles, August 31, 1846.

Sir:—I herewith enclose to you your commission as military commandant of this department.

Martial law will continue in force throughout the whole territory, until otherwise ordered by the governor of the same.

Notwithstanding, however, the existence of martial law, you will permit the civil officers of the government to proceed in the exercise of their proper functions, nor will you interfere with their duties, except in cases where the peace and safety of the territory requires your aid or interference.

You will take care that my proclamation of the 17th be strictly observed throughout this department, except as to those persons who may be exempted by your written order from the operation of its provisions.

You are authorized, whenever it can be prudently done, to give written permission to persons known to be friendly to the government to be out themselves, and to send their servants out before sunrise in the morning.

You are likewise authorized to grant permission, where you see fit, to persons known to be friendly, to carry arms with them, whenever it appears to you they stand in need of them for their own or their servants' protection.

I enclose to you, also, some blank commissions for prefects and alcaldes, that, in case the people should fail to elect either of those officers within the jurisdiction of this department, you may fill up the blank with the name of some one you may think is qualified and will accept the office, affixing the date thereto, and transmitting to me at San Francisco, by the first opportunity, the name and date of all appointments made by you.

Whenever opportunity offers, you will write to me as to the state of the country and the feelings of the people within this department.

Faithfully, your obedient servant,

R. F. STOCKTON,
Governor and Commander-in-chief.

To CAPTAIN A. H. GILLESPIE,
Military Commandant of the Southern Department.

P. S.—Sent that you may see how I have tempered the rigours of indispensable military law with the appliances of peace.

R. F. STOCKTON.

Organization of the Army of California.

GENERAL ORDER.

Besides the governor and commander-in-chief, there will be from this day a military commandant of the territory of California, whose duty it will be to superintend and direct all the military operations in the territory, according to the directions that he may from time to time receive from the governor, to whom he will report all his proceedings. The territory will hereafter be divided into three military departments, to each of which will be appointed a military commandant, who will receive instructions from and be responsible to the military commandant of the territory.

R. F. STOCKTON,
Governor and Commander-in-chief of the Territory of California.

CIUDAD DE LOS ANGELES, September 2, 1846.

CIRCULAR.

You are hereby advised that war exists between the United States of North America and Mexico, and are cautioned to guard against an attack from Mexican privateers, and all vessels under the Mexican flag.

The territory of California has been taken possession of by the forces under my command, and now belongs to the United States; and you will find safe anchorage and protection in the harbour of San Francisco during any season of the year.

R. F. STOCKTON, *Commodore, &c.*

UNITED STATES FRIGATE CONGRESS.

UNITED STATES FRIGATE CONGRESS,
BAY OF MONTEREY, September 19, 1846.

SIR:—I am informed by express from Commander Montgomery, at San Fran cisco, that Suter's Fort, on the Sacramento, is threatened by a thousand Indians from the Oregon, of the Walla-Walla tribe.

The cause of their hostility appears to be this: about a year since one of their chiefs was deliberately murdered at Suter's Fort by a man named Cook.

The Erie is under way, and I have only time to say that I shall go after them immediately with the crews of this ship and the Savannah, and I will give them satisfaction or a fight.

Will you please to send to me, by Mr. Norris, a good spy-glass?

Faithfully, your obedient servant,
R. F. STOCKTON, *Commodore, &c.*

To the Hon. GEORGE BANCROFT,
Secretary of the Navy, Washington, D.C.

SAN DIEGO, HEAD-QUARTERS OF, &c. &c.,
November 23, 1846.

SIR:—By the celebrated Mexican armed brig Malek Adhel, which was cap tured and taken out of the harbour of Mazatlan by the boats of the United States ship Warren, I have the honour to send this despatch for you as far as Mazatlan, and to say that several other vessels—perhaps thirteen or fourteen—have been captured by the Cyane and Warren, official reports of which, however, have not yet reached me; but I have reason to hope and believe that every vessel by which our commerce in this ocean could probably be interrupted has been cap tured by Commander Hull, in the Warren, or Commander Dupont, in the Cyane. Those officers deserve praise for the manner in which they have blockaded and watched the Mexican coast during the most inclement season of the year.

The enclosed letters, from No. 1 to 4, will acquaint you with the position of the squadron and the affairs of this territory, as well as with my intentions in regard to the further prosecution of the war up to the 30th September, when the intelligence reached me that all the Mexican officers in the territory, with the exception of one or two, had violated their oaths, and again taken up arms against the United States, with which insurrection, and the consequent altera tion of all my preconcerted plans, it will be the further object of this despatch to make you acquainted.

The war in California being, as I supposed, at an end, and having ordered the other ships of the squadron to the coast of Mexico, there to await my arrival, I was about to transfer the government of California to other hands, and to sail as soon as possible in the Congress for Acapulco, where I expected to land and lend our aid to the war in that part of Mexico, when I was informed by express that the Mexican officers had violated their oaths and commenced anew the war by a midnight attack on the party of fifty men left at Ciudad de los Angeles.

The enclosed proclamation, No. 5, signed by Jose Ma Flores, a captain in the Mexican army, and on parole, will give you some idea of the disposition of those depraved men.

At this time Major Fremont had gone to the Sacramento to enlist men for me to take to Acapulco. I immediately sent to him to come to San Francisco, with as many men and saddles as he could get to embark in the ship Sterling, that we might by prompt action surprise the enemy at Santa Barbara, only three days' march from De los Angeles; while I would go directly to San Pedro and march to the city, where I would certainly be able to calculate within a day or two the time I would receive his co-operation.

While the necessary preparations were making to carry out this plan of sur prise and at once to put down the insurrection, I ordered the Savannah (then under sailing orders for the coast of Mexico) to go immediately to San Pedro, and afford all the aid in her power to our little garrison at the city.

I left San Francisco in company with the Sterling; but, having crossed the bar before her, I hove to till she came out, and then I steered with a fair wind down along the coast. On our way we spoke the ship Barnstable from Monterey with despatches from the commanding officer there, stating that Monterey would probably be attacked, and that he required immediate reinforcement. I went immediately to Monterey, leaving the Sterling with a fair wind on her way to Santa Barbara.

I arrived the next day at Monterey, and landed two officers, Messrs. Baldwin and Johnston, with fifty men and three pieces of artillery; and, having fortified the town against any probable force in California, I left for San Pedro, looking into Santa Barbara, as I passed, to see how the Sterling made out; but she had not arrived, although she ought to have been there several days previous.

I passed on to San Pedro, where I found the Savannah. Captain Mervine, commander of the Savannah, informed me that on his arrival there he found on board of the ship Vandalia the party of volunteers who had been besieged at the Pueblo, and to whose assistance he had been despatched, but who had been permitted by treaty to retire with their arms on board of this vessel; that about two weeks before my arrival he had landed with his men and the above-mentioned volunteers, and marched for the city; that he met a body of mounted men with a field-piece, with whom he had an engagement; that he had not taken any artillery with him, and they had driven him back to his ship, with the loss of four men killed and some wounded; and that he had remained on board since that time waiting for me.

He says that his officers and men behaved well; that they made several efforts to take the field-piece from the enemy, but they could not overtake it. In truth, nothing short of a locomotive engine can catch those well-mounted fellows.

I did not like this proceeding or its probable consequences; but I have no more to say about it at present. Elated by this transient success,—which the enemy, with his usual want of veracity, magnified into a great victory,—they collected in large bodies on all the adjacent hills, and would not permit a hoof except their own horses to be within fifty miles of San Pedro.

I had, however, agreed to land there, to be in readiness to co-operate with the forces under Major Fremont expected from Santa Barbara; and therefore determined to do so in the face of their boasting insolence, and there again to hoist the glorious stars in the presence of their horse-covered hills.

Orders were accordingly given to prepare to land the troops in the morning, and a party of the volunteers, as you will see by a general order here enclosed and marked No. 6, were ordered to land before daylight, to cover the general landing, which was to be made up a very steep bank and in the face of the enemy.

The volunteers failed to land in time, in consequence of a fancied force of the enemy. Not so with the sailors and marines, who were ready in the boats alongside of the two ships, and whom, as soon as I discovered that the volunteers had not succeeded, I ordered to land. The boats of the Savannah were under the immediate command of Captain Mervine; those of the Congress under the immediate command of Lieutenant-Commandant Livingston, and performed the service in a most gallant manner, being myself present.

On our approach to the shore, the enemy fired a few muskets without harm and fled; we took possession, and once more hoisted our flag at San Pedro. General order, marked No. 7, will show you how I estimated the conduct of the troops at the time.

The troops remained encamped at that place for several days before the insurgents, who covered the adjacent hills, and until both officers and men had become almost worn out by chasing and skirmishing with and watching them, and until I had given up all hope of the co-operation of Major Fremont. Besides, the enemy had driven off every animal, man and beast, from that section of the country, and it was not possible, by any means in our power, to carry provisions for our march to the city.

I resolved, therefore, to embark the troops, and waste no more time there, but to go down South, and, if possible, to get animals somewhere along the coast before the enemy could know or prevent it, and to mount my own men and march to the city by the Southern route.

I left the Savannah to look out for Major Fremont, and, taking the volunteers on board of the Congress, proceeded down the coast as far as San Diego, where Lieutenant Minor was in command.

Two days after my arrival at San Diego, the Malek Adhel arrived from Monterey, with despatches from Major Fremont, in which he says:—"We met the Vandalia with information of the occurrences below. Mr. Howard represented that the enemy had driven off all the horses and cattle, so that it would be impossible to obtain either for transportation or supplies. Under the circumstances, and in virtue of the discretionary authority you have given me, I judged it of paramount necessity to haul up immediately for this port, with the intention to send for all the men who could be raised in the North and for the band of horses which I had left on the Cosumne. In the mean time we should be able to check the insurrection here, and procure horses and supplies, so as to be in readiness to march to the southward immediately on the arrival of our reinforcements."

On the receipt of this letter, having arranged with Lieutenant Minor to send a vessel down the coast for horses and cattle, I returned to San Pedro, and sent the Savannah back to Monterey, to facilitate, as far as I could, the preparations of Major Fremont.

On my return at San Diego, I found that the expedition South had been successful, that the party had obtained about sixty useful horses, two hundred head of cattle, and five hundred sheep.

On the afternoon of our arrival, the enemy, irritated, I suppose, by the loss of his animals, came down in considerable force and made an attack; they were, however, soon driven back, with the loss of two men and horses killed, and four wounded. Those skirmishes or running fights are of almost daily occurrence; since we have been here we have lost, as yet, but one man killed and one wounded.

One hundred more horses will enable me to mount some of my own men, and, before long, I expect to be a *general of dragoons, as well as commodore, governor, and commander-in-chief.*

I have been thus particular in this despatch, that you may see that all that unflinching labour and perseverance on my part, and inflexible patriotism and courage on the part of my officers and men, could do to suppress this rebellion, has been done, and that, although we may still be for some time annoyed by those daily skirmishes, yet the rebels cannot, in all probability, much longer avert the doom that awaits them.   Faithfully, your obedient servant,

R. F. STOCKTON.

To the Hon. GEORGE BANCROFT,
Secretary of the Navy, Washington, D.C.

UNITED STATES FRIGATE CONGRESS,
HARBOUR OF SAN FRANCISCO, September 30, 1846.

SIR:—You will, as soon as you are ready, proceed to sea under your sealed orders, with this modification, however :—you will, on falling in with the Cyane, send her immediately to San Francisco, instead of detaining her on the coast as heretofore directed.

The Congress and Cyane will, by this arrangement, it is expected, be ready to relieve the Savannah and Portsmouth.

If despatches from the government should arrive at Mazatlan between this and the first of December, you will open them; and, if notice of peace, you will leave copies of the despatches at Mazatlan for me, in case I should arrive there after you have left, and come to San Francisco and prepare the Savannah to return to the United States.

If Mr. Norris should arrive from the United States at Mazatlan before I reach there, you will bring him in the Savannah or send him in the Portsmouth as soon as possible to this place, without opening the despatches. The enclosed letter contains a despatch for the Secretary of the Navy. You will please to make every exertion, without regard to expense, to get it forwarded by Mr. Mott, or some one else.

You will also draw for the use of this squadron any sum of money, not exceeding one hundred thousand dollars, that you may be enabled to get at Mazatlan.

Please to seal the letter to Mott, Talbot & Co. before you deliver it; I leave it open in case you should find it best to deliver the despatch to other hands.

Faithfully, your obedient servant,

R. F. STOCKTON, *Commodore, &c.*

To CAPTAIN WM. MERVINE,
United States Frigate Savannah, harbour of San Francisco.

GENERAL ORDER.

UNITED STATES FRIGATE CONGRESS,
OFF SAN PEDRO, October 26, 1846.

Captain Gillespie, with fifty men, will be landed at four o'clock, A. M., to-morrow, to surprise the enemy.

The oars of the boats must be muffled, and the men pull without the least noise, and perfect silence must be observed.

If Captain Gillespie requires aid, he will fire a rocket, when the boats of the ships will be ready to go to his assistance.

If Captain Gillespie meets no opposition in taking possession of the houses, he will conceal his force so as to shoot any spies that may venture inside of rifle-range (*never shooting too quick*) to oppose the landing of the troops.

If Captain Gillespie does not require assistance, the rest of the troops will not land until after breakfast, which will be taken at seven o'clock, and the forces prepared to disembark at half-past eight o'clock, when a signal to that effect is made.

Captain Gillespie will keep his position until the troops are landed, when he will return on board to breakfast.

If the troops are required to land before breakfast, the force from the frigate Savannah will be commanded by Captain Mervine; those from the Congress by Lieutenant-Commandant Livingston.

The commander-in-chief intends to lead on the attack, if there be one, in person.

By order of the commander-in-chief.

J. ZEILIN, *Brevet-Captain and Adjutant.*

GENERAL ORDER.

UNITED STATES FRIGATE CONGRESS,
BAY OF SAN PEDRO, October 28, 1846.

The commander-in-chief commends the determined courage with which the officers, sailors, and marines landed (in despite of the false alarm as to the enemy's force) and again hoisted the American standard at San Pedro.

The important duties of the commander-in-chief, and the entire want of camp equipage or other necessary accommodation, require him, while the troops are in camp on the beach, to retain his head-quarters on board of the ship; but, brave comrades, be assured that he will superintend and direct all your operations, and when in danger he will be, as he was yesterday morning, in the midst of you.

Every officer and man must be ready at a moment's notice to march to the Puebla to support Major Fremont's volunteers, or to go on board of ship to the relief of our gallant brothers in arms at San Diego and Monterey, who are threatened with an attack by overwhelming forces.

Brave men, however various and different your duties may be, the commander-in-chief is satisfied you will give the most willing aid to all his operations in defence of the honour and glory of our country.   •

By order of the commander-in-chief.

J. Zeilin, Brevet-Captain and Adjutant.

Head-Quarters, Ciudad de los Angeles,
January 11, 1847.

Sir:—My last letter to the department will have informed you of the defeat of Captain Mervine at San Pedro, and the return of Colonel Fremont, with the force under his command, to Monterey, since which time I have not heard from him; and of my being at San Diego, surrounded by the insurgents, and entirely destitute of all means of transportation. We succeeded at last, however, in getting animals two hundred and forty miles to the southward of San Diego, and in driving them, in despite of the insurgents, into the garrison.

I have now the honour to inform you that it has pleased God to crown our poor efforts to put down the rebellion, and to retrieve the credit of our arms with the most complete success. The insurgents, again elated by the defeat of General Kearney at San Pasqual, and the capture of one of his guns, determined with his whole force to meet us on our march from San Diego to this place, and to decide the fate of the territory by a general battle.

Having made the best preparation I could in the face of a boasting and vigilant enemy, we left San Diego on the 29th day of December (that portion of the insurgent army who had been watching and annoying us having left to join the main body) with about six hundred fighting men, composed of detachments from the ships Congress, Savannah, Portsmouth, and Cyane, aided by General Kearney with a detachment of sixty men on foot from the first regiment of United States dragoons, and with Captain Gillespie with sixty mounted rifle-men.

We marched nearly one hundred and forty miles in ten days, and found the rebels on the 8th day of January, in a strong position, on the high bank of the "Rio San Gabriel," with six hundred mounted men and four pieces of artillery, prepared to dispute our passage across that river.

We waded through the water, dragging our guns after us, against the galling fire of the enemy, without exchanging a shot until we reached the opposite shore, when the fight became general, and our troops, having repelled a charge of the enemy, charged up the bank in a most gallant manner, and gained a most complete victory over the insurgent army.

The next day, on our march across the plains of the Mesa to this place, the insurgents made another desperate effort to save the capital and their own necks; they were concealed with their artillery in a ravine until we came within gun-shot, when they opened a brisk fire from their field-pieces on our right flank, and at the same time charged both on our front and rear. We soon silenced their guns and repelled the charge, when they fled and permitted us the next morning to march into town without any further opposition.

We have rescued the country from the hands of the insurgents, but I fear that the absence of Colonel Fremont's battalion of mounted riflemen will enable most of the Mexican officers who have broken their parole to escape to Sonora.

I am happy to say that our loss in killed and wounded does not exceed twenty, while we are informed that the enemy has lost between seventy and eighty.

This despatch must go immediately, and I will wait another opportunity to furnish you with the details of these two battles, and the gallant conduct of the officers and men under my command, with their names.

Faithfully, your obedient servant,

R. F. STOCKTON, *Commodore, &c.*

To the Hon. GEORGE BANCROFT,
Secretary of the Navy, Washington, D. C.

GENERAL ORDER.

HEAD-QUARTERS, CIUDAD DE LOS ANGELES,
January 11, 1847.

The commander-in-chief congratulates the officers and men of the southern division of United States forces in California, on the brilliant victories obtained by them over the enemy on the 8th and 9th instants, and on once more taking possession of the Ciudad de los Angeles.

He takes the earliest moment to commend their gallantry and good conduct, both in the battle fought on the 8th, on the banks of the Rio San Gabriel, and on the 9th instant, on the plains of the Mesa.

The steady courage of the troops in forcing their passage across the Rio San Gabriel, where officers and men were alike employed in dragging the guns through the water, against the galling fire of the enemy, without exchanging a shot, and their gallant charge up the banks against the enemy's cavalry, has perhaps never been surpassed; and the cool determination with which, in the battle of the 9th, they repulsed the charge of cavalry made by the enemy at the same time on their front and rear, has extorted the admiration of the enemy, and deserves the best thanks of their countrymen.

R. F. STOCKTON,
*Governor and Commander-in-chief
of the Territory of California.*

HEAD-QUARTERS, CIUDAD DE LOS ANGELES,
January 15, 1847.

SIR:—Referring to my letter of the 11th, I have the honour to inform you of the arrival of Lieutenant-Colonel Fremont at this place with four hundred men; that some of the insurgents have made their escape to Sonora, and that the rest have surrendered to our arms.

Immediately after the battles of the 8th and 9th, they began to disperse; and I am sorry to say that their leader, Jose M. Flores, made his escape, and that the others have been pardoned by a capitulation agreed upon by Lieutenant-Colonel Fremont.

Jose M. Flores, the commander of the insurgent forces, two or three days previous to the 8th sent two commissioners, with a flag of truce, to my camp to make "*a treaty of peace.*" I informed the commissioners that I could not recognise Jose M. Flores, who had broken his parole, as an honourable man, or as one having any rightful authority, or worthy to be treated with; that he was a rebel in arms, and, if I caught him, I would have him shot.

It seemed that, not being able to negotiate with me, and having lost the battles of the 8th and 9th, they met Colonel Fremont on the 12th instant on his way here, who, not knowing what had occurred, entered into the capitulation with them, which I now send to you; and, although I refused to do it myself, still I have thought it best to approve it. I am glad to say that, by the capitulation, we have recovered the gun taken by the insurgents at the sad defeat of General Kearney at San Pasqual.

The territory of California is again tranquil, and the civil government, formed by me, is again in operation in the places where it was interrupted by the insurgents.

Colonel Fremont has five hundred men in his battalion, which will be quite sufficient to preserve the peace of the territory; and I will immediately withdraw my sailors and marines, and sail as soon as possible for the coast of Mexico, where I hope they will give a good account of themselves.

Faithfully, your obedient servant,

R. F. STOCKTON, *Commodore, &c.*

To the Hon. GEORGE BANCROFT,
Secretary of the Navy, Washington, D. C.

UNITED STATES FRIGATE CONGRESS,
HARBOUR OF SAN DIEGO, January 22, 1847.

SIR:—I have the honour to inform you that the civil government of this territory is in successful operation, that Colonel Fremont is acting as governor and Colonel Russell as secretary, and that I am again on board of the Congress, preparing her for the coast of Mexico.

Lieutenant Gray, who is charged with my despatches, has been my aid-de-camp, and has done his duty with great good conduct and gallantry.

He is the officer whom I sent to relieve General Kearney from his perilous condition after his defeat at San Pasqual, and deserves the consideration of the department.

He will be able to give you the particulars of that unfortunate and disastrous affair.

Faithfully, your obedient servant,

R. F. STOCKTON, *Commodore, &c.*

To the Hon. GEORGE BANCROFT,
Secretary of the Navy, Washington, D. C.

UNITED STATES FRIGATE CONGRESS,
HARBOUR OF SAN DIEGO, February 4, 1847.

SIR:—As the guardian of the honour and services of the navy, I take leave to send to you the following narrative. This case requires no argument; nor will I make a single remark in relation to the extraordinary conduct of General Kearney or the indefensible language of his notes: "*demands,*" "*personal collision,*" "*civil war,*" *and the bold assertion that the country was not conquered until the 8th and 9th of January by the troops under his command,* speak for themselves.

I only desire at this time that you will call the attention of the President to it, and ask that General Kearney may be recalled from the territory, to prevent the evil consequences that may grow out of such a temper and such a head.

Last September I ordered an express mail to be sent in charge of Mr. Carson from the Ciudad de los Angeles to the city of Washington, to inform the President that the territory of California had been conquered and a civil government established therein. Mr. Carson was met on his way, and only within four days' travel of Santa Fe, by General Kearney, to whom he communicated the above intelligence, and that Colonel Fremont was to be governor. General Kearney sent back to Santa Fe a large part of the force under his command, but came himself to the territory with a detachment of dragoons; *he would not permit Mr. Carson to proceed with the express, but insisted that he should return with him to California.* On the 3d of December I received a letter from General Kearney by Mr. E. Stokes, which I now enclose, marked No. 1. I immediately despatched Captain Gillespie and Mr. Stokes, with about thirty-nine mounted riflemen, to the "*Head-quarters of the army of the West,*" with the letter marked No. 2. Mr. Stokes said that the General had informed him that he had about three hundred and fifty men with him.

On the night of the 6th Mr. Stokes returned to San Diego, and informed me that General Kearney had attempted to surprise the insurgents early that morning in their camp at San Pasqual; that a battle ensued, in which the General was worsted, but to what extent he could not accurately state, because he came off immediately after the firing ceased, without communicating with any one on the field of battle; that the General had lost many killed and wounded, and one of his guns had been taken; that the insurgents were commanded by Andres Pico, who had with him about one hundred men. The next day, Mr. Godey came in express from the General's camp, and confirmed the sad intelligence of his *defeat*, bringing the enclosed letter from Captain Turner of the dragoons, marked No. 3.

On Wednesday night, the 9th instant, Lieutenant Beale, of the navy, came in from the General's camp, and stated that the force under General Kearney's command had attempted to surprise the insurgents on the morning of the 6th at San Pasqual; that in the fight which ensued General Kearney had been *defeated*, with the loss of eighteen or nineteen killed, and thirteen or fourteen wounded; that General Kearney and his whole force were besieged on a small hill of rocks, and so surrounded by the enemy that it was impossible for them to escape unless immediate assistance was sent to them; that all their cattle had been taken away from them, and that they were obliged to eat their mules; that they were burning and destroying a quantity of valuable public property—tents, saddles and bridles, and camp equipage of every description, as well as private stores and clothing. Lieutenant Gray was leaving San Diego with two hundred and fifteen men, to go to the relief of General Kearney, at the moment of the arrival of Mr. Beale. He succeeded in bringing the General and his troops safely into San Diego. A few days after the General's arrival at San Diego, I offered to him the situation of commander-in-chief of the forces then preparing for a campaign, and offered to go with him as his "aid-de-camp." He declined this proposition, but said he would go as my "aid-de-camp." Soon after this he handed me his instructions from the War Department, which, having read, I returned to him with the enclosed note, marked No. 4. A short time after this, the General, in a conversation with me, intimated that, under his instructions from the War Department, he was entitled to be the governor of the territory. I replied that his instructions expressly said "*that should he conquer the country* he might establish a civil government therein;" that the country *had been conquered, and a civil government established, before he left Santa Fe,* of which he had been informed, as before stated, by Mr. Carson, when he was only four days' travel from Santa Fe. I also said that his instructions from the War Department, under these circumstances, should in my judgment be considered obsolete and nugatory; that, as the thing ordered to be done had been accomplished already, there remained nothing to be done; that the civil government formed by me was, at the time we were talking about it, in actual operation throughout the territory, with the exception of the Ciudad de los Angeles and Santa Barbara, where it had been temporarily interrupted by the insurgents; besides which, I had informed the government that I would appoint Colonel Fremont governor, and had pledged myself to Colonel Fremont to do so. That the thing was therefore *before the government, and their approval or disapproval was probably on its way to me;* and that if he had not interfered with my express, it probably would have returned from Washington by the middle of January. I supposed from this conversation, in connection with the offer of the General to accompany me as *aid-de-camp,* that he would not again aspire to the chief command of the territory until after the expected despatches had arrived from Washington.

The relations between General Kearney and myself remained in this condition until the morning of the 29th of December, when, after the troops had been paraded and were ready to proceed on the march to the Ciudad de los Angeles, General Kearney came to me and asked who was to command the troops. I said that, as commander-in-chief, I would command in person. "But," said he, "I mean who is to command the troops under you?" I said that I had appointed Lieutenant Rowan, the first lieutenant of the Cyane, to do so. The General observed that he thought he was entitled to that command. I replied, that Mr. Rowan had been appointed merely to relieve me from the details of the march and camp; and that if he (the General) was willing to perform that duty, I did not doubt that Lieutenant Rowan would yield to him, and I would give him the appointment with pleasure.

Lieutenant Rowan yielded, and I immediately summoned the officers around me, who were in readiness to march, and announced to them that General Kearney would take Mr. Rowan's situation, but that I would remain commander-in-chief.

With this arrangement we proceeded on our march, during which I ordered when the troops were to march, the road they were to march, and when they were to encamp, and did all other things belonging or appertaining to the duties as the commander of the forces and the governor of the territory, and no one paid more respect and deference to me as such than General Kearney; and it never was more conspicuous than in the battles of the 8th and 9th of January, as well as during our march into the city.

On the 16th of January I received the enclosed letter from General Kearney, marked No. 5, by the address of which you will perceive that I am still considered by him acting governor of the territory, at the very moment he arrogates to himself the supreme power of *demanding* of me to desist from the performance of my duties. I also send my reply, marked No. 6, and his rejoinder, marked No. 7, with a note subsequently received from him, marked No. 8.

> Faithfully, your obedient servant,
> R. F. STOCKTON, *Commodore, &c.*

To the Hon. GEORGE BANCROFT,
   Secretary of the Navy, Washington, D. C.

UNITED STATES FRIGATE CONGRESS,
HARBOUR OF SAN DIEGO, February 5, 1847.

SIR:—I had the honour to write to you on the 11th of January, by my aid-de-camp, Lieutenant Gray, informing you of the victories gained on the 8th and 9th of January over the insurgent army by the forces under my command; that the insurrection had been put down, and peace and tranquillity restored throughout the territory; that we had again taken possession of the Ciudad de los Angeles; that our flag was once more flying in all parts of California; and that the civil government formed by me last September was in successful operation.

I now proceed (as it is my duty to do) to give you a more detailed and circumstantial account of the battles of the 8th and 9th, as well as of the preparations which preceded them. We came to San Diego with the Congress alone, her resources having been almost exhausted in a previous campaign. The town was besieged by the insurgents, and there were no stores or provisions of any kind in it, and we were reduced to one-fourth allowance of bread. We had to build a fort to mount our artillery, to make our saddles and bridles and harness; we had, in truth, to make an army, with all its necessary appendages, out of the mechanics and sailors of this ship, and to take our horses and beef cattle from the enemy.

The industry, perseverance, and hard work, as well as enterprise and courage necessary for such operations, do not need my poor commendation.

We commenced our march on the 29th of December, with Captain Turner's company of 1st dragoons, dismounted, aided by Lieutenant Davidson; six pieces of artillery under Lieutenant R. L. Tilghman and Passed Midshipman William H. Thompson; Captain Gillespie's squadron of mounted riflemen, acting as the advance, the rear, and vanguards; the marines of the Congress and Portsmouth, under Captain J. Zeilin, adjutant of the battalion; the musketeers of the Congress, Savannah, Cyane, and Portsmouth, commanded by Lieutenant William B. Renshaw, Passed Midshipman John Guest, Acting Lieutenants B. F. B. Hunter and Edward Higgins, aided by Midshipmen George E. Morgan, J. Van Ness

Philip, Theodoric Lee, Albert Allmand, B. F. Wells, Edward C. Grafton, Robert C. Duvall, and Philip H. Haywood, and William Simmons, commodore's clerk; the carbineers of the Congress and Cyane, under the orders of Passed Midshipmen J. M. Duncan and J. Fenwick Stenson, and Sailmaker Reed, aided by Midshipmen Joseph Parish and Edmund Shepherd;—in all, a strength of about six hundred men. Brigadier-General Kearney commanding the division, and Lieutenant S. C. Rowan, from the ship Cyane, major of brigade; Captain W. H. Emory, of the topographical engineers, acting adjutant-general; Lieutenant George Minor, of the Savannah, quarter-master, in charge of the transportation, aided by Mr. Daniel Fisher. Mr. Speiden, the purser of the Congress, performed the duties of commissary, aided by Mr. John Bidwell. Mr. Southwick, carpenter of the Congress, acted as chief engineer at the head of the sappers and miners. Dr. John S. Griffin, of the army, Dr. Andrew A. Henderson, of the Portsmouth, and Dr. Charles Eversfield, of the Congress, attended the troops. Lieutenant A. F. V. Gray and Captain Miguel de Pedrovena, aids-de-camp to the commander-in-chief.

Our men were badly clothed, and their shoes generally made by themselves out of canvas. It was very cold, and the roads heavy. Our animals were all poor and weak, some of them giving out daily, which gave much hard work to the men in dragging the heavy carts, loaded with ammunition and provisions, through deep sands and up steep ascents, and the prospect before us was far from being that which we might have desired; but nothing could break down the fine spirits of those under my command, or cool their readiness and ardour to perform their duty; and they went through the whole march of one hundred and forty-five miles with alacrity and cheerfulness.

During the day of our march to the cayotes, we learned that some of the enemy were in our rear following us; and as we approached the cayotes several of them made their appearance in front of the house upon the hill, and waved their lances in angry defiance; but on the approach of the advance guard they rode off and left us to encamp on the hill near the house without molestation.

Being quite satisfied that we were in the neighbourhood of the enemy, during the night a confidential person was sent to ascertain, if possible, their position; he returned, and informed me that the enemy were in force between us and the Rio San Gabriel, and I was satisfied that the enemy intended at last to make a stand against us, and to fight us on the 8th day of January. The day suited me. Before moving that morning, the arms were fired and reloaded, and each officer and man was assigned his position for the fight, and was reminded that it was the 8th day of January and the anniversary of the battle of New Orleans.

We marched at nine o'clock. Immediately on reaching the plain we formed a square, our baggage-packs, spare oxen, and beef cattle in the centre. The advance guard under Captain Hensley, company C, first dragoons, under Captain Turner, and company D, musketeers of the Cyane, under Acting Lieutenant Higgins, occupied the centre, with two pieces of artillery on each flank, under Lieutenant Tilghman. The right flank composed of marines, company C, musketeers of the Portsmouth, Acting Lieutenant Hunter; company C, carbineers, Passed Midshipman Duncan; company A, carbineers of the Cyane, Acting Master Stenson; and company A, carbineers of the Congress, Sailmaker Peco; the whole under command of Captain Zeilin. The left flank composed of company B, musketeers of the Savannah, company A, musketeers of the Congress, under Acting Master Guest; the whole under the command of Lieutenant Renshaw. The rear composed of two pieces of artillery, under Acting Master William H. Thompson. The guard of the day, forty-nine strong, under Midshipman Haywood; one company mounted riflemen, under Lieutenant Renshaw; and Captain Santiago E. Arguello's company of Californians, under Lieutenant Luis Arguello; the whole under the command of Captain Gillespie. When within about two miles of the Rio San Gabriel, the enemy appeared in sight upon the hills on the opposite side; they were six hundred in number, in three divisions, their right about two miles down the river. As we approached, our column closed up and moved steadily on towards the ford, when, within a quarter of a mile of the river, a halt was ordered and dispositions made to meet the enemy.

A detachment of marines, under Lieutenant H. B. Watson, was sent to strengthen the left flank of the square. A party of the enemy, one hundred and fifty strong, had now crossed the river and made several ineffectual attempts to drive a band of wild mares upon the advance party. We now moved forward to the ford in broken files; Captain Hensley's command was ordered to dismount, and, acting as skirmishers, it deployed to the front and crossed the stream, (which is about fifty yards in width,) driving before them a party of the enemy which had attempted to annoy us. The enemy had now taken their position upon the heights, distant six hundred yards from the river and about fifty feet above its level; their centre or main body, about two hundred strong, was stationed immediately in front of the ford, upon which they opened a fire from two pieces of artillery, throwing round and grape shot without effect. Their right and left wings were separated from the main body about three hundred yards. Our column halted upon the edge of the stream; at this time the guns were unlimbered to return the enemy's fire, but were ordered again to be limbered and not a gun to be fired until the opposite bank of the river was gained. The two nine-pounders, dragged by officers as well as men and mules, soon reached the opposite bank, when they were immediately placed in battery. The column now followed in order under a most galling fire from the enemy, and became warmly engaged on the opposite bank, their round shot and grape falling thickly among us as we approached the stream, without doing any injury, our men marching steadily forward. The dragoons and Cyane's musketeers, occupying the centre, soon crossed and formed upon a bank about four feet above the stream. The left, advancing at the same time, soon occupied its position across the river.

The rear was longer in getting across the water; the sand being deep, its passage was delayed by the baggage carts; however, in a few moments the passage of the whole force was effected with only one man killed and one wounded, notwithstanding the enemy kept up an incessant fire from the heights.

On taking a position upon the low bank, the right flank, under Captain Zeilin, was ordered to deploy to the right; two guns from the rear were immediately brought to the right; the four-pounder, under Acting Master Thompson, supported by the riflemen under Lieutenant Renshaw. The left flank deployed into line in open order. During this time our artillery began to tell upon the enemy, who continued their fire without interruption. The nine-pounders, standing in plain view upon the bank, were discharged with such precision that it soon became too warm for the enemy to remain upon the brow of their heights; eventually a shot told upon their nine-pounder, knocked the gun from its trail, astounding the enemy so much that they left it for four or five minutes. Some twenty of them now advanced, and, hastily fastening ropes to it, dragged the gun to the rear. Captain Hensley's skirmishers now advanced and took the hill upon the right, the left wing of the enemy retreating before them. The six-pounder from the rear had now come up; Captain Hensley was ordered to support it, and returned from the hill. This movement being observed, the enemy's left made an attempt to charge the two guns; but the right flank of the marines, under Captain Zeilin, being quickly thrown back, showed too steady a front for the courage of the Californians to engage, who wheeled to the left and dashed to the rear across the river. At this time the enemy were observed collecting on our left and making preparations to charge our left flank. General Kearney was now ordered to form a square with the troops on the right flank, upon which the left flank, in case of being worsted, might rally. The right wing of the enemy now made an unsuccessful attempt to charge our left, but, finding so warm a reception from the musketeers of the Savannah and Congress, under Lieutenant Renshaw and Acting Master Guest, as also the small party of marines under Lieutenant H. B. Watson, they changed their purpose and retired, when a discharge of artillery told upon their ranks. The guard of the day, under Midshipman Haywood, protected the animals in the rear, awaiting with patience for the enemy to give them an opportunity to open a fire.

The dispositions for charging the heights were now made. The troops having been brought into line, the command forward being given, on they went, (the artillery in battery,) charging the heights, which the enemy's centre contested for a few moments, then broke in retreat, their right wing charging upon the rear, under Captain Gillespie, encumbered with packs, baggage, horses, and cattle; but, receiving a well-directed fire from the guard, which hurled some of them from their saddles, they fled at full speed across the river we had just left. The other portion of their forces retreated behind their artillery, which had taken position in a ravine, and again opened its fire upon our centre; our artillery was immediately thrown forward, the troops being ordered to lie down to avoid the enemy's cannon-balls, which passed directly over their heads.

The fire from our artillery was incessant, and so accurate that the enemy were from time to time driven from their guns, until they finally retreated.

We were now in possession of the heights where, a short time before, the insurgents had so vauntingly taken strong position; and the band, playing " Hail Columbia!" and " Yankee Doodle," announced another glorious victory on the 8th day of January.

Our loss in this action was ascertained to be two killed and nine wounded. The enemy's loss we could not ascertain with any certainty, as they carried away both killed and wounded upon their horses.

We moved down the heights until they brought us near the river, where we encamped, having our cattle, horses, and mules under the bank, safely protected. Tattoo was beat at an early hour, and the camp retired to rest. At about twelve o'clock, the picquets having been fired upon, the camp was soon under arms in the most perfect order. Finding the enemy made no further demonstration, after remaining under arms a short time, we again sought our blankets, and nothing disturbed our repose until the sounding of the reveillé on the 9th told us to be stirring.

At daylight, Captain Zeilin was despatched with a party of thirty marines to a rancho about three-quarters of a mile from camp, to ascertain if there were any persons concealed about it, or whether there was any barley or provisions to be found there; finding none, he returned with his party about sunrise, without meeting any of the enemy.

At nine o'clock our column commenced its march, taking a direct course over the plain of the Mesa, towards Ciudad de los Angeles. We had advanced some six miles when the enemy appeared in front, deployed in open order, their line extending nearly across our road. Approaching a ravine to the left of their line in front, the enemy opened a fire from their artillery, masked upon the edge of the bank, but with no other effect than killing an ox and mule in the centre of the square. Our artillery soon returned the fire while still continuing the march; the enemy now brought up two other pieces of artillery; our column halted; our artillery on the two flanks in front was now placed in battery. The six-pounder under Acting Master Thompson, upon our right flank in front, now opened its fire upon the enemy's nine-pounder, the shot telling upon it and cutting away the fixtures about the gun at every fire. The enemy in front and upon the right was now distant about six hundred yards; the nine-pounders, one of them in charge of Mr. Southwick, soon made it so warm for their artillery in front that the enemy bore it off to their rear.

A reinforcement now joined them, and, soon after, down they came upon us, charging upon the left flank, front and rear. A shower of lead from the musketry under Renshaw and Guest, and Passed Midshipman Duncan's carbineers, (who had to-day taken post on the left flank,) being well delivered, at a distance of eighty yards, did so much havoc that their courage failed, and caused them to draw off more to the rear, which had until this moment stood firm without firing a shot. The four-pounder now poured forth a charge of grape upon a party of the enemy about thirty yards distant, hurling four from their saddles, and they again retired.

The Californians now retreated, and we pursued our march along the Mesa and crossed the Rio San Fernando about three miles below the town, where we encamped for the night.

During the day we lost but one killed and five wounded, notwithstanding the shot from the enemy, both round and grape, and from the carbines of the horsemen, fell thick among our men, who undauntedly pursued their march forward. On the 10th our tents were struck at an early hour; but, the morning being cold and the town being distant but three miles, our march was delayed until about ten o'clock.

We entered the City of the Angels, our band playing as we marched up the principal street to the square, our progress being slightly molested by a few drunken fellows who remained about the town. The riflemen, having been sent to the heights commanding the town, were soon followed by Lieutenant Tilghman, with two pieces of artillery, supported by the marines under Captain Zeilin, the enemy, in small force, retiring out of sight upon their approach.

Captain Gillespie, having received the order, now hoisted the same flag upon the government-house of the country which he hauled down when he retreated from the city in September last.

Enclosed I send the report of our killed and wounded. Our loss was three killed and fourteen wounded; that of the enemy between seventy and eighty, besides many horses.

My narrative is done. Our friends and the territory have been rescued. I will only add that we had, of course, to simplify military tactics for our own use. We had, therefore, but five orders,—viz.: form line, form square, fire, repel charge, charge. The celerity and accuracy with which they could perform these evolutions were remarkable, and bade defiance even to the rapid movements of Californian cavalry.

I have thus truly exhibited to you, sir, sailors, (who were principally armed with boarding-pikes, carbines, and pistols, having no more than about two hundred bayonets in the whole division,) victorious over an equal number of the best horsemen in the world, well mounted and well armed with carbines and pistols and lances. I have nothing to bestow on these gallant officers and men for their heroism except my poor commendation, which I most sincerely give to them, individually and collectively. I must, therefore, recommend them to you for the greatest reward a patriot may claim,—the approbation of their country.

Faithfully, your obedient servant,

R. F. STOCKTON,
Commander-in-Chief.

To the Hon. GEORGE BANCROFT,
  Secretary of the Navy, Washington, D. C.

CIUDAD DE LOS ANGELES, January 11, 1847.

SIR:—I have the honour to furnish a statement of the killed and wounded in the actions of the 8th and 9th instants, and also a report from the senior surgeon present John S. Griffin, viz.:—

January 8.

Killed—Artillery, 1 private, (U. S. seaman.)

Wounded—Artillery, 1 private, (volunteer from the California battalion;) foot, 7 privates, (United States seamen;) marines, 1 private.

Total—1 killed, 9 wounded.

January 9.

Wounded—1st dragoons, 1 private; foot, 1 officer, (Lieutenant Rowan, United States navy,) 2 privates, (United States seamen;) California battalion, 1 officer, (Captain Gillespie.)

I am, sir, very respectfully, your obedient servant,

W. H. EMORY.
Lieut. Topographical Engineers
and Acting Adjutant-General.

His Excellency R. F. STOCKTON,
  Governor of California, &c.

CIUDAD DE LOS ANGELES, CALIFORNIA, January 11, 1847.

STATEMENT.

Killed and wounded in the action of the 8th January, 1847.

Killed—Frederick Strauss, seaman, United States ship Portsmouth, artillery corps, cannon-shot in neck.

Wounded—1st, Jacob Hait, volunteer, artillery-driver, wound in left breast—died on evening of the 9th; 2d, Thomas Smith, ordinary seaman, ship Cyane, company D, musketeers, shot by accident through the right thigh—died on night of the 8th; 3d, William Coxe, seaman, United States ship Savannah, company B, musketeers, wound in right thigh and right arm, severe; 4th, George Bantam, ordinary seaman, United States ship Cyane, pikeman, punctured wound of hand, accidental—slight; 5th, Patrick Cambell, seaman, United States ship Cyane, company D, musketeers, wound in thigh by spent ball—slight; 6th, William Scott, private, United States marine corps, United States ship Portsmouth, wound in chest, spent ball—slight; 7th, James Hendy, United States ship Congress, company A, musketeers, wound over stomach, spent ball—slight; 8th, Joseph Wilson, seaman, United States ship Congress, company A, musketeers, wound in right thigh, spent ball—slight; 9th, Ivory Coffin, seaman, United States ship Savannah, company B, musketeers, contusion of right knee, spent ball—slight.

Wounded on the 9th.

1st, Mark A. Child, private, company C, 1st regiment of dragoons, gunshot wound in right heel, penetrating upwards into the ankle-joint—severe; 2d, James Cambell, ordinary seaman, United States ship Congress, company D, carbineers, wound in right foot, second toe amputated, accidental discharge of his own carbine—severe; 3d, George Crawford, boatswain's mate, United States ship Cyane, company D, musketeers, wound in left thigh—severe.

Lieutenant Rowan, United States navy, and Captain Gillespie, California battalion, slightly contused by spent balls.

I am, sir, most respectfully, your obedient servant,

JOHN S. GRIFFIN,
Assistant Surgeon, United States Army.

To CAPTAIN WM. H. EMORY,
Assistant Adjutant-General, United States forces.

From Executive Document No. 1, accompanying the President's message at the 2nd Session of the Thirtieth Congress, December, 1848.

REPORT OF COMMODORE STOCKTON OF HIS OPERATIONS ON THE COAST OF THE PACIFIC.

WASHINGTON, D. C., February 18, 1848.

SIR:—On my return from California in November last, the circumstances of the times seemed to present reasons for delaying a full report of my transactions and operations on the coast of the Pacific.

The authority under which I had acted was questioned or denied; the validity of much that had been done was doubted, and investigations were on foot in which the propriety of my proceedings might be brought to the especial notice of the Executive.

After a full consideration of the circumstances, to which it is unnecessary here further to allude, it appeared to me decorous and respectful to withhold, for a brief period, my own views of the questions in which I was to some extent implicated, and to leave the Executive to learn the details of those transactions from other quarters. The period, however, has now arrived in which I feel that

I can, without the imputation of improper feelings or motives, lay before the Executive, in a tangible and official form, a narrative of the occurrences which I directed in California; explain the circumstances which induced the course which I pursued, the motives by which I was guided, the objects which I designed to accomplish, and thus to put the President in possession of ample means to form a judgment upon my conduct. It appears now to be no longer questioned that I actually possessed and exercised the powers of governor of California and commander-in-chief of the forces of the United States in that quarter, and that, whether rightfully or wrongfully, I executed the duties and administered the functions appertaining to these high offices, for the administration of which I am alone responsible. The despatches which were from time to time addressed to the Department were designed to furnish the government with accurate information of what transpired; but, under the circumstances in which they were prepared, it did not enter into my purpose to give a general narrative of the entire operations. Opening a full view of the circumstances which influenced my judgment in selecting the course which was adopted, and the policy by which that course was determined, with your permission I beg leave, at this time, to perform this duty; the obligations to do which, at this juncture, seem to me more imperative, since it appears that in an official communication addressed to the Department by my successor in command, I am in the most explicit terms censured for premature as well as injudicious action. With what of propriety or of professional courtesy this condemnation has been passed by an officer of equal rank with myself, without any report or communication to him of what had occurred, or the reasons by which I was governed, is not so apparent. Under the instructions from the Department, I arrived, in command of the United States frigate Congress, at the harbour of Monterey, about the middle of July, 1846. The American flag was there flying. I immediately went on board the United States frigate Savannah, then lying off that town, and, in conformity with my orders, I reported myself to Commodore Sloat as forming part of the squadron then under his command. From him I learned that in the preceding month of June, while lying off Mazatlan, he had received intelligence that war had commenced between the United States and Mexico; that he had forthwith proceeded to Monterey, landed a force, and hoisted the flag of the United States without resistance. In the course of our interview, Commodore Sloat apprised me of his intention to return in a short time to the United States, whereby the command of the squadron would devolve upon me. In this position it became my duty to examine into the state of affairs, and, in view of the responsibility which was about to rest upon me, to obtain all the information which would enable me to exercise a proper judgment as to the ulterior measures to be pursued. The result of my inquiries and investigations showed me that the position I was about to occupy was an important and critical one. The intelligence of the commencement of hostilities between the two nations, although it had passed through Mexico, had reached Commodore Sloat in advance of the Mexican authorities. When he made his first hostile demonstrations, therefore, the enemy, ignorant of the existence of the war, had regarded his acts as an unwarrantable exercise of power by the United States, and the most lively indignation and bitter resentment pervaded the country.

The public functionaries of the territory were not slow in availing themselves of this feeling, and endeavoured to stimulate it to the highest possible degree. A proclamation was put forth, denouncing in the most unmeasured terms all foreigners; but it was unquestionably aimed principally at the citizens of the United States, and such others as sympathized with them. Two or three were, in fact, murdered, and all were led to apprehend extermination from the sanguinary feeling of resentment which was everywhere breathed.

The local legislature was in session. Governor Pio Pico had assembled a force of about seven hundred or one thousand men, supplied with seven pieces of artillery, breathing vengeance against the perpetrators of the insult and injury which they supposed to have been inflicted. These hostile demonstrations were daily increasing, and, by the time that the command devolved on me by the departure of Commodore Sloat, the situation of things had assumed a critical and alarming appearance. Every citizen and friend of the United States throughout the territory was in imminent jeopardy; he could count upon no security for either property or life. It was well known that numerous emigrants from the United States were on their way to Upper California. These, marching in small and detached parties, encumbered with their wives and children and baggage, uninformed of the war and consequently unprepared for attack, would have been exposed to certain destruction.

It was also ascertained that, in the anticipation of the eventful conquest of the country by the United States, many of those in the actual possession of authority were preparing for this change by disposing of the public property, so that it might be found in private hands when the Americans should acquire possession, believing that private rights would be protected and individual property secure. Negotiations were in actual progress thus to acquire three thousand leagues of land, and to dispose of all the most valuable portions of the territory appertaining to the missions at nominal prices, so that the conquerors should find the entire country appropriated to individuals, and in hands which could effectually prevent sales to American citizens, and thus check the tide of emigration, while little or no benefit would result to the nation from the acquisition of this valuable territory.

All these considerations, together with others of inferior moment, seemed to make prompt and decisive action an imperative duty. To retain possession merely of a few seaports, while cut off from all intercourse with the interior, exposed to constant attack by the concentrated forces of an exasperated enemy, appeared wholly useless. Yet to abandon ground which we had occupied, to withdraw our forces from these points, to yield places where our flag had been floating in triumph, was an alternative not to be thought of, except as a last resource. Not only would all the advantages which had been obtained be thus abandoned, and perhaps never be regained without great expenditure of blood and treasure, but the pride and confidence of the enemy would be increased to a dangerous extent by such indications of our weakness and inability to maintain what we had won.

Previous to the departure of Commodore Sloat, he had, at my instance, and upon my representations, placed at my disposal the United States sloop-of-war Cyane, as well as the forces on shore. I immediately apprised Captain Fremont, then of the topographical corps, with whom I had previous communications, of the position in which I was placed, and that I had determined upon my plan of operations.

Captain Fremont and Lieutenant Gillespie, of the marine corps, had already raised a body of 160 volunteers, prepared to act according to circumstances. I informed those gentlemen that if they, together with the men whom they had raised, would volunteer to serve under my command so long as I should remain in California and require their services, that I would form them into a battalion, appointing the former major and the latter captain. These arrangements were all completed in the course of the 23d of July, and my letters of that date to Commodore Sloat, to Commander Du Pont, and Captain Fremont, on file in the Department, will have apprised you of my movements.

It was thus that the battalion of California volunteers was organized, which subsequently, under its gallant officers, took so patriotic and efficient a part in the military operations in that territory. It was received into the service of the United States to aid the navy, as essential as well to the maintenance of the position we then occupied as to execute the plans which I had contemplated in the interior.

A few days subsequently, Commodore Sloat sailed in the Levant, thus devolving upon me the command of the entire force, both afloat and on shore. That force then consisted of the frigates Congress and Savannah, sloops-of-war Portsmouth, Cyane, and Warren, and the store-ship Erie. The Portsmouth was at San Francisco, the Congress and Savannah at Monterey, the Cyane had been sent with the California battalion to San Diego, the Warren was at Mazatlan, and the Erie at the Sandwich Islands. The force to be employed on land consisted of 360 men, furnished from the Congress, provided with about 90 muskets and bayonets, some small cannon procured from the merchant-vessels, and the battalion of volunteers, all indifferently provided with the appendages of an army.

Leaving the Savannah at Monterey, for its protection, I sailed about the first of August, in the Congress, for San Pedro. This town is situated about 28 miles from Ciudad de los Angeles, in the vicinity of which the enemy was stated to be. On the way to San Pedro, we landed at Santa Barbara, of which we took possession, and, leaving a small force for its defence, proceeded to San Pedro, where we arrived on the 6th of August. Here information was received of the arrival of the Cyane at San Diego, of the landing of the battalion, and that Major Fremont had experienced great difficulty in procuring the necessary supply of horses. We immediately commenced the landing of our forces from the frigate. On the following day two persons arrived representing themselves to be commissioners sent from General Castro, authorized to enter into negotiations with me, and bearing a letter from the General, which is already in possession of the Department. Before, however, they would communicate the extent of their power or the nature of their instructions, they made a preliminary demand that the further march of the troops must be arrested, and that I must not advance beyond the position which I then occupied. This proposition was peremptorily declined. I announced my determination to advance; and the commissioners returned to their camp without imparting further the objects of the proposed negotiations. Independently of the character of the preliminary conditions insisted upon by these commissioners, various considerations induced me to be averse to any negotiations in the existing state of affairs, and to press forward for the purpose of dispersing the forces which had been collected to oppose my progress. Some of these considerations I feel it my duty to submit to your notice, that my objects and designs may be properly appreciated by the government. From the brief period which had intervened since the commencement of hostilities, it was obvious that the central government in Mexico could not have been apprised of the existing state of affairs; and, therefore, could not have communicated to this remote quarter orders and instructions accommodated to these circumstances. The local functionaries, therefore, who proposed to negotiate with me, must have acted upon their own authority, and their proceedings with a foreign power must depend for their validity upon the subsequent ratification and approval by the general government. Such ratification, it was confidently believed, would be given or withheld, according as the exigencies of the times made advisable. Any arrangements, therefore, by which the further progress of the American arms would be stayed, would have left all the advantages to the one party. It was further manifest that the single act of entering into negotiations with this local authority would have been a recognition of its power to act definitively upon other subjects. If it could treat with us, a foreign foe, it would be impossible to deny its authority in matters more obviously within its sphere of action. The transfer of the public domain and property could scarcely have been questioned by us; and, as was well understood, arrangements were in progress to transfer all of it that was valuable to private hands, bitterly inimical to the United States and its interests. To prevent the accomplishment of this design was one of the chief objects which had been contemplated from the organization and march of the forces under my command; to enter into negotiations without the entire dispersement of the local government, and of the troops which it had assembled for its defence, would have been absolutely to relinquish this highly important design. In addition to this, preservation of American interests, and of the lives and property of our citizens already in California and on their way to this territory, imperatively demanded that the troops which had been assembled under General Castro should be defeated or dispersed. The condition insisted upon as a preliminary clearly indicated that no arrangement would be acceded to which did not leave the Mexicans in the full possession of power throughout the province; and, if left in this possession, relieved from all apprehensions of molestation on our side, they would have been enabled to direct all their energies and force to the accomplishment of other objects.

The extermination of the Americans, which had been threatened in the proclamation already referred to, was too much in accordance with the feelings which pervaded the country and with the policy which governed its rulers not to have been the immediate and certain result of any opening of negotiations begun under such inauspicious signs as were insisted upon as preliminary conditions. Every evil consequence which I had apprehended would result from leaving things as they were found on my arrival in California was still to be feared; and even the movements which had already been made, unless pressed to a successful close, would have tended only to aggravate and precipitate them. There was, further, every reason to believe that the principal, if not the only, object which the Mexicans were sincerely desirous to obtain, was to gain time; and this would have been accomplished with entire certainty by the mere commencement of negotiations and the arrest of our advance, without reference to its final termination.

Our march would necessarily have been suspended at the outset; the sailors and marines must have re-embarked; the California battalion, so prompt and energetic in volunteering to aid us, must have been abandoned to its own resources, and, thus insulated and unsupported, must either have dispersed or fallen a sacrifice to an exasperated and powerful enemy. In the meanwhile, the Mexican General, relieved from all danger of disturbance from us, might, and certainly would, have increased his numerical force, augmented still more its efficiency, until he had acquired the capacity of expelling us from the places which had submitted to our arms.

The foregoing were among the prominent reasons which determined me to reject the Mexican proffers of negotiation, and I trust they are such as recommend my proceedings to the favourable consideration and approval of the President.

The commissioners were dismissed to their own camp, with an intimation that I should immediately follow them, and that the result of a battle would speedily determine whether General Castro and Governor Pio Pico, or myself, were to exercise authority over the inhabitants and territory of California.

Two or three days afterwards, other persons arrived from the camp of General Castro, with a communication from that functionary, stating his determination to defend the country to the last extremity, and indulging in the most extravagant language.

Having completed all the arrangements which time and circumstances permitted, and despatched a courier to Major Fremont, apprising him of my movements, we commenced our march towards the camp of the enemy on the 11th of August. In the course of the afternoon of that day information reached us that the enemy's force, instead of awaiting our approach, had dispersed; that they had buried their guns, and that the governor and general had retreated, as was supposed, towards Sonora. We continued our march towards Ciudad de los Angeles, and on the 13th, having been joined by Major Fremont with about 120 volunteers under his command, we marched into the city, which we quietly occupied.

After the dispersement of the army of the enemy, the flight of the general and governor-in-chief out of the territory, a number of the officers of the Mexican army were captured and made prisoners of war. Among these were Jose Maria Flores, whose name will hereafter appear prominently, and Don Andres Pico, brother of Governor Pio Pico. These officers were released upon their parole of honour not to bear arms against the United States pending the war, unless exchanged; with what of fidelity they performed this obligation will appear in the sequel. The people in general came in, tendered their submission to our authority, and promised allegiance to our government. Every indication of a hostile force had now disappeared from the country, tranquillity was restored, and I forthwith determined to organize a temporary civil government to conduct public affairs and to administer justice as in time of peace. Various considerations prompted to this course. It appeared to me that the existence of such a government, under the authority of the United States, would leave no pretence upon which it might be urged that the conquest of the country had not been accomplished. While merely the military power exercised power, enforcing its authority by martial law and executing its functions through the instrumentality of a regular military force, nothing could be regarded as settled, and opposition to its power would be considered as a lawful opposition to a foreign enemy. When, however, the whole frame of civil administration should be organized,— courts and judges performing their accustomed functions—public taxes and imposts regularly collected and appropriated to the ordinary objects and purposes of government,—any opposition might be justly deemed a civil offence, and the appropriate punishment inflicted in the ordinary course of administering justice.

Indeed, the law military appeared to me wholly inadequate to the emergency. It could not reach many of the objects over which a salutary control ought to be exercised. It could not effectively administer the property or sufficiently guard private rights. A civil government which should, through its various functionaries, pervade the entire country, exercise a superintendence over all the inhabitants, discover, restrain, and punish all acts of insubordination, detect and check all attempts at a hostile organization, recognise and sanction the possession, use, and transfer of property, inflict upon criminals the appropriate punishment, and remedy injuries inflicted upon individuals, seemed not only an important instrument in the accomplishment of the objects which I had in view, but essential to the attainment of the ends of the government. It appeared to me desirable that the actual possession and exercise of power should be transferred, with the least possible delay, from the military to civil functionaries.

Under our institutions the military is regarded as inferior to the civil authority, and the appropriate duty of the former is to act as auxiliary to the latter. Such being the general character of our institutions, it seemed in the first degree desirable that the inhabitants of the country should, as soon as practicable, become familiar with them, that they might perceive and appreciate their importance and their value, their capacity to maintain right and redress wrong, and, in the protection afforded to persons and property, to recognise a guarantee of all their individual rights. The marked contrast which would thus be afforded to their former institutions and rulers would reconcile the Mexican portion of the population to the change; while the American inhabitants would gratefully witness an administration of law and justice analogous to that to which they had been accustomed at home. Actuated by such considerations, I gave my immediate attention to the establishment, upon a permanent basis, of a civil government throughout the country, as much in conformity with the former usages of the country as could be done in the absence of any written code. A tariff of duties was fixed, and collectors appointed. Elections were directed to be held for the various civil magistrates; Major Fremont was appointed military commandant of the territory, and Captain Gillespie military commandant of the southern department. The battalion of volunteers was ordered to be augmented to three hundred; and, contemplating soon to leave the territory, I determined on my departure to appoint Major Fremont Governor of California. He was apprised of these intended arrangements, and instructed to meet me at San Francisco on the 25th of October, for the purpose of consummating them. These acts and intentions were officially communicated to the Department in my several despatches.

This exposition of my operations and acts will, I trust, prove satisfactory to the executive, and be a sufficient reply to Commodore Shubrick's charge of premature action. In a state of actual war against a foreign enemy, I found myself at the head of a force and in command of means competent to take and hold possession of an important part of the hostile territory. I found that before the command had devolved upon me the flag of my country had been raised in some parts of California. Important interests were involved; to stop short would have led to their absolute sacrifice, accompanied by great individual loss and suffering. No middle course was open to my choice. The alternative was the subjection of the entire province to our authority, or its total abandonment. In such a position I could not hesitate as to the line of duty. Empowered to conduct the war against Mexico according to the exigency of circumstances and my own judgment, I determined to support the honour of my flag and to promote what I regarded as the best interest of the nation. Having achieved the conquest of the country, and finding my military strength ample to retain it, the establishment of a civil government naturally and necessarily resulted. The omission to do this would have marred the entire plan and stamped a character of imbecility and instability upon the whole operation. My views of the interests of my country were decisive; as to the expediency of my measures, the estimate I entertained of my authority impressed upon them the sanction of duty. The arrangements having been thus completed, I determined to leave California under the administration of the civil authority, and with the squadron under my command, aided by a volunteer corps raised for the purpose, to sail for the southern part of Mexico, capture Acapulco, and, having secured proper positions on the coast, to march into the interior, advance towards the city of Mexico, and thus to co-operate with the anticipated movements of General Taylor, or produce a powerful diversion which would materially aid him in his operations. My despatches have already put the department in possession of these plans.

About the 2d of September I left Ciudad de los Angeles, embarked on board the Congress on the 3d, and on the 5th sailed for Santa Barbara. Having taken on board the small detachment which had been landed at this place, we proceeded to Monterey, where every thing was found tranquil. The people appeared to be quite satisfied with the state of affairs. Information was here received leading to the apprehension that Suter's settlement on the Sacramento was threatened with an attack by a body of one thousand Walla-Walla Indians. The Savannah was immediately ordered to San Francisco; Lieutenant Maddox, of the marine corps, appointed military commandant of the middle department, and, other necessary arrangements having been made, I proceeded in the Congress to San Francisco, which place I reached in a few days. It soon appeared that the reports in regard to the Walla-Walla Indians had been greatly exaggerated. They were not so numerous as had been represented, nor had they any hostile intentions. The inhabitants of San Francisco, on my arrival, received me *en masse*, with every demonstration of joy on the conquest of the country, and with every manifestation of personal respect as the governor of the territory and commander-in-chief of the United States forces.

About the 30th of September, a courier arrived from Captain Gillespie, despatched by that officer to convey to me the information that an insurrection had broken out at Ciudad de los Angeles, and that he was besieged in the government-house at that place by a large force. I immediately ordered Captain Mervine to proceed in the Savannah to San Pedro, for the purpose of affording aid to Captain Gillespie. Major Fremont was at Sacramento when the news of the insurrection reached him, and, having formed the determination to march against the insurgents with the force he could muster, amounting to about one hundred and twenty men, was preparing to move. I sent a request to him forthwith to join me at San Francisco with his command, and to bring with him as many saddles as he could procure. While awaiting the arrival of Major Fremont I detached officers in various directions for the purpose of procuring volunteers to join the battalion, and engaged the merchant-ship Sterling to take them down to Santa Barbara.

About the 12th of October, Major Fremont arrived at San Francisco, and immediately embarked on board the Sterling, with about one hundred and sixty volunteers. He was directed to proceed to Santa Barbara, there to procure horses to march to Ciudad de los Angeles, while I, with the Congress, was to sail to San Pedro, and by that route advance towards the same point. The insurgents were represented to be encamped in the neighbourhood of that city. The Congress and Sterling sailed in company from San Francisco, but separated the same evening in a fog. Between San Francisco and Monterey we spoke a merchant-vessel from the latter port, with despatches from Lieutenant Maddox, apprising me that Monterey was threatened with an attack, and that he was in want of immediate assistance. We ran into the Bay of Monterey, landed two officers with fifty men and some ordnance. Having thus strengthened that post, I proceeded to San Pedro. On my arrival at that place, about the 23d of October, I found the Savannah frigate. Captain Mervine informed me that Captain Gillespie, with the volunteers under his command, was on board his vessel, having left Ciudad de los Angeles under a capitulation entered into with General Flores, the leader of the insurrection,—one of the Mexican officers who, having been made prisoner of war, had been released on his parole.

Captain Mervine further informed me that, about two weeks before, he had landed with his sailors and marines for the purpose of marching in conjunction with Captain Gillespie and his detachment of volunteers to Ciudad de los Angeles. He had not carried any artillery with him; that about twelve miles from San Pedro he encountered a party of the insurgents with one piece of artillery; a battle ensued; that several charges had been made upon the insurgents' gun, but it was impossible to capture it, as, whenever he approached, they hitched their horses to it and retreated. Having sustained a loss of several men killed and wounded, he retired with his force and re-embarked.

Proper arrangements having been made during the night, in the morning we landed a strong force with several pieces of artillery, once more hoisted the flag of the United States at San Pedro, and formed our camp there. The insurgent force in the vicinity was supposed to number about eight hundred men. Our authority was necessarily limited to the portion of territory in our actual possession or within the range of our guns. The insurgents, in the undisturbed occupancy of the interior, and watchful of our every movement, could, at their pleasure, threaten us with an attack by night or day, and had the precaution to remove beyond our reach every horse and all the cattle which might have been available either for food or transportation.

The roadstead at San Pedro was also a dangerous position for men-of-war, being exposed to the storms which at that season of the year rage with great violence upon the coast.

This consideration decided me to proceed to San Diego, which, although the entrance was obstructed by a bar which had never been passed by a vessel of equal draught of water with the Congress, might, I hoped, be crossed; and, if the passage should prove practicable, would be found a convenient and safe harbour. We did not, however, leave San Pedro until I had been compelled to relinquish all expectation of the co-operation of Major Fremont, from whom I had not heard a word since we parted off San Francisco, nor until the officers and men had become completely exhausted by their incessant duties on shore, in guarding the camp from attack and pursuing small parties of the insurgents who approached us. Having embarked the men belonging to the squadron, and volunteers under Captain Gillespie, I sailed for San Diego in the Congress.

On my arrival off the harbour of San Diego, I received information from Lieutenant Minor that the town was besieged by the insurgents, that his stock of provisions was small, and that he was in want of an additional force. He gave it as his opinion that the Congress might be got over the bar. In attempting this, however, the ship struck, and her position was so dangerous that we were compelled to return to the anchorage outside.

On the following day the Malek Adhel, a prize to the United States ship Warren, arrived from Monterey with despatches from Lieutenant-Colonel Fremont. I thus received information from that officer that on his way to Santa Barbara he met the merchant-ship Vandalia, from San Pedro, by whom he was informed of the state of affairs at the South; that it would be impossible for him to procure horses at Santa Barbara, in consequence of which he had proceeded to Monterey, and would employ all diligence in preparing his force to march for Ciudad de los Angeles.

Lieutenant Minor was directed to send the ship Stonington, then lying in the harbour of San Diego, with as many volunteers as could be spared, to Ensanada, about ninety miles below San Diego, for the purpose of procuring animals, which he was instructed to have driven into San Diego. Without a supply of horses and beeves, it was not prudent to commence our march. Captain Mervine was despatched in the Savannah to Monterey, to aid Lieutenant-Colonel

Fremont in his preparations to march, and, having myself gone to San Pedro, returned with all convenient speed to San Diego.

About thirty or forty miles from that place our progress was arrested by a calm. My anxiety on account of Lieutenant-Colonel Fremont, and my desire to go to his assistance was so great, that a boat was immediately despatched with Lieutenant Tilghman, the bearer of a communication addressed to Lieutenant George Minor, in command at San Diego, apprising that officer that on my arrival I would be ready to take the field in person, and, with an additional force of two hundred and fifty men from the ship, to take up the line of march for Ciudad de los Angeles. Lieutenant Minor was directed to arrange with Lieutenant Tilghman, the commanding officer of the artillery, and Mr. Southwick, commanding officer of the engineers, to have the horses necessary for the transportation of the guns and ammunition.

Notwithstanding my first unsuccessful attempt to get into the harbour of San Diego, it was an object of too great importance to be abandoned, unless from the absolute impossibility of effecting it. The bar and channel were again, on my return, examined and buoyed, and a second attempt made. After crossing the bar, the ship grounded, and in such a situation that it became expedient to prepare her spars to shore her up, to prevent her from tumbling over. While thus occupied, the insurgents commenced an attack upon the town, and, notwithstanding the perilous condition of the frigate and the necessity of employing the crew in extricating her from her position, a portion of them was simultaneously engaged in landing from the ship, in boats, to take part in the fight. In executing my orders in reference to those two distinct objects at the same time, the conduct of the officers and men under my command was such as to command my warmest commendation. Every thing was performed with the regularity and order of the ordinary duties of the vessel. Having accomplished a landing of the men from the ship, the attack of the insurgents was successfully repelled by the combined force under the command of Lieutenant Minor and Captain Gillespie.

The situation of the place was found to be most miserable and deplorable. The male inhabitants had abandoned the town, leaving their women and children dependent upon us for protection and food. No horses could be obtained to assist in the transportation of the guns and ammunition, and not a beeve could be had to supply the necessary food; some supplies of provisions were furnished from the ship. The expedition to the southward for animals, under the command of Captain Gibson, of the battalion, had succeeded in driving about ninety horses and two hundred head of beef-cattle into the garrison.

The horses were, however, much worn down, and it was supposed a fortnight's rest would be required before they would be fit for service. During the time required for resting the horses, we were actively employed in the construction of a fort, for the more complete protection of the town, mounting guns, and in making the necessary harness, saddles, and bridles. While the work of preparation necessary for our march to meet Lieutenant-Colonel Fremont at Ciudad de los Angeles was thus going on, we sent an Indian to ascertain where the principal force of the insurgents was encamped. He returned with information that a body of them, about fifty strong, was encamped at San Bernardo, about thirty miles from San Diego. Captain Gillespie was immediately ordered to have as many men as he could mount, with a piece of artillery, ready to march for the purpose of surprising the insurgents in their camp. Another expedition, under command of Captain Hensley, of the battalion, was sent to the southward for animals, who, after performing the most arduous service, returned with five hundred head of cattle and one hundred and forty horses and mules. About the 3d of December, two deserters from the insurgents, whose families lived in San Diego, came into the place and reported themselves to Lieutenant Minor, the commander of the troops. On receiving information of the fact, I repaired to Lieutenant Minor's quarters, with my aid-de-camp, Lieutenant Gray, for the purpose of examining one of these men. While engaged in this examination, a messenger arrived with a letter from General Kearney, of the United States army, apprising me of his approach, and expressing a wish that I would open a communication with him and inform him of the state of affairs in California.

Captain Gillespie was immediately ordered to proceed to General Kearney's camp with the force which he had been directed to have in readiness, carrying a letter which I wrote to General Kearney. Captain Gillespie left San Diego at about half-past seven o'clock the same evening, taking with him one of the deserters to act as a guide in conducting General Kearney to the camp of the insurgents. The force which accompanied Captain Gillespie consisted of a company of volunteers, composed of Acting Lieutenant Beale, Passed Midshipman Duncan, ten carbineers from the Congress, Captain Gibson, and twenty-five of the California battalion. Mr. Stokes, who was the bearer of the letter from General Kearney, was also of the company. In the evening of December 6, Mr. Stokes returned to San Diego, to inform me that General Kearney, on the morning of that day, had attempted to surprise the insurgents, under the command of Captain Andres Pico, in their camp at San Pasqual; that he had been worsted in the action which ensued, but to what extent he was unable to say, as he had left the field before the battle was concluded. He, however, was under the impression that General Kearney had lost a number of men killed and wounded.

The following morning, Lieutenant Godey, of the California battalion, with two men, came into San Diego with a letter from Captain Turner, of the dragoons, informing me that General Kearney had had a fight with a considerable body of the Mexicans; that he had about eighteen killed and fourteen or fifteen wounded, and suggesting the propriety of despatching, without delay, a considerable force to his assistance. Preparations were immediately made to despatch a detachment for this purpose. Captain Turner had not mentioned the strength on either side, and Lieutenant Godey was not able to inform me. From the information, however, I deemed it advisable to proceed in person, with all the force that could be spared from the garrison, to form a junction with him. Two days' provisions were ordered to be prepared, and the advance, with two field-pieces, under Acting Lieutenant Guest, was directed to march forthwith to the mission of San Diego, where it was my intention to join it with the rest of the force the next morning. Before, however, the advance had moved, an Indian came in from General Kearney. From the information he gave, I judged that the necessity for immediate assistance was much more urgent than had been previously supposed. Anticipating great difficulty and delay from the want of animals to drag the artillery, should I march with my entire force, and believing, from the representations now made, that the force of the Californians was less than had been supposed, and consequently that a portion of my command would be sufficient for the purpose, I determined not to move in person, but to send on as rapidly as possible an effective body of men. About ten o'clock at night, Acting Lieutenant Beale, of the Congress, arrived from General Kearney's camp, and confirmed the worst accounts we had received and the importance of prompt assistance. The advanced body, increased to the number of 215 men, was placed under the command of Lieutenant Gray, my aid-de-camp, with orders to proceed directly to the camp of General Kearney. The order was successfully performed, and Lieutenant Gray, having accomplished it, returned to San Diego accompanied by the General. On their arrival, General Kearney, his officers and men, were received by all the garrison in the kindest and most respectful manner. So far as my observation extended, no civility or attention was omitted. Having sent with Captain Gillespie every horse that was fit for use to General Kearney, I was without one for my own accommodation. I was therefore compelled, on foot, to advance and receive the General, whom I conducted to my own quarters, until others more agreeable to him could be prepared. The arrival of General Kearney was to me a source of gratification, although it was my decided opinion—which as yet I have seen no reason to change—that, under the circumstances that existed, I was entitled to retain the position in which I was placed of commander-in-chief; yet, in consideration of his high standing in the army, his long experience as a soldier, the importance of military science and skill in the movements that were to be made in the interior of the country, I immediately determined to yield all personal feelings of ambition and to place in his hands the supreme authority. In accordance with this determination I tendered to General Kearney the position of commander-in-chief and offered to accompany him as his aid.

This proposition was on more than one occasion renewed, and with all sincerity and singleness of purpose. The responsibility of moving from San Diego, and leaving the safety of the ships, deprived of so large and efficient a portion of their crews, was of itself a momentous one. This, however, in the discharge of duty, I felt no inclination to shrink from. But the fate of the territory itself might depend upon the issue of a battle to be fought on shore against an army organized to encounter us. The nature of the service and the importance of the stake, it seemed to me, appertained rather to a general in the army than a captain in the navy. Whatever ambition I might feel for distinction, either on my account or on that of the gallant officers and men under my command, was voluntarily and deliberately offered as a sacrifice to a paramount sense of duty. The offers thus made were, however, on every occasion distinctly and positively declined by General Kearney, who, on his side, offered to accompany me in the capacity of my aid, and tendered to afford me the aid of his head and hand.

A day or two after his arrival at San Diego, General Kearney removed from my quarters to others which at his instance had been provided for his accommodation. Before leaving, however, he handed me his instructions from the War Department. On reading them, I came to the conclusion that he had submitted them to my perusal to afford me the gratification of perceiving how entirely I had anticipated the views of the government in the measures which I had adopted. In return, I exhibited some of my own despatches to the Department. Subsequently, and before leaving San Diego, General Kearney mentioned the subject of his instructions from the War Department, and seemed to intimate that he ought of right to be the governor of the territory. His language, however, though perhaps sufficiently explicit, was not very intelligible to me, as I was at a loss to reconcile the assertion of such a claim of right with his repeated refusal to accept the offer, which I had more than once made to him, to devolve upon him the supreme command in the territory. The subject, however, was discussed between us without any interruption of that harmony which had commenced on our first interview.

A few days before I expected to take up the line of march, I addressed a note to the General, expressing a wish that he would accompany me. In his reply he repeated the language which he had before employed:—that he would so accompany me, and afford me the aid of his head and hand. Accordingly, on the morning of our departure he appeared upon the ground. After the troops had been paraded, and were nearly ready to commence the march, as I was about to mount my horse, General Kearney approached me and inquired who was to command the troops. I replied, Lieutenant Rowan was to have the command. On his expressing a wish that he should himself command them, I replied, that he should have the command. The different officers were at once convened, and informed that General Kearney had volunteered to command the troops, and that I had given him the appointment, reserving my own position as commander-in-chief. This arrangement having been made, we proceeded on the march.

During our march I was informed by Captain Gillespie, who was sent by General Kearney, who was in the advance, that two commissioners had arrived with a flag and a communication addressed to me. Repairing to the front, I received the commissioners, who bore a letter, signed by General Flores as governor and commander-in-chief, addressed to the commander-in-chief of the American forces. Upon reading it, and ascertaining from whom it emanated, I replied to the commissioners, substantially, that I perceived the letter was written by General Flores, whom I had captured and held as a prisoner, but whom I had released on his parole of honour; that in appearing now in hostile array he had violated his parole, and could not be treated as an honourable man; that I had no answer to return to his communication but this:—that if I caught him I should shoot him. With this reply the commissioners departed, and we proceeded on our march to meet the enemy.

The battles on the Rio San Gabriel and on the plains of the Mesa took place on the 8th and 9th of January, 1847. On the morning of the 8th, we crossed the river under a galling fire from the enemy, who were posted, with their artillery, on the opposite bank, about fifty feet above the level of the river. Having crossed the guns, we placed the two nine-pounders in battery, and commenced the fire. As soon as the troops had passed the river, they commenced forming the squares. At this time I perceived the insurgents were about to make a charge upon our left flank, and I ordered the men of that flank to be kept in line, that we might have a more extended line of fire. At this time, observing that the insurgents had withdrawn their artillery from the hill, I sent Lieutenant Gray, my aid-de-camp, to General Kearney, to move the square, with one field-piece, up the hill. At this moment the insurgents charged the left flank, but were received with such a shower of lead that they were soon repulsed. We immediately moved the line up the hill with the two nine-pounders, which I placed in battery in advance of the troops. I ordered the troops to lie down to avoid the insurgents' cannon-balls, as the fight was kept up by the artillery alone.

On the morning of the day we marched into Ciudad de los Angeles, General Kearney came to me with Mr. Southwick, who was acting as engineer, to ascertain from me by what road I intended to enter the city. He requested Mr. Southwick to mark on the sand the position of the city, and the different roads leading into it. I selected the plainest and broadest road, leading into the main street of the city; and when we marched into the city I led the way with the advance-guard. My position as commander-in-chief was again distinctly recognised in a letter of January 13, addressed to me by General Kearney, as *Governor of California, commanding United States forces.*

A few days after we had taken Ciudad de los Angeles, Lieutenant-Colonel Fremont arrived with his part of the battalion.

With the firm convictions which existed upon my mind as to my rights and authority as commander-in-chief, and the obligations which all officers and men under my command were under to obey implicitly all my orders, I should not only have felt it to be my right, but a matter of imperative duty, to assert and maintain my authority, if necessary, by a resort to force. I continued this exercise of the power of commander-in-chief without its having been denied or questioned by any person, as far as I was informed, up to the 16th of January, when I received a letter of that date from General Kearney, which is now on file in the Department, in which he demands that I will cease all further proceedings relating to the formation of a civil government for the territory. In my reply of the same date to that letter, (which, I think, is also on file in the Department,) I suspended General Kearney from his volunteer command under me, when he again became Brigadier-General Kearney, over whom I never attempted or desired to have any command or control.

I exercised no authority in the territory after I left San Diego, except that which was induced by the receipt of a letter from Lieutenant-Colonel Cook, informing me that he had received information that a French schooner had been landing some guns on the Southern coast, and that General Bustamente, with 1500 Mexicans, was approaching the territory. I wrote to Lieutenant-Colonel Cook that I would go in search of them as soon as possible. I went down the coast 120 miles, landed and mounted some of my men, and went in pursuit. It turned out to be a false alarm. After performing this last service in California, I returned, *via* San Diego and Monterey, to San Francisco, where I gave up the command of the frigate Congress, and returned to the United States by way of the Rocky Mountains.

The California battalion was organized under my own personal direction and authority, under a special condition that it should act under my orders as long as I might remain in California and require its services. It was paid by my orders, as long as I had any thing to pay with. The officers derived their appointments exclusively from me. It was never, in any form or manner, mustered into the service of the United States as a part of the army or connected with it. It was exclusively and essentially a navy organization. The battalion was entirely composed of volunteers, organized under my authority, but with their own free consent, according to the terms of a distinct and specific agreement to obey my orders and to serve while I should require their services. These men were not of that kind of *personnel* which sometimes compose regular armies: they were principally free American citizens who had settled in California; they were men of respectability, of influence, and of property; they were no ordinary men, because, when told that I had offered them as pay ten dollars a month, they said that they would not accept that pay,—that it would not pay their expenses,—but that they would volunteer to serve under my command without compensation.

This was the origin, character, and position of the battalion when engaged, in co-operation with the squadron under my command, in accomplishing the objects which I had in view.

Such was the posture of things when General Kearney arrived in California, and when he joined me in San Diego. He brought with him a very inconsiderable force,—wholly insufficient of itself to accomplish the important objects of tranquillizing the province and subjecting it to the authority of the Union, by the suppression of the insurrection which had been organized for the purpose of recovering the positions we occupied, overthrowing the government we had organized, and expelling us from the country, if, indeed, it had proved itself able to defend itself without our aid. When General Kearney declined the proffers I made to him of devolving upon him the high and responsible position of commander-in-chief; when he volunteered to act as my aid in the march against the enemy; when, at his own request, I assigned to him the position of commander of the troops; when the battles were fought which broke and dispersed the army of the insurgents; when, finally, we entered in triumph Ciudad de los Angeles, during this entire period I had not received any intelligence of the movements of Major Fremont.

The battalion was never placed under the command of General Kearney by me, and was not subjected to his orders. It still remained in immediate subordination to me and to my authority. Up to the period last mentioned,—viz.: the date of our occupation of Ciudad de los Angeles, the only authority which General Kearney had exercised, while he accompanied me, was simply that authority which he had asked me to give him, and which he had voluntarily accepted at my hands.

No one has ever pretended—I certainly never claimed—that I possessed any right or authority to command General Kearney as such. All the power which I ever claimed or exercised over him was derived from his volunteering to aid me and to act under my orders. This connection, being purely one created by mutual consent, was, at any time, dissoluble at the will of either of the parties. As I could not originally have compelled General Kearney to assume the position he held, neither had I any authority to detain him in it one moment against his inclination. He might, at any time, have laid down his character as a volunteer under me, and resumed his official rank and rights as brigadier-general in the army of the United States.

In his capacity of brigadier-general, however, he had no authority to command me or any portion of my force. I was as independent of him as he confessedly was of me. If the force which I had brought ashore from the squadron constituted a portion of the navy,—if the California battalion, which I had raised and organized, was ever rightfully subject to my orders,—both were as independent of General Kearney, or any other officer of the army, as I myself was.

Nor have I ever questioned, much less denied, the authority of General Kearney to assume command over and give his orders to Lieutenant-Colonel Fremont. He might, at any time, without my controverting his power, have directed Lieutenant-Colonel Fremont to leave my command, to terminate his connection with me as a volunteer under my command, and to report to him for orders. With any such exercise of authority I should never have interfered; whether rightfully or wrongfully exercised was not for me to judge. That was a matter dependent upon the relative rights and duties of the parties themselves, as fixed by the military law, and to be decided by military authority.

I did, however, and do still, deny that General Kearney, while occupying the position of volunteer under my command, had any authority whatever, as brigadier-general, over any portion of the forces serving under me. I deny that after the character of volunteer was laid down, and that of brigadier-general resumed, he had, as such, any authority, nor could the Secretary of War give him any such authority over any portion of the force which I had organized. Whatever authority he might lawfully exercise over Lieutenant-Colonel Fremont personally, I deny that it reached to the battalion organized under me and by me placed under the command of that officer. And, finally, I deny that General Kearney could rightfully control me in my conduct as governor of California, more especially after having explicitly refused to accept the supreme authority when voluntarily tendered to him.

I have the honour to be, faithfully, your obedient servant,

R. F. STOCKTON.

To the Hon. JOHN Y. MASON,
    Secretary of the Navy, Washington, D. C.

APPENDIX B.

Instructions of the Secretary of War by virtue of which General Kearney proceeded to California, dated June 3, 1846.

WAR DEPARTMENT, WASHINGTON, June 3, 1846.

SIR:—I herewith send you a copy of a letter to the Governor of Missouri for an additional force of one thousand mounted men.

The object of thus adding to the force under your command is not, as you will perceive, fully set forth in that letter, for the reason that it is deemed prudent that it should not at this time become a matter of public notoriety; but to you it is proper and necessary that it should be stated.

It has been decided by the President to be of the greatest importance, in the pending war with Mexico, to take the earliest possession of Upper California.

An expedition with that view is hereby ordered, and you are designated to command it.

To enable you to be in sufficient force to conduct it successfully, this additional force of a thousand mounted men has been provided.

Should you conquer and take possession of New Mexico and California, or considerable places in either, you will establish temporary civil governments therein.

Instructions sent to Commodore Sloat, and received by Commodore Shubrick in February, 1847, and not communicated to Commodore Stockton. (See Proceedings of Court-martial, p. 59.)

UNITED STATES NAVY DEPARTMENT,
Washington, July 12, 1846.

COMMODORE:—Previous instructions have informed you of the intention of this government, pending the war with Mexico, to take and hold possession of California; for this end, a company of artillery, with cannon, mortars, and munitions of war, is sent to you in the Lexington, for the purpose of co-operating with you according to the best of your judgment, and of occupying, under your directions, such post or posts as you may deem expedient in the Bay of Monterey, or in the Bay of San Francisco, or in both. In the absence of a military officer higher than captain, the selection of the first American post or posts on the waters of the Pacific, in California. is left to your discretion.

The object of the United States is, under its rights as a belligerent nation, to possess itself entirely of Upper California.

When San Francisco and Monterey are secured, you will, if possible, send a small vessel of war to take and hold possession of the port of San Diego; and it would be well to ascertain the views of the inhabitants of the Puebla de los Angeles, who, according to information received here, may be counted upon as desirous of coming under the jurisdiction of the United States.

If you can take possession of it, you should do so. The object of the United States has reference to ultimate peace with Mexico; and if, at that peace, the basis of the *uti possedetis* shall be established, the government expects, through your forces, to be found in actual possession of Upper California.

This will bring with it the necessity of a civil administration. Such a government should be established, under your protection; and, in selecting persons to hold office, due respect should be had to the wishes of the people of California, as well as to the actual possessors of authority in that province.

It may be proper to require an oath of allegiance to the United States from those who are intrusted with authority.

You will also assure the people of California of the protection of the United States.

In reference to commercial regulations in the ports of which you are in actual possession, ships and produce of the United States should come and go free of duty.

For your further instruction, I enclose to you a copy of confidential instructions from the War Department to Brigadier-General S. W. Kearney, who is ordered, overland, to California. You will also communicate your instructions to him, and inform him that they have the sanction of the President.

The government relies on the land and naval forces to co-operate with each other in the most friendly and effective manner.

After you shall have secured Upper California, if your force is sufficient, you will take possession and keep the harbours on the Gulf of California, as far down, at least, as Guaymas; but this is not to interfere with the permanent occupation of California.

A regiment of volunteers, from the State of New York, to serve during the war, have been called for by the government, and are expected to sail from the first to the tenth of August. This regiment will, in the first instance, report to the naval commander on your station, but will ultimately be under the command of General Kearney, who is appointed to conduct the expedition by land.

The term of three years having nearly expired since you have been in command of the Pacific squadron, Commodore Shubrick will soon be sent out in the Independence to relieve you.

The department confidently hopes that all Upper California will be in our hands before the relief shall arrive. Very respectfully,

GEORGE BANCROFT.

COMMODORE JOHN D. SLOAT,
Commanding United States naval forces in the Pacific Ocean.

Extract from Defence of Colonel Fremont, as published in Proceedings of the Court-martial of November, 1847.

I will first call attention, under this head, to what relates to the expedition of December and January, 1846 and 1847, from San Diego to Los Angeles, and especially with reference to the testimony concerning *the command of the troops* in that expedition. This is a matter on which General Kearney lays great stress throughout, bottoming, at one time, his claim to chief authority in the province mainly on the results of that expedition and his alleged command of it. I shall, consequently, examine and test what he says in relation to it, with some minuteness.

1. And first, as to the point, *at whose instance was the expedition raised and marched?* There is great discrepancy here. In General Kearney's letter of 17th January to the Department, he says:—

"I have to state that *the march of the troops from San Diego to this place was reluctantly consented to by Commodore Stockton, on my urgent advice* that he should not leave Lieutenant-Colonel Fremont unsupported to fight a battle on which the fate of California might, for a long time, depend; *the correspondence to prove which is now with my papers at San Diego, &c. &c.*

In his cross-examination on the fourth day of the trial, he says:

"In the latter end of December, an expedition was organized at San Diego to march to Los Angeles, to assist Lieutenant-Colonel Fremont; *and it was organized in consequence, as I believe, of this paper, which is a copy of a letter from me to Commodore Stockton,*" (referring to his letter of December 22, hereafter quoted.)

Let us contrast this first positive assertion, and second more reserved declaration of belief, with facts, with other testimony, and finally with the "proof" which General Kearney tenders.

Commodore Stockton testifies:—

"After General Kearney arrived, (on the 12th December,) and in my quarters, and in presence of two of my military family, I offered to make him commander-in-chief over all of us, and I offered *to go* as his aid-de-camp. He said no; that the force was mine; and he *would go* as my aid-de-camp, or accompany me."

Now, "*to go*" where? to "*accompany*" where?

This, if not sufficiently explicit, is made entirely so by the certificate of Messrs. Spieden and Moseley, of the navy, offered by Commodore Stockton, in corroboration, under the sanction of his oath, and, of course, forming a proper interpretation of his words. This certificate is as follows:—

"We, the undersigned, were present at a conversation held between Commodore Stockton and General Kearney, at San Diego, shortly after the arrival of the General, in which conversation the Commodore offered to give General Kearney the 'command-in-chief' *of the forces he was preparing to march with to the Ciudad de los Angeles, and to act as aid-de-camp. This offer the General declined,* but *said he would be most happy to go with the Commodore as his aid-de-camp,* and assist him with his head and hand.

"WILLIAM SPIEDEN, *U. S. N.*
"SAMUEL MOSELEY, *U. S. N.*

SAN DIEGO, February 5, 1847."

Again, Commodore Stockton testifies that, at a subsequent interview, a few days afterwards, he made to General Kearney "the same offer, in pretty much the same language, and received pretty much the same answer."

It is certain, then, that General Kearney's letter of the 22d December was *not* the inducing cause of the expedition, as "*believed,*" in General Kearney's testimony, and that "the march of the troops" was *not* a matter that Commodore Stockton "reluctantly assented to," as *asserted* in General Kearney's official letter; and is also certain that General Kearney could not have supposed either to be the case, for he had been informed ten days before of the design to send the expedition; that it was "preparing to march;" and he had been twice offered, and had twice declined, the command of it.

Commodore Stockton further testifies:—

I now set to work to make the best preparations I could to commence our march for the Ciudad de los Angeles.

During this time an expedition that had been sent to the South for horses returned, and brought with it a number of horses and cattle. Captain Turner was allowed to take his pick of the horses for the dragoons. After he had done so he wrote to me this note:—

SAN DIEGO, December 23, 1846.

COMMODORE:—In compliance with your verbal instruction to examine and report upon the condition of the public horses turned over to me for the use of C company, 1st dragoons, I have the honour to state that in my opinion not one of the horses referred to is fit for dragoon service, being too poor and weak for any such purpose; also, that the company of dragoons under my command can do much better service on foot than if mounted on those horses.

I am, sir, with high respect, your obedient servant,

H. S. TURNER,
Captain 1st dragoons, commanding company C.

COMMODORE R. F. STOCKTON,
United States Navy, commanding, &c.

The exact day of the return of this expedition for horses and cattle does not appear. But, as there had been time for Captain Turner to be allowed to "take his pick" from the horses, examine them, and make a report upon them by the 23d of December, it is nearly certain that it must have returned by the 22d; and hence it would seem that General Kearney's letter, sent to Commodore Stockton in the night of the last-mentioned day, in which he "recommends" the expedition, and in which he claims the whole merit of the march and to have induced Commodore Stockton reluctantly to consent to it, was not written till he had not only been repeatedly informed that the expedition was in preparation and he had been twice offered the command of it, but not till the horses and cattle for its use had actually arrived, and probably a part of them turned over to his own company of dragoons. This, indeed, is rendered nearly certain by the fact that the preparations for the expedition were so far advanced that Commodore Stockton's general orders for the march were issued on the day next following General Kearney's letter, which he pretends, under oath, to have been the inducing cause of the expedition.

But General Kearney is entitled to the benefit of the *"proof"* which he vouches to the Department in this passage of his letter:—

" I have to state that the march of the troops from San Diego to this place was reluctantly consented to by Commodore Stockton, on my urgent advice that he should not leave Colonel Fremont unsupported to fight a battle on which the fate of California might for a long time depend; *the correspondence to prove which is now with my papers at San Diego,* and a copy of which will be furnished to you on my return to that place."

This " correspondence," as he certifies it on the twelfth day of the trial, consists of three letters and Commodore Stockton's general orders for the march. I will set out all of them:—

SAN DIEGO, December 22, 1846.

DEAR COMMODORE:—If you can take from here a sufficient force to oppose the Californians, now supposed to be near the Pueblo and waiting for the approach of Lieutenant-Colonel Fremont, I advise that you do so, and that you march with that force as early as possible in the direction of the Pueblo, by which you will either be able to form a junction with Lieutenant-Colonel Fremont or make a diversion very much in his favour.

I do not think that Lieutenant-Colonel Fremont should be left unsupported to fight a battle upon which the fate of California may, for a long time, depend, if there are troops here to act in concert with him. Your force as it advances might surprise the enemy at the St. Louis mission, and make prisoners of them.

I shall be happy, in such an expedition, to accompany you, and to give you any aid, either of head or hand, of which I may be capable.

Yours, truly,

S. W. KEARNEY, *Brigadier-General.*

To COMMODORE STOCKTON,
Commanding United States forces, San Diego.

HEAD-QUARTERS, SAN DIEGO, December 23, 1846.

DEAR GENERAL:—Your note of yesterday was handed to me *last night* by Captain Turner of the dragoons.

In reply to that note, *permit me to refer you to the conversation held with you yesterday morning at your quarters.* I stated to you *distinctly* that I *intended* to march upon St. Louis Rey *as soon as possible*, with a part of the force under my command, and that I was *very desirous* to march on to the Pueblo *to co-operate with Lieutenant-Colonel Fremont;* but my movements after, to St. Louis Rey, would depend entirely upon the information that I might receive as to the movements of Colonel Fremont and the enemy. It might be necessary for me to stop the pass of San Felipe, or march back to San Diego.

Now, my dear General, if the object of your note is to advise me to do any thing which would enable a large force of the enemy to get into my rear and cut off my communication with San Diego, and hazard the safety of the garrison and the ships in the harbour, you will excuse me for saying I cannot follow any such advice.

My PURPOSE *still is* to march for St. Louis Rey *as soon as I can get the* DRAGOONS *and riflemen mounted*, which I hope to do in two days.

Faithfully, your obedient servant,

R. F. STOCKTON,
*Commander-in-chief and Governor
of the territory of California.*

To BRIGADIER-GENERAL S. W. KEARNEY,
United States Army.

SAN DIEGO, December 23, 1846.

DEAR COMMODORE:—I have received yours of this date, repeating, as you say, what you stated to me yesterday, and in reply I have only to remark that, *if I had so understood you*, I certainly *would not have written* my letter to you of last evening.

You certainly could not for a moment suppose that I would advise or suggest to you any movement which might endanger the safety of the garrison and the ships in the harbour.

My letter of yesterday's date stated that "if you can take from here," &c., of which you were the judge, and of which I knew nothing.

Truly yours,

S. W. KEARNEY, *Brigadier-General.*

COMMODORE R. F. STOCKTON,
Commanding United States Navy, &c., San Diego.

GENERAL ORDERS.

The forces composed of Captain Tilghman's company of artillery, a detachment of the 1st regiment of dragoons, companies A and B of the California battalion of mounted riflemen, and a detachment of sailors and marines, from the frigates Congress and Savannah and the ship Portsmouth, will take up the line of march *for the Ciudad de los Angeles* on Monday morning, the 28th instant, at 10 o'clock, A. M.

By order of the commander-in-chief.

J. ZIELIN,
Brevet Captain and Adjutant.

SAN DIEGO, December 23, 1846.

The character of this correspondence entirely destroys General Kearney's asseverations,—both the one in his report that Commodore Stockton "reluctantly consented" to the march of the troops, and the one before the court that he "believed" that the expedition was organized in consequence of his letter of advice.

Commodore Stockton's letter is explicit both of his present and previous "*intention*," "*desire*," and "*purpose*," to march "*as soon as possible;*" while the reference to the dragoons, which were General Kearney's especial corps, shows that the subject of the expedition must have been previously entertained between the two correspondents. Allow General Kearney, however, the benefit of any misunderstanding, touching Commodore Stockton's disposition and intentions, that he may have been under when he wrote his letter; the Commodore's reply corrects all such mistakes, and leaves General Kearney's subsequent assertions on this head direct contradictions of the declarations of Commodore Stockton.

The next question in connection with this expedition is, *who was its commander?* General Kearney says *he* was; Commodore Stockton, sustained by the testimony of many others, says *he* was. As it could not have had *two commanders* at the same time, I will compare the testimony. General Kearney's claim first comes to attention in a letter to the Department, of which the following is the first paragraph:—

HEAD-QUARTERS, ARMY OF THE WEST,
CIUDAD DE LOS ANGELES, January 12, 1847.

SIR:—I have the honour to report that, at the request of Commodore R. F. Stockton, United States Navy, (who in September last assumed the title of governor of California,) I consented to TAKE COMMAND of an expedition to this place, (the capital of the country,) and that on the 29th December, *I left San Diego* with about five hundred men, consisting of sixty dismounted dragoons, under Captain Turner, fifty California volunteers, and the remainder of marines and sailors, with a battery of artillery; Lieutenant Emory (topographical engineers) acting as assistant Adjutant-General. *Commodore Stockton accompanied us.*"

Here the claim to have been the commander is plain, unequivocal, and unconditional. In his letter to me, however, of the same date, (January 12th,) he expresses it perhaps even more strongly; since Commodore Stockton is not mentioned at all, and the pronoun "I" and "me" exclude the idea of any participant in the "possession" or command:

PUEBLA DE LOS ANGELES,
January 12, 1847.—Tuesday, 6 P. M.

DEAR FREMONT:—*I am here in possession of this place, with sailors and marines.* We met and defeated the whole force of the Californians the 8th and 9th. They have not now to exceed three hundred men concentrated. Avoid charging them, and come to *me* at this place.

Acknowledge the hour of receipt of this, and when *I* may expect you. Regards to Russell.   Yours,

S. W. KEARNEY, *Brigadier-General.*

LIEUTENANT-COLONEL FREMONT.

At the next step, General Kearney slightly varies his claim, and admits some qualification to the completeness of his command. This is on his cross-examination.

Fourth day of the trial.

In the latter end of December, an expedition was organized at San Diego to march to Los Angeles, to assist Lieutenant-Colonel Fremont, and it was organized in consequence, as I believe, of this paper, which is a copy of a letter from me to Commodore Stockton, (referring to his letter to Commodore Stockton of December 22.) Commodore Stockton at that time was acting as Governor of California, so styling himself. * * * * He determined on the expedition, and on the morning of the 29th December the troops were paraded at San Diego for the march. The troops consisted of about five hundred sailors and marines, about sixty dragoons, and about forty or fifty volunteers. While they were on parade, Commodore Stockton called several officers together; Captain Turner, of the dragoons, and Lieutenant Minor of the navy, I know were there, and several others. He then remarked to them to the following purport:—

"Gentlemen, General Kearney has kindly consented to take the command of the troops on the expedition; you will, therefore, look upon him as your commander. *I shall go along as* GOVERNOR *and commander-in-chief in* CALIFORNIA." "We marched towards Los Angeles," &c. * * * * "The troops, *under my command*, marched into Los Angeles on the 10th of January," &c.

At the next stage, in reply to a question of the judge-advocate, he returns to the positive and unconditional assertion of command:—

" By the act of Commodore Stockton, who styled himself Governor of California, the sailors and marines were placed UNDER MY COMMAND, on the 29th December, 1846, for the march to Los Angeles. I COMMANDED THEM ON THE EXPEDITION; Commodore Stockton accompanied us. I exercised no command whatever over Commodore Stockton, *nor did he exert any whatever over me.*"

Afterwards (fourteenth day) under examination by the court, and when information had been received here of the arrival of Commodore Stockton in the country, the witness greatly modified his position on this point, and admits several acts of authority done on the march by Commodore Stockton, and that he "felt it his duty" to "consult the wishes" of the Commodore.

"I found Commodore Stockton, on my arrival at San Diego, on the 12th December, 1846, in command of the Pacific squadron, having several ships, either two or three, in the harbour at that place. Most of his sailors were on shore. He had assumed the title of Governor of California in the month of August previous. *All at San Diego addressed him as 'Governor.'* I DID THE SAME.

"After he had determined on the march from San Diego to Los Angeles, the troops being paraded for it on the 29th December, he in the presence of several officers, among whom were myself, Captain Turner of the dragoons, and Lieutenant Minor, of the navy, and others, whose names I do not recollect, remarked to them, 'Gentlemen, General Kearney has kindly consented to take command of the troops in this expedition; you will, therefore, consider him as your commander. *I will go along as* GOVERNOR *and commander-in-chief in* CALIFORNIA.' *Under Commodore Stockton's directions every arrangement for the expedition was made. I had nothing whatever to do with it.* We marched from San Diego to Los Angeles. While on the march, a few days before reaching Los Angeles, a commission of two citizens, as I believe, on behalf of Governor Flores, came to Commodore Stockton with a communication to him as the governor or commander-in-chief in California. *Commodore Stockton replied to that communication without consulting me.* On the march I at no time considered Commodore Stockton under my direction; nor did I at any time consider myself under his. His assimilated rank to officers of the army at that time was, and now is, and will for upwards of a year remain, that of a colonel.

"Although I did not consider myself *at any time, or under any circumstances, as under the orders of Commodore Stockton*, yet, as so large a portion of my command was of sailors and marines, I felt it my duty on all important subjects *to consult his wishes, and, as far as I consistently could do so, to comply with them.*"

But it was not till the fifty-first day of this trial, when he had had the benefit of several weeks' reflection, added to information of the character of the testimony delivered by Commodore Stockton and others, and when he came into court fortified with his own questions, drawn up by himself to square with prearranged answers, that he could be brought to the point of admitting that, during the march, the Commodore had exercised the prerogative of sending him what he calls "messages" but the Commodore calls "orders," and had directed many movements of the expedition. But even this day's admissions are so reluctant, and with so many reservations, that for the plain fact other testimony must necessarily be brought in.

General Kearney recites twice, and with much particularity in his testimony to this point, *his* version of what Commodore Stockton said to the troops before marching from San Diego on the subject of the command; labouring, by an ingenious turn of the last clause, to draw a distinction between the commander-in-chief *in the territory* and the commander-in-chief *of the troops.* This is his precise version of Governor Stockton's remarks:—"Gentlemen, General Kearney has kindly consented to take command of the troops in this expedition; you

will therefore look upon him as your commander. *I shall go along as* GOVER-
NOR *and commander-in-chief* IN CALIFORNIA.

This fine-spun distinction seems, in fact, the corner-stone of General Kearney's
claim to have been the Commander of the expedition ; for, while he constantly
persists in that pretension, he as constantly admits that Commodore Stockton
was the Governor and commander in the territory.

I do not refer to this because I attach any value to the point in itself. For
any argument that I desire, the version given by General Kearney would answer
as well as any other; for, if Commodore Stockton was Governor and commander-
in-chief *of California*, his authority was sufficient for my case, since Los Angeles, where I believe the charges are all laid, is certainly within that province.
But the distinction drawn in the version given by the witness was considered
important by him, and that version is contradicted: and this is the point of
view in which I present it. It is contradicted by Commodore Stockton, Lieutenant Gray, Lieutenant Minor, and the certificate of Lieutenant Rowan, all
whose concurrent testimony affirms that Commodore Stockton's reservation of
authority related to the commander-in-chief of the *expedition*, without the words
of qualification to which General Kearney testifies; and it is worthy of note
that, though a witness of the prosecution, Captain Turner, was present at the
address, the prosecution have not thought proper to bring him to sustain General Kearney thus contradicted.

A few detached passages from the testimony will show how materially General Kearney is contradicted, in other respects, upon this point of the command:—

General Kearney.—"By the act of Commodore Stockton, the sailors and marines
were placed under *my command. I commanded them* on the expedition."

Commodore Stockton.—"During which march I performed *all the duties* which
I supposed devolved on the *commander-in-chief."*

General Kearney.—"I exercised no command whatever over Commodore
Stockton, *nor did he exert any whatever over me."*

Commodore Stockton.—"I was *in the habit* of sending my aid-de-camp *to General Kearney* to inform *him* what time *I wished* to move in the morning; and I
always decided on the *route* we should take, and *when* and *where* we should
encamp."

General Kearney.—"The troops *under my command* marched into Los Angeles on the 10th of January."

Commodore Stockton.—"And when we marched into the city, *I led the way, at
the head of the advanced guard."*

General Kearney.—"On the march I at no time considered Commodore Stockton under my direction, *nor did I, at any time, consider myself under his."*

Commodore Stockton.—"I observed the guns being unlimbered; I was told it
was done *by order of General Kearney* to return the fire of the enemy ; *I
ordered the guns limbered up,* and the forces to cross the river before a shot was
fired." "I observed that the men of the right flank had been formed into a
square, *and General Kearney at their head.* I sent my aid-de-camp, Mr. Gray,
to General Kearney, *with* INSTRUCTIONS *to move that square,* and two pieces of
artillery, immediately up the hill."

General Kearney.—"During our march many messages were brought to me
from Commodore Stockton; those messages I looked upon as *suggestions* and
expressions of his wishes. I have *since then* learned that he considered them in
the light of orders."

Commodore Stockton.—"I sent for Captain Emory; I asked him by whose
order the camp was making below the hill. He said *by General Kearney's order.*
I told him to go to General Kearney and tell him that it was *my order* that the
camp should be immediately moved to the top of the hill." "I sent my aid-de-
camp, Mr. Gray, to General Kearney, *with instructions* to move," &c. "The
witness, (Commodore Stockton,) in enumerating *some* of the *orders given* and
some of the details executed by himself, meant merely to cite instances in which
General Kearney recognised and acknowledged his (the witness's) *command-in-
chief on the field of battle* as well as *in the march."*

General Kearney.—"During our march, his (Commodore Stockton's) authority and command, *though it did not extend over me, or over the troops which he had himself given me,* extended far beyond," &c.

Commodore Stockton.—"Commodore R. F. Stockton begs leave to add, &c., that he wishes to be understood as meaning distinctly to convey the idea that General Kearney was fully invested with the command of the troops in the battles of the 8th and 9th of January, SUBJECT *to the orders of him, the witness, as* COMMANDER-IN-CHIEF. Most and nearly all the execution of details was confided to General Kearney as SECOND in command." "He could not attempt to enumerate and specify the many and important acts of General Kearney *as* SECOND *in command.*" "When the troops arrived at San Bernardo, I made my head-quarters a mile or two miles in advance of the camp; and *I* SENT *to General Kearney to send me the marines and a piece of artillery, which was immediately done.*" "*I* ORDERED *the troops all to lie down,*" &c. "*After having* DIRECTED *the troops* to be formed, &c., *I took* the *marine guard* and two pieces of *artillery,*" &c. "On my return, *I* gave ORDERS where the different *officers* and *troops* were to be quartered, and ORDERED the same *flag,*" &c.

General Kearney.—"I exerted no command whatever over Commodore Stockton, *nor did he exert any whatever over me.*"

Lieutenant Gray.—"Question.—Did you bear an *order* from Commodore Stockton on the 8th of January, in the field, to General Kearney? if so, state the order and all the circumstances.

"Answer.—I did bear *an order* from Commodore Stockton to General Kearney on the 8th of January, on the field of battle. The enemy had been observed to withdraw his guns from the height. The Commodore directed me to go to General Kearney, and say to him to send a square and a field-piece immediately up on the height, to prevent the enemy's returning with their guns. I went and gave him *the order,* and, on my return to Commodore Stockton, observed the division or square of General Kearney moving towards the hill.

"Question.—Did you bear that order to General Kearney in your character of aid-de-camp to Commodore Stockton, the commander-in chief?

"Answer.—Yes.

"Question by the judge-advocate.—Do you recollect the words and manner in which you delivered that order; did you deliver it so that General Kearney must have received it as an order, or merely as a suggestion?

"Answer.—I carried it *as an order,* in the usual respectful way. How General Kearney received it, I, of course, cannot say. He did not show, by his manner, that it was disagreeable to him, according to the best of my recollection."

Finally, I shall conclude this point by showing that General Kearney did not, and could not, at any time, have considered himself the commander of the expedition, or of the troops composing it, and was not so considered by the army officers who had accompanied him into California, and were there. Because,

1. The place which General Kearney held in the expedition was that which had been before assigned to a lieutenant of the navy, serving under Commodore Stockton, and this General Kearney knew. This is the testimony of Commodore Stockton:—

"After the forces had been paraded preparatory to the march, and I was about mounting my horse, General Kearney came to me and inquired, who was to command the troops. I said to him, *Lieutenant Rowan, first lieutenant of the Cyane, would command them.* He gave me to understand that *he* would like to command the troops, and, after some further conversation on the subject, *I agreed to appoint him to the command,* and immediately sent for Lieutenant Rowan," &c.

2. Because, at the moment of receiving the appointment, he was informed that the command-in-chief was reserved by Commodore Stockton. This is Commodore Stockton's testimony to this point:—

"I immediately sent for Lieutenant Rowan, and, assembling the officers that were near at hand, stated to them that General Kearney had *volunteered* to take command of the troops, but that I *retained my own position as commander-in-*

chief. I directed my aid-de-camp, and the commissary who was with me, to *take a note* of what I said on the occasion."

And to the same effect is the testimony of Lieutenant Gray and Lieutenant Minor, and the certificate of Lieutenant Rowan.

3. Because both General Kearney and the officers under him received and obeyed the orders of Commodore Stockton, in some instances in opposition to those first given by General Kearney, both on the march and in the battles. The evidence on this point need not be recapitulated. Commodore Stockton testifies to it, Lieutenant Gray testifies to it, Lieutenant Minor testifies to it, and Lieutenant Emory testifies to having received and obeyed orders from Commodore Stockton.

4. Because Lieutenant Emory, attached to General Kearney's dragoon escort, and acting as assistant adjutant-general, did not make his official report of losses in action in the expedition to General Kearney, but to Commodore Stockton. True, General Kearney says this was done "without his knowledge or consent;" but that is only the stronger proof that he was not regarded or respected as the commander-in-chief, even by his confidential supporters and military family.

5. Because he admitted to Colonel Russell, as appears repeatedly in Colonel Russell's testimony, that he was serving *under* Commodore Stockton, and had been serving under him from San Diego.

6. Because, when I delivered to him, and he read in my presence, my letter to him of 17th January, in which is this passage:—

"*I learned also in conversation with you that on the march from San Diego, recently, to this place, you entered upon and discharged duties implying an acknowledgment on your part* OF SUPREMACY *to Commodore Stockton,*" he made no denial of it, or objection to it.

7. Because, on the 16th of January, he applied, in writing, to Commodore Stockton, "advising" and "offering" "to take one-half" of the command, and march to "form a junction," &c., addressing Commodore Stockton in that letter as "Governor of California, *commanding United States forces.*"

On the eighth day of the trial General Kearney testified as follows:—

"Question.—Do you know whether the officers of the battalion raised it and marched it under commission from Commodore Stockton?

"Answer.—I have always understood that Lieutenant-Colonel Fremont had raised that battalion under the direction of Commodore Stockton.

"Question.—With what commission?

"Answer.—*I never heard of Commodore Stockton conferring a commission on Lieutenant-Colonel Fremont further than having appointed him military commandant of California.*"

The object of this inquiry was not, by any means, to get an opportunity to discredit the witness. The object was to ascertain before the court that the battalion was enlisted, organized, and officered exclusively under naval authority, and so, of course, subject to the orders of the naval commander; and also to ascertain if these facts were not within the knowledge of the witness when he attempted to get command of the battalion in opposition to Commodore Stockton; both being inquiries pertinent to the issues of the trial, and the facts being what was desired. But the nature of the last answer was such as to leave the original inquiries unsettled and to open a *new one.*

The answer was this:—"*I never heard* of Commodore Stockton's conferring a commission on Lieutenant-Colonel Fremont further than having appointed him *military commandant* of California."

And the new question raised was whether, in fact, the witness had "*never heard*" of a matter so notorious in that country. Accordingly, on the next day, General Kearney having mentioned the receipt on the 16th December, 1846, of a certain communication from Commodore Stockton, this question was put:—

"Question.—Did not Commodore Stockton, in that communication, *inform you* that Captain Fremont had been appointed by him MAJOR, and Lieutenant Gillespie, of the marines, captain, in the California battalion?"

And, a copy of the paper having been shown to the witness, he answered:—

"Answer.—Among the papers sent to me by Commodore Stockton on the 16th

December, *was* a copy of his letter to the Navy Department, dated August 28, 1846, the second paragraph of which states that he had organized a California battalion of mounted riflemen, by the appointment of all the necessary officers, and received them as volunteers in the service of the United States ; *that Captain Fremont was appointed major, and Lieutenant Gillespie captain of the battalion.*"

Again, on the 13th day of the trial, two other papers were shown to the witness, with this question :—

"Were not copies of these two papers, describing him (Fremont) as Major Fremont, among those furnished to you by Commodore Stockton at San Diego? And were not copies of them filed in the War Department by you since your return from California and after your arrival in this city in September last?

"Answer, (after reading over the papers.)—I think that copies of these papers *were furnished to me by Commodore Stockton.*"

To the latter part of the question, "Were they not filed by you in the War Department since your return from California and after your arrival in this city in September last." "I see on the papers the certificate of Captain Townsend that I did so; *I think Captain Townsend is mistaken.*"

But on the following day he admitted that Captain Townsend was *not* mistaken ; that the papers had been put into his hands by Commodore Stockton in December, 1846, and had been filed by him in the War Office as late as the 21st September last? From all this, however, it only resulted that he had *seen* of the appointment of Fremont as major; that he had "*never heard*" of it was not yet disproved.

This was accomplished in his testimony on the ninth day, when he admitted as follows :—

"Commodore Stockton *did* inform me, in the conversation alluded to between us, that California had been conquered in July and August of the same year, (this conversation was held in December,) and that *Major Fremont* had gone to the North to raise men," &c.

In the same connection and for the same purpose the question arose whether Lieutenant Gillespie, of the marine corps, was not also an officer of the battalion ; and the answer of the witness was again such as not only to leave the original question open, but to raise the new one, which brings the subject within this branch of my defence. The witness's answer was as follows :—

"Captain Gillespie had marched with me from San Diego to Los Angeles, and was serving under me. *If his company was with the California battalion* I DID NOT KNOW IT."

It appeared, however, on examination, that the same communication (of 28th August, 1846) that informed the witness that Fremont had been appointed major of the battalion also informed him that Gillespie had been appointed captain in it. It further appeared that, in the surgeon's list of killed and wounded in the actions of 8th and 9th January, furnished by Lieutenant Emory to General Kearney, and by him sent to the department, Captain Gillespie is reported as an officer of the California battalion ; and Captain Gillespie himself gave the following emphatic testimony :—

"Question.—Did you at any time communicate to General Kearney your rank and position in the California battalion? If so, when and where was that communication made?

"Answer.—*I did communicate to General Kearney my position in the battalion* on the 5th of December, 1846, about one o'clock in the day, in the mountains about half-way between Santa Maria and Santa Isabel. When I met him I was at the head of a detachment of volunteers and sailors, I having been ordered by Commodore Stockton to proceed to Warner's Pass to communicate with General Kearney."

These inquiries concerning the raising and officering of the battalion were to matters connected intimately with the issues of the trial, and the answers of the witness seemed to indicate a consciousness of it. But I do not desire to present them in any other light than as instances of defective and equivocating memory, and in that view affecting the general credit of his testimony.

Under the same infirmity of memory I am willing to class the extraordinary facility of *omission* betrayed by the witness in his manner, which seems to be habitual, of *half-telling* where *whole-telling* is essential. Thus: On the third day of the trial he commences an answer in these words:—"About the 14th January, 1847, *I received* from Lieutenant-Colonel Fremont a communication, dated," &c.—the inference being, of course, that my communication was voluntary; the fact (and most important one, too) being that it was drawn out by no less than *four* importunate letters that I had before received. Again, in continuation of the same narration:—" On the day subsequent, viz., on the 17th January, Lieutenant-Colonel Fremont *came to my quarters*, and in conversation," &c.—the inference being, of course, that I went at my own instance, whereas the fact (most material and relevant, and deciding the character of the interview) turned out that I went in compliance with the written request of the witness to see me "on business." Again, same day:—"I was first *met* by a detachment from Commodore Stockton," &c. . . . . . " It *came* from Commodore Stockton *to give* me information," &c.; . . . . . the inference being that it went voluntarily or was sent by Commodore Stockton of his own motion,—the important fact appearing, however, when Commodore Stockton came on the stand, three weeks after, that it was sent out at the written request of General Kearney for a party "to open communication with him," &c. So, in the same letter making this application, he writes to Commodore Stockton as follows:—"*Your express, by Mr. Carson, was met on the Del Norte, and your mail must have reached Washington at least ten days since*"—omitting the material fact that Mr. Carson, in addition to being *met*, was likewise *turned back*, and leaving the inference that he had gone on. Again, in his testimony on the sixth day of the trial, speaking of his position on the hill of San Bernardo, the witness says:—" I stated to the doctor and others that we would leave next morning, which we accordingly did; *Lieutenant Gray, of the navy, with a gallant command of sailors and marines, having come into our camp the night previous*"—the inference being that Lieutenant Gray and his command came voluntarily or by chance into the camp, the fact being that it was a detachment of two hundred and fifteen men sent from San Diego expressly for the relief of General Kearney's camp and in pursuance of his repeated urgent calls for succour—one of them (that by Lieutenant Beale, Mr. Carson, and the Indian) conveyed through the enemy's lines and an insurgent population under circumstances of devotion and courage unsurpassed, but no mention of which is found in the official report or in any part of the testimony of General Kearney.

APPENDIX C.

The following statement is appended in a note to Mr. Benton's Speech, July, 1848, on the brevet nomination of General Kearney. See Appendix to Congressional Globe, 1848.

Mr. CARSON has since arrived in Washington and given me the following statement in relation to the turning back, the truth of which, as of every thing else that he says, I underwrite:—

Statement of Mr. C. Carson.

I met General Kearney with his troops on the 6th of December, a short distance below Santa Fé. I had heard before of their coming, and, when I met them, the first thing I told them was that they were " too late"—that California was conquered, and the United States flag raised in all parts of the country. But General Kearney said he would go on, and said something about going to establish a civil government. I told him a civil government was already established, and Colonel Fremont appointed governor, to commence as soon as he returned from the North, some time in that very month, (October.)

General Kearney said that that was no difference,—that he was a friend of Colonel Fremont, and he would make him governor himself. He began from the first to insist on my turning back to guide him into California. I told him I could not turn back; that I had pledged myself to Commodore Stockton and Colonel Fremont to take their despatches through to Washington city, and to return with them as far as New Mexico, where my family lived, and to carry them all the way back if I did not find some one at Santa Fé that I could trust as well as I could myself; that I had promised them I would reach Washington in sixty days, and that they should have return despatches from the government in one hundred and twenty days. I had performed so much of the journey in the appointed time, and, in doing so, had already worn out and killed thirty-four mules; that Stockton and Fremont had given me letters of credit to persons on the way to furnish me with all the animals I needed, and all supplies to make the trip to Washington and back in the one hundred and twenty days; and that I was pledged to them and could not disappoint them; and, besides, that I was under more obligations to Colonel Fremont than to any other man alive. General Kearney would not hear any such thing as my going on. He told me he was a friend to Colonel Fremont and Colonel Benton, and all the family, and would send on the despatches by Mr. Fitzpatrick, who had been with Colonel Fremont in his exploring party, and was a good friend to him, and would take the despatches through and bring them back as quick as I could.

When he could not persuade me to turn back, he then told me that he had a right to make me go with him, and insisted on his right; and I did not consent to turn back till he had made me believe that he had a right to order me; and then, as Mr. Fitzpatrick was going on with the despatches, and General Kearney seemed such a good friend of the Colonel's, I let him take me back; and I guided him through, but with great hesitation, and had prepared every thing to escape in the night before they started, and made known my intention to —— Maxwell, who urged me not to do so.

More than twenty times on the road General Kearney told me about his being a friend to Colonel Benton and Colonel Fremont, and all their family, and that he intended to make Colonel Fremont the Governor of California; and all this of his own accord, as we were travelling along or in camp, and without my asking him a word about it. I say more than twenty times, for I cannot remember how many times, it was such a common thing for him to talk about it.

This statement I make at the request of Senator Benton, but had much rather be examined in a court of justice, face to face with General Kearney, and there tell at once all that I know about General Kearney's battles and conduct in California.

APPENDIX D.

Extract from Appendix to Senator Benton's Speech in Executive Session, on the brevet nomination of Brigadier-General Kearney for Major-General, delivered July, 1848, *and printed in Appendix to Congressional Globe of that date.*

QUESTION OF SUPREMACY BETWEEN COMMODORE STOCKTON AND GENERAL KEARNEY IN CALIFORNIA.

1. Note from Mr. Robert Semple, editor of the "Californian," dated April 24, 1847, asking him to state the circumstances of the march and campaign from San Diego to Los Angeles, taken from the "Californian" of July 17, 1847.

MONTEREY, April 24, 1847.

DEAR SIR:—Some facts have come to my knowledge, which make it proper for me to request you to write the facts which occurred at San Diego previous to the march of the American forces on Los Angeles, and the manner of conducting the campaign; not for publication, or to be used without your permission, but to be kept, that it may be used, should such necessity arise.

Very respectfully, your obedient servant,
R. SEMPLE.

S. W. KEARNEY,
   Brigadier-General and Governor of California.

2. Statement of Mr. Semple in the "Californian" of the 17th of July, near three months after writing the above note, showing that it was written to General Kearney in consequence of a communication from Commodore Stockton of the 10th of March previous, asserting his supremacy of command in the San Diego and Los Angeles expedition; and that General Kearney made no answer to it, but held the editor to his accountability if he should publish Stockton's statement and the vouchers which accompanied it.

The above letter was written on my return to Monterey, and after the receipt of Commodore Stockton's letter and the accompanying documents. Several days passed, and, having received no answer, I called on the General and informed him of the purport of Commodore Stockton's letter, and he refused to release me from responsibility in the publication of the papers alluded to. I immediately wrote to Commodore Stockton, informing him of the fact, and asking if he insisted on their publication. My great object in delaying the papers was, that it was a personal difficulty between Kearney and Stockton, and might be much better settled in the United States, and would be productive of no good here, either to the parties or to the country.

3. Commodore Stockton's letter to the Editor of the "Californian," 10th of March, 1847, asserting his own command in the expedition, and contradicting an editorial article of the 13th of February, in that paper, claiming the command for Kearney.

United States Frigate Congress,
Harbour of San Diego, March 10, 1847.

TO THE EDITORS OF THE "CALIFORNIAN," MONTEREY:—

Gentlemen:—In an editorial article in the "Californian" of the 13th February, you may find the following paragraph:— .

"Commodore Stockton announced to the officers that the *whole expedition* was placed under the command of General Kearney, himself holding his station as Commander-in-chief of California, and General Kearney did command the *whole expedition.*"

I take the first opportunity to say to you that the above paragraph is not true in any one of its important particulars. It is not true that I placed the *whole expedition* under the command of General Kearney, nor did I so announce it.

On the request of General Kearney, and with the consent of Lieutenant Rowan, (to whom, with the consent of Lieutenant Minor, who had previously held it, I had given the command only the night before,) I appointed General Kearney to command the troops, and so announced it; at the same time, stated distinctly that I still retained my own position as Commander-in-chief. The word California did not pass my lips upon that occasion.

Now, Messrs. Editors, if you say that I delegated, or intended to delegate, to General Kearney, or to any one else, any part of my duty or authority as the director of the expedition or Commander-in-chief of the forces, or that General Kearney, or any other person but myself, exercised, or pretended to exercise, any such power or authority from the time we left San Diego until we arrived at the Ciudad de los Angeles, then I must say to you that all such statements are false.

But, Messrs. Editors, it is quite true that "Commodore Stockton did leave San Diego at the head of the forces at his command," and marched into the Ciudad de los Angeles in the same way.

There are other most glaring misstatements in the editorial referred to, which, no doubt, in due season, will be corrected. In the mean time, go on.

Sic iter ad astra.

Your obedient servant,
R. F. Stockton.

P.S.—This communication has been delayed in the hope that I could be at Monterey before this time.

---

4. Letter from Purser Speiden, of the 16th of March, to the same Editor, contradicting the same editorial, avowing himself the author of a letter in which an account of the expedition was given, and Commodore Stockton treated as the Commander-in-chief.

United States Ship Congress,
San Diego, March 16, 1847.

TO THE EDITORS OF THE "CALIFORNIAN," MONTEREY:—

Gentlemen:—I have noticed, in an extra sheet of your paper, under date of the 28th of January last, an account of the battles of the 8th and 9th of January, on the banks of San Gabriel and plains of the Mesa, taken from a communication from an officer of the Congress, dated Ciudad de los Angeles, 14th January.

On referring to a "Californian" of the 13th February following, I find in the editorial column of that paper the following sentences, having reference to the communication referred to:—

"Our object in referring to this letter is to do justice to two brave and distinguished officers, General Kearney and Captain Mervine."

The writer of this letter states that, in the march from San Diego to Los Angeles, the whole was under the immediate command of Commodore Stockton; while the truth is, that previous to taking up the line of march, Commodore Stockton announced to the officers that the whole expedition was placed under the command of General Kearney, himself holding his station as Commander-in-chief of California, and General Kearney did command the whole expedition, and Captain Turner the dragoons alluded to.

As the writer of the communication referred to is the subscriber, he now requests you to publish the enclosed papers, marked A and B, that the public may judge who the party is, dealing in error and untruths.

Should the truth of the communication, a copy of which is herewith enclosed, be sustained by the evidence adduced, the editors must see, and the public too, the palpable misrepresentation of the editorial report.

The undersigned has nothing to do with the notices of the editors in defending the military character of General Kearney and Captain Mervine, which it was not his intention to attack, and he leaves it with the public to judge how far his expression in the communication, "*The success attending the Californians in their fight with Captain Mervine, and afterwards with General Kearney, made them very bold and arrogant,*" is a matter of notoriety.

The only object of the undersigned in making the communication was that you, sirs, might give publicity to an event that would be interesting to your American readers, at least, not dreaming it would call forth so unjust an attack by you upon his veracity.

Very respectfully, your obedient servant,

WM. SPEIDEN.

---

5. Statement of four naval officers, of the 9th of March, attesting that Commodore Stockton was Commander-in-chief in that expedition:—

SAN DIEGO, March 9, 1847.

SIR:—In answer to your letter of the 8th instant, we have to state that the expedition from San Diego to the Ciudad de los Angeles was conceived and fitted out by Commodore Stockton, and commanded by him as Commander-in-chief, and as such he was recognised from its conception to its successful termination at the Ciudad de los Angeles.

Commodore Stockton gave all orders and directions during the march comporting with the dignity of Commander-in-chief, and all flags of truce were referred to him. Commodore Stockton replied to General Flores (who signed himself Commander-in-chief and Governor of California) that he would have nothing to do with any man, or set of men, who did not acknowledge him (Commodore Stockton) as Commander-in-chief and Governor of California.

We consider General Kearney as second in command from the time we left San Diego to the termination of the expedition; and we believe he was so considered by all the officers of the expedition.

With the highest respect, we remain your obedient servants,

S. C. ROWAN, *Lt. U. S. N. and Major.*
GEO. MINOR, *Lt. U. S. N. and Q. M.*
J. ZEILIN, 1*st Lt. U. S. N. and Bt. Capt. and A. Bat.*
W. SPEIDEN, *Purser U. S. N. and Com'y.*

---

6. Statement of fifteen naval officers, including the other four, attesting the truth of the narrative contained in the letter of Purser Speiden to the Editor of the "Californian." The letter is a detailed narrative, written immediately after the expedition, and, in recounting events, always speaking of Commodore Stockton as Commander-in-chief, it not being known at Los Angeles at the time of writing that letter, (14th January,) that General Kearney claimed to have been the commander.

We the undersigned, officers of the United States Ship Congress, who accompanied the troops under the command of Commodore R. F. Stockton, in the march from San Diego to the Ciudad de los Angeles, and who were present during the fight of the 8th and 9th of January, do certify to the correctness of the above narration.

J. GUEST, *Acting Lieutenant.*
W. H. THOMSON, *Acting Lieutenant.*
J. ZEILEN, *1st Lieut. and Bvt. Capt. U. S. M. C.*
J. M. DUNCAN, *Acting Master.*
C. EVERSFIELD, *Assistant Surgeon.*
T. LEE, *Midshipman.*
B. F. WELLS, *Midshipman.*
P. H. HAYWOOD, *Midshipman and Acting Lieut.*
             on the march.
R. C. DUVAL,   "   "   "
W. SIMMONS, *Com.'s Clerk.*
J. SOUTHWICK, *Carpenter.*
J. PEED, *Sailmaker.*

I cheerfully coincide in the opinion expressed by the above-named officers.
G. MINOR, *Lieut. U. S. N. and Quartermaster*
             on the march.

I believe the written account of our march on the Ciudad de los Angeles to be circumstantially correct.
S. C. ROWAN, *Lieut. U. S. N. and Major of Brigade.*

We do hereby certify that we have compared the above copy with the communication made by Purser Speiden to Walter Colton, Editor of the " Californian," and find it to be a correct copy.
J. W. LIVINGSTON, *Lieut. Com'g United States*
             Frigate Congress.
S. MOSELY, *Surgeon, United States Frigate Congress.*
UNITED STATES SHIP CONGRESS,
    SAN DIEGO, March 11, 1847.

---

7. Official Letter from General Kearney to Commodore Stockton, at Los Angeles, January 13, applying to Commodore Stockton, as his Commander-in-chief, for leave to take part of the command, and to go to the relief of Lieutenant-Colonel Fremont.

HEAD-QUARTERS, ARMY OF THE WEST,
    CIUDAD DE LOS ANGELES, U. C., January 13, 1847.

SIR:—I fear, from the armistice which I this morning saw, signed by Lieutenant-Colonel Fremont, and sent to me by you, that our countrymen under Colonel Fremont are entirely ignorant of our being here; that they are embarrassed in their movements. And I further fear that, unless something is done *at once* to inform them of the true state of affairs here, they may capitulate and retire to the upper country.

To avoid so serious an evil, I advise and offer to take one-half of this command,—from 250 to 300 men,—and march at once to form a junction with Lieutenant-Colonel Fremont.

Very respectfully, your obedient servant,
S. W. KEARNEY, *Brig.-General.*
COMMODORE R. F. STOCKTON,
    Governor of California, commanding U. S. Forces.

A true copy.   E. D. TOWNSEND,
                                   Assistant Adjutant-General.

8. Letter of Purser Speiden, referred to in his letter of the 16th March, 1847, above set forth.

(*From the California Extra, of January* 28, 1847.)

The following letter is from an officer attached to the *command of Commodore Stockton*, and describes with graphic force the engagements which took place on the march to the Puebla:—

"CIUDAD DE LOS ANGELES, January 14, 1847.

" I seize the moment to write you a few hasty lines, which may possibly reach you through the agency of a friend. In my last you were informed of the outbreak of the insurgents of California, and the trouble we should have for our Commodore to quell them. *The plan of Commodore Stockton, of which I informed you a few weeks ago, has been fully carried out. At the head of the forces at his command, amounting to about six hundred, including the detachment of the first regiment of United States dragoons, under General Kearney, he left San Diego on the morning of the* 29th *December, determined again to enter the capital, take possession, and put down the insurrection.* Our line of march was through a rough and mountainous country of nearly one hundred and fifty miles, with impediments on every side, to say nothing of the constant apprehensions of attack, both day and night, by our enemy on the way. Our march was, notwithstanding, rapid, and, although performed mostly by sailor troops, would have done credit to the best-trained army in the world.

" On the morning of the 8th of January we found ourselves, after several days' hard marching and fatigue, in the vicinity of the river San Gabriel, on the north bank of which the enemy had fortified themselves, to the number of five hundred well-mounted men, with four pieces of artillery, and in a position so commanding that it seemed impossible to gain any point by which our troops could be protected from the most galling fire of their artillery. They had formed, as I before said, on the north bank, within three hundred yards of the river, and presented a front, consisting of their whole force, in three divisions, one on our right, the other on our left, and the third in front of the artillery. Our whole line advanced, while a skirmish was kept up by a party of the enemy and a detachment of our riflemen. *On reaching the south side of the river, the Commodore dismounted, forded the stream, commanded the troops to pass over, which they did promptly, under the brisk fire of the enemy's artillery on the opposite bank. The Commodore ordered that the artillery should not unlimber until the opposite side of the river was gained. As soon as that was effected, he ordered a charge, to take the hill directly in the teeth of the enemy's guns, which soon resulted in the entire possession of the prominent point they had just occupied.* An attempt was made by the Californians to cut off our pack-horses and cattle in the rear, all of which, however, with the exception of a few horses, were protected by our rear in the most creditable manner. I am not sufficiently skilled in military tactics to give a definite account of the battle; *but the skill in management and determined courage and bravery of our Commodore gave to all the fullest confidence of a victorious result of this brilliant affair.* The first gun fired was aimed by the *Commodore* before the charge was made up the hill, (his superior skill in gunnery and fondness for exercising 'big guns' never appeared to greater advantage than on this occasion,) overthrowing the enemy's gun, which had just poured forth its thunder in our midst. Finding the hill in our possession, and our artillery having gained the desired point, a cannonading was now kept up for some time, *the Commodore continuing to aim the guns, ordering his men to lie down until the moment he was ready to fire, by which means many valuable and brave fellows' lives were saved, as the Californians continued for some time to fire their artillery with much effect.* For brevity, I must leave out many particulars. Having driven our enemy before us, we now made our camp for the night on the very hill they had tried so hard to defend, and where they intended (as they said) ' to eat us up.' The number of their killed and wounded it was not possible for us to ascertain, as they carried away immediately on their horses all who fell.

"*9th January.*—The enemy met us again to-day on the plains of the Mesa, near the city, and with bold and determined effort tried our lines on every side in a brisk cannonading, with several attempts to charge in upon us. The battle was kept up spiritedly for two hours and a half, when General Flores said to his men, 'I have but another discharge of artillery to make, and my last request is that you will make a bold and determined charge as our last resort.' This they attempted; but the firm and steady course in which our troops continued to defend themselves repelled the attempt at a charge, and we found ourselves again victorious in the second day's fight. The first day's fight lasted one hour and a half. At night we encamped near the battle-ground, and on the morning of the 10th marched into the city, and took possession while the adjacent hills were glistening with the lances of our enemies, whom we forced to disperse. When it is recollected that all our work to defend ourselves, our baggage-wagons, cattle, horses, and pack-mules, had to be done on foot, while our enemies were mounted on first-rate horses, is it not remarkable that we should have been so successful? But it was done on the glorious 8th of January, together with the following day. Of the result of both days we are proud to boast; but the 8th was indeed a brilliant affair: our war-cry was 'New Orleans!' I can say nothing here of the officers and men individually; *but no doubt full justice will be done to all by the official report of the Commodore.*

"I give the above facts, being myself an eye-witness to the events of the two days, and glad that I live to write you.

"The success attending the Californians in their fight with *Captain Mervine* at San Pedro, and afterwards with *General Kearney at San Pasqual*, made them very bold and arrogant; and every man of us was determined to retrieve, if possible, the credit of the American arms in this country.   Yours, &c."

From the Correspondence of the Richmond Inquirer.

We have never known more regret to be expressed upon the retirement of any Senator than that which has followed the announcement of the resignation of Stockton. All parties, sects, and factions are united in opinion on this matter. All lament the loss of his ability, whole-souled patriotism, and experience to the country; and all deplore the event because of those excellent qualities of head and heart which have shone so conspicuously in the social world. Many now regard it as a foregone conclusion that the gallant Sailor-Senator is to be Secretary of the Navy. There are no two opinions about his being pre-eminently the man for the place.

From the Alexandria (Va.) Age.

ON DITS.

The resignation of Commodore Stockton, the notice of which was published in our last issue, has given rise to much speculation—some asserting that it was occasioned by the pressure of his own private business, which is said to be sufficiently overwhelming to occupy his whole time, and others that it was predicated upon the assumption of still higher honours in the councils of the nation. The latter class of speculators assign to him the position of Secretary of the Navy, in the Cabinet of General Pierce; and the Baltimore American and Washington Republic, acting upon the hypothesis that they speak by authority, give utterance to the opinion which they entertain of the distinguished Senator, in terms as creditable to themselves as to the object of their commendation. Read:—

The Washington Republic, referring to the resignation of United States Senator Stockton, says:—

"While we regret to lose the Senatorial services of this distinguished gentleman, we hope that the country will enjoy the benefit of his abilities and varied experience in some other position."

We join in the expression of the same wish. If the present able head of the Navy Department could be continued in the station which he has filled with such hearty acceptance to the country at large, it would indeed be a happy circumstance; but, as this is a thing not possible, we are rejoiced that his place is probably filled by so worthy a successor.

We are not advised whether there is any foundation for this speculation, but, if there is really any authority for it, we are persuaded that the choice of the President could not possibly fall upon a gentleman more competent to discharge the arduous duties of that responsible post, or whose elevation to it would be more generally acceptable to the country. Senator Stockton has won for himself a leading position in the most dignified assembly of statesmen in the world; and the reputation which he has thus acquired as a civilian, coupled with the renown he enjoys as one of the bravest and most chivalric of our naval heroes, eminently fit and prominently point to him as the man for the post to which public sentiment has already assigned him.

From the National Democrat, (N. Y.)

SENATOR STOCKTON.

Doubtless there are wiseacres who fancy the resignation of his Senatorship by R. F. Stockton indicative of a seat awaiting him in the cabinet of General Pierce. Stranger and far worse things might happen; but, as this step has long been contemplated, owing to the pressing demands of his private business and interests, we can see abundant reason for his resignation other than a cabinet seat. Commodore Stockton was a candidate for the Senate more in obedience to the solicitation of his friends, and they include pretty much all New Jersey—the New Jersey Democracy especially,—more than from his own desire or predilections. We can only regret that, having done so bravely in the Senate, he is, perforce of private or other interests, induced to resign a post which he has so dignified and honoured. Just at this time, especially, we regret it; for his voice, it strikes us, as the potent one to carry through a thorough reform in that great arm of the national service with which the best energies of his past life have been connected—the navy. At any rate, he has boldly set forth the inefficiency of our present naval system, and, in or out of Congress, we believe he will labour for a reorganization until it is accomplished. He is not one to take hold of the plough and look back. Stockton will be missed from the Senate, both as a legislator and as a man.

From the Newark Eagle.

COMMODORE STOCKTON—SECRETARY OF THE NAVY.

The whole nation seems unanimously to point to Commodore Stockton as the future Secretary of the Navy under Franklin Pierce. The whole world acknowledges his naval pre-eminence, and accords to him the merited renown of marine skill and heroism.

It is gratifying to Jerseymen to see such testimony as the following, from the remotest bounds of the Union, in commendation of one of whom they are instinctively proud. The *New Orleans Delta* of November 16, in speaking of those who will probably compose the new Cabinet under Franklin Pierce, says:—

"Should it be deemed expedient to fill the post of Secretary of the Navy with one who would infuse new energy and spirit into a department of the Government which has suffered so much from old fogyism,—who would bring to the discharge of its duties an *esprit de corps* which would insure reform, energy, and some degree of progress in the present old grannyisms of our naval bureaus,—we know no prominent Democrat of better qualifications than R. F. Stockton, of New Jersey."

We know of no other man whose appointment would receive such universal approbation; and all parties in New Jersey would feel a proud gratification at his selection.

From the Hunterdon Gazette, (Whig,) N. J.

COMMODORE STOCKTON AND THE NAVY DEPARTMENT.

It is pretty generally understood that Commodore Stockton is being warmly pressed by his friends as a candidate for Secretary of the Navy. Of all the gentlemen we have heard mentioned in connection with that station, we look upon the Commodore as the one best qualified to fill the post. We say this from no feeling of partiality for Mr. Stockton, personally or politically, but because we believe he is abundantly capable, from his knowledge of naval affairs, to fill, with credit to himself and honour to his native State, the position alluded to.

From the Trenton True American.

Commodore Stockton stands without a rival in naval exploits, and the nation unanimously accords to him pre-eminent qualifications to discharge the duties of that position which, the signs of the times indicate, will at no distant day demand his naval skill, dauntless courage, and unflinching patriotism.

From the Philadelphia Saturday Evening Courier.

DOINGS IN WASHINGTON AND BALTIMORE.

DEAR COURIER:—   WASHINGTON, D. C., June 11, 1852.

Congress has been in session near seven months, at an expense to the country of one million at least, and without accomplishing any important public business as yet. It will probably adjourn on the 16th of August, that having been designated as the day. On Monday, the election for Mayor of Washington resulted in favour of John M. Maury, Democrat, by eight hundred and ninety-three majority.

Having been present during the sitting in Baltimore of the recent Democratic Convention for nominating a Presidential candidate, I partook of the intense excitement which the occasion inspired, and will furnish such facts, in relation to the closing scenes, as will be likely to interest those of your numerous readers who have sought in vain for any mention of the name of the "Conqueror of California" in the Convention.

The public mind, outside the Convention, had settled down to the conviction that Commodore Stockton was to be the successful favourite, and so he unquestionably would, had his name been simply announced in compliance with the universal anticipation. There are different explanations given as to the neglect to fulfil the general expectation in reference to the Senator from New Jersey. The Public Ledger of your city, under the head of "A narrow escape from being a Candidate," credits the Trenton State Gazette with the assertion that Commodore Stockton had a narrow escape from being the Democratic candidate for the Presidency in this way:—"On Friday, a number of the States, among which was Virginia, became tired of voting for the old candidates, and satisfied that it was necessary to go for some new man, they determined to vote upon any one whom the Virginia delegation might agree upon. That delegation discussed the question on Friday night and till an early hour on Saturday morning. They were nearly equally divided between Stockton and Pierce; but, on taking the vote among themselves, Pierce obtained a majority of *one*, and the delegation therefore led off for him. It adds, that a majority of the New Jersey delegates were opposed to him, and two of them steadily refused till the last to vote for him. We know not how much of this statement agrees with the facts, but more unlikely things have happened in the Convention."

This is incorrect, inasmuch as there was at no time "a majority of the New Jersey delegates" opposed to their Senator, though the objection of one or two ultras did, it is true, prevent that entire unanimity in the State delegation without which the friends of the Commodore unwisely determined to withhold his name. This course was understood to be in compliance with the known wishes of Mr. Stockton himself, who had determined that no movement should be made in his behalf without the entire acquiescence of the delegation.

Thus it may justly be said that the presentation of the name of Commodore Stockton, and his nomination as a candidate for President of the United States by the Convention, was solely prevented by his own independent decision. Had his name been but mentioned before the Convention, it would have been hailed with acclamation, for those who were present agree that the strongest feeling prevailed in his favour, both within the Convention and without. At a large meeting held in Monument Square during the previous evening, the mention of the name of Stockton drew forth such rounds of applause as clearly indicated the public sentiment in the city which he once so gallantly aided in defending. The want of the entire unanimity on the part of the New Jersey delegation originated from the fact that the Commodore had, on the recent visit of Mr. Webster to Trenton, highly eulogized that eminent statesman, and also expressed his estimation of the principles of one of the signers of our ever-glorious Declaration of Independence.

These offences were still further heightened by the daring assumption that the labour of his own native State deserved better encouragement than it received. Such were the very grievous offences which alone prevented the unanimity that would have made a gallant, high-minded citizen of the State of New Jersey the next President of the United States.

Yours, truly.

From a New Jersey Paper, June, 1852.

COMMODORE STOCKTON.

The position of Commodore Stockton before the country is one of which he and the State may well be proud. For some time prior to the National Convention, by the spontaneous action of his friends in various parts of the Union his name was connected, in view of certain contingencies, with the Presidency; but, with consistent dignity, he stood aloof, and refused, even by the lifting of a finger, to promote what some might have considered a move calculated to make more intricate the already confused game on the Presidential board. On the eventful Friday, when every thing seemed to be chaos, some of his friends in New Jersey, New York, and the South, desired to bring forward his name as the rallying-point for the Convention. He was applied to, and promptly answered—"*It is not for me, gentlemen, to stir in this matter!*" Still, notwithstanding this, we learn from good authority, that when Virginia cast the die, the present illustrious nominee of the party only led our own favourite son ONE vote.

From the Richmond Whig, March, 1852.

COMMODORE STOCKTON.

A correspondent of the Washington Union communicates to that paper a long biographical sketch of Commodore Stockton. The gallant sailor has had a life of splendid heroism and adventure, and, we have no doubt, if nominated, would make a tall run for the Presidency. Who knows but the Democrats may compose their personal feuds by eventually uniting upon STOCKTON? Geographically, he stands midway between North and South, and perhaps politically he stands midway between Old Fogyism and Young America. His advocates could no doubt convince men of all sections and parties that he is decidedly a *Northern Southern* man, and emphatically a *Conservative Progressive.* They might also deny that the *soldiers* should always be put on the field for the Presidency in total exclusion of the *sailors.* The Navy is the favourite arm of the nation, and ought to come in, now and then, for a share of the Presidential prize-money. Mr. Stockton asked, in a late speech, "Did you ever see Jack on horseback?" We would not be greatly astonished if the next Democratic Convention, in case they are satisfied that General Scott will be the Whig nominee, should set Jack astride of the resolutions of '98, and then—*nous verrons.*

From the Newark Mercury.

COMMODORE STOCKTON AND NEW JERSEY.

We notice that some journals are engaged in slurring the position which Commodore Stockton occupied in the Democratic Baltimore Convention, and we think this in exceeding bad taste. Commodore Stockton would have been the nominee of the Democratic party but for his strict adherence to the interests of his native State. It was openly stated by the Virginia delegates that they would have preferred Stockton to Pierce but for the tariff sentiments of the former, and the nomination of Virginia would have made him the candidate of his party. We rejoice to say that political elevation cannot, now or prospectively, change the firm and decided attachment of our Democratic Senator to a principle which he believes to be identified with the interests of the country, and in which he is supported by the Democracy of his State. We feel that his devotion to the interests of New Jersey is not a fit subject for censure even in a Whig press.

While we are far from coinciding with Commodore Stockton in all his views, and while we think him essentially wrong on the Slavery question, we do admire his real ability, his generous impulses, his straightforward manliness of purpose, and his wearing his party principles loosely about him when they come in contact with the interests of the country. For his course in the Senate of the United States he is entitled to the thanks of Jerseymen. He has ably represented the humane sentiments of our people in his opposition to the restoration of the sailor's lash; he has nobly vindicated New Jersey interests in demanding ampler protection for her iron and her manufactures; he has never swerved from upholding in his position the character and claims of his native State; and, if this course has been instrumental in defeating his .political prospects, far be it from us to join in his condemnation. The truth is, we cannot conceive how Commodore Stockton could have been controlled sufficiently to have got one foot on such a platform as that made at Baltimore.

The Washington correspondent of the *New Orleans Delta* thinks that Commodore Stockton stands a chance for the nomination for the Presidency by the Baltimore Convention. He writes:—

"I find that many persons in and out of Congress think that Commodore Stockton has a very good chance for the nomination at Baltimore. He will not be brought forward until the prominent candidates shall have been tried and shall have failed. No one of them, it is believed, could, under present circumstances, obtain a vote of two-thirds; and it is not likely that in sixty days the state of things will be much changed. The rivalry of the prominent men, of which we have such strong evidence here, will probably prevent their friends from combining in favour of any one of them. They must, therefore, compromise upon some new candidate. The New York delegation will settle the matter by leading off for Stockton. The two-thirds will soon follow."

The correspondent of the *New York Journal of Commerce* expresses a similar opinion.

From the New York Times.

For President, R. F. Stockton.

Very much stranger things have happened than the nomination of such a ticket. The chances for Mr. Polk were far less respectable in 1844. The name of that gentleman had been unheard of, until announced by the Baltimore Convention. His life was unwritten and but half lived. His claims to Presidential honours were so many drafts upon an uncertain future.

Present circumstances seem to flush the prospects of the Captain with the hues of success. He stands high with his party. His temporary following of strange gods in the days of Harrison and Tyler has only served to set off his subsequent fidelity. He has the means at his disposal to pay the most extravagant of costs in the prosecution of the campaign. He is free from the priggishness of old fogyism, and equally free from the crazy vagaries of Young America. Upon the Slavery question he is sound to the core—entirely sound. His family connections, his Carolinian inheritance, his Virginian gold-mines, are deposited collaterals for his reliability upon all questions in which the peculiar institution is involved. His positions upon foreign policy are remarkably safe and conservative. Indeed, as a public man, it would be difficult to pick out another so entirely spotless in all that relates to partisan qualifications. His style of talk out-doors and on the stump is irresistible. There is something so free, candid, and nautical, in his manners, such a winning disregard of partisan ties, a contempt so lofty for conventionalities and formalities of every kind, so many piquant inconsistencies, so much of confiding *naïveté*, that he springs close to and at once clenches the popular heart. That his spirit spurns and soars immeasurably above the littleness of party, is demonstrated at every fitting opportunity. How frank and manly his panegyric of the man who may, in a few short months, be his rival in the race of fame?

APPENDIX E.

Address of Commodore R. F. Stockton to the People of New Jersey, in relation to the existing contracts between the State and the united Delaware and Raritan Canal and Camden and Amboy Railroad Companies, September 24, 1849.

FELLOW-CITIZENS:—Upon the faith of a contract made with the State of New Jersey in the years 1830, '31, '32, I invested a very large amount of my property in the enterprise of constructing a Canal and Railroad across the State of New Jersey.

I have been from the first, and I am at this day, I believe, the largest stockholder of the united Delaware and Raritan Canal and Camden and Amboy Railroad and Transportation Companies.

On my return from California, I found that suits had been commenced against the Railroad Company by persons alleging that they had been overcharged some small amount in the transportation of articles of merchandise between New York and Trenton, in the companies' lines. These suits were founded on an act of the Legislature, passed in 1839, and they question a construction of the company's charter, which for fifteen years had been unquestioned, and was supposed to be free from doubt.

The question involved is clearly one of law. The first case is now pending before the highest judicial court in the State. I have been early taught that causes pending in a court of justice were only to be discussed at the bar of the court. But I have read long and laboured legal arguments in the *public newspapers*, attempting to sustain the claims of these persons against the company, and in *one newspaper*, at least, published in New Jersey, it has been stated that the editor has "*authority*" for saying that the case will be decided against the company.

I am not surprised; for I presume this mode of dealing with causes in court affecting private property is part of the new-born code of rights of which I propose to speak. Cotemporary with these lawsuits, a series of abusive articles has been commenced and continued in the public newspapers, in and out of the State, full of false charges against the companies and slanderous accusations of their officers. In reference to these it is sufficient to say at present that, at the request of the companies, commissioners have been appointed by the Legislature, who have the subject of these charges under examination. But certain political agitators, who have been labouring to poison the public mind against the companies, have at length come before the people with an address and resolutions, emanating from what they call a State Convention, in which the ground is broadly and deliberately taken that *a part of the existing contract between the State and the companies is null and void;* and the public are called upon to make *this* the great question in the election of members of the ensuing legislature.

This is the first time in the history of New Jersey, I believe, that her citizens have been called upon to settle the rights of private property and the validity of contracts *at the polls,* amid the conflict of party politics and through the machinery of party organization; and as I am one of the chief victims marked for the sacrifice, and it is proposed to begin this career of improvement in legal science by divesting me of my property without judge or jury, and through my purse sweat the public treasury, it is proper perhaps that I should ask a hearing, and say that I do not mean to be an unresisting victim.

But, first of all, I feel that I ought to say to you, my fellow-citizens, that this address is not prompted by any doubt of your intelligence or integrity.

I was born among you, as were my ancestors. Through many years of public service, in scenes of difficulty, privation, and danger, the thought of my native State, her honour, her interest, and her glory, have been the lights that led me in the path of duty; and I cannot, and will not, doubt her fidelity to law and principle and justice. But facts misrepresented, falsehood and slander often repeated and not contradicted, in time come to be received by the public as truth; and history, and principle, and common justice, are hence liable to monstrous perversions.

I was not in the State of New Jersey in 1830, when the acts incorporating the Delaware and Raritan Canal and Camden and Amboy Railroad Companies were passed, and had nothing to do with framing their charters. I was always opposed to the present system. I said that the State had a valuable farm and ought to work it herself, and it was not until the people had deliberately, after years of agitation on the subject, determined in the first place to lease the right of way, and, in the second place, to give all necessary protection to secure the construction of her various improvements, that I came forward to give my aid to these well-settled principles and the people's wishes. This principle of protection, falsely called monopoly, was settled and adopted many years before the canal and railroad charters were passed. The Delaware Bridge, the bridges over the Passaic and Hackensack Rivers, the Morris Canal, and the charter for the Delaware and Raritan Canal, passed in 1824, are monuments to show that this policy of protection was no new thing, introduced for the first time in our charters. I repeat that the present policy is, as it always has been, *protection*, not *monopoly*. I am no more a monopolist than the man who rents my farm; we both rent under written agreements, and are both protected in our rights by the same laws. But it is an odious cabalistic word, well suited at all times for the use of the political demagogue, especially for the bar-room and tippling-houses. It can be pronounced by the ignorant or the wise, by the drunkard or the sober man, and means about as much in the mouth of the one as of the other.

Returning to the State some time after the charters were passed, I learned that the stock of the railroad company had been subscribed; that of fifteen thousand shares of the canal stock only eleven hundred and thirty-four shares had been taken. The books had been closed—the hope of digging the canal abandoned. There was no difficulty about the *railroad;* that was considered a safe enterprise, with the protection already stipulated for in the charter.

My private fortune was at this time safely invested, yielding me an ample income; I was absorbed in my profession, and desired no other business.

I was importuned for aid. I was assured that if the canal failed now it was lost forever; and, deeming the canal of infinite importance to the State and the nation, I subscribed the balance of the stock necessary to preserve the charter, amounting to over four hundred thousand dollars. From that time to the meeting of the next Legislature, 1831, every effort was made to enlist capitalists in New Jersey, New York, Pennsylvania, and elsewhere, in the enterprise, but in vain. Aid was solicited from the General Government and refused.

These facts were laid before the Legislature, and they were asked to invest the company with the power to construct a railroad in connection with and on the bank of the canal, as the means of inducing the subscription of the balance of the stock. This the Legislature refused. There was a protection contained in the charter of the railroad company. But they passed an act, in 1831, which, while it required the proposed dimensions of the canal to be increased from fifty to seventy-five feet in width, at an additional expense of more than a million of dollars, held out the prospect of a railroad grant, if the company would first complete the canal. This act alarmed the stockholders of the railroad company. The two companies came in conflict. The case stood thus:—

The canal company could not go on without railroad privileges. The railroad company would not proceed with their work if another railroad was to be authorized to compete with them. Both enterprises were in jeopardy, when the compromise was finally effected by the act of 1832, consolidating the stock of the two companies, and thus securing the success of both. The stock of both companies was now subscribed. But it was soon perceived that the increase in the size of the canal, stipulated by the late act, and other unforeseen contingencies, would render a loan of more than two millions beyond the whole capital stock subscribed, necessary to complete the two works. The faith of capitalists was shaken by this announcement. It was found that something more definite in the way of protection was necessary to restore it. The companies came to the Legislature again, and to meet the exigency—*to hold out a sufficient inducement to moneyed men* to loan the funds necessary to complete the works, and in consideration of the transfer of one thousand shares of the joint stock to the State, and the guarantee of at least thirty thousand dollars a year transit-duties and the dividends on their shares—the act of March, 1832, was passed, completing the contract as *it now stands between the State and the companies.*

What is the Contract?

New Jersey has leased the right of way across the State to these companies for the purpose of a canal, for fifty years—for the purpose of a railroad, for thirty years. The canal and railroad to be built at the expense and risk of the lessees, and, at the end of the leases, the State to have a right to take the works at an appraised valuation, not to exceed the cost. The lessees pay the State, for this lease, the dividends on two thousand shares of their stock, and transit-duties on every passenger and ton of merchandise carried across the State, amounting already to eighty thousand dollars a year; and the whole amount which has been received by the State from the companies, up to the present time, exceeds eight hundred thousand dollars, besides two thousand shares of stock, the first cost of which was two hundred thousand dollars. Let me again remind you that *the fee* is in the State; *we* are merely the lessees, and no more monopolists than any farmer who leases a piece of land, or any mechanic who leases a dwelling-house or shop: and, on the other hand, the State agrees that no other railroad shall be authorized during the continuance of the charter, to compete with *these lessees* in the business of carrying between New York and Philadelphia.

It is a contract, therefore, in which there is a perfect mutuality. *Both parties are bound, and both benefited.*

How was it made?

By the people, through their representatives in the Legislature; by solemn laws deliberately passed through all the constitutional forms, after many years' excitement and discussion throughout the State, and accepted by the companies.

When made?

Before the works were commenced, and during their progress, on the faith of the State, I invested nearly my whole fortune, as have others, in these works. On the faith of the State the company borrowed three millions of dollars, to enable them to fulfil their part of the contract; and I have spent nearly twenty years of my life in doing all I could for the interest of the State as well as my own. The State has had not only the use of my fortune, but of eighteen years' hard work, without paying me one dollar for either. And will you, fellow-citizens, after all this, permit socialists, speculators, or demagogues of whatever degree, to bring this matter into party politics, and to affix a foul blot on your fair fame, by plundering my family, my friends, and myself, in the name of the State?

It is an executed contract.

The companies have performed their part of it; have completed the works as required, and paid the consideration-money annually to the State for seventeen years, according to the terms of the contract. The State has never questioned its validity. For seventeen years under this contract, the State has received every year the money-consideration which the contract called for; thus re-affirming it every year. Your State-prison, your lunatic-asylum, your very capitol, stand as witnesses of the validity, as the benefit of the contract, for they were built by the consideration-money paid and received under it. Besides all this, the Legislature have, at various periods within these seventeen years, re-affirmed its validity by Acts and Resolutions:

1. In 1835, the Legislature passed this resolution with only two dissenting voices in the Council.

"Resolved, by the Council and General Assembly of the State of New Jersey, that the passage of any act by this Legislature, authorizing or recognising any other railroad or roads, which shall be intended or used for the transportation of passengers or merchandise between the cities of New York and Philadelphia, would *be unjust*, impolitic, in violation of the plighted faith of the State, and deeply injurious to its interests."

2. In the preamble and resolutions passed in 1835–36, raising a committee to ascertain upon what terms the companies would surrender their works to the State, reciting that "whereas, by the laws heretofore passed by the Legislature of this State, certain exclusive privileges were conferred upon the Delaware and Raritan Canal and the Camden and Amboy Railroad and Transportation Companies, and whereas, it is represented that a large portion of the people of New Jersey are desirous that those privileges should be extinguished in some just, honourable, and legal manner, and whereas, it is *manifest* that this desirable object *can alone be obtained by and with the consent of the said companies*, therefore resolved."

3. By an act passed 1837, proposing "with the consent of the companies to alter the contract, allowing them to charge the sum of *four dollars* for each passenger carried on any of the railroads of said companies to and from the cities of New York and Philadelphia by day, and *five dollars* by night, provided, that they shall pay into the Treasury of this State *one-half* of any sum over three dollars they may charge each passenger so carried. That the revenue which may from time to time be received from the said companies, after paying the State-tax out of the same, shall be invested by the treasurer of this State, under direction of the Governor, Vice-President of Council, and Speaker of House of Assembly for the time being, as a specific fund for the redemption of the railroad and railroad-appendages of the said companies, as soon as the same shall become redeemable." This act the companies have not as yet thought proper to accept.

4. By an act of the same date, allowing the companies to construct a railroad from Bordentown to New Brunswick, with a branch to the Delaware Bridge at Trenton, reciting that, "for the purpose of enabling them to construct said roads, the said united Delaware and Raritan Canal and Camden and Amboy Railroad Companies be, and they hereby are, invested with all the power and authority which they now possess, and entitled to *all the privileges* and emoluments to which they are now entitled, under an act entitled an Act to incorporate the Delaware and Raritan Canal Company, and an act entitled an Act to incorporate the Camden and Amboy Railroad and Transportation Company, and the *several acts supplementary to said acts*, or either of these, as far as the provisions thereof are now in force and not repealed, altered or amended by subsequent acts."

Notwithstanding the united companies were to make the road thus authorized, they deemed it necessary to insert in this act two important provisions:—

1st. "That nothing in this act contained shall be construed, held, deemed, or taken in any way to affect, impair, or defeat the right of the State of New Jersey of, in, or to, *the shares they now hold* of the capital stock of said companies, or the interest accruing therefrom—or the transit duties or the right of redeeming said works. And 2d, that the act should not become a law until formally accepted by said companies, and the assent duly filed."

These references show that successive Legislatures coming fresh from the people have over and over again affirmed and re-affirmed the binding validity of the contract between the State and the companies, by repeated solemn acts and resolutions at various times, and under various circumstances, since 1830.

So that if a contract solemnly made by public laws—passed, affirmed and re-affirmed by successive Legislatures, approved by the people, accepted by the party contracted with, uniformly recognised—the consideration paid and received annually for seventeen years—executed by the parties, up to the present time—is a binding valid contract, upon which the citizen can rely for the security of property invested under it, *this is such a contract.*

The two following propositions will not be denied by any one.

1. That this is in form a legal contract: a valuable franchise is granted by one party, a valuable consideration paid for it by the other.

2. That this contract was made and entered into by both parties upon full advisement. There was no misunderstanding about it; there is no ambiguity in it. *Both parties intended to become solemnly and legally bound by it, the one to the other.* The Legislature agreed, if we would invest our fortunes in the construction of a canal and railroad across New Jersey, pay them the annual dividends on $£00,000 of stock, transit-duties on every passenger and ton of merchandise we carried on these works across the State, and allowed them to redeem the works at cost, in thirty and fifty years, that they would not during these periods allow other roads and canals to be chartered to compete with us. We agreed, on our part, to accept these terms. We invested our fortunes in making the canal and railroads; we have paid semi-annually the consideration stipulated for seventeen years; we recognise the State's right to redeem according to the agreement.

Now if any citizen of New Jersey will stand up and say to me, *I repudiate this contract; the Legislature had no right to make it; I will not abide by it;* I beg leave to ask him, Were not the Legislatures of 1830, of '32, of '35, and '37, your Representatives? Did you not elect them? Did you not know that they in your name made, affirmed, and re-affirmed these contracts with me and my associate stockholders? Did you not stand by and see me invest my fortune in these works upon the faith of these agreements? Did you give me notice that you would not abide by them? Have you not, through your agents, received from us every year for seventeen years the consideration we agreed to pay in conformity with the stipulations of this contract? and have you not, through your agents, expended this money in the erection of your public buildings and in the support of your State government? And when he has answered these questions, I ask him by what code of morals he reconciles his conduct with his conscience.

But is the contract legal?

I am no lawyer, but we have not failed to inquire of those who are. I refer to the brief extracts which follow, taken from opinions long in my possession. Horace Binney and the late Charles Chauncey say, that the clause granting protection in the act of 1832 is substantially a promise by the Legislature that no law shall be passed to authorize the construction of a railroad contrary to the import of the engagement, *is free from doubt.* This species of engagement is not without precedent in the legislation both of the United States and the States.

That it is within the competency of the States, generally seems to have been the opinion from the time of the Revolution. Thinking, as we do, that the Legislature of New Jersey may lawfully grant an exclusive franchise of making a railroad for the transportation of passengers and merchandise between certain points,—that they have done so for a valuable consideration by the supplemental charter in question, and that the law by which they have done it is in the nature of a contract with the canal and railroad companies,—we are of opinion that a repeal of that law, and the incorporation of another company to compete in business with these companies, *would be a violation of the faith of the State, and of the Constitution of the United States,* and would therefore be without legal effect.

George Wood, Ogden Hoffman, and the late David B. Ogden of New York, say, we are satisfied that the Legislature of New Jersey were clothed with sufficient power to pass such an act, (1832,) and that the Legislature, having thereby entered into a compact with the companies not to permit the construction of another railroad within the prescribed period and the prescribed local limits, it was competent for them to do so, and falls within the scope of their legitimate and constitutional power. It is true that no such power is given to them by the Constitution in express terms, nor was it necessary. That instrument contains a broad grant of sovereign power, in the following language:—

"The Government of this Province shall be vested in a Governor, Legislative Council, and General Assembly." This general grant of sovereign power unquestionably embraces the power alluded to. The late Isaac H. Williamson and Garret D. Wall say, "after deliberate consideration of the act of the Legislature of March 2, 1832, they are clearly of opinion that the act is constitutional and a valid exercise of legislative power, and that the Legislature is legally restrained from passing any laws impairing the privileges thereby granted. The prohibitory clause in the Constitution of the United States extends to contracts with a State as a party, as well as to contracts between individuals; and when a law is in its nature a contract, a repeal of this law cannot divest those rights, *and a party to a contract cannot pronounce its own deed invalid,* although the party be a sovereign State." And *Chief-Justice Marshall* says "that the principle that one legislature is competent to repeal any act which a former legislature was competent to pass, and that one legislature cannot abridge the powers of a succeeding legislature, is correct *as far only as respects general legislation;*" and *Judge Story* says:—"It has been decided upon solemn argument, in the Supreme Court of the United States, that contracts and grants made by a State are not less within the reach of this prohibition of the Constitution against impairing the obligation of contracts, than contracts and grants of private persons." The late Samuel L. Southard says:—"I have examined with proper care the several laws of New Jersey relating to the Delaware and Raritan Canal and Camden and Amboy Railroad Companies, and am of opinion that the Legislature had the clear constitutional power to pass those laws, and that they are obligatory upon the people, judicial tribunals, and the Legislature of the State. These laws, and the proceedings had under them, create a valid contract, founded on good and valuable consideration, which the Legislature of the State had a right to make, and which it cannot now violate without a disregard of legal obligations and good faith, and a forfeiture on its part of the benefits secured by the contract with the State." These opinions, and others in my possession, fortified by numerous legal authorities, can leave no doubt in any candid mind—if indeed such a mind could ever upon due reflection have entertained a doubt—as to the validity of our contract with the State. Among them are names high in the esteem and dear to the memory of Jerseymen,—names that adorn the annals of American jurisprudence, and whose opinions are of the highest authority.

I am not aware that those who have sought at different times to divest us of our property have ever been able to produce the opinion of any lawyer of established reputation as a jurist, favourable to their views, except the present Chief-Justice Taney, given when at the bar; and he admits that this is a contract, and, if the Legislature had power to make it, it is binding. He admits that "there would appear to be high authority for regarding this power as an incident to the power of legislation." In the Act of Congress incorporating the Bank of the United States, there is, he says, "an agreement on the part of the United States not to authorize any other bank out of the District of Columbia during the existence of that charter; and similar pledges may be found in similar cases in the Legislatures of different States, where the Constitution has not conferred on the Legislature the power to make them."

This is his own language; and yet, without citing a single adjudicated case to support him, or pretending that any one of these similar contracts made either by Congress or any of the various States have in a single instance been ever doubted, he ventures his naked opinion that as the Constitution of New Jersey did not expressly, in very terms, authorize the Legislature to make such a contract, it could not do it.

With unfeigned respect for Mr. Taney, if I understand his argument, it answers itself. He says, "It is now too well settled to be disputed that a charter granted by a State to a Company incorporated to make a road or canal, where the funds for the work are provided by individuals, is *a contract* on the part of the State; and the *public cannot* by subsequent legislation, without the consent of the corporation, alter the terms of the charter." He says, further, "that the power claimed by the Legislature in this instance is that of *restricting* the *power of succeeding Legislatures* in the exercise of certain legislative functions, and they have by *a contract with individual corporations* engaged that the Representatives of the people of New Jersey shall not for a specified time exercise the power of incorporating a Company for the purpose of making a railroad in a certain part of the State." Then he adds, "The question is, Have the people of New Jersey delegated to the legislative body the power of making such a *contract?* There is no clause in the Constitution of New Jersey which gives this power specifically;" therefore, he concludes that the Legislature had not the power.

Now, this is the argument:—the grant by the Legislature of a charter *is a contract which a subsequent Legislature cannot repeal.* But this contract *limits the power of a succeeding Legislature,* and therefore is not binding. The answer is, The *first case* is as much a limitation of the power of the Legislature as the second; he admits one is a good contract, and thinks the other bad. If both are contracts, if both limit the power of succeeding Legislatures, if no power to make either one or the other is specifically given in the Constitution, as is admitted, it seems clearly a *non sequitur* to say that the law is invalid for *a reason* that applies equally to the first, which is admitted to be valid. In fewer words, he admits that the Legislature have *power* to make a contract.

2d. That a contract made between the Legislature and a corporation is irrepealable.

3d. That the protection clause in the act of March, 1832, is a contract between the Legislature and the companies, but, because the Constitution gives no specific power to make *such a contract,* they have no power to make it.

The idea that one Legislature has as much power as another seems to be as potent a knot-cutter, in the opinion of some men, as the sword of Alexander. Nobody denies the proposition. What I maintain is that no Legislature in New Jersey ever had *the power to repudiate a contract without compensation to the parties injured.*

I have as much power to-day as I had yesterday. The joint companies have as much power to-day as they had in 1832. The Legislature of 1850 will have as much power as any Legislature which preceded it. But that power will not enable me to-day with impunity to repudiate a contract I made yesterday, nor the companies, nor the Legislature, to repudiate theirs. The Constitution of the United States says to the States, as the law says to me, and as authoritatively, You shall not *impair,* much less destroy, the *obligation of contracts.*

Upon the whole, I think Mr. Taney's opinion is more in our favour than against us. Be that as it may, I am quite ready to appeal from Mr. Taney the Advocate to Mr. Taney the Chief-Justice of the United States. Mr. Taney the Advocate, interested and excited, is not Mr. Taney the Chief-Justice, mild, amiable, and philosophical.

I have read the address and resolutions which the assembly calling themselves an anti-monopoly convention recently adopted at Trenton. If I understand these papers, they put their whole case within a very small compass; the address says, "We are as jealous of the honour of the State as any one; we would resist every attempt to violate its *plighted faith;* whatever *contract* the State may have with the companies, we wish to see executed to the very letter "

Very well: be it so. But the address proceeds :—" The act of 1830 and the supplement of 1831 contain *contracts.* But the *supplement of* 1832, *which creates the monopoly power, does not.* It is a mere law enacted by one Legislature and of course repealable by any Legislature." The whole case then is put upon the solution:—Does the act of 1832 contain a contract? What difference in principle is there to be found between the supplements of 1831 and 1832? In both supplements a valuable franchise is granted by one party and a valuable consideration paid for it by the other; if one is a contract, the other must necessarily be so; there is no difference in the principle.

Let us see how it is. Section 1 of the act of 1832 stipulates *for the companies* that they shall transfer one thousand shares of their stock (one hundred thousand dollars) to this State, with all the instalments paid in full. Section 2 stipulates *for the State* that it shall not be lawful at any time during the railroad charter to construct any other railroad or roads to compete with the company in transportation between New York and Philadelphia. Section 3 stipulates for the companies that they shall guarantee thirty thousand dollars a year to the State from the dividends on their shares and the transit-duties required by the act of 1830. Section 7 requires the assent of the companies to the stipulations of this act; and that assent is executed in due form of law and filed.

The stock was transferred in 1832, the thirty thousand dollars guaranteed, met and paid annually, and for seventeen years both parties have treated it as a contract. If it is not a contract, the original charter is not a contract. It is a part of the charter; it is another feature added with the consent of the companies to the charter. If any part of the charter be violated, the whole is violated: the charter and the supplements are one and inseparable. If it is not a contract, I should like to know what it is. And this is all I have to say about the legal doctrines of their address.

A word as to the wishes of those who thus come before the public. They say in their address, "We wish to have *free* roads, *free* ferries, *free* ingress and egress and *free* transit in, out, and over the State. We wish to be equally free from the tyranny of railroad kings, ferry kings, and turnpike kings; this is what we aim at, and what we call upon the people of the State to unite in achieving." And the preamble to their resolutions, setting forth the rights and wrongs asserted and complained of, enumerates among those rights the making of roads where they please and over anybody's land they please; among their wrongs, "that sundry persons, on pretence of grants alleged to have been obtained at remote periods, have obtained control of *exclusive bodies of land,* embracing landing-places, and ferries, and all the places at which such ferries could be established." A great deal has been said in like phrases, by similar rhetoricians, about the somewhat extensive monopolies of property of other descriptions, particularly of a class of lords familiarly known in this State as *landlords.* But it seems that turnpikes, ferries, and railroads, possess the exclusive power of constituting kings; though, for myself, I never could perceive how the possession of a certificate of road or ferry stock made a man a king.

But is this doctrine of free rights any thing more or less than the specious idea of socialism rife in our day? Is it not of the same species as the cant about *free* farms, *free* houses, *free* corn-cribs, and *free* pockets? All property is held by contract. Every farmer has a monopoly in his farm, if the "*exclusive right"* to it is a monopoly; and it may be well for the citizens to consider whether the doctrine of treating contracts as things, in derogation of popular rights, will stop with the crusade against railroad, ferry, and turnpike contracts. It will be well for them to remember that it is as easy to put a firebrand to a dwelling-house or a barn as it is to put a pickaxe to a railroad.

These reformers in substance say, Let the Legislature pass an act declaring the contract by which these stockholders hold a portion of their property, invalid, and we will take the risk of getting our share of railroad property; and may they not, if they succeed, say next, Let the Legislature pass a law declaring all title-deeds invalid, and we will take the risk of taking our share of the land? The complaint against the *large land proprietors,* bodied forth in the preamble to the resolutions, foreshadows this idea already. I trust, therefore, my fellow-citizens, who are invited to join in the business of achieving the enterprise of making common stock of my property, will pause, and consider whether they have not some *exclusive privileges* in houses or farms or factories, in banks or mills, in bridges or shops or fisheries that may by-and-by be sought after, as equally convenient and proper articles to be turned in as common stock in order that the area of freedom may be still farther enlarged. They want free roads. But it costs money to make roads, particularly railroads and turnpikes. Money is property, and when invested in roads by private individuals, roads become property, and, unless a mode be discovered of making roads *without money*, the vast multiplication proposed would probably result in the multiplication to an indefinite extent of the odious article of *railroad kings, turnpike kings, and ferry kings;* and indeed their publications intimate that they propose to go largely into the business themselves.

But a few words more. Constitutions are the *contracts* mutually agreed upon by associations or masses, defining individual rights and guaranteeing their protection in the name of the whole.

The men of the Revolution who framed the Constitution of this republic are in their graves. But their work still lives. "May it be perpetual!" The life-blood of our Revolutionary fathers secured it. The life-blood of their sons will be shed freely in its defence. *"No State shall pass any law impairing the obligation of contracts,"* is its language; and I doubt not, whatever demagogues and pretended reformers of our institutions may say, there are few true Jerseymen who will not respond with a hearty *Amen!*

I make this appeal to you, fellow-citizens, in behalf of a principle affecting the security of my property and yours. I make it to you because your power is invoked to aid in the repudiation of a contract to which this state is a party. I make it to you as honest men, intelligent, law-abiding, conservative men, and feel confident that you will not be found willing to do an act as *citizens* which you would scorn to do as *men.*

It has been and shall be my constant aim and desire, as a stockholder and officer of the joint companies, to do whatever I can to meet the public wants and conform to the wishes of my fellow-citizens. This sentiment pervades the companies. We have removed all reasonable causes of complaint, as fast as we have, on examination, been satisfied it was practicable to do so. The fares and freights have both been put down to a point, as far as I can learn, satisfactory to the great mass of the people.

It is our intent and desire to accommodate the people to the best of our ability. And we shall not fail to do so. We have invested, and have induced others to invest, millions of dollars in Jersey property, in canals and railroads, works of public improvement and universal benefit, long desired and clamoured after, but never ventured on till we took the hazard of their construction on the faith of a clear and explicit agreement with the State.

Our improvements have added millions to the value of property in New Jersey. They have made the treasury rich and erected public works of necessity and charity. They have relieved the people from the burden of a State tax. They have afforded facilities for travel and transportation equal to those possessed anywhere on the continent. A few years only remain, and then the State has the *right* to take them.

We encountered the risk and the labour. The State risked nothing, and reaps a large share of the profits, with a reversion of the whole. These great works completed rest in the bosom of New Jersey, and there they will remain forever. They have a place in the history of the past, and they will have a place in the history of the future. If that future history shall point to them as memorials of the broken faith and violated contracts of New Jersey, it shall record on the same page that so foul a stain upon her escutcheon was not impressed without resistance from her sons.

Fellow-citizens—I submit this last appeal to your patriotism and to your honour with undoubted confidence—with these two remarks:—

1. It is clearly shown that the right of way across this State has been leased to the joint companies under a contract which cannot with honour or safety be destroyed without the consent of both the contracting parties.

2. The joint companies are satisfied with the contract, but they are willing to yield any thing and every thing to the public which can be demanded by justice or accepted with honour.

If therefore the people of New Jersey are of opinion that the experiment has been sufficiently tried, and are desirous to take immediate possession of all the railroads of the companies, I think (though I speak for myself alone) that an arrangement can be made by which the State may be enabled to do so, and to pay for them, within fifteen years, without the hazard of a dollar, and without any sacrifice of her own unsullied honour, or the property of individuals who have confidingly pledged their all on the integrity of their fellow-citizens.

R. F. STOCKTON.

September 24th, 1849.

From the National Intelligencer of September 6, 1824.

WE avail ourselves of the first spare room to render justice to Lieutenant R. F. Stockton, who presided at a meeting at Princeton, July 14, 1824, at which an auxiliary colonization society was formed, selecting from the account of the meeting the Address which he delivered on that occasion. On motion made and seconded, Robert Field Stockton, Esq., of the United States Navy, was requested to take the chair; and, on taking the chair, opened the meeting with the following Address :—

The promptness with which I accept this high honour which you, my fellow-citizens, have conferred upon me, arises not from any presumption of my own worthiness, but from an unwillingness to slight, in the least degree, the smallest mark of your esteem. The usual embarrassments which are experienced upon the first occasion of a young man's addressing a public assembly are much increased by the peculiar circumstances under which I am called upon to fulfil the duties of your chairman; and, perceiving among this audience some of the most learned and distinguished men, before whose age and experience it would better become me to be silent, I confess my confidence has almost forsaken me; and my mind would surely sink under the weight of this exertion, did I not know that all the deficiencies of the person addressing you will readily be made up by the intelligence and sagacity of those who hear him.

In conformity with the common practice upon such occasions, I beg your indulgence while I shall endeavour, in the briefest manner, to give an outline of the design, commencement, and progress of the AMERICAN SOCIETY FOR COLONIZING THE FREE PEOPLE OF COLOUR OF THE UNITED STATES, and in aid of which this public meeting has been called, leaving it to be filled up by gentlemen who are much more competent, and no doubt prepared, to give this matter a thorough investigation.

Slavery, with all its unprecedented atrocities, had, for many years, been the constant theme of reflection and discussion among the philanthropists of the world; and in no country were their exertions to put an end to that traffic and to make amends for the mistaken policy and cruel inhumanity of our progenitors more zealous and sincere than in this our own. Various had been the suggestions and plans of the friends of justice and humanity, to put a stop to that trade, and for the gradual abolition of slavery throughout the country. But no man was found sufficiently bold and able to lay before the public a well-digested plan, obviating the objections which had always been raised against this effort of benevolence, (the greatest of which was the letting loose upon the community of the United States such a body of men who had no important interest at stake, nor any common concern in the permanency of our institutions,) until the Rev. Mr. Finley, of this State, with the assistance of others, made known the present scheme of the American Colonization Society

The remembrance of Mr. Finley's exalted virtues and steady perseverance in the paths of rectitude and honour and humanity swell my bosom with emotions not easily to be checked; for to none were they better known than to myself, having been one of his pupils; and may I be permitted on this occasion to offer my humble, but sincere, tribute of respect to the memory of one so great and so good? His object was national as well as humane and religious. The nation ought, and I have no doubt will, honour him. If those, then, who are connected with him by no other tie than that of national pride, will respect and cherish his memory, where would you draw the limits to that ardent and enthusiastic regard which every friend may be allowed to entertain for his character? I have said he was a good man; and, as it is the highest eulogium that can be bestowed upon any one, I will leave this subject, pleasing as it is, for the purpose of performing my duty and relieving you, as soon as possible, from the fatigue of hearing me, and be myself relieved from that perturbation of mind which arises from the novelty of my situation.

It has been stated that the objects of the authors of that institution were national and religious; but, perhaps, it will not be amiss to be a little more particular and minute, as there appears to be some misunderstanding of that particular.

Their first and great object was a gradual abolition of slavery. They perceived the dangers that would result from the liberation of slaves in any number until some suitable place beyond the limits of the United States had been prepared for their reception, and, therefore, proposed the plan which is now in successful operation.

A second motive was to reclaim the inhabitants of Africa from savageness and brutality. That vast continent is said to contain fifty millions of inhabitants, whose pleasures are sloth and idleness; their employment, rapine and murder; their knowledge, treachery; their government, force, cruelty, and oppression; their religion, a blind devotion to the most profane and bloody superstitions; and, in truth, the whole of that immense population vitiated and debased by the most profound ignorance and unrestrained barbarism. To civilize this degenerate people, to change their ignorance into knowledge, their horrible superstition into a right understanding of the Christian religion, their treachery into good faith, and their slothfulness into industry, are among the results contemplated by the proposed plan of the American Colonization Society.

A third motive, that was strong in its operation upon the mind of Mr. Finley and his coadjutors, was the suppression of the slave-trade. I need not detain you by any comment upon the wickedness and barbarity of that trade; it has been so often the theme of just reproach and severe invective, and all Christendom seems to have settled down upon the principle that such traffickers are "hostes humani generis." But, as the first founders of that institution have so often been accused of extravagant and visionary expectations, it may not be unbecoming in me to state how it was expected that the establishment of a colony on the coast of Africa would operate upon that trade.

All the inhabitants of that region, south of the Great Desert, have been for ages constantly supplied with rum, tobacco, pipes, &c. &c. through the instrumentality of the slave-traders; and, having been led to believe that their supply of those articles depended entirely upon the prosecution and prosperity of that trade, they are continually engaged in wars for the purpose of its continuation. They have been led from the cultivation of their rich and luxuriant soil, and even from the chase, the legitimate pursuit and manly employment of savage life, to the unnatural practice of speculating in human blood! No rational mind can believe that the feelings of relation, and friend, and tribe, and countryman, could have been originally denied to this people; but rather that it had been paralyzed by the prospect of gain, the removal of which powerful principle would restore to the African, in full force, his natural regards and friendships. It was, therefore, believed that the establishment of a colony in the heart of the slave-trade would lead them to the cultivation of their land and the ardour of the chase as a more quiet and easy mode of obtaining those articles of European luxury which have become almost necessary to their existence.

Such were the views and intentions upon which the American Society for Colonizing the Free People of Colour in the United States was instituted. This scheme had no sooner been promulgated than an attack was made upon the purity of its principles. It was thought by the inhabitants of the Southern section of the country to be a plan generated in the North to operate against the institutions of the South; and in the North it was thought to be a Southern project to get rid of the free blacks only that they might tighten the chains of slavery. Steady perseverance, however, overcame misrepresentation and calumny, and they both yielded to the irresistible force of truth and humanity. A cry of visionary enthusiasm was, however, still heard. The constant exclamation was, "Show us that your plans are feasible; convince us that the thing can be done."

The managers went to the experiment elated with hope and joy, and, after great exertion, fitted out an expedition to the island of Sherbro. Intelligence from that expedition of a most disastrous nature soon reached the United States. It wrung the hearts of every friend of the society and checked, for a time, (until the true cause of that melancholy misfortune could be clearly understood,) the exertions of the managers.

Although it was necessary at that time that the cause should be explained, it is not so now in the present advanced state of the society's affairs; for the pestilence of the island of Sherbro, or the treachery and infamy of Kezzell, has no more to do with the climate of Montserrado, or the character of its inhabitants, than a Southern fever can affect the State of New Jersey. I will not, therefore, dwell upon that lamentation and grief longer than to pay a proper tribute of respect to the memory of Mills and of Bacon, and the others who fell in the exercise of the most magnanimous and disinterested humanity. Their bodies are on the coast, but their memories are embalmed in the hearts of their countrymen. May their names and their exertions be perpetuated!—the one for praise and the other for imitation.

On the first intelligence of this disaster, the whole plan was denounced as impracticable; and, without looking into the causes of that melancholy fatality, the opponents of the institution would persuade that the Almighty had placed impassable barriers to the civilization of Africa, and that, therefore, the scheme of the Colonization Society must fail. But whence came this important conclusion?—this would-be prophecy?—this knowledge of the future? Was it the result of careful examination and the deduction of sound philosophy? or did the great Jehovah let them into the secrets of his unfathomable designs? or was it written in the sunbeams of heaven?

No; they would not undergo the labour of inquiry and rational investigation; they were unworthy of inspiration; nor had they any knowledge of the future; but it was the force of inveterate prejudice, the violent effusions of hasty thought.

In this distress, the first attention of the society was directed to a complete and impartial investigation of the causes which produced it. Their misfortune was traced to the deceit of persons in whom they had a right to confide and to the unfortunate location of the first settlement. They arose from this painful inquiry with minds harassed with grief; but, fortified with confidence and relying upon that Almighty Power who said, "Let there be light, and there was light," they made another appeal to their friends and the public, and were enabled, in the course of a year, to obtain an agent of great enterprise and merit, who was directed, with a public vessel to assist him, to make a careful examination of the whole coast of Africa, to ascertain if there was not some part thereof which, from the salubrity of the climate and the fertility of its soil, would afford a well-grounded hope of future prosperity. The success which rewarded the courageous enterprise and the disinterested sacrifices of Dr. Ayres is known to the public, and, as the particulars can be found in the reports of the society, I will not detain you with a relation of the difficulties and privations endured by him, but be satisfied with stating that, overcoming all difficulties pronounced to be insurmountable, he succeeded in establishing a colony at Cape Montserrado, which is called Liberia, and which is now flourishing and happy, and is a clear demonstration of the feasibility of the plan of the Colonization Society, and a practical answer to the common exclamation, "Convince us that the thing can be done."

The successful establishment of the colony at Liberia has silenced all doubts in respect to the practicability of the colonizing system, and the improbability of its future success is now the principal ground of objection. These doubts are founded chiefly upon the insalubrity of the climate, the barrenness of the soil, the obstacles to its cultivation, the want of capacity in the negro, and, lastly, the great expense attending their transportation thither.

There is not a greater misapprehension in relation to this whole matter than that which has arisen from the want of proper information in regard to the climate of that part of the coast of Africa. It is unnecessary to enter into any speculation upon that subject. It is now placed beyond reasonable doubt by this most convincing evidence that the colony of Liberia has been settled for three years, during which time twenty-five deaths only have occurred,—fourteen by fever, five killed in battle, one by falling from a tree, two drowned, and the rest casualties. The greatest obstinacy cannot ask more incontrovertible proof on this point.

The soil of that part of the coast of Africa is exceedingly fertile. It is capable of producing rice, cotton, sugar, and indigo; and gold-dust, hides, gums, and camphor, can be procured in great abundance. The facilities which are offered for cultivating the soil at Liberia are, at this time, very great. For a few years past, the slave-trade (through which channel, as I before mentioned, the natives have been in the habit of receiving their supplies of rum, tobacco, &c. &c.) has been much interrupted, and in some places, on that part of the coast, entirely stopped; for instance, at Liberia and its neighbourhood, once a great mart for that trade. This has rendered their supplies precarious, the pressure of which uncertainty is felt by all, and they are desirous for some more regular and certain means of procuring those necessaries, and are ready and willing to engage in any employment offered to them by which they may be obtained. There are thousands of people there whose energies may be directed in any course, either for good or evil. Enhance the value of slaves by a brisk demand, and you will produce war, rapine, and murder. Create a demand for what their soil can produce, and they will use the hoe. Give them a pound of tobacco, a yard of muslin, a string of beads, a pair of shoes or a hat, in exchange, and you will get the valuable productions of their rich and fertile soil.

As to the intellectual qualifications of the negro, it is unfair to judge him, in that respect, as he is seen here in a state of servitude. At the English settlements upon the coast of Africa, natives have been taught all the mechanic arts. In Regent's Town, young natives are making rapid progress in the Latin and Greek languages, who, six years ago, were wild and ignorant. It is found they acquire a knowledge of the arts and sciences with as much facility as any other people, and it is only here, in their state of degradation, that such a question has been agitated.

With regard to the expense of transportation, it is by no means so great as has been represented. I have the authority of Dr. Ayres, of whom I have before spoken, for stating that the last company of one hundred and five persons were taken out for $26 each; and, when the prosperity of the colony shall enable them to furnish a return cargo, it will unquestionably reduce the average price to a much lower rate, and, in fact, a great many will be able to work their own passages as soon as a brisk trade shall be opened with the colony.

In this manner of viewing the affairs of the American Society for Colonizing the Free People of Colour of the United States, I think you will yield your hearty assent to the purity and philanthropy of its principles; for you, no doubt, desire the abolition of slavery and are anxious for the civilization of Africa, and cannot but rejoice in the destruction of the slave-trade. I think, also, that you must be satisfied that the climate is sufficiently salubrious for our black population; that the soil is good; that the facilities for cultivation and improvement are great; that the intellect of the negro, in a state of natural freedom, is strong enough; that the expense of transportation is not much; and, finally, that the plan of the American Society for Colonizing the Free People of Colour of the United States is not only practicable, but there is great probability that, with moderate assistance from the nation, it will succeed to the utmost expectations of its first friends.

To appeal to your feelings upon an occasion like the present, and to offer inducements to a popular assembly to aid in so good a work, presents a fine field for declamation. But I believe there is too much intelligence in this meeting to bear with such presumption from me, and that all you require is a fair understanding of the subject to induce you to advocate, with zeal and alacrity, the views of the parent institution and to form a society auxiliary thereto.

Speech at Washington, 1825.

In the *African Repository* of March, 1825, appears a report of the annual meeting of the Colonization Society held in the Supreme Court Room of the Capitol at Washington on the preceding 19th of February. A number of distinguished individuals were present; among them General Lafayette, Chief-Justice Marshall, and others. The African Repository publishes the following extracts from a speech delivered on this occasion by Robert F. Stockton, Esq., on the presentation of certain resolutions of the New Jersey Colonization Society, of which the then Lieutenant was a delegate:—

" Why is it, sir, that the people of these United States have thus far enjoyed a happiness and prosperity unexampled in the annals of nations? Is it exclusively to be attributed to the wisdom of her statesmen? to the upright and independent administration of her laws? to the physical strength and resources of the country? to the prowess of her sailors? No, sir! All this is well, is excellent, is admirable; but more than this is, nevertheless, required. It is because—whatever may be the cancerous and alarming evils which, by its early masters, have been entailed on the finest country in the world—her institutions of modern times, dating their birth with the American Revolution, are based substantially on moral rectitude and the equal rights of man. But, sir, let me not be misunderstood on this delicate and important question. With the enthusiasts of the North, I embark not in the wild and destructive scheme which calls on the South for immediate and universal emancipation. With the South,—but, sir, I will not offend against the talent, and refinement, and magnanimity, by which all, who have the happiness to know it at all, know it to be distinguished, by suggesting the possibility that what long-lived error has made indispensable for the present she can wish to increase, and strengthen, and perpetuate. No, sir! There is a golden mean which all who would pursue the solid interest and reputation of their country may discern at the very heart of their confederation and will both advocate and enforce,—a principle of justice, conciliation, and humanity,—a principle, sir, which is not inconsistent with itself, and yet can sigh over the degradation of the slave, defend the wisdom and prudence of the South against the charge of studied and pertinacious cruelty, and, yet, with an eye of warning and a voice of thunder, invoke them to be stirring in the great cause and claims of Nature. Thus, sir, it is that, although inheritors of difficulties of no ordinary complexity, these United States, in their separate as well as their federal relations, are substantially based on those elevated maxims, which, if they continue to maintain, will not fail to reward them with unparalleled liberality.

" Nor, sir, in the future application of these great principles, do I presume to counsel the statesmen of the day, or to instruct them in their creed of political morality. But surely, sir, as a citizen and a freeman, yielding to no one in ardent devotion to my country's honour, I may be allowed to conjure those distinguished individuals upon whose talents, integrity, and patriotism, we repose, not to lose sight of those beacon-lights which are calculated on the one hand to protect us from danger and on the other to lead us to prosperity. Is it unbecoming in me to beseech them not to mistake sin for expediency, and to be instructed by the philosophy of history? What, sir, in the rearing and advancement of a young, reflecting, and enterprising people, are the real advantages of the age in which we live? Are they that architecture is rebuilding her proudest temples? that music swells its unequalled harmony? that painting bids fair to rival the works of its ancient masters? or that all the arts, whether useful or ornamental, guided by the light of liberal science, are rapidly striding to perfection? No, sir; it is because we have before us the experience of so many ages and the philosophy of so many human experiments and human failures to humble and enlighten us.

"But unfortunately, sir, history is rarely examined as it should be. Of what avail is it, in the pursuit of the speculator, that cities and empires have been reared and overturned, and that so many towering and intrepid spirits have, with all their schemes, been tumbled from their elevation, if he fail to consider the moral influence upon human events and to look for their accomplishment beyond the boundary of human means? There are, sir, crimes of nations as well as of individuals ; and, while the immortal essence of the latter is reserved for judgment when time shall be no more, the former shall account in the only sphere to which their physical conformation is adapted and beyond which their identity is forbidden by the imperishable requisites for eternity. Spain, sir, has had her day of glory and of happiness, and why is it not so with her now? The short-sighted politician will trace it no higher than to the natural infirmities of human institutions, the scarcity of her patriots, the exhaustion of her re-sources, and the gradual progress of bloated luxury, to eventual want and general degradation. But, sir, can we be satisfied with this trite array of se-condary causes—this blind and, therefore, hopeless grasping after truth and wisdom? It is indispensable that we should answer, No. It would be inte-resting to analyze the history of Spain in support of the position I would main-tain, but time does not permit; and if it did, to the present assembly it would, in all probability, be more than superfluous. But, sir, can there be hazard in the assertion that Spain has even now, however inglorious, inactive, or subdued, her abundant resources, her port of dignity, her romantic chivalry, her armies of patriots? Cast your eye upon her fertile regions, breathe in the luxuries of her delicious climate, calculate the value of her exhaustless colonies—her ad-vantages for commerce and the number of her inhabitants, and who shall deny to her abundant resources?

"As for her patriots,—for the moral and intellectual energies that might be expected to excite them in the great causes of national and individual inde-pendence,—need they be mentioned that they may be remembered? The accents of her gallant defenders expiring on the scaffolds of her own erection are still piercing our ears; and yet, with all her elements of worth, and pride, and chivalry,—with all nature to cheer her, all art to aid her, all science to instruct, all example to rouse, and all wrongs to madden,—Spain is still poor and wretched, spiritless and ignorant, the ruinous and crumbling corner of a splendid continent. But how? Spain, sir, has been arraigned before the King of kings, and is now writhing in agony under the torture of his retributive justice. The curse of successful, but insatiate, avarice, of unintermitted wrong, of unbending insolence and unsurpassing cruelty, is upon her! She made 'unto herself a golden calf and fell down and worshipped it.' She did more, and the 'filthy witness' of it stains her hands. The blood of thousands of unoffending natives is still smoking for vengeance ; and when shall the ruth-less deeds of Cortez and Pizarro be forgotten? When it shall comport with the mysterious dispensations of Heaven to be appeased and forgive her, Spain may again be free and glorious and happy.

" There are other nations, sir, yet in the pomp and confidence of ascendency, to whom a lesson of national justice and moderation would be useful ; but 'iniquity in years,' and with strength undiminished, must be left to abler cor-rection. Time, the arbitrator of the destinies of the world, will do his duty, and the Ruler of the universe, ' before whom every knee must bow,' will be at hand to decide and punish. But, sir, returning from abroad, with these serious warnings from ancient communities, to the nurture and accomplishment of our useful and interesting country, let us not be wanting in the manly exer-cise of self-examination. We, too, have a moral debt, contracted by our ancestors, formidable in its origin, and which has been daily accumulating; and, if we desire that this young day's happiness may not be succeeded by a wretched imbecility, and that our Constitution (the sublimest structure for the promulgation and protection of human rights the world ever saw, the very capital of human freedom) shall be first completed, and then endure through the lapse of ages, let us not presume on the tranquillity of to-day. This may be the calm out of which bursts the tornado, this the smooth and deceptive water on the edge of the cataract. The time may come when, in the dispensation of Providence, this great people, too, may be stretched in death before the scrutiny of posterity.

"Let it not be said that, in the pride of youth and strength of manhood, she perished of a heart blackened by atrocity and ossified by countless cruelties to the Indian and the African. I will trespass no longer. If, sir, I have said a word by which the objects of our institution and the humane recommendation of our venerable Executive for the colonization of our aborigines is likely to be promoted, I shall be happy."

Letter of Commodore Stockton on the Slavery Question.

MR. WEBSTER TO COMMODORE STOCKTON.

WASHINGTON, March 22, 1850.

MY DEAR SIR:—

I send to you, as an old friend, a copy of my late speech in the Senate. It relates to a subject quite interesting to the country, as connected with the question of proper governments for those new territories which you had an important agency in bringing under the power of the United States.

I would hardly ask your opinion of the general sentiments of the speech, although I know you are a very competent judge, but that, being out of the strife of politics, your judgment is not likely to be biassed, and that you have as great a stake as any man in the preservation of the Union and the maintenance of the Government on its true principles.

I am, dear sir,
With great respect, yours,
DANIEL WEBSTER.

COMMODORE STOCKTON.

REPLY OF COMMODORE STOCKTON.

PRINCETON, March 25.

DEAR SIR:—

I thank you for your letter and a copy of the recent speech delivered by you in the Senate of the United States.

I need say nothing in commendation of your course, which has been so generally approved, and will proceed (without referring to any difference of opinion that may seem to exist between us on the subject) to communicate to you my candid and long-cherished opinions on the subject of slavery as it exists in the United States, and the duty of the Government and the people in connection with it.

In view of a national crisis in the affairs of Great Britain, one of her eminent statesmen once said, "In order to be prepared for the trials of these times, we should be possessed of a prompt facility of adverting in all our doubts to some grand and comprehensive truth. In a deep and strong soil must that tree fix its roots, the height of which is to reach to heaven, and the sight of it to the ends of the earth."

A great crisis presents itself in the path of the Republic. Interests of incalculable consequence are involved in it—to you, to myself, to every citizen—con-

sequences not limited to our times, but extending onward to all future generations, and, if there is any thing in the hopes that have been cherished of the
universally progressive principles of liberty, to the world for ages to come.
"There are times (says another eminent person) when the assertion of great
principles is the best service a man can render society," and this is such a time.
We are all called upon to pause at the present crisis and consider well what
are the demands of duty. It is no time to palter about party distinctions or
sectional differences; now, if ever, it becomes us to feel that we are Americans
—*only Americans.* It is no time to calculate questions of personal popularity;
that sacrifice which any citizen may make is as nothing, if it contributes to save
his country. A Jerseyman myself, born on one of those proud battle-fields
where American liberty was purchased, bearing a life devoted to the service of
the Union, I can withhold nothing from the cause of that Union with which I
solemnly believe liberty is herself identified, "one and inseparable."

It appears to me that the polar truth to which the view of our fellow-citizens
should be directed in the present emergency is this:—that God works in the
affairs of nations, and shapes them to his purposes; and that to ascertain his
will we must study in the school of his providences, and take counsel from the
observation of his ways to regulate our own. The destinies of men and of nations are in the bosom of the Most High. He lives in the history of the past;
he will live in the history of the future; and he who has most deeply reflected
upon the records of the past has most clearly seen that the great characteristics
which have marked the progress of every nation, in every age, have eventually
resulted in the accomplishment of some grand design in which the hand of
Providence, though for a time obscured by shadows, has been at last clearly
and distinctly seen.

Of this our own history furnishes a luminous example. The preparation for
the erection of the great temple of civil and religious liberty we now inhabit
began in the discoveries and convulsions of the fifteenth century. The materials
for it were found in men schooled by providential trials and disciplined to the
work they were to commence; and it is as rational to suppose the world was
the production of chance, as to suppose that the combination of events which
led them to this continent, which cherished and protected their infant colonies,
which brought about the Revolution and its results, and has made us what we
are, was the work of chance; it is this which inspires me with hope that He
who founded the Republic will save it—that he has great purposes to accomplish yet, and that they will be unfolded through successive years for ages to
come, in perfecting the institutions of a rational freedom here, and in extending
them to all other continents.

Though men were the instruments, the American Revolution was the work
of an unseen Power; the actors in it themselves looked back with astonishment
at the course they had taken and the results that had been accomplished. The
greater the event, the more clearly has the hand of Providence always been
seen in it; the greater the hero, the more heartfelt always has been his acknowledgment that a superior destiny controlled his actions. The American Constitution is the result of a fearful struggle. Its full price was by no means the
sufferings undergone in the conflict. The series of events by which it was accomplished we are now able to trace distinctly back, through the privations
and trials of the early colonists, to the days when popular freedom first began
the contest with arbitrary power in the civil wars of England; and its pathway
is everywhere marked with patient endurance and costly sacrifice.

Things permanently good are of slow growth: the offspring of hardship, they
are made strong through suffering. So universal is this law, that the most
hasty minds have a secret misgiving of the efficacy of hasty products; and we
would as soon expect undisciplined troops to be equal to the hardships and
perils of a dangerous campaign, as that an undisciplined community could
triumph in that fiercest of all warfares,—the warfare which marks everywhere
the pathway to national existence, greatness, and virtue.

More than two centuries have passed since the events which were to result in
founding the Republic were put in motion; and who does not perceive, both in

our colonial and constitutional history, that the process by which we have, within a comparatively few years, come to the full achievement of a distinctive nationality, has been one mainly of forbearance and self-denial? Nor have we been the only sufferers. When our ancestors came to this country, they found it in the possession of another race. That race has had their day. A great continent, fitted by nature for large developments in the progress of humanity, had been for centuries committed to their keeping, and they had proved faithless to their trust. It was manifest, from the commencement of the struggles, that one of the two races must give way to the other, and no one doubts the beneficence of that Providence which decided for the Anglo-Saxon race. Yet how touching is the story of the red man's wrongs! We commiserate his sufferings, while we clearly see that the decree by which his race wastes away before the advancing footsteps of civilization is the fiat of Infinite Wisdom.

The same all-pervading Providence has brought us in contact with still another race,—the *African*,—but under widely different circumstances. Out of this circumstance, and the events connected with it, the crisis we are now considering has grown. Three millions of that race, scattered through fifteen of the States of the Union, are in the condition of servitude. Individuals in the non-slaveholding States have not only been long in the habit of denouncing the holding of slaves as a sin, as, indeed, among the worst of crimes, but have insisted on immediate and unconditional abolition—have carried on the work of agitation—have encouraged slaves to desert their masters—have protected fugitive slaves from pursuit and reclamation, and have even gone so far as to declare that it was cause for separating from the South altogether.

The General Government has been agitated ; compromise after compromise has been made, and proved, as was to be expected, only the means of postponing rather than of settling the question, until at last things have reached a condition that real danger to the Union seems to be apprehended by the wisest men of both sections of the country. It is time for men now to speak out, calmly, but fearlessly. Whatever has been wrong should be made right, and the question settled now and forever. We should not meanly shrink from our just responsibilities and put them upon our children.

Now, in reference to the relation of master and slave, it is proper we should bear in mind that African slavery was introduced into this country by *no act of ours*. For its introduction the American people are in no just sense responsible. Its introduction here was the act of Great Britain while we were her colonies. She engrafted this system into our communities at a time when these communities (then in their infancy) were unable to make any effectual resistance. Our ancestors, at the time, and through all the process by which it was accomplished, remonstrated and protested against it; but their remonstrances and protests were unheeded. Its introduction was considered by the early colonists an evil—a measure of oppression to them as well as to the slave ; but they were as powerless to resist it as the slave himself.

So far as we are concerned, this circumstance in our condition is providential. If we would presume to scrutinize and judge the ways of Providence, we are driven back to first principles. God rules in the affairs of nations and of men as an absolute sovereign, and shapes all human events to his great purposes. The purposes he designed to accomplish in all this may be involved in comparative darkness now ; but if it shall appear hereafter *that this was the means by which, in the lapse of centuries, he accomplished the redemption of Africa herself*, who will say that the means he chose were inconsistent with his wisdom or his goodness?

This fact, then, is undisputed, that when the battles of the Revolution had been fought—when the North and the South had passed shoulder to shoulder through that long and bloody and self-sacrificing struggle, and the independence of their country was achieved, the institution of slavery, planted by other hands in our midst, existed. A very large number of our citizens, both in the North and South, were slaveholders. Property is the creature of the law, and slaves had been made property by law—been so held for ages. What was to be done? The general welfare—the preservation of all that had been gained—the law of self-defence—required that a Government should be established, and that this Government should embrace and combine in one indissoluble union all the liberated colonies. If that had not been accomplished, all would have been shipwrecked together.

The men of the Revolution saw this plainly. They were men equal to the crisis. They considered the question as a whole. They sacrificed on the altar of concession their different views and interests as to particulars, that they might reach harmoniously the grand result. The articles of confederation, and subsequently the Constitution, were the results of compromise; and whatever politicians may say—the spirit—the intent—the fair construction of that compromise—is, *that the institution of slavery belongs exclusively to the States, as a matter of State regulation, and that the General Government has nothing to do with it.*

No power over it was delegated by the Constitution to the General Government, (except as to the importation of slaves into the States,) nor was any such power prohibited by it to the States. It was expressly provided that persons held to service or labour in one State under the laws thereof, escaping into another, should not be discharged from such service or labour, but should be delivered up on claim of the party to whom such service or labour might be due; and by an amendment to the Constitution, adopted in 1791, it was provided that the powers not delegated to the United States by the Constitution, nor prohibited by it to the States, are reserved to the States respectively, or to the people. Such is the Constitution—such the compromise upon which it was formed—such the imperative necessity of that compromise: and even if that compromise and that Constitution were the result of a *mistake*, it is binding now, and as long as it shall remain unaltered, on every law-abiding man.

If the *toleration* of slavery—if the permission for its existence in any part of the Union—was a great national *crime*, when and by whom was that crime committed? At the formation of the Government, at the adoption of the Constitution, and by the Washingtons, the Roger Shermans, the Hamiltons, the Madisons, the Franklins, the Pinkneys, of the land—by such men as Livingston and Paterson, Brearly and Dayton, of my own native State, approved and sanctioned with unparalleled unanimity by the North and South. Under its auspices, I need n t say with what giant strides the Republic has advanced to greatness and prosperity, nor that heaven has smiled propitiously upon our common heritage.

Now, the question which has come up with such a threatening aspect before the country is, in my judgment, one of *morals*, not of politics,—questions always the most difficult and dangerous to deal with, because they do not lie in notions of expediency, but in matters of conscience. They are always liable to run into fanaticism, and are always mingled with questions of religious faith and moral obligation. The question is one of morals, and as such it is to be settled, if settled permanently at all. Out of this aspect of the case have sprung, as incidents, all the questions that have heretofore been and are now the subjects of discussion. The Convention of '87, the Missouri Compromise, the contested question of abolition petitions in Congress, the agitations in the North, the recriminations of the South, the difficulties about fugitive slaves, and latterly, the California question and the Wilmot Proviso, are all but branches of one fruitful tree—the question as to the moral character of slavery as it exists in the States, and the moral duty consequent upon that character. In reference to those phases or incidents of this question, which involve the action of the Government, they never would have been unsettled, or at any rate never would have come up in their present embarrassing forms, if the General Government had adhered, as it ought in my opinion to have adhered, from the beginning, to a strict construction of the Constitution. The framers of this instrument meant to exclude, and by the language of the instrument did exclude, the national Government from all action upon the subject.

They granted no such power; they expressly excluded all powers not granted. Whenever the doctrine of inferential powers—that latitudinarian doctrine—comes fully to be insisted on and adopted, the Constitution will become itself a thing of wax, to be moulded, by the ever-changing opinions of men, into whatever shape those opinions happen to take; the majority will become supreme; its will, the Constitution, and every thing conservative, will be liable to be broken down. Suppose a measure oppressive—ruinous—to one portion of the Union, is adopted by a mere constitutional majority, and in constitutional form: it is said the party complaining and denying its constitutionality has an appeal to the Supreme Court. But to argue that that is always to be regarded as a place of absolute security, is to argue that it is infallible. It undergoes the process of change by death; the new incumbents are apt to partake of the views of the Constitution held by a majority of the Government, and the Court to become itself the advocate of those views. Beyond this are the rocks, the breakers of revolution—the dernier resort of an oppressed people. The Constitution itself was originally intended to be the cable and anchor of the Union and all its parts; and nothing, you may rely upon it, but the doctrine of a strict construction, can ever preserve it what it was intended to be.

Upon the question of domestic slavery in the States and in the territories, nonintervention is the true principle. There the letter of the Constitution placed it, and there it should be left. The law of nature, fixing the bounds of the institution by the unalterable constitution of the coloured race, the temperature of the climate and nature of the soil, and the will of the people acting through the State Legislatures upon their several States, are the true and legitimate regulators; and all interference, except moral suasion, the power of argument, the free expression of opinion, ought to be excluded.

I now come to the main question—the question which lies back of all the others. 1. Is domestic slavery a sin, or an unmitigated evil? and, 2. What is the duty of the people of the non-slaveholding States respecting it? These questions go to the root of the whole difficulty.

1. Is domestic slavery a sin, or an unmitigated evil? In order to arrive at an intelligent conclusion respecting the right or the wrong of any complex scheme or any existing institution, we must be careful not to array our feelings against our reason; nor ought we to allow our displeasure at particular cases of excess to interfere with a fair and deliberate consideration of the general working and tendency of the system as a whole. It belongs to this question to consider,—1. The condition of the coloured man as it would have been had he been left in Africa. 2. The circumstances under which we find him here. 3. The necessity, if such there be, of his present continuance in the condition in which we find him. 4. The ultimate tendency of what may seem to be a providential arrangement of this state of things.

1. Of all the races of men with which history and travel have acquainted us, there is none so sunk beyond all hope of self-restoration as the African on his wide continent. In ignorance so utter that he is elevated little above the brute, in superstition so gross that it drags him even lower than the brute, without a thought of liberty, he is the sport of tyranny in its lowest, meanest, and most cruel forms; he has nothing he can call his own; he has no idea of God, of justice, of moral obligation, of the rights of persons or property. In a word, "Africa has long forgotten God, and God has abandoned Africa"—but not, I trust, *forever*. From such a land and such a condition—sold, bartered away by his countrymen—the slave was brought to these shores while we were colonists and subject to British law. Here he is in a civilized and Christian country; he has more opportunities of enlightenment than he would have had in Africa; he is, as a general rule, treated with kindness; he is protected from want in sickness and old age, and is, on the whole, better off, safer, happier, than he would have been in his native country.

2. But in the second place, with the moral character of the act bringing the slave to this country we have now nothing to do. We find him here; the thing is done. So far as the slave-trade is concerned, we have acted on that, and abolished it. Slavery was introduced in other times and under other auspices. It existed when the Government was established; an institution which could not be got rid of—which had of necessity to be tolerated. Slaves had been made property in the Colonies by British law. The Government found it an existing

institution, and the Constitution left it so—of necessity, imperative and uncontrollable—to be enacted on exclusively by the States, subject to the moulding and changing and controlling opinions and consciences of those concerned. These have not been inactive. In many of the States the institution has been abolished; in others, meliorated; in all, it is a question for opinion and conscience to act upon. As the General Government has no power to abolish it, so it has no power to prevent any State from abolishing it.

3. In the third place, every considerate man sees that in the present condition of things slavery cannot be immediately and absolutely abolished. We must reason about things as they are—not as we might wish them to be. The slave is property; he became so by a law of our common ancestors; he was left in that condition by the law of our common fathers who founded the Republic. The burden of this purchase should be borne in all justice, equally by our citizens, and we are not ready to pay the price. But, if we were ready, he is not in a condition to take care of himself. He has not the culture, the training, the experience, necessary to self-dependence. And where is he to go? No reflecting man is prepared to say he is willing to have three millions of slaves turned loose in the States, to fill the prisons and poor-houses and alms-houses of the country, or to live by plunder on the community. What, too, is to be his lot for the future in such a case? Is he to live in our midst as a marked and degraded being, through all time, or are we prepared to place him on an equality with us, civilly and socially. Are we ready for amalgamation?

There seems under those circumstances to be a necessity for his continuance at present in the condition in which he is placed.

In the fourth place, the hand of Providence seems to be clearly pointing out an ultimate design in all this arrangement of things. Yonder is Africa, with her one hundred and fifty millions of miserable, degraded, ignorant, lawless, superstitious idolaters. Whoever has stood upon her sands, has stood upon a continent that has geographical and physical peculiarities which belong to no other of the great divisions of the globe. The latter appear, upon the face of them, to have been adapted to draw out the energies of the natives in their inequalities of temperature, soil, and surface, inviting the ingenuity and enterprise of man to overcome them, and in the varieties of their products tempting the interchanges of commerce; thus affording ample encouragement to the progress of civil and social improvement. But Africa is still, as of old, a land of silence and of mystery. Like the interminable dreariness of her own deserts, her moral wastes of mind lie waiting for the approach of influences from abroad. No savage people have ever advanced to a civilized state without intercommunication with others. All the continents of the world have, in their turn, been occupied and civilized by means of colonies; but in no one of them did it appear so inevitably necessary, from a previous examination of circumstances, as in that of Africa. It is plain to the very eye that Africa is a land to which civilization *must be brought.* The attempt has been made over and over again, by devoted missionaries and others, to penetrate that land and seek to impart the blessings of civilization and Christianity to her savage hordes. But the labour has been spent in vain. The white man cannot live in Africa. The annals of the Moravians, of Cape Colony, of Sierra Leone, of Liberia, contain the records of the sacrifice of some of the best men that have lived to grace the pages of any people's history, in the vain attempt to accomplish something for her redemption through the instrumentality of white men. *Who, then, is to do this work?*

Let now any calm, reflecting spectator of the present state of the world be asked to look at Africa, and then, from among the nations, point out the people best calculated to do this work; and when his eye falls upon the descendants of the sons of that continent now in America, will he not say, *These are the people appointed for that work?*

The ways of God are mysterious. So Joseph was sold a slave into Egypt; so his father and his brethren were driven thither by providential circumstances; so their generations remained as slaves in Egypt for four centuries and a half; and, when the appointed time had come, in His own appointed way the Ruler of nations led them to the accomplishment of His great purposes. And it is not to be forgotten that it was not the act of holding this people in bondage for so many years, that Pharaoh and the Egyptians were punished; but their crime was this: that when the Divine Being had prepared all things for the event he proposed to accomplish, and demanded, by an accredited ambassador, that they should be allowed to depart, "they would not let the people go."

The great progenitor of the Israelites was a slaveholder; the Israelites, after their emancipation, became slaveholders. Nothing is clearer than that under the Mosaic dispensation slavery was lawful; the institution was recognised and regulated by the law of Moses; and the founder of Christianity and his disciples (though Judea and all the provinces of the Roman empire were in their times full of slaves, and slaves subjected to the most rigid laws) never forbade or even denounced the relation as sinful, or exhorted masters to liberate their slaves; but enjoined on masters the principles of humanity and justice, and on slaves obedience and contentment; and those notions of morality may well be questioned which in our days disallow what Christ and his apostles did not disallow.

Such an Exodus as that of the Jews from Egypt may not be within the purpose of the Deity in relation to the children of Africa now in this country, or their descendants. But has He no purpose in all this arrangement that has been going on,—in the gathering of a vast family of these people here,—in their condition of servitude, endurance, discipline,— in the difficulties with which their emancipation is surrounded,—in the natural impossibility that the whites ever will or can consent to raise them to a condition of equality? No purpose in casting their lot in a country so free for the interchange of opinion, and where opinion is so enlightened and progressive and there is so much benevolence and Christian enterprise? Has he not a purpose in all this, to accomplish (in some way of his own, through this instrumentality) the regeneration of the millions of benighted Africa? The germs of colonies are already planted there as the fruits of this system of servitude. But the free African among us clings to this country still, under all his disabilities, regardless of the claims of the land of his fathers upon him; and may not *slavery and the necessity of migration as the condition* of his release be the appointed instrument to produce compliance? The colonies we have settled in Africa would, ere this day, have become a Republic of power, had the free negroes of the North been willing to become citizens of it. But, like the Israelites of old, who would, but for the Divine interposition, have sacrificed their liberators in the wilderness and returned into Egypt, these liberated descendants of Africa cannot be persuaded to look towards the land of their fathers. The millions of their coloured bondmen *there* awaken no sympathy in their hearts. Their fixed and resolute purpose appears to be to remain among the whites and force themselves by progressive steps into a civil and social equality with them; and it is chiefly with a view to strengthen themselves in these particular views and aspirations, that they band together under the abolition flag, and fill our cities with threats of vengeance against the white race if they shall dare to execute the laws in relation to fugitive slaves.

Now, when we came to reflect calmly and candidly upon all these circumstances, in connection with the question, "Is domestic slavery, as it exists at the South, *a sin?*" it seems to me that question must be answered in the *negative.* The relation of master and slave may be, and doubtless is, sometimes the occasion of cruelty and injustice. But this is also true of the relation of husband and wife, parent and child, master and apprentice, and of employer and employed in our system of labour. But the abuses of a system or relation form no sound argument against the system or relation itself. I am no apologist for abuse. I am as ready as any man to denounce cruelty, unnatural separations, a disregard of the domestic relations, or a deprivation of the means of moral and religious culture to the slave, under our system of slavery, as a crime. But the correction of these belongs to the duties of the State Governments. We, in New Jersey, have no more right to interfere with South Carolina than she with us, in such matters; nor in fact have we in New Jersey any more right to interfere with the slaves of South Carolina or Georgia than we have with the slaves of Russia or Austria,—each Southern State being, in respect to this question, as absolutely sovereign as are Russia and Austria. We are to reason about the institution of slavery as we reason about every other human institution, from its proper, humane, conscientious and lawful *use*, when both parties discharge their mutual obligations.

Having established, as I think, that domestic slavery, as it exists in the Southern States, is not in itself sinful or an unmitigated evil, this subject is relieved from its greatest embarrassment; and now I proceed to consider: *What is the duty of the people of non-slave-holding States respecting Slavery?*

Shall we attempt forcibly to break down this institution of slavery? To make the attempt is:—

First. To violate the Constitution and its compromises. I care not whether under colour of inferential instruction—assuming the Constitution to imply the power of interference—(which, by-the-way, I unconditionally deny)—or acting regardless of it. In either case it is, at best, the appeal to the mere majority power, acting upon and forcing the minority.

Second. It is to attempt the liberation of the slave, and fail. For by the effort the most we can do is to drive the South with its slaves out of the Union without liberating a single slave; and,

Third. It is to *compel a dissolution of the Union.* Have the people considered the consequences implied in this branch of the alternative? Suppose, after all, that, in opposition to the plain teachings of the Bible and the judgment of God's holiest men, they still hold that slavery is in itself *sinful, and the owners of slaves are men-stealers, robbers and pirates,* then, indeed, this question assumes a more serious aspect, and Mr. Calhoun may no longer be denounced as either unpatriotic or extravagant in calling for an amendment of the Constitution, or any other means that will secure his constituents from imminent peril and his posterity from the calamities of civil war. But—

Is there not, in this view, a crime of deeper and redder dye, in marching over a desecrated Bible and a broken compact to shed oceans of fraternal blood? Is it lawful, on their own principles, to do evil that good may come—even if good could by it be accomplished? If they succeed in driving the South to a secession, they inevitably kindle the fire of a conflagration which will burn over this whole Republic until it reduces to ashes the structure which Providence has for centuries been preparing and rearing up on this continent; and, in the conflagration, their own homes and hopes will be mingled with the sacrifice.

"One great principle," says Dr. Channing, "which we should lay down as immovably true, is, that if a good work cannot be carried on by the calm, self-controlled, benevolent spirit of Christianity, then the time for doing it has not come. *God asks not the aid of our vices.* He can overrule them for good, but they are not the chosen instruments of human happiness." But if we would adopt, as I sincerely do, the other alternative—that with the institution of slavery as it exists in the South we have nothing to do—that we are not only prohibited by the Constitution from meddling with it, but that it is a question of conscience to be settled by Southern men for themselves—a question upon which good men may differ, and must be left to differ if they will, whether in the North or South—a new train of thoughts, a new field of benevolent and Christian enterprise, opens before us. Going back to the great truth from which we started, and regarding all the circumstances of the present state of things as a part of the design of Providence to accomplish a great result for Africa, there is a work, and a great work, for us to do. Let the great heart of Christian benevolence in the North and the South unite in selecting from this vast African family—this nursery planted and growing on our shores—the proper subjects to be sent upon the mission of redemption to the land of their ancestors, until the last slave shall have departed, and Africa's long night shall have been dispelled by the sun of freedom and civilization. The philanthropist will find here enough to do to satisfy the largest benevolence, in acts, in personal sacrifices, in contributions to the cause of humanity, without the violation of personal or legal rights—doing *good* that *good* may come.

Let the General Government, then, retrace its steps; and instead of provisos, and compromise lines, and agreements to keep up the balance of power, fall back upon the literal construction of the Constitution—adopt the principle of *total non-intervention*, now and forever—leaving the laws of nature and the voice of public opinion to adjust the limits of the institution, free, uncontrolled, and uninfluenced by the action of Congress, and all will be safe. The Gordian knot will be dissolved—not cut—and the ark of the covenant, with its sacred deposit, be borne on safely to its destination.

The measures, in short, which I would propose, are—

1st. A declarative act, in such form as may be deemed proper, that the Constitution gives no power to the General Government to act on the subject of domestic slavery, either with respect to its existence in the States, the Territories, or the District of Columbia.

2d. The most efficient act that can be framed to enforce the provisions of the Constitution in relation to fugitive slaves.

3d. That California, in consideration of the peculiar circumstances of her case, be admitted without the approval or disapproval of that part of her Constitution which relates to slavery.

I believe these three positions, carried out, would settle the question forever. They involve no concessions—no compromise; they are no temporary expedient. They put the solution of the difficulty on the eternal principles of right—the law of the Constitution.

I think the great majority of the North and South are prepared to place it there, and, having placed it there, to stand by and maintain the Union at all hazards.

I feel that I have already trespassed too long on your patience. But it is a subject of vast importance, and I cannot close this letter without a few general remarks in reference to the foregoing views.

At such a time all good men will forbear, exchange opinions, and reason in the spirit of conciliation.

Conscientious differences of opinion among men will always exist in relation to moral questions.

Some conscientious men believe slavery to be a sin; other conscientious men believe that the law of property which enables one man to hold what they insist is the common gift of the Creator to his creatures, is sin. Again, still, other conscientious men hold that to take a glass of wine is sin; and so on, through an endless variety of subjects.

If these conscientious opinions, or any of them, pervade the majority, are all who do not hold them to be driven with fire and sword out of the Union, or compelled to yield their opinions, equally conscientious, to the majority? These notions are inconsistent with a wise moderation; they come from an abuse of reason in the first place, and a proposed abuse of power in the second.

Such arguments are always drawn principally from the *excesses* of a system, rather than from the system itself, and there lies the error; it is the error of *fanaticism*, which always puts in the plea of conscience, whether it burns the supposed heretic at the stake, or hunts down witchcraft, or impales the Nestorian, or fans the flame of civil war.

Instead of railing with infuriated declamation against a system because of its excesses, which are incident to every human institution, we should calmly and dispassionately seek to extract the truth from the general rule rather than from its exceptions. The system of slavery, like every human system, has its excesses—its exceptions from the general rule. But it is quite probable that there may exist in the one, as in the other, an absolute law, which is working out a beneficent result. If a man wishes to fall under the delusion of a universal fanaticism, it is only necessary that he adopt the method of looking at the special attendants of every system to the exclusion of the general law which regulates them, and the work is done; while he is intent with some accident of the train, the train itself has long since passed on, leaving him to grow more and more inflated with conceit, indignation, unholy zeal, and misanthropic railing,—all the natural results of so narrow-minded a procedure. Let every man run off with particular features out of the general complexion of any subject or thought, and gaze at those features long enough and absorbingly enough, and the best thing within the range of human experience will become to him a bug-bear. The individual, however, who neglects the "great law of compensation" in judging of human affairs, has only to apply the same method of judging to himself; and, passing by his redeeming qualities and looking only at his own excesses and defects, he will find in himself, if he is honest in the search, enough to satiate his appetite for condemnation and hate. It is far easier to condemn than to judge correctly—far easier to get into a passion about a subject than to get a comprehension of it.

The idea that out of the institution of domestic slavery in this country is to spring the regeneration of Africa, derives, it seems to me, great force from the recurrence to past history.

We invariably find that, in the dispensation of Providence, nations which have been called to act an important part in the work of human progress have been led through a long previous discipline of trial; the restraints and endurance of youth have preceded the power and efficiency of manhood. Primary subjection is the law of stable growth, and seems an indispensable condition of the advancement of our race.

We have only to look back through a few centuries to find the evidences of this in the annals of our race. Our ancestors were for centuries a down-trodden, enslaved, and toiling people. The Anglo-Saxon race have become what they are by a long training in the school of patient endurance; in the case of England, under oppressive servitude to the Roman and the Norman; in the case of America, under the oppression of our mother-country and the trying discipline of Colonial suffering. In the life of a nation, hundreds of years may be as a day in the life of an individual. It is often necessary for many generations to pass, before a new influence can be made to affect the mass. If all were willing, the work of national preparation might be more rapid; but thousands are to be made willing, and by the providential adaptation of the means to the end.

It is conceded, on all hands, that the probation of the African people now in bondage on our shores is to come to an end.

That, while there is an interchange of benefits between the parties, there is at the same time a community of evil, which renders it better, both for the whites and the blacks, that it should come to an end.

When shall that time be? is the great question before the American people.

In seeking an answer to this question, we may be sure there is some safer ground on which to take our stand than that of political chicane, of fanatical prejudice, or of any merely temporary or prudential expediency.

If slavery is to be abolished now, then it is to be done in a moment. That is to say, at one stroke a community of three millions of people, habituated to a certain way of life, are to be thrown into new circumstances:—a thing plainly preposterous, because no kind of society changes its customs suddenly and succeeds in doing well. Great changes in society must come in with previous preparation, or they come in to little purpose. Seven years sufficed to fight the battles of the Revolution, but many more were spent in preparation for that event, and many more will be required to perfect its results. If Providence rules in the affairs of nations, the existence of slavery has some prospective purpose, only to be accomplished by prior preparation for it.

Let us not be impatient or presumptuous. These African people are passing to their destiny along the same path which has been trod by other nations, through a mixture of hardship, of endurance, but in a land of light and amid a civilized society. They are preparing to accomplish a work for their native continent which no other people in the world can accomplish. Their plain mission is ultimately to carry the gifts of society, of religion, of government, to the last remaining continent of the earth, where these blessings are totally unknown. Their work is a great one, as it would seem to be connected essentially with the final and universal triumph of civilization and Christianity in the world. It is our duty to follow, not to attempt to lead in the ways and purposes of Providence. We are to move forward when the pillar of fire and cloud moves forward, and to rest when it rests.

Doubtless there is a time for action; but it is characteristic of all great changes that they make known their own seasons. That time, in the present instance, has not yet come—for the manifest reason that the way is not yet open for it. When the time shall come, the way will come with it, the preparations for it be complete. The North settled this question easily, quietly. Surely, it is no great stretch of charity for us to suppose that in due time the same thing will be accomplished in the South. We of the North have given no peculiar evidence of superior goodness, that we should suppose the South not to be possessed of as much justice, charity, and good sense, as ourselves.

I firmly believe that the hour for the complete enfranchisement of the Southern Slave will be the hour of the complete preparation for the work of African redemption and civilization; and that hour will make itself known *in the removal of all obstacles here and there*, in the preparation of the workmen and the work; and I earnestly hope that guided by happier influences than seem now to pervade the country, the pulpit, the press, the people of the North and the South may give their thoughts and efforts to this subject in the spirit of Him whose mission to our earth was heralded by the proclamation of peace and good-will.

With great regard, yours,

R. F. STOCKTON.

ADDRESS

Delivered at Elizabethtown, July 4, 1851.

FELLOW-CITIZENS:—

For the honour you have done me I tender you my most cordial thanks. If I could have foreseen the imposing ceremonies of this morning, I should have thought it wise and prudent, had time permitted, to have prepared a written address for this occasion. As it is, all that is left to me is to do the best I can, and to wish that you may meet with no disappointment to-day. You have known me, more or less, from my youth up. You have known that my life has been rather a life of action than of words; that I have not been educated a speech-maker—that I am no orator—that I have not learned the art of seductive eloquence. I come here for no oratorical display or effect. I come to address you to-day, because you invited me to do so, and because I was ambitious of the honour of being introduced to you. It was but a few days since that I received your invitation, and I was more willing that my reputation as a public speaker should suffer, than that I should seem to be indifferent to your kindness. But, fellow-citizens, I bring with me that which will, perhaps, answer my purpose on this occasion better than the highest order of eloquence or the most elaborate preparation. I bring with me a heart full of devotion to my country and her institutions. I bring with me an habitual veneration for the memory of all our distinguished patriots who have contributed so largely to the glory of their country and the happiness of mankind; especially for those good and fearless men who, appealing to God for the purity of their intentions, declared the Colonies free and independent of British rule; and those great and incomparable statesmen who framed the Constitution of the United States, and inbound the States in one Union by the adamantine chain of Constitutional Law.

On the 4th of July, 1776, the Declaration of Independence was signed by our patriotic forefathers, and delivered into the hands of the people, for the benefit of themselves and their posterity, to the remotest generation; and, as Mr. Adams predicted, the anniversary of that day has been ever since celebrated by bonfires, firing of cannon, public orations, and all other manifestations of a nation's triumph and a nation's joy.

Fellow-citizens, that was no small thing done in a corner. It was a mighty work, done in the broad light of day. It was no small candle hid under a bushel. It was a great fire built on the top of the mountain, to show the way that the great Anglo-American family were taking to God and Liberty. It has been burning brighter and brighter, till it has illumined this continent from the Atlantic to the Pacific Oceans, and I hope it will burn, and continue to burn brighter and brighter, and ascend higher and higher, until it lightens up the dark cavern of Terra del Fuego, and redeems even the Patagonian wanderer to liberty and civilization.

I congratulate you, fellow-citizens, on this auspicious day, and that we are permitted once more to celebrate this anniversary under the broad banner of the Union,—under that flag whose gorgeous stripes, with its mysterious *E Pluribus Unum*, we were wont, in our boyish days, to hail with so much joy, as it waved from our village liberty-pole. Yes, that flag, planted on the ramparts of liberty by the immortal Washington, and drenched with the blood of Mercer at Princeton, and that liberty-pole, raised by our fathers and consecrated by the prayers of our mothers, have always been, in my mind, one and inseparable. What wonder that I should be a Union man? My morning matin and my evening lullaby were tuned to the praises of the Union; and I have lived for the Union, the whole Union, and nothing but the Union. I can remember nothing before the Union, and I desire to know nothing and to remember nothing after it shall be dissolved. May the great arbiter of nations—He who guided the adventurous footsteps of our pilgrim fathers to these shores, and who has since watched over the preservation and glory of the Republic—continue us a united people, henceforth and forever.

Our lot has been cast in pleasant places, but we have fallen upon evil times. At the North, a fanaticism, the wildest and most indefensible that ever swayed the passions of men, is at work to strike down all that is valuable upon earth of human liberty, in the vain and delusive expectation of reconstructing upon its ruins some utopian system of beatific bliss and of the equality of the white and black races of men. At the South, the watch-fires of the Revolution have been rekindled in the preparation for the defence of their homes and firesides. Groaning under the pressure of apprehended wrongs, and writhing under the lash of constant and reiterated insults, the men of the South are preparing for war, in the hope of redressing their wrongs and avenging their insults by an appeal to the sword. Every north wind goes southward freighted with libels and insults, and every southern breeze bears on its wings notes of defiance and revenge. Thus two great principles, never before in the history of our race reconciled or appeased but by blood, stand in hostile array to each other. Yet there are those who say that there is no danger of a conflict—no danger to the safety of the Union. With the thunders of secession roaring along the Southern coast and the billows of insurrection breaking on the Northern shores,—sure presages of a storm,—they tell us there is no danger to the ship of State, that the sky is clear and the sea is smooth. But, fellow-citizens, be not lulled into fatal security by these siren voices. Take heed; be warned, by the roaring thunder and the forked lightning, that this may be the calm which precedes the tornado—the smooth and deceitful surface on the edge of the cataract.

It must be admitted on all hands that there is great excitement among our people in regard to public affairs, not unmixed with a degree of apprehension respecting the safety of the Union. In the violence of party and sectional strife, there seems to be a confusion of ideas in regard to the motives and objects which induced our forefathers to seek an asylum on these western shores, and in regard to the principles which they avowed when they first established the government, and none the less in relation to the teachings of the Constitution. Instead of detaining you by a recital of the early history of the country, —the events of the Revolution, and the heroic achievements of the actors in that great drama of human effort, with which you are all familiar,—I will ask your attention to some of the principles upon which our political system has been constructed.

Our forefathers left Europe to seek a home on this continent, to avoid religious persecution and despotic power, and to establish freedom of religion and civil liberty. It is a very important as well as an interesting fact, that, when the first colonists landed from the Mayflower, they had prepared a constitution for their government. The sufferings and hardships arising from the climate, and the want of necessary supplies, were not the only difficulties with which our fathers had to contend; but those which grew out of their contact with the aborigines of the country were more hazardous and distressing. I will not dwell upon the conflicts between the white and the red man. The story of the Indian is too sad and too well known to make it necessary or agreeable to dwell on the subject. But I must remind you that that race is fast wasting away before the march of civilization. I do this merely for the purpose of illustrating this principle, namely:—That the advancement of civil and religious liberty is so important to the happiness of the human race, that no considerations connected with the temporary misfortunes of any portion of the human family can be permitted to interfere with its progress.

No one can read the history of the Indian and fail to see that amalgamation with the white race was utterly impracticable, and that the only question seemed to be, which of the two races should suffer most in the approaching conflict. The result is known; and while we may shed a tear of sorrow at the sufferings of the Indian, or on the ashes of his wigwam, we may at the same time thank our God that he has thus made us the instruments to forward his purposes towards our race.

It must be remembered that the history of the Indian is not the only record of human sufferings in the cause of civil and religious liberty. Look back on its pathway: see it marked with national and individual sufferings, and many costly sacrifices; see it covered with blood mingled with lamentation and wo. But who will gainsay it? It is the fiat of omnipotent power, goodness, and truth, before whom every knee must bow and every tongue be silent.

I will not detain you by noticing any of the occurrences of the intermediate time, but will hasten on to that period when our fathers felt themselves strong enough to assert their right to all those privileges of free and independent men which by a common heritage they had derived from their ancestors, and when they published to the world that declaration of their principles which you have just heard read. That declaration contains these great principles:—1st. That all civil government is of divine origin. 2d. That every nation or community which have united for mutual protection, and for the pursuit of happiness, have an inalienable right to make laws for their own government. 3d. That every nation has a right to alter or amend those laws whenever they may see fit to do so. These appear to me to be the great principles of our Declaration of Independence. Now, in violation of every rule of fair criticism, there are persons who say that the practice of our government is inconsistent with the principles of the Declaration, because, while that instrument proclaims that all men are born free and equal, we keep in bondage a portion of the human family. It is an error to say that the general expression of a sentiment contained in an instrument of that kind is to control the sense of that instrument. It must be taken as a whole, and any single or isolated passage must be construed by the obvious intent and meaning of the instrument itself. It is quite obvious that the general expression alluded to is applicable only to men in their *national* and not in their *individual* character; because any other construction would be opposed to all our knowledge of human affairs, as well as to the universal common sense of mankind.

In the formation of our government the pre-existing institution of domestic servitude was recognised as lawful. When the Constitution of the United States was framed, we are informed that the convention was sitting in Philadelphia at the same time that the Congress of the Confederation was in session in New York. In some cases the same person was a member of both bodies; their proceedings were known to each other, and the same questions were in several instances simultaneously discussed: and the question of slavery was then, as it is now, an exciting and absorbing subject. During the sittings of these respective bodies the ordinance of 1787, interdicting slavery in the Northwest Territory, was passed, and with the full knowledge of the Constitutional Convention. With these historical facts, it is inconceivable that the framers of the Constitution should not have well considered the ordinance referred to, or that its provisions could have been omitted from the Constitution by inadvertence. But, on the contrary, it is manifest that the framers of the Constitution *refused* to insert it, preferring to leave all the consequences of slavery, whether for good or for evil, exclusively with the States who saw fit to tolerate the institution. It was known, of course, not only by the Convention which formed the Constitution, but by the people who adopted it, that when it went into operation it became the supreme law of the land, not to be controlled by the feelings of individuals, or by any act of the Congress of the Confederation. The ordinance of '87, so far as it respects slavery, was virtually abrogated by the adoption of the Constitution, because there is no authority conferred by that instrument on Congress to re-enact it. I need hardly add that I am, therefore, opposed to the Wilmot Proviso, and all kindred measures.

In a letter written by me last fall, declining to enter the arena of competition with others as a candidate for the post of senator, I expressed very naturally a hope that, whoever might be selected, he would be a man pledged to the Union and to the execution of the laws. The expression of that sentiment has provoked the most angry, bitter, and unrelenting denunciation. I have not been convinced, however, by any thing which has been said on the subject, that the sentiment then avowed was improper or not justified by the existing state of things. I will here repeat that I go for the Union, the whole Union, and nothing but the Union, and the compromises of the Constitution at all hazards, at all sacrifices, and in defiance of all consequences.

I am not, fellow-citizens, in the habit of using equivocal language or ambiguous inuendoes. I say now that I not only considered the Union in jeopardy then, but that I am of opinion that it continues to be menaced by dangers imminent and formidable, and that I entertain no doubt that, unless the aggression of the Northern and Eastern agitators be arrested by the controlling power of public opinion and authority, a dissolution of the Union is still probable, to say the least. How can it be otherwise, if the country continues to be infected by intestine factions, whose criminations and recriminations shall drive its people to a mutual hatred, only to be appeased by blood?

Fellow-citizens, I dislike much to speak of the dissolution of the Union. I loathe the term. But it may come despite of all our efforts to avert it. Therefore it may be proper for me to say a word or two in anticipation of such a result, and for the purpose of turning the attention of my fellow-citizens to the course which New Jersey should take under consideration. For one, if such a calamity should occur, I hope that New Jersey, following the dictates of duty as well as interest, will unite for better or for worse with those who are willing to abide by and respect the compacts of the Constitution. You may depend upon it, that no reliance is to be placed upon the faith of those who refuse to acknowledge the obligation of the common compact of the present Union. If a dissolution of the Union is inevitable, then I would prefer that the lines of separation should be drawn along the Hudson and the Lakes, rather than the Potomac and the Ohio. I have no doubt that in such an event the Northwestern States would unite with New Jersey, Pennsylvania, and the South. The South is their common customer; there is their market. The republic so constituted would have no natural repugnance to the spread of civilization and reformed religion over that portion of the continent which seems now to be but imperfectly subjected to their influence. Great Britain, while we were yet colonies, attempted to limit our settlements to the Alleghanies—a vain and fruitless attempt; and any similar policy now would be equally vain. Already has the Anglo-Saxon avalanche descended the western slope of the Rocky Mountains to the Pacific shores. Hitherto the impulse has been westward, and westward chiefly has been the march of empire, until at last it has met resistance in one of those vast oceans which cover so large an area of the globe. Rebounding from the contact, it will and must naturally soon take another and more southern direction.

I am only stating what I consider the *law* which governs the progress of the Anglo-Saxon race. I will not attempt to impeach or defend what I believe to be the inevitable destiny of my country and my race. But I am under no obligation to shut my eyes on the vista through which it reveals itself. I am satisfied with the limits, the grandeur, the capabilities, of my country. I justify no wars of aggression, no inordinate and lawless desire for extension of territory, no infraction of treaty-stipulations, no violation of the laws of nations or the rights of man to aggrandize the Republic. With her present boundaries and the certain growth and development of her resources, I feel assured that my country, if she remains united in all her integral parts, will, within fifty years, acquire more wealth and power than any sovereign potentate or dominion which now sways or ever before swayed any portion of the destiny of mankind. Nevertheless, I am unwilling to say to my countrymen that you shall go no farther East or West, or North or South. I am unwilling that the Anglo-American race shall perpetually recoil from any given boundary, and that any portion of this continent not now in their possession shall forever be impenetrable to their civilization, enterprise, and industry. Any such exercise of authority would be as ineffectual as that of the Danish monarch over the Atlantic tides. Faithfully let us perform all our treaty stipulations with our neighbours, punish marauders and lawless adventurers who within our borders marshal forces in hostile array against a friendly power. But let us not attempt to prevent the peaceable progress of our countrymen over a continent which Providence seems to have designed for their occupation and civilization.

The position which would practically limit the Republic at the South, assumed by a great Northern statesman, for whom I have the most profound regard, and whose virtues and patriotism are better known to no one than myself, I cannot approve. That position is assumed under the plausible idea of limiting the area of slavery. The assumption that would not permit the admission of a State into the Union, without a restriction on slavery, is an aggression on the South which finds no warrant in the Constitution. We have as much right to say that the population of a State shall be all Protestants or all Catholics, as to prescribe the *kind of labour* to be employed by its people. We have as much right to force slavery upon a State as to interdict it. If the South shall obtain a majority in Congress, they would have as much right to introduce slavery into the free States, as the North have to force the Wilmot Proviso upon new States. There is no such power in the Constitution. That incomparable production of human wisdom nowhere gives authority to Congress to prescribe to an emigrant, going to the public lands, what kind of property he shall take with him or what kind of property he shall not take with him. The attempts to exercise any such authority can only be made in virtue of a latitudinarian construction of the Constitution, which would invest the General Government with unlimited powers. The paramount duty of the small States consists in restraining the General Government within its delegated limits; because, as soon as the National Government refuses to recognise the obligations of the Constitution, the small States will only hold their sovereignties by the sufferance of their neighbours.

For these reasons, and others, I deny that the Government, or Congress, or the North, have any right to say that a State asking to be admitted into the Union shall be refused admission unless she discards from her borders a portion of the property of fifteen sister States. I have no fears of the increase of the slave States over the free States, no matter what their latitude or multiplication may be. I have heretofore indicated what I believe to be the destiny of the African race. Whether I am right in these views or not, or whether the evils of slavery are such as the abolitionists represent them to be, no considerations connected with those evils, nor any growing out of the balance of power, will warrant a violation of the compacts of the Constitution. The Constitution is neutral on the subject of slavery. To make it aggressive or defensive is to violate it. The Union can only be preserved by a strict adherence to the Constitution. If that be violated, the bonds of the Union are broken, and the aggrieved parties will seek redress and compensation without regard to its obligations.

In conclusion, fellow-citizens, I will express the hope that wise and beneficent councils may everywhere prevail—that wild fanaticism may be arrested in its mad career—that its folly may be made manifest to all men—and that in all coming time the stripes and stars our patriot fathers followed to victory or death may wave, as they wave to-day, over a united people.

Speech of Mr. Stockton, of New Jersey, on flogging in the Navy.

DELIVERED IN THE SENATE OF THE UNITED STATES, JANUARY 7, 1852.

THE memorial in relation to flogging in the Navy being before the Senate, Mr. Stockton said:—

Mr. PRESIDENT:—The subject of this memorial, in my judgment, is equal in importance to any which is likely to occupy the attention of Congress. It was therefore, sir, that I asked the Senate, on its first presentation, to permit it to lie on the table for a few days, that I might have an opportunity to examine it. At the same time I promised the Senate, when it next came up, that I would express my views in relation to it. It is my purpose now to redeem that promise.

The memorial upon the table presents for the consideration of the Senate nothing less than the whole foundation of our naval structure,—the human material by which your ships are worked and fought, your guns levelled and their thunders pointed at your foes. Good ships, well built, well rigged, and fully equipped, are magnificent and perfect specimens of human science and art. But unless they are manned by good men they will sail only to become prizes to your enemies. If you do not desire to build ships for your enemies, you must give them crews worthy to defend them. Sir, the difference between sailors is as great as the difference between other classes of different nations. There is as much difference between the American sailor in our whaling and coasting service and the sailors of other nations, as there is between the raw European emigrant and the sturdy son of one of our frontier pioneers. The emigrant will, in some cases, almost starve, while the pioneer is building his log-house, enclosing his corn-field, and making himself an independent and useful man.

I am of opinion that the nation whose service is supplied with the best common sailors will excel in naval warfare, as well as in all maritime pursuits. I am further of opinion that in versatility, education, courage, and industry, our sailors in the whaling and coasting service excel those of all other nations. I am furthermore of opinion that the superiority of the American sailor has decided the battle in our favour in many a bloody conflict, when, without that superiority, it might have been otherwise. I desire to secure and preserve that superiority. To that end, and for humanity's sake, I am utterly and irreconcilably opposed to the use of the lash in the navy, or anywhere else. The longest, the most arduous voyages are made in the merchant service without the use of the lash. In the Polar seas—among the icebergs of the Arctic and Antarctic Oceans—the intrepid New Englander pursues his gigantic game and hurls his harpoon, and, after a three years' voyage, returns with the oily spoils of his adventurous navigation. But he owes none of his success, his patient endurance, his exemplary discipline, and his indefatigable industry, to the guardian ministrations of the lash. To say that men who can make such voyages, and endure such hardships cheerfully and contentedly, cannot navigate their own national ships without the infliction of the infamous lash, is a libel. Is their nature changed the moment they step on the deck of a national vessel? Are they less men—less Americans—as soon as the custody of the American flag or the national honour is intrusted to their keeping? No, sir; it is a libel. I do not mean to use the word in an offensive sense, nor shall I to-day use any word in that sense. It is one of those inconsiderate, thoughtless opinions, which mankind seem to think they have a perfect right to express in regard to sailors. It was not long since, sir, that I had a conversation on this subject with a gentleman who had for several years commanded a fine ship in the merchant service, but who is now an honourable, active, and efficient man of business in one of our large cities, and to whose integrity, generosity, and humanity, I would intrust anybody *but a sailor.* After he had heard my views on this subject, he instantly replied, "Why, you mean to treat them like human beings!" The theory that the navy cannot be governed and that our national ships cannot be navigated without the use of the lash, seems to me to be founded in that false idea that sailors *are not men*—not American citizens—have not the common feelings, sympathies, and honourable impulses, of our Anglo-American race.

I do not wonder, when I look back on the past history of the sailor, at the prevalence of this idea. His life has been a life of habitual—I will not say of systematic—degradation. The officers who command him—the oldest, the bravest, and the best—have been accustomed from their boyhood to see the sailor lashed about the ship's deck like a brute. He who by the laws of the service in which he is engaged is treated, or liable to be treated, like a brute, soon comes to be thought of as at least but little better than a brute. Who in social life respects a man whose back has been scarred at the whipping-post? Into what depth of contempt does such punishment sink its victim? And here is one of the worst evils of the system. It destroys those feelings of respect and kindness which officers ought to entertain for the sailors under their command. But this is only one of the worst evils of the system. It destroys those feelings of regard and respect which the sailors should entertain for their officers. The truth is, there are no relations of affection and regard between them. The one is the oppressor, and the other the oppressed. Sir, a man may fear or hate; but he neither loves nor respects his tyrant. The worst government upon earth is that of fear; the best, that of love and affection. These sentiments, by a law of our nature, must be mutual sentiments. Bonaparte was the idol of the soldier, because the soldier was his idol. They loved him because they supposed he loved them. There is nothing that gallant and brave men will not do and suffer for a commander whom they love. Difficulties and dangers and death have no terrors for such men. In great battles, where the contest has been doubtful, those soldiers have always fought most desperately whose devotion to their commander was the greatest. It has always been considered as an essential element in the character of a successful commander, that he should be able to excite and encourage the confidence and affection of the men under his command. But what confidence or regard can be expected under the government of the lash? But more than this: this punishment destroys the sailor's own self-respect. What has honour—what has pride—what has patriotism—to do with a man who may be, at the caprice of another, subjected to an infamous punishment, worse—ay, sir, in some cases worse a thousand times—than death? Can nobleness of sentiment, or an honourable pride of character, dwell with one whose every muscle has been made to quiver under the *lash?* Can he long continue to love his country, whose laws degrade him to the level of a brute? The infamous "question" of torture now only remains as a blot on the page of Anglo-Saxon history. The whipping-post, where the worst vagrants used to expiate their offences, has been discarded from society. The worst offences in our State prisons are no longer punished by the lash. Why is all this? Why are those punishments now condemned as the shameful relics of a barbarous age? It is because the light of a better day has dawned. It is because the pecepts of the gospel of Christianity have ameliorated our laws. It is because society has made the discovery that if a man is fit to live at all he ought not to be divested of all the qualities which make a man, by the infamous mutilation of his body. What is the answer which is given to all this by those who seek to restore this relic of barbarism to the navy? Why, they tell us, We intend only to apply this system of punishment to seamen—we intend only to flog sailors. That is quite true. It is only sailors who are to be treated like brutes —ay, sir, worse than brutes. No man who hears me would permit his dog to be thus treated. There is no spot on the habitable globe known to me, where a man would be permitted to seize up his dog, and lash him until he cut the flesh from his ribs and the blood should be made to run down from his backbone to his heels. But, sir, it is only the sailor for whom this punishment is to be reserved.

Who, O senators! is the American sailor, that he is to be treated worse than a dog? He has been my companion for more than a quarter of a century—through calm and storm, privations, sufferings, and danger. In peace and in war I have lived with him, and fought with him side by side by sea and land. I have seen him in the Northern Ocean, where there was no night to veil his deeds. I have seen him on the coast of Africa, surrounded by pestilential disease. I have seen him among the West India Islands in chase of pirates, with his parched tongue hanging almost out of his mouth. I have encamped with him on the California mountains—and on the plains of the Mesa have seen the rays of the morning sun play on his carbine and his boarding-pike. I have seen him march one hundred and fifty miles through an enemy's country, over mountains and through rivers, with no shoes on but those of canvas, made by his own hands, and with no *provision* but what he took from the enemy. I have seen his feet scarified by the projecting rocks, as he hauled his cannon over the hills. I have seen him plunge into the Rio San Gabriel, and drag his guns after him in the face of a galling fire from a desperate foe. And, finally, I have lain beside him on the cold ground, when the ice has formed on his beard. Sir, his heart has beat close to my own. I ought to know him. I do know him. And this day—now, before the assembled Senate of the Republic—I stand up to speak in his behalf. I hope he will find an abler advocate. Nay, I am sure he will find abler advocates on this floor. But, nevertheless, hear me.

Mr. President, the American sailors, as a class, have loved their country as well, and have done more for her in peace and war, than any other equal number of citizens. Passing by for a moment their antecedent glorious achievements, let me remind you that he has recently gained for his country an empire. Through perils by land and perils by water he has gained a golden empire, which has added to his country's renown and greatness, and perhaps saved his fellow-citizens from almost universal bankruptcy and ruin. And what has his country done for him? When the fighting was over, the battles won, the conquest achieved, you sent a band of Mormons to California to drive him to his ship and rob him of his glory,—and historians, too, to prove once more that history is a *lie.* You refused to give him "bounty lands," which you give to the soldier,—his comrade fighting by his side; and you have neglected to give him even your thanks. And now, to cap the climax of his country's ingratitude, these memorialists would have him scourged. They would scourge him for drunkenness, when they put the bottle to his mouth. They would scourge him for inattention to his duty, when injustice and wrong have made him for an instant discontented and sullen. Shame! Shame! You would scourge him while living, and when dead consign him to a felon's grave. That I may not be supposed to have drawn upon my fancy, or to have exaggerated his country's inhumanity, I ask the Secretary of the Senate to read these documents.

The Secretary read them, as follows:—

" *To the Honourable the Senate and House of Representatives in Congress assembled*

" The undersigned, President and Trustees of the Boston Marine Society, of the city of Boston, in the State of Massachusetts, beg leave to represent to your honourable bodies that, having had their attention for many years directed to the condition of seamen, abroad and at home, they have been much impressed with the fact of the sufferings of this valuable class of our citizens by sickness and accidents, and from poverty arising from these circumstances, connected with their proverbial improvidence for the future, with their pecuniary means.

" The benefits of medical aid and comfort in foreign ports enjoyed by others are hardly ever obtained by them, and, in consequence, after receiving such comforts and attentions as the ships they are attached to and their officers can give, they are frequently brought home and placed in our marine hospitals, where no seaman can remain beyond the time limited by the laws regulating those institutions.

" It is very often the case that they are dismissed from these hospitals when not sufficiently restored to render them fit for their active service, and, in consequence, they become paupers or tenants of public almshouses, though most of them would rather die than suffer this degradation.

" It is well known to all observant of seamen, that they are always ready to answer the call for their services, whether it be in the service of the naval or of the mercantile marine—as ready to fight with valour for their country as to aid in its commerce ; and so true is this, that very few seamen advanced in years can be found who have not served in both our public and private ships.

" Your attention is respectfully called to the fact that there is at this moment in the public treasury, as your memorialists have been informed, money to the credit of seamen who have been attached to the government marine and to the mercantile marine, amounting to more than a million of dollars.

" This large amount has accrued from unclaimed sums due to deceased seamen, from unclaimed prize-money belonging to seamen of private as well as public armed vessels, and to the contributions made by all seamen of twenty cents per month in the name of hospital-money.

" In view of these facts, your memorialists beg leave to solicit from your honourable bodies that measures may be taken to ascertain the amount accumulated from these sources in the United States Treasury, and that therefrom suitable provision may be made in the principal seaports in the United States for the further maintenance of seamen, citizens of the United States, who are infirm and unfit for service, from sickness, advanced age, or any other cause. All which is respectfully submitted.

" PRESIDENT AND TRUSTEES, B. M. S."

" Z. RING, ESQ.—DEAR SIR :—I herewith furnish you with the information desired. During the year 1850 there were one hundred and six deaths of seamen ; of which number forty-five were buried by friends ; the balance (sixty-one) were taken by the Almshouse to Potters' field ; for the latter class the Government allow us $5 each—($3 for coffin, and $2 for ground,)

" Not one in ten have money to provide for themselves.

" Very respectfully,

" JOHN L. ROOME,
" Superintendent of the City Hospital, N. Y."

POTTERS' FIELD.—The grand jury for the September term examined two hundred and seventy-six complaints, and found one hundred and thirty-three bills of indictment. They visited the various public institutions, but made no presentment. Previous to being discharged by the court, the foreman, Henry Erben, Esq., at the request of the grand inquest, stated to the court that the jury had visited Potters' Field, and found it in a horrible condition. One pit was about half-filled. The coffins were exposed to the sun. The stench from them was very great. They directed Mr. Webb, the keeper, to come before the grand jury on the following day. On the 19th he made the following affidavit :—

" GRAND JURY ROOM, September 19, 1851.

" William O. Webb, being duly sworn, saith, that he is the keeper of Potters' Field ; that the ground on Randall's Island, used for a burying-place, is not at all suited for it ; that it is full of rocks ; pits are dug for the dead, where they are put in layers of six deep. The bottom of the pits being solid rock, when decomposition takes place, the liquid not being able to go in the ground, passes through the top, causing a horrible stench, which can be smelled for more than a mile.

" There is no earth between the layers of coffins, and there are only about eighteen inches of earth over the top layer of coffins ; that it frequently happens that at high tides and heavy rains the water gets into the pits, so that the

coffins are floating. He further saith that in less than three weeks there will be
no room left in the yard to bury another person. He also states that the south
end of Ward's Island is a suitable place for a Potters' Field, the soil being good
and free from rock.

"Sworn this 19th day of September, 1851.

"HENRY ERBEN, *Foreman.*"

Mr. STOCKTON.—Mr. President, to whom in time of peace are intrusted the
lives of the thousands who traverse the ocean? Whose energy and skill, and
hardy, self-denying toil, carry the products of your soil through the world, and
bring back the rich return? It is the American sailor. By his superior qualities as a man, he has enabled you to rival in commerce the boasted mistress of
the ocean. Where is the coast or harbour in the wide world accessible to human enterprise to which he has not carried your flag? His berth is no sine-
cure. His service is no easy service. He is necessarily an isolated being; he
knows no comforts of home and wife and children. He reaps no golden rewards for the increase of treasure which he brings to you. When on shore, he
is among strangers and friendless. When worn out, he is scarcely provided for.
Making many rich, he lives and dies poor; carrying the arts of civilization and
the blessings of the gospel through the world, he is treated as an outcast from
the mercies of both. But look to your history—that part of it which the world
knows by heart—and you will find on its brightest page the glorious achievements of the American sailor. Whatever his country has done to disgrace him
and break his spirit, he has never disgraced her; he has always been ready to
serve her; he always has served her faithfully and effectually. He has often
been weighed in the balance, and never found wanting. The only fault ever
found with him is that he sometimes fights ahead of his orders. The world
has no match for him, man for man; and he asks no odds, and he cares for no
odds, when the cause of humanity or the glory of his country calls him to fight.
Who, in the darkest days of our Revolution, carried your flag into the very
chops of the British Channel, bearded the lion in his den, and woke the echoes
of old Albion's hills by the thunders of his cannon and the shouts of triumph?
It was the American sailor. And the names of John Paul Jones and the *Bon
Homme Richard* will go down the annals of time forever. Who struck the first
blow that humbled the Barbary flag, which for a hundred years had been the
terror of Christendom, drove it from the Mediterranean, and put an end to the
infamous tribute it had been accustomed to extort? It was the American
sailor. And the name of Decatur and his gallant companions will be as lasting
as monumental brass.

In your war of 1812, when your arms on shore were covered by disaster—
when Winchester had been defeated—when the army of the Northwest had surrendered, and when the gloom of despondency hung like a cloud over the land,
who first relit the fires of national glory and made the welkin ring with the
shouts of victory? It was the American sailor. And the names of Hull and
the Constitution will be remembered as long as we have left any thing worth
remembering. That was no small event. The wand of Mexican prowess was
broken on the *Rio Grande*. The wand of British invincibility was broken when
the flag of the *Guerriere* came down. That one event was worth more to the
Republic than all the money which has ever been expended for the navy.
Since that day the navy has had no stain upon its escutcheon, but has been
cherished as your pride and glory. And the American sailor has established a
reputation throughout the world—in peace and in war, in storm and in battle—
for unsurpassed heroism and prowess.

Mr. President, I am no painter. I cannot draw with artistical skill the scene
I would have you look upon. But it requires no artist. Picture it to yourself,
sir. See the gallant, bold sailor who has served his apprenticeship with Hull
in the Constitution, or one who helped to drag the guns across the San Gabriel,
stripped, and lashed worse than a dog. Can you stand it, sir? Yet your laws
have authorized it to be done—it probably has been done. And now it is proposed to give authority to do it again. Will the American people stand it?

Will this more than Roman Senate long debate whether an American citizen, as he is—the sailor—shall be entitled to all his rights as an American citizen or not; whether, freeman as he is, he shall be scourged like a slave? Cicero's climacteric, in his speech against Verres, is, that though a Roman citizen, his client had been scourged. And shall an American citizen be scourged? Forbid it, God of humanity, forbid it! For my own part, I would rather see the navy abolished, and the stars and stripes buried with their glory in the depths of the ocean, than that those who won its glories should be subjected to a punishment so ignominious and brutalizing. Sir, if I had the power vouchsafed to others, to impress my own feelings upon the hearts of those who hear me, I would rouse in the minds of senators such a sense of national pride and human sympathy that they would with one voice demand that the memorial which seeks to rob the American sailor of his rights as an American freeman should be thrown under your table and trampled beneath your feet.

Mr. President, the object of all our legislation for our seamen should be to elevate them as a class, and not to degrade them. In proportion as you do this, and teach the sailor to respect himself, you will bring him to the performance of his duty with cheerfulness and alacrity. You best appeal to his patriotism by showing him that he is honoured and respected by his country. You best appeal to his sentiment of native pride by presenting motives to his emulation. You can do infinitely more with him by rewarding him for his faithfulness than by flogging him for his delinquencies. Whatever the peculiarities of the sailor may be, he is still a man, with all the impulses, wishes, and hopes of a man. And, if there is one trait more peculiar to him than another, it is the sentiment of gratitude. He never forgets a kindness, and would take his heart out of his bosom, if he could, to save a friend. Let him only see that he is honoured and respected by his country, and her honour and interest will always be safe in his hands.

I believe that many of the officers of the navy have fallen into the error of supposing that sailors are more influenced by their fears than by their affections. They do not rightly appreciate his character. If they would take more pains to think for him, to keep him out of temptation, to attend to his wants, to see that he was fairly and justly dealt by, and properly to consider the fair allowance which ought to be made for him, they would find it much less difficult to enforce discipline, to gain his confidence, and find him much more tractable. It is not by the severity of discipline as much as it is by a firm, just, and generous government, that he is to be controlled. It is so among men everywhere. It is rather by humane and judicious laws, than by the severity of penal enactments, that good government is established and maintained. Again: in the training and governing those men who are to fight your battles and face every danger with courage, their fear should seldom be appealed to. You ought not to cultivate the emotions which make men cowards and teach them habitually to shrink from the fear of personal suffering. You ought rather to teach them to despise all honourable suffering. True heroism is an intellectual quality. It is moral intrepidity that makes the man of true and reliable courage. And this can only co-exist with a proper sense of personal honour and self-respect. Degrade a man by an infamous punishment, which destroys his personal honour and self-respect, and you do all that human ingenuity can to make him cowardly.

But it is said that the navy cannot be governed without the lash. As a general proposition, I express my utter dissent to it. I admit that among sailors, as among other classes, there will always be found some who are vicious and troublesome. That is the case in the army as well as in the navy; and they have abolished the lash in the army. It is as easy to get other and less offensive punishments for the navy as for the army; and, if those punishments will not answer, the refractory person had better be driven in disgrace from the navy. He is not fit to be trusted in the hour of peril; he is unworthy to have the honour of the flag confided to him. Sufficient inducements should be offered to the better classes to enter the navy; and a part of those inducements should always be good treatment. A free use of the lash—nay, its probable use, its permission by law—has always been an objection urged by the better classes to entering the navy. They prefer the merchant service, where they can at least select their own commander, while in the navy they know not into whose hands they may fall. Thus you see that the very necessity which is pleaded creates, in a great degree, the circumstances out of which it is supposed to spring. You flog because there are bad men in the navy, and the fact that you do flog excludes the better class of sailors from entering the service; so that the mischief is self-perpetuating. But again, it is said that a large majority of the officers of the navy are of opinion that the lash is necessary and indispensable.

Well, there are differences of opinion about it. We all know, however, that old notions and opinions are hard to be rooted out, and that men are very apt to love arbitrary power when they are to exercise it and not be subject to it. All history shows this, and the experience of all reformers confirms it. Lord Denman, late Chief-Justice of England, in a letter on the subject of legal reform, complains that everywhere he met the objection that the judges were opposed to it. And Lord Brougham, in a speech delivered in Parliament on the same subject, expresses a similar sentiment. Yet it was not long before the judges and the bar and the people concurred in opinion as to the beneficial effects of the same reforms. It would seem, sir, that it is a part of man's nature to yield with great reluctance the smallest atom of power with which he may be invested. He is unwilling to admit that he can abuse it. Its safest depository, he considers, is his own hands. For these and similar reasons, I think that the opinion of the officers of the navy on this subject should be taken with many grains of allowance. I find no fault with the independent expression of their opinions. It is the opinion itself which I propose to combat. Their argument is as brief as it seems to some minds formidable. They declare the lash to be necessary and indispensable. If they are right in this opinion, there is an end to the matter. Necessity has no law. But I beg leave to inquire into this alleged necessity.

And first, I ask for what offences has this lash been so freely used? Has it been inflicted for serious or atrocious crimes, which involve the honour of our flag or the safety of our national vessels? Or rather, let me ask, has it not been inflicted for offences which, if they had been entirely overlooked, would not have injured the proper discipline of the navy? Has the lash ever been used in the hour of battle or in that of preparation for a battle? Is it reasonable to suppose that a coward or traitor would face a cannon-ball to avoid the lash? It would seem, then, without multiplying words, that, so far from the lash being necessary for the maintenance of discipline in the most important duty of a ship-of-war, it never has been and never will be used. How is it, then, in regard to the most important matter concerning the discipline of a man-of-war? Has it ever been used for the suppression of mutiny? No, sir; the law has provided for that offence, as well as for cowardice, the punishment of death. Having thus briefly stated what the lash has not been used for, let me inquire, what are the offences for which it is deemed so absolutely necessary? We may derive some information in this particular from the published reports of the offences and punishments which have actually occurred on board our ships-of-war. By reference to the report of the Secretary of the Navy on this subject, you will perceive that one of the offences for which it has been used is that of suspicion of theft. One would hardly say it was either necessary or proper in that case. The offence for which, however, there seems to have been more lashes inflicted than for all other offences, is that of drunkenness. Now, sir, the Government furnishes the liquor for the sailor, and if he gets drunk upon his allowance the Government itself is responsible, and the sailor ought not to be flogged. If he procures it on board of a ship by theft or bargain, it is evidence of a laxity of discipline, for which others are responsible, and for which the sailor ought not to be flogged. The lash, therefore, is not necessary to prevent drunkenness, not only for the reasons just stated, but because it must be universally admitted that it never has and never can prevent the offence of drunkenness, if he who is habituated to it is permitted to have liquor.

The offence of disobedience of orders will be found frequently in this report.

But we are not informed of the precise nature of the offence. Whether it is actual or constructive disobedience of orders; whether it is a serious or trifling matter; whether it is for accidentally spitting on the deck, or neglecting to clean the bright-works of a ship, or not mending his clothes, or leaving his bag on deck; or whether it was a positive refusal to do his duty. We are, therefore, left to infer its seriousness by the punishment inflicted for it. I will hazard the opinion, judging by that standard, that stopping the offender's allowance of tobacco, or rum, tea, sugar, and coffee, would have been, in every case, a much more reasonable and a more efficient punishment. And now, sir, what has become of this plea of necessity,—I will not call it in this connection the tyrant's plea; the officers of the navy do not deserve such a reproach from any one, and especially from myself, because I did, when in the service, execute and permit to be executed the law of the lash, as I hope I did all other laws of the service, which I had sworn to obey and to enforce. And this should be a sufficient answer to those who expect to escape from the grasp of argument and facts by indulging in individual recrimination, and will be sufficient to remind them that there is some difference in the position of those who are called upon to make the laws and those whose duty it is to execute them.

The officers of the navy, in my judgment, are entitled to high commendation. They are, as a class, noble, brave, generous, and patriotic men ; and in all the elements of character which constitute valuable public servants, they have no superiors. But, however much respect I may entertain for them as a class, it is my duty, which I shall endeavour to perform, to deal without reserve or false delicacy with their arguments, and the errors which disgrace and paralyze the service to which they belong. It does appear to me, Mr. President, that the argument, from necessity, has resolved itself simply into this: That the lash is an easy and short way to settle a trifling difficulty with a sailor. And so were the thumb-screw and the rack an easy and short way to get a confession, and the Inquisition settled matters of faith easily and readily. But, sir, there has been a great change in the opinions of mankind on this subject, and I hope the change will go on until the last relic of barbarism shall be banished from the world.

But I care very little for the details of this argument, and will not detain the Senate any longer in relation to them. There is one broad proposition upon which I stand. It is this: That an American sailor is an American citizen, and that no American citizen shall, with my consent, be subjected to this infamous punishment. Placing myself upon this proposition, I am prepared for any consequences. I love the navy. When I speak of the navy, I mean the sailor as well as the officer. They are all my fellow-citizens, and yours; and, come what may, my voice will ever be raised against a punishment which degrades my countrymen to the level of a brute, and destroys all that is worth living for,—personal honour and self-respect.

Mr. President, reference has been made by these memorialists to the example of the British Government. With what propriety such an appeal is made by the citizens of a free republican Government to the institutions of monarchy, let others determine. But, sir, I am not aware that the British Parliament has ever by statute expressly authorised the use of the lash. There is no doubt that it is used in the navy of Great Britain, and has been so used since the restoration of the monarchy under the Stuarts ; but there is no evidence that the practice of flogging prevailed in the republican fleets of the English Commonwealth ; and it is doubted by the best authorities that it ever was tolerated prior to the act of 13th Charles II. We have copied it from their practice, and not from their statute-book. But our Congress did what no British Parliament ever did ; they sanctioned it in express terms by the laws of the United States. And here, Mr. President, you must permit me to call the attention of the Senate to a most singular fact, which is this:—Our law of April, 1800, was principally copied from the statute of Charles II., and is openly and avowedly more severe and arbitrary than the British act, even under the Stuarts, and has remained so until last year, although flogging, as a punishment, was tolerated during the whole of that time, and up to the present moment, on land in England.

The act of Charles II. alluded to was passed when the Duke of York, afterwards James II., was Lord High-Admiral of England, and may be supposed to have been done at his instance. The English historian, the Earl of Clarendon, tells us that when that prince entered on his duties he found the navy too republican for his taste or purposes, and set about reorganizing it by getting rid of the republican officers. In pursuance of this policy, he procured the passage of the act of 13th Charles II. Although that act does not, in express terms, authorize the use of the lash, yet, by virtue of a clause contained in it, the Lord High-Admiral, or the commissioners for executing his duties, issued instructions authorizing the use of the lash in the British navy; and certainly it may be cited to justify any tyranny. I would not have noticed the reference of the memorialists to the practice in the British navy, but that I desire, on this subject, not to leave a peg to hang a doubt upon. But, sir, the example of the British Government, such as it is, is no justification for the United States. The infliction of corporal punishment for certain offences has always, as far as I know, been sanctioned by British laws. The sailor in the British navy receives the same punishment that is inflicted upon landsmen in England; whereas, in the United States, it has been almost universally abolished, and certainly has never been sanctioned by the laws of the United States, except in the army and navy. Justification it has none; and if palliation is to be looked for it could only be found in its infliction by the judgment of the sailor's peers. But the trial by jury is unknown to the naval service. Those great conservative safeguards, so dear to freemen—the arraignment and trial before a jury of his peers indifferently selected, counsel and defence—are unknown to the every-day discipline of a man-of-war. Much less has the sailor any appeal. The process by which he is tried is a short process, and the punishment follows immediately on judgment. Where the power to punish is so absolute, the law should at least protect its victim from an infamous punishment for a petty offence, which may disgrace and ruin him for life. If, when a citizen enters into the service of his country, he is to forego the protection of those laws for the preservation of which he is willing to risk his life, he is entitled, in all justice, humanity, and gratitude, to all the protection that can be extended to him in his peculiar circumstances. He ought certainly to be protected from the infliction of a punishment which stands condemned by the almost universal sentiment of his fellow-citizens,—a punishment which is proscribed in the best prison-government; proscribed in the school-house, and proscribed in the best government on earth—that of parental domestic affection. Yes, sir, expelled from the social circle, from the school-house, the prison-house, and the army, it finds defenders and champions nowhere but in the navy. To say that no laws can be devised for the government of the navy which do not tolerate the lash is an acknowledgment of imbecility which this Senate will never make.

The difficulty in regard to this matter has been that, in framing articles for the government of the navy, three things have been overlooked which ought never to be lost sight of. First, that an American sailor is an American citizen and a freeman, though in the service of his country. Second, that he has yielded no legal right not inconsistent with his obligations of duty. Third, that naval officers are not infallible, and require as stringent regulations for their government as other citizens invested with authority.

And now, Mr. President, I come to the discussion of a part of this subject far from being agreeable. Why is it that naval officers, and even some seamen, as I am told, desire to have the lash restored to the navy? It is a symptom of unfavourable augury. It is an indication that the moral standard by which the navy is estimated is low and degraded. It argues a preference for the exercise of arbitrary power, rather than appeal to those feelings of respect and sentiments of honour which should influence the conduct of honourable men towards each other in the service of their country.

The great Montesquieu has said that, while virtue was the principle of a republic, honour was that of a monarchy. Now the actual government, in peace or war, in your military and naval service, is necessarily, in some degree, monarchical. Within the limits of his command, and in reference to those immediately subject to him, the captain, the colonel, the general, or the commander of a ship-of-war, is a sovereign—a monarch; and I hold that honour is the principle on which the government of his subordinates should be founded. Tell me not that a sailor's heart is insensible to the dictates of honour. I know better. It is there. It may, indeed, slumber and remain passive, and be almost extinguished by sullen revenge or bitter hatred; yet there it is, as real and in as perfect existence as in your breast or mine. By proper appeals to it—by generous treatment—by manly and discriminating excitement—it kindles into activity and becomes the supreme arbiter of the sailor's life and conduct. Sir, if the officers would only believe in the existence of this sentiment of honour, and appeal to it as an instrument for the preservation of discipline, we should not be asked to restore the lash. A requisition for the lash proceeds on the supposition that there is no honour in a common sailor. Now, so far from that dogma having any foundation in fact, it must be known to all who appreciate the character of a true-hearted sailor that honour is almost the only principle by which nine-tenths of them are governed. When an unsuccessful appeal is made to the honour of a sailor, it is not because he is destitute of the principle, but because the appeal has not been properly made.

In the view I take of the subject, then, the argument derived from a low and degraded estimate of the navy is unfounded in any of the characteristics belonging to the common sailor. Has it any foundation in the incapacity of the officers to excite and cultivate those feelings of honour in a sailor which make him obedient and tractable? I hope not. If there be any such they should not be intrusted with any command; *they* are destitute of the faculty of commanding; *they* have not the necessary qualification; *they* are not safe depositaries for such absolute power or for the security of our public ships. How can *they* rouse the sailor's sense of honour in time of battle who have proved themselves incapable of believing in its existence at all other times? I apprehend, if the restoration of the lash be made to hinge upon the question whether the sailor is destitute of honour or the officers of capacity to successfully appeal to that honour, that we should not be troubled with many importunate demands for its restoration. If the desire to restore the lash to the navy is evidence that the standard by which the navy is judged is low and degraded, it is also evidence, to my mind, that the navy has not kept pace with the moral improvement of the age. If it be the general opinion in the navy that the lash is necessary and indispensable for the preservation of discipline, then, I say, we are now just where public sentiment stood in 1660, during the infamous reign of Charles II. Then the thumb-screw and the rack were in vogue, too. And, if we are to go back to the lash, I do not see why we should not retrograde likewise to the boot, the rack, and the torture. What would be thought of the man who would propose to introduce into our penal code those horrible and barbarous punishments of which I have spoken? what would be thought of the civilized community who would approve such a proposition and re-enact punishments in vogue three hundred years ago? Yet the proposition to restore the lash is of a similar character. It takes for granted that the sailor has remained stationary ever since the rack, the thumb-screw, and the boot were abolished as part of the criminal law of civilized nations; it takes for granted that of all the light which has irradiated the human mind during the progress of the world none of it has been poured on the understanding of the sailor; that he alone has remained stationary; that he alone has remained ignorant and incapable of improvement; that he alone is doomed to remain the victim of injustice and cruelty. Look, sir, through the various pursuits of human life, and wherever your eyes rest you find that improvement has advanced with giant strides; you find that it has elevated and enlightened the ploughman in his field—the mechanic in his workshop—the merchant—the professional man—the daily labourer—all have felt the benign influences of improved civilization. If the sailor has not felt it in an equal degree with other classes, it is because you have degraded and abused him by treatment from which other classes have compelled you to relieve them. His voice has not been heard, like that of other classes, in the halls of legislation. He has no representative in such places; he wields no political influence; he has no residence; his domicil is on the ship. If the interests of the sailor had received a tithe of the attention bestowed by legislators on the interests of other classes, we should not now be discussing the question whether or not he should be remanded to the tender mercies of these penal atrocities, from which the progress of modern improvement has relieved all other denominations of men; we should not now be discussing the question whether he should be treated like a man or a brute.

Mr. President, a word or two more and I am done. We hear a great deal of the delinquencies of sailors. There are delinquencies of officers as well as of sailors. There are officers in the navy as well as sailors who ought not to be there. If you desire to prepare the navy for the exigencies of war—if you desire to preserve your ancient renown as a naval power—you must, in my judgment, abolish the lash and adopt a system of rewards and punishments in its stead; you must abolish the liquor ration; you must alter the whole system of the recruiting service; in one word, you must purge the navy of all its foul stuff in high places as well as low places; and you must lay broad and deep the foundation of your naval greatness in the character of the COMMON SAILOR. The bone and sinew of every navy is the common sailor. You require the commanding intellect of scientific officers to direct him, and you require good ships. But, after all, the common sailor is the working power which enables the captain and the ship to gain laurels. 'Tis the sailor who works and sails and fights the ship; and in proportion as he is superior or inferior will be the success of the captain and the ship. Sir, in all the best traits of character which distinguish sailors no nation excels the United States. The American sailor is bold, intelligent, hardy, and enterprising, and in nautical skill is unsurpassed. He shrinks from no danger, he dreads no foe, and yields to no superior. No shoals are too dangerous, no seas too boisterous, no climate too rigorous, for him. The burning sun of the tropics cannot make him effeminate, nor can the eternal winter of the polar seas paralyze his energies. Foster, cherish, develop these characteristics by a generous and paternal government. Excite his emulation and stimulate his ambition by rewards. But, above all, save him, save him from the brutalizing lash, and inspire him with love and confidence for your service; and then there is no achievement so arduous, no conflict so desperate, in which his actions will not shed glory upon his country. And, when the final struggle comes, as soon it will come, for the empire of the seas, you may rest with entire confidence that victory will be yours.

I move you, sir, that it is inexpedient to grant the prayer of the petitioners.

Remarks of Hon. R. F. Stockton, of New Jersey, upon non-intervention.

DELIVERED IN THE SENATE OF THE UNITED STATES, FEBRUARY 2, 1852.

Mr. PRESIDENT:—I hold in my hand a series of resolutions passed by the Legislature of the State of New Jersey, and which by their authority have been transmitted to me. I ask that they may be read and printed.

The Secretary read the resolutions, as follows:—

"JOINT RESOLUTIONS IN RELATION TO GOVERNOR KOSSUTH AND THE DOCTRINE OF NATIONAL NON-INTERVENTION.

"WHEREAS, Louis Kossuth, Governor of Hungary, exiled from his country because he made a gallant but unsuccessful struggle for his country's rights, has come to the United States, an invited guest of the nation:

"1. *Be it Resolved by the Senate and General Assembly of the State of New Jersey*, That Louis Kossuth be invited to visit this Legislature at its present session, that we may extend to him the hospitality of the State, and assure him of our sympathy.

"2. *Be it Resolved*, That in Louis Kossuth we recognise a true patriot, and the able and eloquent expounder of constitutional rights and liberties; that we sympathize with him and his countrymen in the calamities which have befallen their fatherland; that we deeply deplore that the recent glorious struggle for the freedom of Hungary was rendered unsuccessful by the treason of their general, and the armed intervention of Russia, contrary to the principles of justice and international law; and that we trust, by the blessings of Divine Providence, that all his future efforts in the cause of his country may be crowned with success, and that the people of Hungary, now dispersed or down-trodden, may be restored to freedom and happiness, under the protecting care of a constitutional government, erected by themselves.

"3. *And be it Resolved*, That every nation has a right to alter, modify, abolish, or adopt its own form of government, and regulate its own internal affairs, and that an armed intervention of any other nation to control or destroy this right is an infraction of international law.

"4. *And be it Resolved*, That the supremacy of the non-intervention law, acknowledged by all nations, would tend to maintain national rights, prevent national wars, and give a lasting peace to the world.

"5. *And be it Resolved*, That our Senators and Representatives in Congress be requested to obtain the passage of a resolution by Congress, instructing the representatives of the United States to the Governments of Europe to urge upon those Governments a declaration that the forcible intervention of one nation to regulate the internal affairs, or to alter, modify, abolish, or prescribe the form of government, of another nation, is an infraction of the law of nations.

"6. *And be it Resolved*, That the Governor be requested to transmit a copy of these Resolutions to the President of the United States, to Louis Kossuth, and to each of our Senators and Representatives in Congress."

Mr. STOCKTON.—Mr. President, no one need doubt my regard for the old Democratic principle, that the representative is bound by the will of his constituents. No one need doubt the profound respect which any expression of opinion by the Legislature of New Jersey will command from me. I know no higher honour than faithfully to represent my native State. I can enjoy no higher satisfaction than to feel that I merit her approval. My ambition in the discharge of my duties here is to promote her interests. In doing *that*, I know that I shall promote the welfare of our whole country.

Sir, I execrate the oppressors of poor Hungary, and cordially sympathize with the Legislature and people of New Jersey in her sufferings. I am as desirous for her independence and the extension of human liberty as any of my fellow-citizens. Nevertheless, I am constrained to say that, while I agree to every sentiment of freedom and love of liberty contained in the resolutions which you have just heard read, I do not entirely concur in the principles of public law by which the object they have in view is sought to be obtained. I will, therefore, with the Senate's leave, proceed to state, in a few brief remarks, the grounds of my opinion, what, in my judgment, are the responsibilities of this Government, and the course we ought to take in regard to our foreign relations. The course suggested by the resolutions is not precisely the one preferred by me. They do not avow the principles which this Government ought to assert and maintain, which the United States always has asserted, and which I hope she will continue to assert as long as there is a single despotic Government existing whose people rise to demand the blessings of liberty.

Sir, when we cast our eyes over the world, everywhere, with the exception of America, we see the surface of the whole earth appropriated by absolute monarchs. The only country which enjoys Republican Government, and whose people adequately appreciate free institutions, is the United States. Those free institutions comprehend all that survives of free principles and political liberty. In them is concentrated all that is valuable of what man has ever achieved in qualifying himself for self-government.

The Mosaic Republic—Rome and her Empire—the transitory commonwealths of Italy and Germany, which heralded the revival of learning—all stand as beacon-lights to warn and instruct us. All that is of value in the institutions of the Great Alfred or Modern Britain is ours—improved, perfected, and divested of every element which can interfere with or enfeeble the sovereignty of the people. We are, in truth, the residuary legatees of all that the blood and treasure of mankind, expended for four thousand years, have accomplished in the cause of human freedom. In our hands alone is the precious deposit. Before God and the world, we are responsible for this legacy. Not for our own benefit only, but for the benefit and happiness of the whole family of man. What course, then, shall this Government take to perpetuate our liberties and to diffuse our free institutions over the world?

1st. We must guard our Constitutional grant of delegated power from infraction. We must abide within the limits prescribed by the States to the General Government. We must discreetly exercise the powers actually granted, and abstain from the exercise of all powers not granted.

2d. We must so direct the foreign affairs of this Government, that the progress of liberty shall be promoted and not retarded. This progress may not be promoted by war except under peculiar circumstances. Peace, as I said upon a former occasion, is the true policy of this Republic. "Peace is the animating genius of our institutions," and, indeed, ought to be of all nations.

But the whole world, wherever you look, with the exception of a portion of this continent, being under monarchical governments, I desire to know how the oppressed and fettered nations of the earth are to break their chains, and maintain themselves against the armies of despotism, if the law of nations reads that there shall be *no intervention* in their behalf?

I cannot give my consent to any proclamation of principles which may be construed to abridge the right and sacred duty which belongs to this Government to do whatever it may choose to do in aid of any people who are striving to throw off the yoke of despotism.

But, Mr. President, there are, in my judgment, *two extremes*, which should be avoided in the conduct of our foreign relations. 1st. We should not recklessly interfere with the affairs of foreign nations. We should count the cost, weigh well the duty and necessity, and be sure that our objects are practicable and attainable, consistent with the principles of our Government, and promotive of human liberty and happiness. Washington, and the master spirits of that age of great men, knew well that in the infancy of this Government we were not able to cope with the European belligerents who had given us such just cause of offence. But he foresaw the period when this Republic would be able not only to protect itself, but to stand forth as one of the greatest powers of the earth. He foresaw, likewise, that our mission was not compatible with any entangling alliances with other nations. He therefore admonished us to avoid all such connection. Notwithstanding, sir, the able and ingenious manner in which the invitation has been given, that we should entangle ourselves in a coalition with Great Britain to dictate this new law of *non-intervention* to all nations, I am, so far as it respects this overture, for abiding by the advice of Washington; I want no entangling alliances.

2d. The other extreme which we should avoid, and into which so many are desirous that we should rush headlong, without a glance to the future, is, that forgetting all our obligations and duties to the cause of humanity and to the principles of universal freedom, we should, from unworthy fears or a false conservatism, hastily decide that we have no concern in the condition of the world beyond our own boundaries; and precipitately resolve, that in no event and under no circumstances shall we interfere in behalf of oppressed nations.

I cannot consent to yield and abandon this natural right, which all nations from time immemorial have exercised. Sir, I say that intervention—not for the purpose of helping an odious tyrant to put down liberty, because that is against the laws of God and man, but in behalf of "*an oppressed people who implore assistance*"—is not only in conformity with the universal *practice* of nations, but it is sustained and inculcated by the best authorities on *public law*.

Vattel says:—

"But, if the prince attacking the fundamental law give his subjects a legal right to resist him,—if tyranny, becoming insupportable, obliges the nation to rise in their defence—every foreign power has a right to succour an oppressed people who implore their assistance."

Again, the same author says:—

"For, when a people from good reasons take up arms against an oppressor, justice and generosity require that brave men should be assisted in defence of their liberties. Whenever, therefore, a civil war is kindled in a State, foreign powers may assist that party which appears to them to have justice on its side. He who assists an odious tyrant—he who declares for an unjust and rebellious people—offends against his duty."

So much for the law; now as to the practice.

Mr. Wheaton says, in his history of the "Modern Law of Nations:"—

"The first war of the French Revolution originated in the application, by the allied Powers, of the principle of armed intervention to the internal affairs of France, for the purpose of checking the progress of her revolutionary principles and the extension of her military power. That this was the avowed motive of the Powers allied in the continental war of 1792, will be apparent from the examination of historical documents."

He says again:—

"That the measures adopted by Austria, Russia, and Prussia, at the Congress of Troppau and of Laybach, in respect to the Neapolitan Revolution of 1820, were founded on principles adapted to give the great Powers of the European continent a perpetual pretext for interfering in the internal concerns of its different States."

Mr. Wheaton, speaking of that period of time between the peace of Westphalia (1648) and that of Utrecht, (of 1813,) says:—

"Whatever disputes might arise as to its (intervention) application, the principle itself was acknowledged on all hands."

Sir, I well know that the opponents of intervention are in the habit of relying on isolated passages from writers on the law of nations in support of this doctrine. But it will be found, on a thorough examination of those writers, that all they mean to say is that no nation has a right to interfere with the *domestic concerns or the municipal institutions of foreign countries, or to stir up to rebellion their citizens or subjects*. But they all agree to the right to intervene when a people have actually risen and are striving to throw off intolerable oppression.

It is my deliberate opinion, sir, that we not only have the right, but that it would be our duty, under some circumstances, in our own good time, when the occasion is proper and it may be practicable, to assist any people who rise to achieve their liberties and to establish a republican government. Sir, it has been practised by all nations from time immemorial; and all the paper promulgations which will ever be made will never stop this practice among nations. The only way in which it can be arrested is by appealing to their interest and safety—*by boldly declaring that we will interfere whenever it suits us.* Sir, what law will they or do they consult except the law of their own will? You cannot chain up the great Powers of the earth by paper declarations of the law of nations. The law of nations in modern times, as well as of old, is the *law of the strongest*. This we experienced to our loss and sorrow for many years, during which our commerce was plundered by Great Britain and France, and for which redress has been vainly sought up to this time by our suffering fellow-citizens.

It is true, indeed, that nations have generally exercised this right for the purposes of oppression and injustice, and in hostility to the rights of mankind. But a better time is coming, when the United States may interpose against the oppressor and in favour of the oppressed.

Therefore, I am unwilling, *after tyranny has so long had sway*, and lorded it over the destinies of mankind, now to avow a principle which leaves to its tender mercies the happiness of the whole human race.

Sir, an avowal by us of the principle of non-intervention would raise a wall around this Republic as high as heaven, and would shut in the light of liberty from surrounding nations. The avowal of such a principle at this time would be received with one universal shout of joy by all the potentates of Europe, and with one universal wail of lamentation and wo by all true lovers of freedom on earth. I am unwilling to gratify the despots of the world by any such proclamation. What hope would remain to the oppressed after such a declaration? The radiant light which, emanating from this Republic, has so long cheered and animated their hearts, would shine no longer; all would look black and cheerless, and despair would settle darkly on their prospects.

Besides, would not the establishment of the principle of non-intervention as the law of nations be in direct opposition to the principles declared by Mr. Monroe in relation to this continent? Does any one doubt that if this country felt itself bound, under no circumstances and at no time, to interfere with the affairs of Europe, that before many years monarchical governments would be established in the whole Southern portion of this continent? Does any one doubt that, before many years, the island of Cuba would be a dependency of Great Britain? It is, then, palpable that while peace is the policy of this country, and while we should always bear in mind the admonition of Washington against entangling alliances, that it would be suicidal to the honour, to the interests and prospective power, of this Government, if the United States should incur any obligation by which they would forever be forbidden from interfering in the affairs of other nations whenever circumstances in any case might render it necessary, just, and expedient. Therefore it seems to me that this principle of non-intervention would be in direct violation of all the rights and duties of a free and independent republic.

Now, sir, in the practical application of these principles to the important topic of the day, I will take hold of that idea which others seem to have handled with such significant delicacy. I am not afraid to express my opinions on this subject, or, indeed, on any other, although the press (which, God knows, is brave enough) seem to shrink from touching it; and I say, for one, that I am not prepared to go to war with Russia on account of Hungary, partly because Russia is our old and true and faithful friend, and partly because Hungarian liberty, through the instrumentality of the United States, is at present an idea utopian and impracticable. This proposition is self-evident, and requires no demonstration; it is an impossible thing, and what is impossible cannot be— never comes to pass. But, Mr. President, though I am not prepared nor willing to go to war with Russia, or to disturb the present state of things in Hungary, about which we have so little satisfactory information, I will once more repeat, and declare it in the face of the world, as my opinion, that this Government has an indisputable and perfect right to interfere whenever, by such interference, she can promote her own interests and advance the cause of liberty; whenever, by such interference, she may successfully rescue from the grasp of tyranny an oppressed nation, whom she may see fit to assist and to place among the independent nations of the world. This is a principle which we cannot, we dare not, we never will, relinquish. It is an inherent principle of nationality, under no pretence whatever to be surrendered.

Sir, if tyrants have used it heretofore to enthrall mankind, this growing Republic will, some of these days, use it for their freedom. In peace let it be maintained with unfaltering tenacity; in war let it be asserted by all the power of arms; and when the great contest begins, as before 1900 it must, between free principles and the right of self-government and despotic power, then let it be inscribed upon all our banners—everywhere—wherever they float, on every sea, and land, and ocean, and continent, where the warfare rages, let it herald the advent of freedom and national independence, and the discomfiture of tyranny and oppression.

I move that the resolutions be laid upon the table, and printed for the use of the Senate.

Remarks of Hon. R. F. Stockton, of New Jersey, on the Presentation of the Resolutions of the Legislature of New Jersey, upon the Compromise Measures.

DELIVERED IN THE SENATE OF THE UNITED STATES, FEBRUARY 12, 1852.

The following resolutions of the Legislature of the State of New Jersey were presented to the Senate, by Mr. Miller:—

Whereas, the Constitution of the United States is a compact between the several States, and forms the basis of our Federal Union:

And, whereas, the said States, through their representatives, in sovereign capacities as States, by adopting said Constitution, conceded only such powers to the General Government as were necessary "to form a more perfect union, establish justice, insure domestic tranquillity, provide for the common defence, promote the general welfare, and secure the blessings of liberty to themselves and posterity:"

And, whereas, the questions which agitated the country and absorbed so large a portion of the time of last session of the Congress of the United States,— questions in their nature directly opposed to the spirit and compromises of the Constitution, calculated to destroy our domestic tranquillity and dismember our glorious Union,—were happily terminated by the Compromise Measures, it is deemed the imperative duty of this Legislature to express their sentiments in relation thereto: Therefore,

1. *Resolved*, (Senate concurring,) That the Constitution of the United States was framed in the spirit of wisdom and compromise, is the bond of our Federal Union, and can only be preserved by a strict adherence to its express and implied powers; that New Jersey, one of the original thirteen States, has always adhered to the Constitution, and is unalienably attached to the Union, and that she will resist, to the extent of her ability, any infraction of that sacred instrument.

2. *Resolved*, (Senate concurring,) That this Legislature cordially approves the measures adopted by the last session of Congress, known as the "Compromise Measures," and that every patriot in every part of our widely-extended country has cause to rejoice in the adoption of said measures, as a triumph of constitutional rights over a spirit of wild and disorganizing fanaticism.

3. *Resolved*, (Senate concurring,) That New Jersey will abide by and sustain the Compromise Measures, and that her Senators in the Senate of the United States be instructed, and our Representatives in Congress be requested, to resist any change, alteration, or repeal thereof.

4. *Resolved*, (Senate concurring,) That the Fugitive Slave Law is in accordance with the stipulations of the Constitution of the United States, and, in its provisions, carries out the spirit and letter of the Constitution in its compromises, upon which our Union is founded.

5. *Resolved*, (Senate concurring,) That we approve of the patriotic stand taken by the Executive of the United States, in declaring his determination to execute and enforce all laws constitutionally enacted, and that the people of New Jersey will sustain him in so doing.

6. *Resolved*, (Senate concurring,) That the Governor of the State be requested to transmit a copy of these resolutions to the Governor of each State in the Union, and to each of our Senators and Representatives in Congress.

The resolutions having been read, Mr. Stockton addressed the Senate as follows:—

MR. PRESIDENT:—I have also had the honour to receive the resolutions passed by the Senate and General Assembly of the State of New Jersey, which have just been presented by my honourable friend and colleague. Those resolutions, sir, are patriotic and explicit, and need no commendation or explanation or defence from me. Nor is it necessary that I should follow the example of my colleague, and re-state my opinions in regard to the important matters of which they treat, further than to say that I entirely concur in the sentiments which they express. I have heretofore written and spoken as much on this subject as I ought, perhaps, to write and speak on any subject; and, if senators and the country are not sufficiently well informed in regard to my opinions, it certainly is no fault of mine. It would, likewise, be quite superfluous for me to enter upon any vindication of the course which New Jersey has taken in relation to the subject-matter of these resolutions. If, unfortunately, she may, by that course, have alienated from her the affectionate regard of any of her sister States of the North, I can only for her regret such a result, and say that what she has done was intended for the welfare of the Union—the whole Union, and nothing but the Union. It was not that "she loved Cæsar less, but that she loved Rome more." If the men of the South are not satisfied with her course, all that I will say to them is that they are hard to please.

Mr. President, it is a subject of regret as well as surprise to me, that the differences of opinion in regard to the construction of the Constitution should continue to excite in the minds of a portion of our fellow-citizens such strong feelings of bitterness and resentment. Differences of opinion acrimonious and exciting, in relation to the interpretation of the Constitution, are no novelties. Bitter controversies, growing out of such diversities of opinion, disturbed the country long since quite as generally as that which is referred to by these resolutions. Happily, they were not of long duration. They subsided when the will of a majority of the States became known. Why, sir, at the time of the adoption of the Constitution, great diversities of opinion existed among the founders of the Republic. Formidable parties in Massachusetts, in New York, in Pennsylvania, and in Virginia, vehemently opposed its adoption, and in many of the smaller States there were great objections to some of its provisions. It is known that it was not the plan preferred by New Jersey, and different in many respects from the one presented by that pure patriot and eminent statesman and jurist, Judge Patterson, from New Jersey. But that was the age of self-sacrificing virtue. Our fathers sacrificed their feelings, their personal interests and ambition, to the public safety. They magnanimously acquiesced in the will of the majority of the States, and exerted their best faculties to perfect the Constitution and to hand it down to posterity as a bond of Union. Following the example of the wise and patriotic founders of the Constitution and their contemporaries, I can perceive no reason why we should refrain from uniting, as they united, in a spirit of generous conciliation, to preserve the Constitution hereafter from infraction; and to restore that harmony and those fraternal feelings which should exist between the different parties to this compact, and which are so essential to its beneficial existence as well as to the happiness of mankind.

Mr. President, the passage of these resolutions has given me no ordinary satisfaction. They were unanimously adopted in each House of the New Jersey Legislature. They embody the undivided sentiment of that State. *There*, at least, no dissenting voice is now audible in opposition to the Compromise Measures. This unanimous declaration of the opinions of New Jersey is entitled to great respect from the States of this Confederacy. It is a voice from the Flanders of Revolutionary America. New Jersey is that State which, more than any other, was the battle-field of the Revolution. And is it too much to expect that her example should exercise a salutary influence upon Congress and the whole country for all time? Certainly not, if unsparing sacrifices for the achievement of freedom and unfaltering fidelity in maintaining it deserve commendation and respect.

Sir, New Jersey has produced her heroes and her statesmen, but not her historian. When her history is written, *that* will be her eulogy. There is no stain on her escutcheon. Her sons can trace back their ancestry through many generations without finding their blood curdling in the veins of a slave. Her territory was settled by freemen—by men whose pride it was not only to be free, but just. True to themselves, and true to virtue and patriotism, no foot of her soil was wrenched by fraud or force from the original savage proprietors. The last shadow of an Indian claim, a claim to some reserved hunting and fishing grounds, was voluntarily extinguished by purchase many years ago. She has as much pride in looking back to her colonial as to her national history. In the long struggle with insolent governors and royal prerogative, her people were never driven back one hair-line from the assertion and maintenance of all the rights conferred upon them by their original grant; and when the final struggle for independence came she was then among the first to enter the bloody arena. She threw overboard the royal Government and established a free Constitution before the Declaration of Independence, and in advance of her sister States, with the exception, I believe, of New Hampshire and South Carolina. Of the part which she took in that memorable struggle she has memorials which will never perish. Bunker Hill, and Lexington, and Brandywine, and Charleston, were glorious, but not altogether successful, fields. They wear the laurels of Thermopylæ. But the Marathons of the Revolution are in New Jersey. Trenton, Princeton, and Monmouth, commemorate victories. From their bloody fields freedom sprung disenthralled and invigorated. None of the "old thirteen" made more costly pledges to the cause of liberty and the Union. On her territory everywhere may be seen the marks of hostile armies. She was literally baptized in blood. None of her old household homesteads but are rich with the legendary tales of plunder and cruelty suffered at the hands of the enemy. Few of her old families but gave of their best blood to the cause; and when the struggle was ended she reposed on the sacrifices she had made, and left to others the task of boasting of their achievements. She had performed her duty and was satisfied.

Nor has New Jersey been less true to the Union in peace than in war. Among the first in her exertions to achieve our liberties, she yields to none the palm of superior exertions in maintaining them. When the imperfections of the articles of the old confederation became manifest, she was the first to clothe her commissioners to the convention at Annapolis, in 1786, with full powers to remodel the whole form of Government. She united with New York, Pennsylvania, Delaware, and Virginia, in giving the first impulse to the movement which produced the Constitution. She was only second to Virginia in sending delegates to the Constitutional Convention; and when the Constitution was formed she took the lead, with Pennsylvania and Delaware, in its ratification. She was the first, as I stated the other day, to approve the important amendments to the Constitution which secured freedom of religion and of speech, and the right of petition, which have been the safeguards of the States against the encroachments of the General Government. She furnished her full proportion of those great men whose eloquence and wisdom have guided your public councils, and whose heroism has adorned your military annals. The first bright names given to glory in the war of 1812 were those of Pike and Lawrence, true representatives of the Jersey Blues. The first died in the arms of victory at Little York; the other with the memorable words "Don't give up the ship" on his lips. There she is. Though small comparatively in territory, she yields to none in honour, virtue, and patriotism. She has never been at your doors begging importunately for her share of the "loaves and fishes." If in the lifetime of this Government, now embracing a period of three generations of men, she has ever had more than two secretaries of a department and one judge of the Supreme Court, I have forgotten it. She has never had even one foreign minister. With a long extent of sea-coast, and with an imperfect tide-water navigation running into the heart of the State, she has never received any assistance from the General Government worthy a name in aid of her harbours and rivers. With her mountains full of iron, zinc, and other minerals—with her territory dotted all over with manufacturing establishments—she has borne without a murmur her share of the injuries sustained from an ever-changing revenue system. It may be truly said of her that, while she has borne her full proportion of the burdens of the Government, of its direct benefits she has asked little and received less. Still, there she stands, this day as of old, heart and hand, with her treasure and her resources and her blood pledged to a strict construction of the Constitution and to the Union of the States.

In the name of a patriotic, generous, and heroic constituency—ay, sir, if my colleague will permit me to say, in the name of every man, woman, and thinking child in the State of New Jersey—I place my hand on that sacred instrument and declare for me and mine that no letter of it shall be infracted, if we can help it, neither by Northern or Southern unwise counsels. If wrongs exist, they must be redressed by law and according to the Constitution. But this Union of the States—the world's wonder—is the common heritage, as it is the common glory, of all the people of all the States. We must not permit one link of that golden chain to be broken and the hopes and happiness of mankind, for all coming time, to be blighted in the bud by wild fanaticism or hasty passion.

The motion to print was agreed to.

Remarks of the Hon. R. F. Stockton, of New Jersey, on the Bill to increase the efficiency of the Army and Navy.

The Bill to increase the efficiency of the Army and Navy, by a retired list for disabled officers, being under consideration, Mr. Stockton said:

Mr. PRESIDENT:—I have no objection to the postponement of this bill till tomorrow; nay, I desire that it may be postponed to a still more remote period. I do not rise, however, to discuss that question, but simply to ask the chairman of the Military Committee, if he is not willing to leave the business of the Navy in the Senate to the Naval Committee, and whether he will not be kind enough, in the generosity of his temper, to believe that the Naval Committee will use their best exertions in behalf of the navy, and if he will not consent to strike out of the bill the words "the Navy, and to the Marine Corps."

Mr. Shields.—I am perfectly willing to refer the whole matter to the Naval Committee, and they will do me a very great favour if they will take it upon their shoulders. The Committee on Military Affairs have included the navy in this bill, because, on a former occasion, the Committee on Naval Affairs felt it rather hard because we introduced a bill for the army, and did not include the navy. And another reason for including both in one bill, was that they might be precisely upon the same footing; because, if one bill is brought in for the army, and another for the navy, they might differ in principle and in detail. But I will consent, if the senator wishes it, to refer the whole subject to the Naval Committee, and let them investigate it.

Mr. Stockton.—The honourable senator would then commit a greater error still, in my opinion, by referring to the Committee on Naval Affairs an important subject, of which they know little or nothing in comparison with the experience and knowledge which his own gallant services have afforded him. He is well acquainted—no one is better acquainted—with the wants of the army, and no one can or will do it more justice. I have no doubt he is equally disposed to do justice to the navy; but certainly there is a difference between the wants of the army and those of the navy of the United States in many particulars, and perhaps in none more so than in the matters of efficiency and discipline. That the navy of the United States requires some reform in several particulars, I think there are but few who doubt; but this bill cannot secure the reforms adverted to, some of which I will mention before I resume my seat, at the risk of being tedious. Sir, this bill confers but little power that is not already vested by law in the Executive Department of the Government. The President of the United States and the Secretary of the Navy may now put any officer on furlough who cannot perform his duty; and why do they not exercise that power, unpleasant, I grant; yet the efficiency of the navy calls loudly for its exercise, disagreeable as it may be. Why is it that senators ask us to stand between the Executive Government and the people in regard to their proper responsibilities? The law, sir, has already given them power to clear away all this rubbish of which the honourable Chairman of the Committee on Military Affairs speaks.

Such persons as he speaks of have no business in the navy. They ought to have been furloughed long ago. The channel should have been opened before this, and in a different way. The best officers of the navy should have been called up to the performance of the highest duties of the profession, without regard to their rank. The reason that they have not been so called is to be found in the imbecility of the Government. They have the power now, let them take the responsibility of exercising it.

Sir, if it be necessary for the Senate now to interfere, let us have a well-considered system. Let us begin and make a thorough reform. But is it wise to do this now? to do this on the eve of the outgoing of an administration? The Committee on Naval Affairs, I believe, for twelve months, have thought of nothing more earnestly and anxiously than naval reform, and they design to submit, at a proper time, to the Senate, their views of that reform. But they wish to do it thoroughly, and intend to begin at the Navy Department.

Sir, all the members of that committee cherish a regard, a patriotic love, for the navy. They cherish those feelings not only on account of the remembrances of the past, but the anticipations of the future. They remember that this nation is indebted to the navy more than to the army, or to all the other defensive institutions of the country, for its present lofty and prosperous position. That I say without fear of contradiction. Sir, when dismay pervaded this country, when the dark cloud of misfortune was hovering over you, when defeat followed defeat in your army, whose shouts of triumph reanimated and reinvigorated the patriot's heart? It was your gallant navy. And yet, sir, the honourable senator from New Hampshire (Mr. Hale) only on yesterday complained of the expenses of the navy. Sir, the expenses of our navy are nothing in comparison with its importance, its usefulness. They never have been. One battle, the battle of the Constitution and Guerriere, was worth more to this nation than all the treasure that has ever been expended upon the navy. Remember, that at the time of which I speak the British navy and invincibility were, in the minds of most of our countrymen, one and the same thing; and remember, also, that your Executive quailed before the terrors of that invincibility. Your ships were ordered to be laid up, and your coast and mercantile marine abandoned to the enemy.

It was an officer of the navy (Hull) who, against authority, without orders, in opposition to the will of the Government, put to sea, and with his noble ship and gallant crew achieved for you that victory which astonished the world and electrified our own Government and people; and, from its moral effect, was worth, as I have said, all the money you have ever expended upon the navy. The importance, the effect, the value of that fight of Hull's it is impossible to measure or to explain. In fifteen minutes the trident of Neptune was wrested from the grasp of that heretofore invincible navy. At that time, the idea of British invincibility was so common, hardly a man out of the navy, perhaps, who did not believe that one British frigate could take two or three American frigates. Now sir, bearing in mind this state of public feeling, with such odds against them, let me call up before the Senate some reminiscences of the past. Let me state one fact, if no more, to show the obligation you are under, not only to the ship, but to the officer, and to illustrate the cause of this victory to have been the superiority of your men. You have as good materials now, but we must keep up with the progress, the improvement of the age in which we live.

> " See the bold Constitution the Guerriere o'ertaking,
>   While the sea from her fury divides."

See, likewise, that haughty invincible British frigate lying to leeward under easy sail, impatiently waiting the encounter. See her crew, elated with the remembrances of a hundred battles, in the hope, the joy, the expectation of an easy conquest. Hear their shouts of anticipated triumph, only checked by the certainty of too easy a victory. Look again to your own "Constitution." See her bearing down on that frigate, that invincible frigate with St. George's imperious and arrogant ensign streaming from her mast-head. All is silent on the Constitution; no hurrying to or fro, no confusion; all ready to fight and to die for their country. Again, sir, on board the British ship all is bustle, and hurry, and exultation of anticipated victory. All is still as death on board the Constitution. Sir, we can all feel the anxiety of that moment, but I cannot describe it. I speak not merely of their courage, but of their devotion· to their country and to their flag; they had resolved to do or die. She bore down on the British frigate without a whisper being heard on her peopled deck.

They had heard of raking fires; they well knew their destructive effect. They had heard of the memorable tactics of the British navy, and soon perceived that the captain of the British frigate was not to be satisfied with simply taking them, but he would do it in the most approved manner. Steadily Hull goes down, nothing daunted. The British frigate fires a raking broadside, and then wore round and fired another. Steadily Hull keeps his course. By-and-by the first Lieutenant of the Constitution asked Captain Hull if he should return the fire. Hull inquired, "Have you lost any men?" "No, sir." "Wait a while," said Hull. Steadily he keeps his course until he gets within pistol-shot, and then, rounding to as if for a salute, with one broadside decided the victory.

Now, sir, some of these, perhaps, are among the men whom you propose by this bill, unceremoniously, if you please, by the will of the President to put upon a retired list, and with them you would, perhaps, put some of the men who ran from the defence of the frigate Chesapeake. Would you, sir, put men who, when the English boarded their ship, ran below, on the same list with the gallant victors of the Constitution? Is that just? Therefore I say, that the chairman of the Military Committee has, in my judgment, not well considered this bill, so far as regards the navy. If we are to have a retired list, we should have two lists. We should have one which would be for such men as Hull, and such men as Morgan, the gentleman who was before the Senate yesterday on indictment by the senator from New Hampshire. He is one of the most gallant men I ever knew, and when the Constitution got foul of the Guerriere, he went up into the mizen-rigging, and, having looked down, sung out to his shipmates, "They have all run away from their guns; let us board!" And this he did amid showers of musket-shot which fell around him. That was the officer who was arraigned here yesterday.

Sir, I ask the honourable chairman of the Committee on Military Affairs to allow the Committee on Naval Affairs, who perhaps have reflected on this subject as much as any other members of this body, to take care of the interests of the navy for the present—let them have further trial.

But I must in candour say, that that committee, I believe, are not ready to-day to report on so important a matter as the reorganization of the navy. The navy has not only been important, but with these warlike resolutions and these warlike speeches ringing in our ears day after day, I consider it quite as important, at this time, as it ever has been. The navy is now, I will undertake to say, good for nothing for the purposes of war; and I would rather make a motion now to abolish the navy of the United States, than undertake to mend and patch it up by piecemeal. Let us go at it in good earnest, and see what we can do for it. It has happened with the navy, that since its first establishment there has never been any overhauling of its "personnel." The army has been pruned and culled two or three times, but the navy has never been interfered with in that way. The Government has always acted on the presumption that a boy who entered the navy when he was twelve years of age was capable of commanding a ship and wearing the epaulets of a captain whenever he was promoted in turn to that rank. Apply that rule to the pursuits of the world generally; take any hundred men who promised well in their youth, and how many of them will you find who have realized the fond expectations of friends when they arrived at the age of manhood?

The thing speaks for itself. The navy needs reforming, not only because it never has been reformed, but because most of those persons who got appointments in the navy when boys are there now, and some of them totally disqualified for efficient service. The consequence of this system is, all the old officers who are in the service must continue to fill the most important places, fit or unfit. Many of them are of high character, and have rendered the country great services, and should be honoured, but not employed where younger men would do better. They do not belong to the school of progress; they may be old men who have not thought it necessary to keep up with the constant pro-- gress of naval affairs in the world. They may be men of high honour, of great courage, of exalted worth, men who maintained the honour and glory of the country in the battle and the breeze. But, sir, old age has come; they must retire; but for such it should be an honourable retirement. The ardour, the fire of youth is gone; they feel not the same motives to excite them to exertion as younger men, who are in the meridian of life, and who by the present system are kept entirely without employment such as their talents demand, until they, in like manner, are borne down with years.

Sir, I hold that this Government has nothing to do with commiseration or pity in this matter of reorganizing the navy. We are bound to do justice to the country as well as to the officers. I hold that the nation is entitled to the ser- vices, and the best services, of the best men in its employ; and I say that any system which precludes the employment of the best men in any branch of the service is radically wrong, and it ought to be changed; I care not by what pro- cess it is changed. No appeal can be made to my sympathies or feelings. I am willing to pay money to these officers, if that is all that is required; but I am not willing that they should be in the way of others, and thus to balance the account with their country by doing as much harm as good. The Executive has, as I have before observed, the power to correct most of the evils complained of; but he will not do it if the present system is continued. I shall take some proper occasion to recommend an entirely new organization of the Navy Depart- ment. You generally have a Secretary of the Navy who knows nothing in the world about naval matters. He is brought here from his profession, and has to depend upon others for all the information he gets, and those others in nowise responsible for their advice. His word is the law. If a squadron is to be fitted out, he, under the direction of the President, orders the ships and their officers without knowing any thing about them.

Sir, this one-man power will not do in such an establishment. I think that there is no living man that has the intellectual or physical power to perform the duties of the Navy Department as they ought to be performed in justice to the country. Mr. President, I look to the navy as the bulwark of our honour if not safety; and I tell you, sir, that all your famous schemes in reference to Cuba will vanish like mist before the wind, and gentlemen will regret the war- like speeches which they have made, if you do not look to your navy in time. Look at the threatening aspect of France and England. It has amazed me that we are so indifferent about the only means you have to defend your honour. Sup- pose Europe should combine against you, as they would have done long ago, if there had been a monarch there of sagacity and boldness worth the gold in his crown. Every one of your ports would have been blockaded. They would have forbidden you to go on the ocean. They would have declared that, as you had assumed this continent to be your own, you should leave the ocean to them. In such a case how would you have fared twenty-five years ago? It is very easy to bully and boast; but I know the effect of a 32-pound shot at sea at any rate, and I know that a man's heart cannot save his head in such a case. Let me assure senators, while I am discoursing upon this subject, that I am speaking to the most important subject which, in my opinion, can now occupy the attention of American statesmen.

Mr. President, I repeat that the Secretary of the Navy should have responsible advisers, and that in all the details he should have his vote, and that is all. He is a Cabinet Minister. The President has the power of appointing him. I would have it so—he may know all about those duties. But I would have him in- structed in all those branches in which he is deficient, not by casual itinerant teachers, but by known responsible instructors. Sir, I would have a Board established. I would have that Board composed of the heads of all the bureaus. I would have them meet at a given hour every day. I would have the Secretary of the Navy ex-officio president of the Board, and the modus operandi of such organization would be this:—When the President and Congress wanted a fleet to go to the West Indies or to the East Indies, or anywhere else, the order would be presented to the Board, the ships and the officers would be selected by it, and so, through the instrumentality of this Board, the Government and people would have the benefit, as they ought to have, of the best experience and the best knowledge in the navy upon every given question. As it now stands, you have several irresponsible bureaus. The officer at the head of the Ordnance bureau may know more about construction, yet he has nothing to say about it; he is to look to the guns and to nothing else. The officer who has charge of the construction may know more about ordnance, yet he has nothing to say about the ordnance. Now, I say that the whole power of these bureaus should be brought to bear upon every question, not only in regard to the construction of ships, but the appointment of officers. In my judgment, sir, there would be less probability of injustice being done by this process than in any other; especially, you would have some responsible men to look to. Who is responsible now in the navy? Who is responsible for the present condition of the navy? Who is responsible for the building or repairing of the vessels? I must say one word only about that matter. I ask, who is responsible for the failure of the Princeton? They took the name of the most effective and useful ship-of-war that ever floated in our waters, the most formidable man-of-war that was ever put in commission in this country, a ship that could have defied the whole American navy, and gave it to this abortion of which we have heard so much of late. They disregarded her model, her construction, and her engine, and, from being the first ship in the country, she is now the scorn of all seamen and all engineers.

And again, I ask, who is responsible? You may go on and reform the officers. But while the Secretary of the Navy is allowed to remain with his present honours and powers, and in perpetual ignorance, the reform of the officers will not amount to much. Sir, I want to reform the Secretary. I do not allude particularly to the present Secretary. But that will be done before long. Then, if another Secretary cannot, or will not, reform the navy, I hope Congress will take it in hand in good earnest; but, sir, once more I say that it seems to me there is no responsibility anywhere in the navy. The other day they built a dock in Philadelphia, and incurred the expense of fitting a ship in New York or some other Eastern port to be taken to Philadelphia and put in the dock. When she arrived there, it was found, not before, but after, her arrival, that there was not water enough to permit her to be taken upon the dock. Yet, sir, as far as I have been informed, nobody is responsible; and so, after this manner, has the navy of the country been disgraced time after time and year after year.

Mr. President, my object, as one of the Naval Committee, has been, and is, to endeavour to perfect the whole naval system, by beginning at the head, and making everybody responsible that can be made responsible, and to insure, as far as possible, to the people of the United States the benefit of all the experience and knowledge that may be in the navy. And now, sir, I ask my friend, the chairman of the Committee on Military Affairs, whether he will not trust the Committee on Naval Affairs with this matter, and strike out of his bill that portion of it which relates to the Navy and Marine corps?

Mr. Shields.—I wish to assure my honourable and gallant friend, the senator from New Jersey, that we do not want to interfere in any way with the prerogatives of the Naval Committee. But, on former occasions, some difficulties arose in the Senate because the Military Committee brought in one bill and the Naval Committee brought in another, and hence the Military Committee thought it would be better that we should agree on one bill and apply it to both services. We drew up the bill precisely in pursuance of that understanding. We drafted it in accordance with the bills that have been heretofore reported; but if the honourable senator wishes to have charge of the subject, and is not satisfied with this bill, I am, for one, heartily willing that he should take the whole subject into his own charge.

When the honourable senator rose he said he did not mean to discuss this bill, and I think he has kept his word; I do not believe he has discussed the measure before the Senate, although he has discussed the merits and condition of the navy to my delight and satisfaction. But, Mr. President, there is one thing in which I cannot follow the honourable senator, and that is, in drawing a contrast between the navy and the army. That honourable and distinguished senator says that the navy has done a great deal more than the army. Now, I believe that both have done their duty tolerably well, and I am satisfied they will do their duty again, although the honourable senator says that the navy is not worth any thing now. I am inclined to believe that perhaps it has suffered very much since his retirement from the service. His retirement must be partly the reason for its decline.

I agree with him in reference to the necessity of a reformation of the navy; and nothing would give me more satisfaction than to see my honourable friend in a position which would enable him to reform it, root and branch. But, so far as this bill is concerned, it does not aim at any such thing. It does not go into the radical reformation of the navy. It does not contemplate the establishment of an Admiralty Board, and when that proposition comes up I shall have something to say about it. The boards which we have hitherto established in reference to claims, or lands, or for any other purpose, have almost all been failures, and I have doubts whether this Board of Admiralty would not be the biggest and greatest failure of the whole. That is my opinion upon the subject; but that question is not now before the Senate; when it does come up, I for one shall be ready to discuss it.

Although I cannot follow the honourable senator throughout his speech, there is one thing I can say: that, so far as this bill goes,—and I speak in relation to the army,—I think it will be an efficient and a beneficial bill. If the honourable senator takes upon himself the responsibility, in the name of the navy, to move to strike out all that pertains to the navy, he may do so; I will proceed in relation to the army, and let him remain responsible to the navy for striking it out. I shall not make any such motion. The provision is there, and there it will stand, unless he moves to strike it out.

I must say that the speech of the honourable senator was not very logical in some respects. He says that the President has power to do the very thing contemplated by this bill without its passage, and yet he says it would be oppressive. That is not very logical. If the President can do what is contemplated by this bill without its passage, the worst it can do will be nothing; for it will amount to nothing, according to that view of the subject. It is true, the President can turn any officer out of the army or navy; but if he were to turn one of them out,—if he were to turn out one of those gallant and distinguished officers whose names the gentleman has mentioned, in what condition would they be left? Without support—without pay. The President may turn them out in their old age, when they are broken down with service and with sickness, and throw them upon the charities of the world. But this bill provides for the support of those officers who may be removed.

However, sir, I am not disposed to continue the discussion any further to-day. I have moved that the bill be postponed for the purpose of having it printed, and when it comes up again we can dispose of it more advisedly.

Mr. Stockton.—I do not intend to assume any responsibility upon myself as speaking for the navy, but such as belongs to my position. I am here as a senator, and I speak on my responsibility as a senator, and as such I shall move to strike out from this bill its provisions in relation to the navy and marine corps. I presume to speak for no body of men and for no individual but myself.

The senator adverted to my remark that the President had this power now; yet he complains of its severity, and says that the President has power to turn out, but if he exercised it he would turn the officers adrift without any provision for their support. That is not the power to which I alluded; and the gentleman's remark only shows what I apprehended was the case—that he has not looked into the matter in reference to the navy. The President has a right to furlough officers upon half-pay. That is the law to which I alluded; and, therefore, it seems to me that the gentleman has indulged his wit without, perhaps, having a very proper occasion to do so.

There is, however, one part of the gentleman's remarks that perhaps I did not exactly understand, and I should like to have him explain them. He referred to what I said as to the present condition of the navy, and said that it had perhaps retrograded since I left the navy, or in consequence of my leaving it. I did not exactly catch the senator's words, and I should like to hear them again in order to understand his meaning.

Mr. Shields.—I meant the very highest possible compliment to my honourable and gallant friend. I indulged in no wit whatever. I made no effort to be witty. I stated that I presumed the navy had suffered considerably since that honourable gentleman had retired from the service. Could I have paid him a higher compliment? There is no man of whom I have a higher estimate than I have of the gallant and meritorious officer; and I certainly did not mean to reflect on the honourable senator from New Jersey, by saying that the navy had suffered since his retirement from the service.

Mr. Stockton.—I felt under the conviction that I could not be mistaken in the sentiments and feelings of the honourable senator from Illinois towards me, and I am glad that I have not been mistaken.

Speech of Hon. R. F. Stockton, of New Jersey, on Harbour Defences.

DELIVERED IN THE SENATE OF THE UNITED STATES, MAY 11, 1852.

The Senate having resumed, as in Committee of the Whole, the consideration of the joint resolution authorizing the completion of a war-steamer for harbour defence—

Mr. Stockton said:—Mr. President, when the chairman of the Naval Committee announced to the Senate his intention to call up the resolution now under consideration, he stated that the senator from New Jersey—myself—felt great interest in the subject. It is quite true; I do feel great, very great interest in the success of this resolution, and I have no doubt that the result will show that I am not the only senator who feels deeply interested in the prosperity and safety of New York City. I am interested, principally, because I am of opinion that the defences of that city require the immediate attention of Congress, and partly because one of my constituents—a gentleman of reputation and usefulness—has been, in my opinion, unfairly, ungenerously, unjustly treated by the Government. I do not mean by the present Secretary of the Navy, because I understand that this whole matter was, by his remarkable predecessor, placed beyond his control.

There was a report made by the Naval Committee, at the time this resolution was first presented to the Senate. I ask that it may now be read. It will probably relieve me from the disagreeable duty of saying any thing further as to the conduct of the late Administration:—

" The Committee on Naval Affairs, to whom was referred so much of the President's message and accompanying documents as relates to naval affairs, having had under consideration that part of the report of the Secretary of the Navy which refers to the construction of a war-steamer by Robert L. Stevens, report:—

" That on January 13, 1842, the Board of Commissioners of the Navy recommended Mr. Stevens's plan for a steamer, to be ball and bomb-proof, to the consideration of the Secretary of the Navy. Shortly afterwards Mr. Stevens submitted to Congress a printed copy of his plan. The Chamber of Commerce of New York, on the 15th of February, 1842, recommended to Congress the plan of Mr. Stevens.

" A joint board of officers of the army and navy, to wit:—Colonels Totten, Thayer, Talcott, and Captain Huger, Commodores Stewart and Perry, Captain Stringham, and Lieutenant Newman, appointed for that purpose, convened in New York the 8th of July, 1841, to witness, superintend, and report upon Mr.

Stevens's experiments with a bomb and ball-proof target, suited to the sides of a vessel. The experiments were made in their presence, and a report of the Board submitted to the Department in favour of Mr. Stevens's proposed plan of construction.

"On the 14th of April, 1842, Congress passed an act authorizing the Secretary of the Navy to contract with Mr. Stevens for a war-steamer, shot and shell-proof, to be constructed principally of iron, upon the plan of Mr. Stevens, not to cost more than the average of the steamers Missouri and Mississippi, and appropriated $250,000 for the purpose.

"On the 10th of February, 1843, Mr. Stevens entered into contract with Mr. Upshur, Secretary of the Navy, to build a war-steamer, 'to be shot and shell-proof against the artillery now in use on board vessels of war.'

" In order to launch a vessel of the size and description of the one contracted for, Mr. Stevens found it necessary to excavate and erect, at his own and an enormous expense, a dry-dock of capacity sufficient to build her in and float her out. This, of course, involved the necessity of delay in construction; though while engaged in making the dry-dock, he was also assiduously engaged in procuring the materials, fashioning the patterns, and organizing the preliminary details for an undertaking of such magnitude and importance.

"In December, 1843, Mr. Henshaw, who succeeded Mr. Upshur as Secretary of the Navy, declined making the necessary payments for materials. In November following, a second contract, very full, minute, and particular, was made with Mr. Stevens, which was followed by a supplemental contract with John Y. Mason, Secretary, in December, 1844, and which provided for the payments on account of the contract. Mr. Stevens then prosecuted with vigour the performance of his duties; and while so engaged, on the 9th of December, 1845, was again arrested in the execution of his contract by an order from Mr. Bancroft, stopping all further proceedings under the contract, and refusing further payments until the plan for the steamer was furnished. Yet, at this very time, the Department was in possession of the plan of Mr. Stevens, furnished when the original contract was first made, and a further statement of his plan furnished in November, 1844. Thus a second time was he stopped in his work. His health being seriously impaired, he was ordered to Europe by his physician.

"In January, 1847, Mr. Stevens applied to Mr. Mason, then Secretary, for an extension of time in which to complete the steamer, and satisfactorily accounted for the causes of whatever delay had been suffered. After more than eighteen months, an additional contract was made, reciting the former, and extending the time of completion to four years from the date of the last. By these several contracts, the most minute details of the work were given, and the complete security for the execution of the project, and every proper safeguard was provided against loss by the United States.

" Hardly a year, however, was permitted to elapse, when, in August, 1849, Mr. Secretary Preston refused to make any further payments to Mr. Stevens on account, and the work was again stopped. Mr. Stevens was then in Europe, engaged in obtaining better materials for some portions of the steamer than could be obtained in this country. Contracts were made by him in Europe for such materials; after which he immediately returned home, and urged the Secretary to permit him to proceed according to contract. Mr. Preston, however, declined taking any other step than to refer the matter to Congress.

" Whatever delay took place in the performance of this contract, was indispensable to its faithful and successful execution. The necessity for these delays was not, it is believed, properly appreciated by the Navy Department. The experiments necessary to test the quality of the materials, and demonstrate the details of the plan, involved the consumption of much time. The experiments necessary to establish and improve the character of the propeller which was finally adopted, also required much time. Even from this delay the Government derived the advantage of availing itself of this propeller, in the construction of the Princeton, which was thus proved to be superior to any other then in use, or, indeed, since adopted. Workshops, together with a steamboat, were required to be built for those experiments. Also a large dry-dock was constructed, with a steam-engine, punching and drilling-machines, tools, &c., and large pumps, which have kept the dock free from water ever since its completion, at very great expense. One-third of the dry-dock within which the Government iron steamer was to have been built was excavated from solid rock. All this consumed and required unremitting personal exertion and supervision, and large expenditures of money, for which no remuneration has been made. But all delay was satisfactorily explained before the several renewals of the contract, at each period of such renewal.

"When the contractor was first arrested by Mr. Secretary Bancroft, he was in advance, and liable for materials—principally for heavy plates of iron from Pennsylvania—about $40,000, which was subsequently paid to him. He is now in advance about $30,000, also for heavy plates and tubes for the boiler, &c., from England. Yet the Government now proposes to sell his property to reimburse itself for previous payments on his contract, for non-performance of the same, performance of which has been prevented by the action of the Government itself.

"On the 21st January, 1851, Commodore Skinner addressed Mr. Stevens, and informed him that the Navy Department, considering the contract void, designed to sell, shortly, the materials collected by him for the purpose of executing it according to his several agreements.

"To sum up the whole subject, it appears that Congress, by the act of 14th April, 1842, directed a Secretary of the Navy to make a contract with Robert L. Stevens for a war-steamer, and appropriated a specific amount of money towards the construction proposed. The contract was executed. Mr. Stevens, in good faith, proceeded to perform all his obligations. The contract was afterwards made more specific, its minutest details enumerated, and the time for its completion extended by a succeeding Secretary. The amplest security for its faithful execution was required and given. Officers of the United States were appointed to superintend the receipt of materials provided, and payments for such materials were made by the Government from time to time. A subsequent Secretary of the Navy, without any previous notice to the contractor, suddenly suspended the execution of the contract, and refused the payments stipulated therein to be made; leaving the contractor bound to pay large sums for the materials for which he had contracted in the prosecution of his work. Another Secretary renewed the contract, and extended the time for its execution. The contractor again vigorously and actively applied himself to the execution of his contract. While thus industriously employed, another Secretary again arrested his work, and finally suspended all payments, and referred the subject to Congress. The present Secretary considers himself bound by the acts of his predecessor, and treats the contract as at an end; and, Congress having omitted to act on the subject, he has given notice to Mr. Stevens, under the power to sell, contained in the mortgages executed by the contractor, that materials collected by him will be sold for the benefit of the Government.

"It is, therefore, apparent that, without some legislative action by Congress, the contractor, who is willing and desirous of fulfilling all engagements in good faith, entered into by the *direction and under the authority* of Congress, will, by Executive interposition, be subjected (against right, as your committee believe) to very heavy and unjust losses, while the Government will lose the advantages to be derived from the genius, skill, and science of one of the most accomplished naval architects in the country, in the construction of that very sort of war-steamer which the service requires.

"Your committee, therefore, on full consideration of the whole subject, recommend the adoption of the following joint resolution:—

"*Resolved, by the Senate and House of Representatives in Congress assembled,* That the Secretary of the Navy be, and he is hereby, authorized and required to have completed, without any unnecessary delay, the war-steamer contracted for with Robert L. Stevens, in pursuance of an act of Congress passed April 14, 1842."

Mr. President, I should have felt disposed to leave this report, and the unanimous recommendation of the Committee on Naval Affairs, without a word of comment, to the Senate, if I had not been asked to make some explanation, and if the importance of the subject of which it treats, at the present juncture of time, did not seem to require from me some few remarks. Considering the relation which the city of New York bears to this Government and to the whole country, the committee are of opinion that every reasonable preparation for her defence, in time of war with a maritime Power, ought to be adopted.

I will not dilate on the importance, in a military or naval point of view, of that harbour. Its great importance must be obvious to all minds who have given the subject of *national defence* any consideration. But I must say that, while thus important, it is the most exposed, perhaps, of any other important city of the first class on the seaboard. Sir, our defences require immediate attention. The signs of the times are premonitory of war and revolution. Almost every arrival from Europe informs us of warlike preparation by the great Powers of that continent. Upon the throne of France—I say *throne*, for in fact Louis Napoleon is monarch and supreme arbitrator of the destinies of France, as much as Napoleon the Great was in his zenith—upon the throne of France now sits a man, whom the necessities of his position seem to compel to a rivalry of his renowned kinsman and predecessor. If we examine the history of Europe, we will find that since the time of Charlemagne, whenever France was under the control of a bold, restless, ambitious, or unscrupulous monarch, she was invariably engaged in long and bloody wars with her neighbours.

In addition to the national propensity to interfere with the affairs of her neighbours, which modern history shows is characteristic of the French, they have, as we were eloquently told the other day, in the able and instructive speech of the Senator from Tennessee, (Mr. BELL,) as they believe, wrongs to avenge and dishonour to wipe away. France was never more powerful than she is now. Near thirty years have enabled her to recruit the wars of the Emperor ; and for twenty years past she has assiduously exerted all her resources to regain that military efficiency which has always given her a commanding ascendency in the affairs of the world. She has regained it. She is, at present, the cause of disquietude and alarm to all the contiguous Powers. She stands in the panoply and attitude of defiance ; and no one can say how soon, or where, she will not pour her mighty armies.

But all will agree that no great European war can take place without endangering our peaceful relations with one or other of the belligerents. We are admonished, therefore, not to neglect those preparatory defences which, in war, would be indispensable for the protection of our seaboard.

We had some severe lessons on this subject during the late war with Great Britain, and it would be the height of fatuity if another war should find us no better prepared for it than we now are.

And yet, sir, I am not exaggerating when I say that we are at this present time quite as defenceless ; our cities and harbours are quite as much exposed to hostile incursions as they were in 1812. They have grown in wealth and population quadruple what they were then ; but when we consider the increased facilities for attack which foreign naval powers possess, we shall find that, notwithstanding your forts, your most important ports are as vulnerable now as they were in 1812.

While the engines and implements of war have been, of late years, vastly augmented for offensive operations, those for harbour defence have not been correspondingly increased by us. A hostile squadron is no longer dependent on the fickle winds for an opportunity to approach your shores or enter your harbours. They can hover, at their own chosen distance, on your coast, distracting and alarming the whole seaboard, and pounce, with celerity and precision, under the cover of night, upon the devoted place which they doom to destruction.

Steamships of great power and speed have been constructed, infinitely more formidable than any thing which we had to encounter in 1812. Your forts have not been increased or strengthened in proportion to the increase of power with which other nations have fortified themselves.

There have always been great doubts entertained, by the most scientific and experienced men, as to the ability of the best-constructed forts to prevent sailing-vessels, with a leading breeze, from passing them; and there seems to be little or no doubt that steamships may be built, which would pass, unharmed, materially, any fort.

Steamships may, undoubtedly, be built, which, with aid from the tide, may attain a speed exceeding twenty miles per hour. Such a vessel, in six minutes, might approach and pass any of your forts, at night, without being disabled. One such steam-vessel, moored in New York Bay, might kindle that great city into flames, and, screaming the proud note of triumph, leave it a heap of smoking ruins. Nothing could prevent such a catastrophe. Be assured, senators, and let our fellow-citizens everywhere be assured, that nothing could prevent such a catastrophe, in the event of a war with a great naval power, but a steam floating-battery, such as that contemplated by the plan of Mr. Stevens—indestructible, shot and shell-proof, and bearing an armament consisting of such guns, a single shot from which would be sufficient to disable the most powerful man-of-war now launched. One such vessel would be sufficient to defend New York Harbour from any force which could possibly enter it. It would combine the impregnable qualities possessed by stone and mortar fortifications with the advantages belonging to ships-of-war for locomotion. The mere knowledge, by any enemy, that a harbour enjoyed the protection of such a formidable protector, would be sufficient to deter them from hazarding an experiment of its omnipotence.

Now, sir, it seems to me, when one of the most accomplished engineers and naval architects of America is willing to construct a war-ship for harbour defence, that we ought, without hesitation, to avail ourselves of his skill and enterprise for such a purpose.

Mr. Stevens is a gentleman of the highest attainments in those pursuits to which, with hereditary passion, he has devoted the greater part of his life. He is a gentleman of large fortune, and of reputation. He is not an ordinary speculator, seeking a *job* of Government, but a high-minded, patriotic gentleman, who, from elevated and public considerations, and not from motives of pecuniary profit, tenders his skill, science, and experience, (unsurpassed, in his department, by those of any one,) to the service of the Government. He is willing to connect his reputation with the navy of the country. He has acquired, by long years of experience and expensive experiments, a dexterity and felicity in design and execution in nautical architecture, which he is willing to place at the disposal of the Government. He does not want to make money out of you; but he desires to confer on the country the benefit of his superior knowledge,. while, at the same time, he identifies his reputation with the naval history of the country.

He is the builder and proprietor of the yacht Maria, which beat the America —which, under his brother, Commodore Stevens, achieved that victory over all the naval chivalry of Great Britain—a victory worthy to be enrolled with those other glorious triumphs of American naval valour during the war of 1812 which have done as much to elevate the national character, and inspire confidence and self-reliance in American prowess, as all your campaigns on shore, from Canada to the City of the Montezumas.

The offer of such a man to render his skill available to the service of the country ought to be met with promptitude, alacrity, and liberality, by the Government.

It is not proposed by Mr. Stevens to supersede the use of permanent local fortifications. No one thinks of substituting any floating-battery for them. The floating steam-battery which Mr. Stevens has projected is designed, not as a substitute, but as an auxiliary to fortifications. They are fixed and stationary, and invaluable at certain points, where they command the channel of ingress for an enemy. In passing such fortresses, the enemy, except under favourable circumstances, may be destroyed or crippled; yet there is no certainty in any such result. In any such attempt by a powerful fleet of war-steamers, though some might be destroyed, others would be very likely, under the smoke raised by the broadsides from the fort and its opponent, to force an entrance into the interior harbour; then, without such a vessel as that contemplated by the plan of Mr. Stevens, nothing could prevent the most disastrous consequences.

Mr. Stevens's war-steamer, after an enemy had run the gauntlet of the Narrows, and become more or less crippled, would move upon him, and interpose an effectual barrier to his nearer approach.

I have the utmost confidence that Mr. Stevens can accomplish all he proposes, if he is met by this Government in the proper spirit of fairness and liberality. He is no visionary, but a practical engineer and ship-builder, who has a high reputation at stake, and which he is willing to risk for the benefit of the country. He is incapable of undertaking to perform what he knows to be impracticable. I will now read from a work just published by the learned and accomplished President of Columbia College, Mr. Charles King, in regard to Mr Stevens:—

"The extent, variety, and value of Mr. R. L. Stevens's labours and inventions in mechanics should have more fitting commemoration than can be given in any passing notice by one unskilled, as is the writer of this, in the mechanic arts. Yet he cannot suffer this allusion to Mr. Stevens to go forth, without attempting at least to enumerate some of the many services and ingenious inventions and appliances of that gentleman in steam, in gunnery, and in mechanics. From the time when a mere boy, in 1804–05, he was zealously working in the machine-shop at Hoboken, up to the passing hour, he has given his time, his faculties, and his money to what may be justly described as *experimental philosophy;* and the results have been of great public benefit. Of some of them, the following chronological record may bear witness.

"1842. Having contracted to build for the United States Government a large war-steamer, shot and shell-proof, R. L. Stevens built a steamboat at Bordentown for the sole purpose of experimenting on the forms and curves of propeller-blades, as compared with side-wheels, and continued his experiments for many months, the result of which we may yet hope to see in an iron war-steamer that will be *invincible,* and so should be named. While occupied with this design, he invented, about 1844, and took a patent for, a mode of turning a steamship-of-war on a pivot, as it were, by means of a cross-propeller near the stern, so that if one battery were disabled she might, in an instant almost, present the other.

"1848. This year succeeded in advantageously using *anthracite* in fast passenger-locomotives.

"1849. Witnessed the successful application of air under the bottom of steamer *John Neilson,* whereby friction is diminished, and she has actually gone at the rate of twenty miles an hour; this was the invention of R. L. Stevens and F. B. Stevens. The John Neilson also has another ingenious and effectual contrivance of R. L. Stevens, first used in 1849, for preventing ill consequences from the foaming of the boiler. In conclusion of this dry and imperfect chronological recital of some of R. L. Stevens's contributions to the mechanic arts, to public convenience and national power as well as renown, it must be added that Mr. Stevens is himself the modeller of all the vessels built by or for him, and that many of our fastest yachts are of his moulding; and especially the *Maria,* which beat without difficulty the victorious *America,* which, in her turn, carried the broom at her mast-head through the British Channel, distancing all competitors, as she continues to do, I believe, under her new owner, in the Mediterranean.

"Of such a man not the mechanics only of our city, among whom he has worked and is well known, but the nation, may well be proud."

I said that he had an "*hereditary passion*" for those pursuits to which he has devoted most of his life, and here, sir, my State pride may be pardoned, if I advert to the name of his honoured parent, to whose services in practical engineering, mechanics, and other kindred departments, the country owes a debt which it is too late to liquidate now.

Sir, John Stevens, of Hoboken, New Jersey, was one of the most extraordinary men of his age, so prolific of great men. He was the compeer of Fulton, and contributed his full proportion towards making steam that powerful locomotive agent which it has become. Like Fulton and Oliver Evans, he was in advance of the age in which he lived. Near fifty years ago he astonished and confounded a committee of the New Jersey Legislature by the prediction that the time would come when men would travel as fast as a pigeon could fly. They would hear him no longer; they turned from him with pity and incredulity; they told him, as "Festus" told "St. Paul," "Much learning has made you mad." As he was in advance of his age in relation to the use of steam, so he was in relation to railroads. These he used experimentally in his work-yards long before public attention was directed to their importance. He in vain solicited from the New Jersey Legislature permission to connect the waters of the Delaware and the Hudson many years before the Legislature would permit any such enterprise to be attempted. He did as much, if not more, than any other man to bring the steam-engine for locomotion to its present perfection. When his history is written, his name will rank with the names of Franklin, Fulton, Fitch, and Rittenhouse, among the greatest benefactors of his country and the human race. His genius and his fondness for practical engineering he has transmitted to his sons, who are among the most eminent men in their vocation of which this or any other country can boast. It is for Congress now to say whether this Government shall avail itself of the services of such men in constructing just such vessels for national defence as the necessities of the naval service require.

Had this Government taken by the hand Fulton and John Stevens fifty years ago, there is no telling how far we might now have been in advance of our rivals in many important elements of national power.

The proposition now submitted to you is intimately connected with the national defence and the growth and efficiency of your navy; and I avail myself of the opportunity to make some general remarks on that subject.

Sir, the recent victories of your armies seem to have obscured somewhat the splendour of your naval achievements. I entertain no apprehension, however, that the country will ever undervalue the importance of the navy as a sure reliance for the protection of the national honour and the vindication of national injuries. You are destined, (excuse the word,) but if you continue a united people you will be compelled, to become the greatest naval power which the world ever saw. Yet, apparently appalled at the expense to be incurred in any attempt to rival the lavish expenditures of England and France on their navies, we seem to have been embarrassed as to what was the true course to be pursued. Steam has, as you have often been told, revolutionized war upon the ocean. The leviathan ships, with which Nelson annihilated the navy of Napoleon at the Nile and Trafalgar, are no longer invincible.

I have long thought that the improvement of our steam marine has not received from the country and from Congress that attention which it deserves. There can be little doubt that we are at this moment more inferior as a naval power for purposes of immediate defence, compared with the offensive means possessed by other powerful nations, than we were forty years ago; while England, France, and Russia have of late years vied with each other in the creation of a formidable steam navy, we have been standing by comparatively passive. In the admiralty navy-list of 1850 of Great Britain is found one hundred and fifty war-steamers, and she is constantly building and launching others. In addition to these, she has between sixty and seventy mercantile steamers capable of being converted into war-steamers, and whose war-equipments are all prepared. In further addition, she has upwards of eight hundred steamers capable of furnishing formidable assistance for coast defence.

France, since 1815, has never lost sight of the importance of maintaining a navy; she is, next after England, now the greatest naval power of the world. She had at the commencement of the present year one line-of-battle ship of ninety guns, with screw propeller; fourteen steam frigates, mounting from eight to sixteen guns of heavy ordnance, and many others of smaller size. We shall have in the navy of this great Republic—in a navy of a country whose people, and patriots, and statesmen, (some of them,) are ready to dictate a new code of laws for the nations of the earth and to throw a firebrand into Europe, regardless of all consequences, war or no war—I say, sir, we shall have in our navy, when completed, five steam-frigates and two steam-sloops, mounting from six to ten guns. Sir, we had better be prepared for a fight before we attempt to bully. This disparity between our naval steam force and that of other powers is growing greater every year. Yet the tonnage of the United States engaged in foreign or domestic commerce, if we include that of our lakes and large rivers, is about equal to that of Great Britain, and far exceeds that of France or Russia.

Now, these three facts being ascertained—first, our defenceless condition; second, the disparity of our naval power compared with that of the other great powers; third, the equality or superiority of our mercantile tonnage—it becomes a question of great magnitude what policy is it proper for us to adopt, so as to guard against immense and incalculable losses in case a sudden war should break out with any of the great powers.

My mind has been anxiously directed to this subject for many years, and I avail myself of this occasion to throw out a few other suggestions in relation to it.

This gigantic species of warfare it is utterly useless and impracticable, at any cost, to wage with the old-fashioned ships-of-the-line and frigates. Indeed, such vessels would only be built and sailed for the benefit of the enemy. In the present improved condition of naval tactics and steam superiority of Great Britain, there can be no doubt that we must take new observations—a new latitude and departure—if we expect to protect our own shores. We must build a sufficient number of war-steamers which shall exceed any which she may have built: first, in celerity; second, in their invulnerability; and third, in their superior destructive qualities.

We must build vessels which, in speed and power, will enable one of ours to cope with half a dozen of hers; vessels, any one of which would be sufficient to enter any of her harbours and sail through or around any of her fleets.

Now, Mr. President, all this is neither impracticable nor difficult; and in Mr. Stevens you will find not the only American engineer and naval mechanic who can accomplish this great object. We have the coal and iron and all the raw materials which will enable us, with the aid of all the experience obtained by England and France in steam naval architecture, to commence, *now*, efficient steps for the creation of a steam navy fully equal to any thing now afloat.

But, sir, for this purpose you must adopt an entirely new system of constructing your national vessels. By this I do not mean to reflect on the constructors in the navy; by no means. All of them whom I have known would favourably compare with other naval architects; especially, sir, would I place no one ahead of the able and accomplished naval constructor in Washington, Mr. Lenthal. You must appeal to the emulation of all the naval mechanics of the United States, so as to draw out the utmost capacity of that sagacious, skilful, and enterprising class.

You must invite them all to enter the field of competition. I do not see why, by the offer of a bonus for each separate class of war-steamers proportioned to the magnitude of each vessel, or by some other plan similar in principle, you should not make available all the skill possessed by any of our American mechanics for the purposes of the Government. They are superior to those of any other nation. I have some knowledge of and entire confidence in the genius, the enterprise, and indomitable superiority of the American mechanic and artisan. My avocations and favourite pursuits have brought me into personal, familiar, and confidential contact with them. I honour and respect them; and I speak with a confidence founded on knowledge when I say that they *are superior to those of any nation or age;* and I say, furthermore, that the interests of our country in all those great pursuits in which we are most closely pressed with the rivalship of other nations, enjoying the benefit of cheap labour and more abundant capital, may be safely intrusted to their hands. But then you must give them the advantages which our own resources supply in the cheap raw materials of coal and iron. This you can readily do. You have only to adopt the home valuation, or to assess your present *ad valorem* duty on the actual sales in this country. By doing this you will violate no principle of the Constitution, no precept of the resolutions of 1798. You will only be obeying the dictates of an enlarged patriotism. Do but this, and you will rekindle your forge-fires and reopen your workshops, and our constituents in New Jersey and Pennsylvania and all over the country will once more hear the merry ring of the anvil. Do but this, and no foreign war-steamer, nor English, nor French, nor Russian, will scream the hoarse notes of defiance on your coast or in your harbours; do but this, and you will put a fulcrum in the hands of the American mechanics, by means of which they will move the world.

Sir, that they are superior has been proved over and over again. Let the following extracts from a newspaper received this morning be added to the proofs. It has been proved by our clippers, whose unparalleled voyages round the world have recently astonished Europe; it has been proved by the speed and superiority of the Collins line of steamers; and it has been proved by the glorious victory of the yacht America:—

"*Quick Passage of the Witch of the Wave.*

"One of the London papers says:—A large American clipper-built ship, named the Witch of the Wave, Captain Millett, commander, has recently arrived in the East India Docks, London, from Canton, having made one of the most extraordinary and rapid voyages on record. She has also brought one of the most valuable cargoes of tea that, perhaps, ever entered the port of London, having on board no fewer than nineteen thousand chests of the choicest quality. She is nearly fourteen hundred tons burden, the size of our largest Indiamen, and was built at Salem, Massachusetts, in the course of last year. She proceeded to California, thence to Hong Kong, and sailed from Whampoa, near Canton, on the 5th of January; made the passage to Java in seven days and twelve hours, then had the wind W. S. W. to N. W. for several days, with light trade-wind, and made the Cape in twenty-nine days. Then encountered strong easterly winds from the Western Islands, and took a pilot off the Dungeness on the 4th of April, making a passage from China to the Downs in ninety days, a trip surpassing the celebrated runs of the Oriental and Surprise, American clippers. Had she not encountered the strong easterly winds up the Channel, she would have accomplished the voyage several days earlier. As it was, she was only four days beating up from the chops of the Channel to reaching the river, while some of our large vessels were nearly a fortnight doing the distance. The Witch of the Wave is the object of much interest as she lies in the dock. Her bows are similar to a large-sized cutter yacht. By the above it will be seen that she sailed round the world in ten months and a half, including loading and discharging at the above ports. The greatest distance she ran in twenty-four hours, on the voyage to London, was three hundred and thirty-eight miles."

Another paragraph is in these words:—

"Quite a sensation has been created in the English commercial world by the arrival of the American clipper-ship Witch of the Wave, at London, after a run of ninety days from Canton to the Downs—the shortest passage on record. Up to this period the British have retained a nominal advantage in the navigation of this route, one of their traders having accomplished the distance in a few days shorter than any American or other craft; but by this recent achievement of one of our clipper fleet, their last dream of fancied superiority has been dispelled."

And another is as follows:—

"*The Yacht America in Parliament.*

"Colonel Peel, in a recent discussion of the Navy estimates, in the British House of Commons, took occasion to express his surprise that not one word had been said in reference to the circumstance of a foreign yacht having come to England, and, in the presence of the Queen herself, beaten some of the crack English sailing-vessels! That, Colonel Peel said, appeared to him a deeply-humiliating event. She was an American yacht, and was described as 'the race-horse of the ocean.' Colonel Peel confessed that he was wholly ignorant of nautical matters, although he was conversant with the pastime of horse-racing, and he flatters himself that he could appreciate such an expression as the 'blue ribbon of the turf,' as used by Mr. Disraeli. Whatever might be the sailing qualities of the American yacht, Colonel Peel declared that if such a defeat had been sustained by the English sailing-vessels at the Isle of Wight, there was not a true sportsman in England but would go to any expense to recover back the lost laurels. Colonel Peel stated that it was part of his creed that 'Britannia rules the waves,' but what became of the goddess on the day to which he alluded he could not say; but if she 'ruled the waves' at all on that occasion, she must surely have done so with a downcast look. Colonel Peel's remarks were received with cries of 'Hear, hear.'"

I have alluded to those great sources of national wealth—iron and coal; and, as they are so intimately connected with the defence of the country, a few more words in relation to them may not be amiss. It has been those products of her soil which has chiefly made Great Britain what she is, or was. These enabled her to fight the battles of despotism in Europe. These were the conquerors of a Napoleon. They are indispensable for *defence*, if not for national existence. The nation which possesses them in the greatest abundance, and can produce them the cheapest, must excel all others. They are infinitely more important now, as elements of national greatness and power, than ever before. The race of competition in this age, between civilized nations, depends upon their respective facilities for the use of steam. Steam on the ocean is to fight the battle of supremacy *there;* and steam on land, in the factory and on the rail-road, is to decide the question of superiority in all the diversified pursuits of human life.

Sir, we should look to them; we have them in abundance. There in the mountains of my own native State, and of her neighbour and sister, old Democratic Pennsylvania, are the weapons with which alone your victory can be achieved. There are the materials from which your thunderbolts must be fabricated. There is the armory from which to clothe your warriors in an invincible panoply. Strike the rocks of these pregnant mountains, and streams of victorious legions will come forth at your bidding. There slumber the unforged fetters of the seas. You have but to fabricate them from the materials there abounding, and you may fling your chains upon old ocean's mane at will, *and then* you will need "no bulwarks, no towers along the steep."

But I may be told, advocating the policy of encouraging the promotion of the production of iron, I am running counter to the principles of my party. Sir, I yield to no one in my sense of abiding obligation, while I represent a Democratic State, faithfully to adhere to the Democratic standard of faith. But surely no one can justly accuse me of not being true to the Democratic party, while I act in accordance with the often-declared principles of Andrew Jackson, and of old Democratic Pennsylvania. There is nothing in the Democratic creed which forbids encouraging the promotion of that which is essential to national defence. Democracy, in my estimation, does not consist in giving or withholding a per cent. above or below the average revenue duty. God help the Democracy measured by such a standard! With me, it is the first duty which I acknowledge to provide for the national defence. It was this elevated view of his duty which impelled the great Chatham to say that he would not permit America to manufacture a hob-nail. Sir, I hope the period is not distant when the cheapness of American iron and coal will not permit Great Britain to manufacture a hob-nail for us, or for any market where we can compete with them on equal terms. Democracy, as I understand, has more immediate reference to the construction of the powers of the Government rather than to the fluctuating policy of discriminating respecting the imposition of duties. That must be controlled by questions of expediency—by the changing modifications of the commercial and restrictive policy of other countries. But it is in the construction of the powers of the Government where Democracy has proved itself the bulwark of the Constitution and the Union. When the reign of terror was upon them—when the fathers of the Democratic party saw, under the rule of the elder Adams, the rights of the States endangered, and every thing tending to the consolidation of all power in this Central Government—they promulgated what I have always considered, since I have directed my mind to political subjects, the true standard of Democratic faith. I allude to the Virginia and Kentucky resolutions of '98 and '99. Sir, I know that it is a custom with some politicians to indulge in sneers in relation to those resolutions, and to taunt those who respect them with being abstractionists, impracticables, and dreamy theorists.

Sir, I care little what terms—whether Federalist, State-Rights, or Abstractionist—are applied to me; but I will say what I believe, at the hazard of every consequence, personal or political, and without regard to popularity or unpopularity. The one has no charms to swerve me from what I consider right, and least of all has the other any terror.

I will not say of popularity what Horne Tooke said,—that if it was to come in my way "I would kick it out of my way;" but I will say that I trust I shall always have courage enough, of whatever sort may be needful, to despise any popularity, purchased by any dereliction of principle or any sacrifice of personal honour or independence.

But, sir, the resolutions of '98 and '99! the resolutions! I have to say of them that, in my opinion, they are the most valuable legacy, next after the Constitution, which the early patriots of the Republic have bequeathed to the country. They have, in my opinion, done more to preserve the Constitution from infraction, and to keep this Government within its limits, than any other production of political wisdom from the day of their origin to this time. They have been the touchstone by which wild and visionary theories have been tested and found to be valueless or dangerous. They have been the light-houses along the stormy shoals and breakers of politics—warning us of the only safe and smooth channel of navigation for the ship of state.

I know well that their enemies have pretended to find in them the germ of nullification. But, sir, I perceive no such dangerous heresy in any of them. I see in them a plain, common-sense, practical scheme for the administration of this Government:—a scheme by means of which the Union and the Constitution may be preserved inviolate, the rights of the States respected, and the Government enabled to exercise all those national functions designed to be performed by it; while it is preserved and restrained within those barriers with which it is invested by the Constitution.

Sir, as a citizen of a small State, which has as much to dread from a dissolution of the Union as any other State of this Confederacy, I acknowledge my gratitude to the great men who promulgated those doctrines, and to their disciples, who, since that time, have remained steadfast to the Democratic principles they contain. Those are the principles by which I would have my Democracy estimated; by them I will consider myself bound; upon them and the Constitution, a long time ago, I planted my standard.

Thus much, sir, I have felt bound to say in vindication of myself as well as of the Democracy of the patriotic State which sent me here, in relation to the encouragement of the product of iron.

"I hope I don't intrude," as Paul Pry said. I hope that I have not interfered with the prerogative of others—that I have not trespassed on the premises either of Young America, or old——

A SENATOR.—Fogy.

[Mr. STOCKTON hesitated; and, looking around to see who addressed him, continued,]

I thank you, sir; but my memory did not fail me. No, sir; my tongue refused to utter the ungracious phrase. The instinctive power of my heart forbade it.

Thank God for the inspiration!
[Turning to Gen. Cass, he said:]
No, no, "*Conscriptus pater.*" I have, as an American citizen, neither the heart to conceive nor the tongue to speak any sentiment but that of the greatest personal respect and the highest admiration and appreciation of your long and faithful public services. May God prolong your life, and health, and mind, and may the spirit of your country's gratitude rest upon you!

Mr. President, some time since, in another place, I was as unexpectedly called upon as I have this moment been to say a few words in commendation of a distinguished public man. That was put down an "*explosion*," and this may be recorded as "*explosion second*." Well, sir, I can have but little left, and I propose now to finish the business of blowing myself up by making this declaration before the Senate and the country. Sir, I acknowledge my responsibility to the national Democracy with reference to national questions, respecting the rights of the States and the powers of this Government; but to New Jersey alone I hold myself responsible with reference to questions of a local or transitory character.

Mr. President, I am done; and if your able reporter will do me the justice which he has heretofore done to myself and all others, why then, sir, political quackery may make the most of it.

Remarks of Honourable R. F. Stockton.

In the Senate, on the 21st July, 1852, the resolution of the House in regard to the adjournment of Congress was taken up and elicited a spirited debate. In the course of it, Mr. Stockton rose and said:—

Mr. President:—Being one of the humblest members of this august body of the Representatives of the Federal Republic, I have been slow to participate in this discussion, and certainly should have said nothing on the subject if it had been confined to the mere question of agreeing to a day of adjournment. But a question has been connected with this discussion which seems to render it my imperative duty, as a Representative of the State of New Jersey, to say a few words in relation thereto. In the first place, however, I must say that I do not concur in the reproaches which have been cast upon the other branch of Congress on account of any supposed delay in their business. If any delay has occurred, the reason is to be found in the great amount of business which Congress has had to consider and to act upon.

Nor am I disposed to find fault with any of the discussions which have taken place on the subject of Presidential candidates. They have been mostly interesting, and I do not know that they have interfered with the business of Congress. The business of Congress requires reflection and information, which is not to be attained in this chamber alone. So far as I am concerned, sir, my mind has been more devoted to the consideration of the public business in my own than in the Senate Chamber. Therefore, so far as my voice goes, I am ready to acquit both Houses of Congress of any neglect of their appropriate duties. The delay, if any, has been caused by the amount and the importance of the business we have had before us. Though I am as desirous of returning to the bosom of my family as any member of this body can be, I would prefer that the resolution should lie on the table for the present, and until I can see more clearly the probable time when we may hope to finish the public business in a satisfactory manner to our constituents as well as ourselves.

Mr. President, I had no disposition to discuss this question, and but for the exciting speech made by the senator from South Carolina, (Mr. Butler,) I should have remained silent. The senator from Tennessee (Mr. Bell) spoke of the importance of the harbour and river bill; and another senator spoke of the importance of the tariff bill. With regard to the first I have but little to say at present, except to concur in its importance. With regard to the tariff, I must be permitted to say that I regard it of more consequence to my constituents than any other bill which has been, during the session, or is now, pending before Congress. The tariff—ay, sir, the tariff!—the mere mention of which startles gentlemen from their propriety, and drives them headlong into the question of the dissolution of the Union.

I have to tell such gentlemen, let them come from where they will, or represent whom they may, that there are two sides to the question of the tariff; and, Democrat as I am, I intend that, on all proper occasions, my voice shall be raised in the Senate and out of the Senate in behalf of the poor labourer of the North ; and he who represents the slave-labour of the South may raise his voice as potential as he sees fit, he will not alarm, but find me prepared, to the best of my poor ability, to defend the interest of the free labourer of the North. *But, sir, do not misunderstand me. I repudiate the doctrine of a tariff for the purpose of protecting one interest more than another interest, one section more than another section.* We are not to consider the interests of fragments, but of THE WHOLE PEOPLE ; not of States, but the nation. Sir, we must seek for some sound, well-settled principle upon which to rebuild this theory of a tariff.

The President.—The Chair must remind the senator from New Jersey that the question is not upon the tariff, or upon any other bill.

Mr. Stockton.—I am aware of that, sir.

The President.—The senator can allude to the subject of the tariff generally ; but it will not be in order, upon the present question, to go into the merits or demerits of any tariff.

Mr. Stockton.—What I mean to say is this: that the tariff bill is a matter of so much consequence that it behooves Congress not to adjourn without modifying it; and I give that as a reason why we cannot now fix a day for adjournment. Besides, sir, the tariff bill to which I allude is not for protection of manufacturers ; it is not to be a tariff exclusively for revenue ; but it is intended to protect millions of our fellow-citizens who earn their bread by the toil of their own hands.

I can tell the senator from South Carolina that their interests are not much longer to be disregarded. Sir, this Government may survive the effects of the most disastrous battles ; we may regain lost territory ; but I tell him and others to be warned in time that we may not be able to resist the importunate remonstrances of a free but impoverished and degraded people.

Mr. Butler.—The senator from New Jersey is under a great mistake. I made not the least allusion to the tariff. However, I suppose he may as well hang his speech on what I said as on what was said by any other senator. I certainly made no allusion to the tariff—not in the least.

Mr. Stockton.—What I meant to say is this: that the tariff belongs to the business of Congress, and is entitled to as much of our time as any other matter. If the senator from South Carolina did not speak of "free trade," if he did not make use of that expression which naturally leads to the consideration of the whole subject of a tariff, then I stand before the Senate corrected.

Several senators.—He did—he did.

Mr. Butler.—I wish to correct the gentleman. I believe that, if he chose to take the remark which I made in that view, he might have used it for the purpose of dilating upon the subject. I think, however, that the subject of the tariff was freely spoken of by the senator from Alabama ; and the remarks of that senator, it appears to me, might have afforded the senator from New Jersey a better text than my remark in regard to "free trade." The connection in which I spoke of free trade—and I hope the senator from New Jersey, while he is in favour of the tariff, will not undertake to controvert the great doctrines of free trade—was in relation to California. Though that, as far as I know, does not involve the tariff, yet, in candour to the senator, I must admit that I did speak of California as a probable ally against one which might be a proscriptive and protective tariff. My remark may allow that interpretation, but I used it at the time with no such purpose.

I did not wish to introduce into this debate any topic which did not properly and legitimately relate to the subject. I did, perhaps, manifest some little temper, because I thought that some topics had been introduced here which ought not to be introduced, I will not say deliberately, but perhaps inadvertently. I think the senator from New Jersey is at liberty to make his remarks both in regard to what was said by the senator from Alabama and myself; for I believe we both, in some measure, said something in relation to the question of a tariff, though all that I said was a mere allusion, in the most casual way, to the subject of free trade.

Mr. Stockton.—All that was necessary to fill the measure of my surprise on hearing the senator's explanation was for him to have added, that what he did say was said in the most amiable and unexcitable and courteous manner. He put some interrogatory in regard to free trade. I do not remember its precise purport. But, sir, I am willing to confess my homage to the sublime and simple truths of Adam Smith and the disciples of that school of political economists. I will go further, and say that I believe all the efforts that have been urged against his leading doctrines and those of Ricardo on rent have failed; but their application to this country in its present condition, in relation to the rest of the world and in reference to the commercial policy of other nations, is an entirely different question—the great question.

It does appear to me (not designing any thing offensive) the most absurd thing in the world is to be wrangling and quarrelling about the abstract theories of free trade when we have staring us in the face the necessity of raising fifty millions of annual revenue, which has, since the origin of Government, and must continue to be, almost entirely obtained from duties on imports. Now, sir, what I claim is the right, as a Representative of New Jersey, interested as she is in the development of her iron, not to allow any reproach as to its importance, any insinuation as to its unconstitutionality, or any sneer at efforts made to modify the tariff without remarks from me. I hope, before the session is over, that gentlemen will have to face the music on that same question of the tariff. We mean, if we can, to get it up before the Senate, and we intend to explain to the Senate and to the people our objects, views, and motives in doing it. New Jersey means to insist that you shall unlock the hoards of treasure which slumber in the mountains that traverse her territory as that of a sister State.

She means to insist that, by doing so, you will not violate the Constitution. You will only be fulfilling your obligations to further other interests besides those of commerce and agriculture ; and I say this to show the importance of sitting two months longer rather than avoid this great question.

Mr. Hunter.—I am constrained to ask if it is in order to debate the tariff on this resolution ?

The President.—Certainly not; but the Chair was unwilling to interrupt the honourable senator.

Mr. Stockton.—I am very much obliged to the senator ; but if he had taken the same trouble to arrest the extraordinary excitement of his own friend he would not have had occasion to interfere in my behalf. (Laughter.) I did not intend to say a word about the day of adjournment. But, sir, you may expect to wake up New Jersey whenever the tariff is agitated ; you may then look out for her. (Laughter.) I will now relieve you, Mr. President, by no longer persisting in this debate.

Remarks of Mr. Stockton, of New Jersey, on the Indian Appropriation Bill.

DELIVERED IN THE SENATE OF THE UNITED STATES, AUGUST 11, 1852.

The Senate proceeded to consider, as in Committee of the Whole, the bill from the House of Representatives " making appropriations for the current and contingent expenses of the Indian Department, and for fulfilling treaty stipulations with various Indian tribes, for the year ending June 30, 1853."

The first question was on concurring in the following clause, adopted as in Committee of the Whole, in relation to the California superintendency :—" for presents and provisions for Indians visiting the superintendency, $3000."

Mr. Weller.—Mr. President, I move to strike out that clause, and to insert the following :—

" For the purpose of purchasing supplies and presents, to be distributed to the Indians in the State of California, under the direction of the President of the United States, the sum of $100,000."

In my judgment this appropriation will be absolutely necessary in order to prevent a large body of Indians in California from starving during the approaching year. They have been brought down from the mountains, from their accustomed homes, and settled upon the reservations that were made by the Indian commissioners, in the eighteen treaties that were negotiated with the different tribes. Those treaties have all been rejected by the Senate, and it is therefore necessary, in my judgment, that some provision should be made for them in order to avoid hostilities. It will be a very difficult thing to explain to these Indians how it comes that these treaties which they entered into with persons who represented themselves as agents of the Government have now been repudiated. They will be compelled, as a matter of course, in consequence of the rejection of the treaties by the Senate, to leave these reservations upon which they have been placed by the Indian commissioners. It is, therefore, proposed in lieu of a confirmation of those treaties ; the object being to appease the Indians by providing them with subsistence. They have been driven, as I said, from that section of the State where it was their habit to live on acorns and the fruits found in the woods, and they must inevitably starve unless some provision be made for them. For that purpose I hope the Senate will adopt the amendment.

After an interesting debate, in which Messrs. Weller, Dawson, Badger, Bell, Butler, Mallory, Hunter, Cass, and Underwood, participated,—

Mr. Stockton said :—

Mr. President, I approved of the proposition first made by the senator from California (Mr. Weller) to amend the amendment now before the Senate, and I regret that he has seen fit to accept any modification of it whatever. It did appear to me, that the principles on which he founded his application were based on such grounds as we may well suppose would govern the understanding and the heart of a distinguished American senator or an American statesman.

Sir, I have not been much surprised at the course which the debate on this proposition has taken. Having heard the discussions in regard to these Indian appropriations from the first, I was prepared for opposition to any donation to them. But, I have been astonished by the enunciation of some of the principles on which the judgment of senators relative to the course best to be pursued as to the Indians has been predicated. It has been stated here that this Government is under no obligations, no responsibility, to the Indians; that my friend—the friend of the California Indians—seeks to obtain from this Government a donation for them, which the Government is under no sort of obligation to give. Ay, sir, the little, which by the great exertions of their friends, has been extorted from you, has been only yielded with growls and threats that you were under no obligations to grant it. I dissent from all the reasonings founded upon the proposition as amended by the senator from Virginia. Sir, I go for that proposition which acknowledges in their length and breadth our obligations as American citizens to repair, as far as we may, the wrongs of an injured people. You *have* obligations which it is not quite so easy to get rid of, either in your national or in your individual character, as senators or as Christians. Sir, let me tell you that you have responsibilities with regard to the Indians that it would be well for you if all the money in your Treasury could satisfy. Ay, sir, we might well thank God if money could enable us to appease the great spirit of retributive justice. The principle contained in the amendment, which negatively pledges us to do no more, is one which I repudiate from the bottom of my soul. Do gentlemen ask if we design by this amendment to establish a principle that shall govern this country in all time to come? I answer, and say, *Yes*. I go further, and say, that so long as there is a dollar in your Treasury, half of it, if necessary, should go to relieve the distress of the aborigines of the country.

Mr. President, while I stand here in this Capitol and remember that it has been erected upon the soil, the blood, and the bones of the Indians, and on the ashes of their wigwams, am I to be told, here in this Senate, that the laws of the land—of this Christian land—will not permit me to vote money from the public Treasury to ease their distress and relieve the misery of that unfortunate race? Sir, under no obligations to take care of the California Indians! What do senators mean? You are under most indissoluble bonds to take care of them. Justice —justice—inexorable justice—demands it. It is not for me to express in words your obligations. They may be seen in bloody tracks over the mountains and across the plains; they are engraved on every Christian heart. Sir, it may do in the general course of legislation, for those who have a clean bill of health, to make such prescriptions for the body politic as may be found in the strict construction of the Constitution. But, sir, when we come here, in this temple of liberty, our hands reeking with the blood of the savage, does it become us to prate about law, constitutional or divine, in defence of violent aggression? No, no; we have nothing to do but to relieve, fully and substantially relieve, the misfortunes we have been the means (innocent, if you please) of creating, and feel consoled if in that way we can alleviate the distresses we have inflicted.

But, sir, with regard to the proposition now immediately before the Senate, I will say that, if I understand the object of the senator from California, it is to place at the disposal of the President of the United States the sum of $100,000 for the purpose of preventing starvation among a certain portion of the Indians in that State. Now, sir, considering the responsibility of that gentleman as a senator from California, and that this money is to be disbursed by the President, I am ready to give my vote for the appropriation of $100,000, or any other reasonable sum, for such a purpose. But we are told that this donation of $100,000 to-day, will establish a precedent which will bind this Government ever after to do the same thing. That is just exactly the thing I desire to do—the principle which I desire to establish. It is exactly the principle which I think we should proclaim to the world. Sir, wherever money will save the life of an Indian, or wherever or whenever it can secure his confidence and friendship, it should not be withheld. But, after all, the difficulty is not, as it seems to me, so much in any difference of opinion as to what is due the Indians, as how it is to be paid. The real difficulty has not yet been pointed out in regard to the Indians. The fault is not with the Indians, but in the Indian agents; and, sir, if money has been improperly expended, it is the fault of the Government officers or agents, and they should be held accountable, and not let the Indians suffer in consequence of their delinquencies. Will you, then, make the Indian suffer because your Government does not employ agents who are sufficiently just, wise, and honest, properly to expend the money which is appropriated? Certainly not; you cannot do that. You will not commit so great a wrong!

Mr. President, the simple question is, whether, under all the circumstances of this case, the Indians are entitled to our protection; and whether, if you cannot make him work, or keep the peace without, you are bound to protect and feed him? Sir, having taken his lands from him, how can you complain if he will not work and feed himself? Having taken all that you saw fit to take, you ease your conscience for taking what he did not want to give, by offering him land which he does not wish to receive. Sir, no one can appreciate the sufferings and sacrifices of the Indians, but those who, like myself and the senator from California, have witnessed them in joy and in sorrow, who like us have seen them in their prosperity, in their freedom, and in the free enjoyment of all their possessions, given to them by God; have seen them in the haughty independence of their nature—and in their servile attitude of petitioners—bowing the knee to their white, despotic, and cruel masters.

Sir, if chance, or accident, or any other thing, had taken you across the Rocky

Mountains some few years since, you would have passed through tribes of men—Indians you may call them: aborigines they are of this country; proud, hospitable, high-minded, noble, gallant men: men as free as I was—ay, sir, freer. The Snakes and Sioux were as free as the air they breathed, and walked with as proud and mighty a step as any of God's created beings. Let senators not suppose that I am drawing on my fancy for this picture of the Sioux and the Snake Indians. They were at that time as gallant, as noble, as generous, and as hospitable men as any who live, or I know nothing of human life or character. I go further: they were in the full possession and unannoyed enjoyment of their hunting-grounds, in the enjoyment of peace, tranquillity, and happiness, under the direction of their own independent and brave chiefs. From St. Joseph's, in Missouri, to the Pacific, there was one great community of nature's children, happy and content. But, alas, what is their condition now? Sad, sad! Your armies of emigrants have traversed annually their territory, and driven away their game, and eaten up their pastures, until death and starvation stare them in the face. They have lost their game, and they are sorrowful; they have lost their country, and they are indignant and revengeful. I persuaded them to peace; they agreed, but implored that their great father,—a father, indeed,—as he had destroyed their hunting-grounds, would, at least, give them lands fit for agriculture, and implements of husbandry, and persons to instruct them in the art of raising bread. But what has the father done? These people must all leave their usual hunting-grounds, and who is to care for them?

Sir, after these armies of men have crossed the mountains, and arrived in California, their first business seems to be to drive off or kill the Indians. There is not a brute that walks on the face of the earth that has been so much contemned and despised and cruelly treated as have been these Indians from the time of the first invasion up to the present time. These Indians of California are spread over the whole mountainous part of that State. When we took possession, we found them a kind and docile but not a warlike people, comparatively contented and happy, and friends. We have driven them from their homes; have despoiled them of their property, and expelled them from the mines. What wonder that they are hostile? From this very land of theirs we have taken millions on millions of gold, and now, when we are asked to appropriate $100,000 to save them from starving, the Constitution of the United States is invoked to prevent it. Yes, sir, that sacred instrument is invoked, and thrust between us and our consciences and our dearest sensibilities. It was invoked yesterday to save the white man, and to-day it is invoked to destroy the Indians. If the Constitution of the United States forbids me from aiding, by an appropriation of money, to save the California Indians from starving,—if it should step, with blasphemous intrusion, between me and those sacred feelings of our nature which God and nature's God has planted in the breast of poor human nature,—then I say that (here the senator paused)—my friends will know where to find me in regard to the construction of that instrument.

But, sir, the Constitution of my country tells me no such thing. Its whole spirit breathes a spirit of philanthropy and love to men everywhere. It is universal love, as well as universal freedom, which is taught by the Constitution of the United States. Sir, so far from considering this as a donation,—so far from considering this proposition, which asks you to give but $100,000, as an extravagant donation,—I hold that you are bound by all your responsibilities as men and as Christians, by all your responsibilities as senators and statesmen, to protect them, cost what it may.

That there may be no misapprehension about this amendment, I will repeat what I take to be its object, its essence. It is to save the Indians in California from starvation. We are told that there are seventy thousand Indians in a starving condition in California. I believe it; and these are the Indians of whom I have endeavoured to draw a feeble picture, and to whom I feel that we are so much indebted, and for whom we cannot do too much. But it is said that this bill has not come up in a proper shape; that if we pass this appropriation we shall be setting a precedent hereafter to be followed, and therefore that it ought not to be passed. We are further informed that even if it were a thing proper to be done, that $100,000 would not be enough to answer the purpose, and therefore it should not pass. Some gentlemen would not have it done because it is not entirely in accordance with their parliamentary notions and their technical ideas; others say that it is opposed to their views of proper economy in the administration of this Government. Well, sir, are these sufficient reasons to defeat the passage of this bill, or to retard for a single day the passage of the proposed amendment? No, sir!

Let me again remind senators that, while we are endeavouring to settle differences of opinion on matters of form and parliamentary etiquette, the Indians in California are starving.

In concluding these wholly unpremeditated remarks, I must be permitted to reiterate these painful truths:—that you have destroyed the homes of these people, devastated their villages; you have taken away their occupation, and have extracted millions of gold from their mines; and that you are bound by every principle of duty to make this appropriation of $100,000—ay, sir, and $500,000 more, if necessary, to *preserve peaceful relations with them, or to keep them from starvation.*

Remarks of the Hon. R. F. Stockton, of New Jersey,

DELIVERED IN THE SENATE OF THE UNITED STATES, DECEMBER 14, 1852,

On the adoption of the following resolutions offered by the Hon. John Davis, of Massachusetts:—

" *Resolved,* That the Senate has received with profound sensibility the annunciation from the President of the death of the late Secretary of State, Daniel Webster, who was long a distinguished member of this body.

" *Resolved,* That the Senate will manifest its respect for the memory of the deceased, and its sympathy with his bereaved family, by wearing the usual badge of mourning for thirty days.

" *Resolved,* That these proceedings be communicated to the House of Representatives."

Mr. Stockton said:—

Mr. President:—I was prevented from coming to Washington until this morning. After travelling all night, I hastened here to take my seat, wholly unapprised of the intention of the senator from Massachusetts to introduce the resolutions now before the Senate.

It would, therefore, not become me, nor the solemnity of the occasion, to mingle, unprepared as I needs must be, my voice in the eloquent lamentation, which does honour to the Senate, for any other purpose than merely briefly to express my grief, my sorrow, my heartfelt, unaffected sorrow, for the death of Daniel Webster.

Senators, I have known and loved Daniel Webster for thirty years. What wonder, then, I sorrow? But now that I am on my feet for that purpose, and the Senate, who knew and loved him, too, are my listeners, how am I to express that sorrow? I cannot do it. It cannot be done. Oh! sir, all words in moments such as these, when love or grief seeks utterance, are vain and frigid.

Senators, I can even now hardly realize the event, that Daniel Webster is DEAD—that he does not "*still live.*"

I did hope that God, who has watched over this Republic, who can do all things, "who hung the earth on nothing," who so endowed the mind of Daniel Webster, would still longer have upheld its frail tenement, and kept him as an example to our own men and to the men of the whole world.

Indeed, it is no figure of speech when we say that *his* fame was " world-wide."

But, senators, I have risen to pronounce no eulogy on *him.* I am up for no such vain purpose. I come with no ceremony. I come to the portals of his grave, stricken with sadness, before the assembled Senate, in the presence of friends and senators, (for whether they be of this side of the Chamber or the other side of the Chamber, I hope I am entitled to call every senator my friend,) to mingle my grief with the grief of those around me. But I cherish no hope of adding one gravel-stone to the colossal column he has erected for himself. I would only place a garland of friendship on the bier of one of the greatest and best men I ever knew.

Senators, you have known Mr. Webster in his public character, as a statesman of almost intuitive perceptions, as a lawyer of unsurpassed learning and ability, as a ripe and general scholar. But it was my happiness to know him, also, as a man, in the seclusion of private life; and in the performance of sacred domestic duties, and of those of reciprocal friendship, I say, in this presence, and as far as my voice may reach, that he was remarkable for all those attributes which constitute a generous, magnanimous, courageous, hospitable, and high-minded man. Sir, as far as my researches into the history of the world have gone, they have failed to discover his superior. Not even on the records of ancient Greece, or Rome, or of any other nation, are to be found the traces of a man of superior endowments to our own Webster.

Mr. President, in private life he was a man of pure and noble sentiments, and eminently kind, social, and agreeable. He was generous to a fault. Sir, one act of his—one speech of his made in this chamber—placed him before all men of antiquity. He offered himself—yes, you all remember, in that seat *there*, he rose and offered himself a living sacrifice for his country. And Lord Bacon has said that he who offers himself as a sacrifice for his country is a sight for angels to look upon.

Mr. President, my feelings on this occasion will not surprise senators who remember that these are no new sentiments for me; that when he was living I had the temerity to say that DANIEL WEBSTER was the greatest among men and a true patriot—ay, sir, when the expression of such opinions might have interfered with political aspirations imputed to me. Well, sir, if an empire had then been hanging on my words, I would not have amended or altered one sentiment.

Having said thus much for the dead, allow me to express a word of thanks to the honourable senator from Michigan, (Mr. CASS.) Sir, I have often had occasion to feel sentiments of regard, and, if he will permit me to say it, of affectionate regard for him, and sometimes to express them; but the emotions created in my heart by his address this morning are not easily expressed. I thank him—in the fulness of my heart I thank him; and may God spare him to our country many years. May he long remain here in our midst as he is at this day, in all the strength of manhood and in all the glory of matured wisdom!

Remarks of Mr. Stockton, of New Jersey, on Mr. Merriwether's Resolution.

DELIVERED IN THE SENATE OF THE UNITED STATES, AUGUST 11, 1852.

The following resolution of Mr. Merriwether was taken up for consideration by the Senate on the 14th of August:—

"*Resolved*, That the President of the United States be requested to inform the Senate what amount of public money has been paid to General Winfield Scott and General Franklin Pierce, respectively, from the time of their first entrance into the public service up to the present date, distinguishing between regular and extra compensation; also, for what said amounts were paid, whether for pay proper, rations, forage, horses, mileage, transportation, servants, quarters, fuel, medical attendance, or commutation for any of the preceding items; also, that he inform the Senate what amount of extra compensation has been claimed by either, the items of each and every such claim when first presented, and when and by whom allowed or rejected, and the official reasons given at the time for such allowance or rejection, and whether any item or items, claim or claims, once disallowed, were subsequently presented for payment, and if so, how often and when, and if subsequently allowed or paid, by whom and when, and the amounts thereof, and the reasons for such allowance, and the amounts thereof; and that he also inform the Senate whether either of the above-named generals has received from the public treasury pay or emoluments for discharging the duties of more than one office or employment at the same time, and if so, what offices or employments, and the amount of such pay and emoluments, and the time when paid, and whether any claim or claims have been presented for the discharge of the duties of two or more offices or employments at the same time by either of them, and disallowed, and if so, by whom disallowed, when and for what reasons then given; and that he also inform the Senate whether either of the above-named generals has ever, under colour of charging for percentage, or for extra compensation, or for any other reason or reasons, or in any manner or form, applied to his own use, or retained in his hands, any of the public funds or property without authority of law, and if so, when and the amount or value thereof, and whether the amount thus applied or retained, or any part thereof, has ever been repaid to the United States, and if so, what amount and when so repaid, and whether any amount of public money or property, which has ever come to the hands or possession of either of them, remains unaccounted for, and if so, in whose hands and how much."

The resolution having been discussed by Senators Douglas, Weller, Bradbury, Jones, Soule, Underwood, Butler, Clemens, and Adams,

Mr. STOCKTON said:—

This is not the first occasion, Mr. President, that I have had the misfortune to differ from views expressed by my political friends. It has always been a source of some regret to do so; it is especially grievous to me to-day. I find myself compelled to dissent from the course which my distinguished friend from Louisiana (Mr. Soule) has indicated that his duty constrains him to take. I have some relief, however, from this embarrassment in the persuasion that his own sentiments of personal honour and patriotism, as far as they are connected with this subject, do not differ materially from mine. If they did, I should certainly distrust my own instincts and judgment, so far at least as to remain silent. But, supposing that my honourable friend, in following the example of others, has mistaken his true position, and placed the defence of his vote on political and party grounds alone, and believing likewise that others of my honourable friends here have taken the same erroneous view of this subject, and have looked upon it only in one aspect, I shall venture, even though I have already heard from them a general expression of opinion in favour of the resolution, to make an appeal to both sides of this chamber to uphold the dignity of the Senate, and to lay both the resolution and the amendment upon the table.

Sir, gentlemen have discoursed upon this subject as if they had no other obligations in the world except those which are due as party men to General Scott and General Pierce, or to their respective political parties.

Now, sir, permit me to say that I stand here this morning as a senator of the United States, and not merely as a politician; and that while I bear in remembrance the long line of grave, dignified, and distinguished men and patriots who have served their country in this Senate, I cannot consent to act or vote upon any measure arising in this body solely on party grounds, or upon any such principles as those assumed by some of my distinguished friends upon this occasion. I have, as a senator, nothing to do with the party interests or affinities of General Scott or General Pierce in the discussion of this question. I care but little about either one or the other in comparison with my duty to the Senate and the country. In this matter I care nothing about party politics. Mr. President, upon another occasion and in another place I said that my party robes hung loosely upon my shoulders whenever the honour, the interest, and the welfare of my country were at stake; and now, sir, here before this Senate

22

and before the people I say that my party robes will hang loosely upon my shoulders whenever the honour, the dignity, and usefulness of this august body, in my judgment, may depend upon any vote of mine.

Sir, is this the arena to discourse on the subject of party politics, or to indulge in personal commendation or vindictive aspersion? I say no. Party politics is a business that our constituents never expected or desired us to waste their time upon here. It is a small business, which the Democratic party do not expect or wish us to meddle with; and, if I have not wrongly estimated their virtue, and wisdom, and patriotism, they would prefer that we should lay the resolution and the amendment upon the table rather than that we should do any thing to impair public confidence' in the exalted reputation and dignity of this body. But it is said that there is a Whig precedent for this resolution. Then let us put the brand of Democratic disapprobation upon it. I move that the whole subject be laid on the table.

Mr. Underwood.—Will the honourable senator allow me to say a word? It will be very short, and I will renew the motion.

Mr. Stockton.—No, sir; I cannot withdraw the motion.

Mr. Bradbury and Mr. Merriwether asked for the yeas and nays on the motion; and they were ordered, and, being taken, resulted—yeas 20, nays 23—as follow:—

Yeas—Messrs. Adams, Bayard, Bell, Brooke, Butler, Chase, Davis, De Saussure, Foote, Geyer, Hunter, James, Mallory, Pearce, Smith, Stockton, Sumner, Underwood, Upham, and Wade—20.

Nays—Messrs. Atchison, Borland, Bradbury, Bright, Cass, Charlton, Clemens, Dodge, of Wisconsin, Dodge, of Iowa, Douglas, Downs, Felch, Hamlin, Jones, of Tennessee, Merriwether, Norris, Sebastian, Seward, Soule, Spruance, Toucey, Walker, and Weller—23.

So the motion was not agreed to.

Before his death, Mr. Cooper wrote a "Continuation of his Naval History," from which we make a brief extract.

Mr. Cooper, giving a detailed account of the operations of the navy in the "Conquest of California," says:—

"Throughout the whole of the foregoing movements, Commodore Stockton exhibited great activity, energy, and spirit. He and his ship seem to have been everywhere; and, whatever may be the decision of military etiquette as between the rival competitors for the command of this successful expedition against the enemy's capital, there can be no misapprehension on one subject, and that is, that Commodore Stockton was in the thickest of the fight and animated his men not only by his presence, but by a very brilliant personal example.

"Commodore Stockton virtually assumed the command near the close of July, and the whole of the succeeding five months was, on his part, a scene of as great exertion and of as bold assumption of responsibility as ever characterized the service of any man under the flag. We conceive the whole of those movements, marked as they were by so much decision and enterprise, to have been highly creditable to the American arms, and particularly so to that branch of the service of which we are writing."—*Naval History.*

Speech of Commodore Stockton, delivered in the State-House, Trenton, New Jersey, at the reception of Mr. Webster by the members of the Legislature, March, 1852.

SENATORS AND GENTLEMEN OF THE ASSEMBLY, AND FELLOW-CITIZENS:—You may perhaps imagine that I am very fond of making speeches. It is, therefore, proper for me to say that this is not the time or the occasion I should have selected for such a purpose. I am altogether unprepared; I did not, I could not have anticipated this event, or that any power on the face of the earth could have dragged out of me a speech or an attempt at a speech upon this occasion so worthily appropriated to your distinguished visitor.

If senators and members of the House of Assembly require any additional proof of my regard for them or my desire to serve them, or of my willingness to sacrifice myself for them, you have it in this prompt but hazardous compliance with your wishes.

This venerable hall, distinguished by so many proud reminiscences and hallowed associations connected with the early history of New Jersey, has this day been honoured in a way that, if the spirits of our fathers are hovering over us, they will applaud the spectacle.

Friends and Fellow-Citizens:—If there is any thing that can rouse up the best emotions of the human mind, it is the contemplation of the spontaneous affection which gratitude sometimes bestows upon the possessor of high virtues and great intellectual attainments. When we can lay down on the altar of patriotism all our selfish and unworthy feelings, forgetting party predilections and sectional differences, to pay just homage to the great and good, we may feel that we have achieved a triumph over human infirmity of which we may well be proud.

This is a proud day for New Jersey. I feel it as a Jerseyman, as a man, as a patriot. This day, here in this Hall of the Representatives of the people, the men and women of New Jersey have assembled to testify their regard for the talent, the patriotism, and the worth of Daniel Webster, one of the wisest and best of mankind. Whenever I contemplate the character of Daniel Webster— his extraordinary endowments—my heart goes to heaven in thanks to God that he has made such a man, that he has thus endowed one of our species. It is not simply that manly form or noble brow (which seems to have been placed as a crown to mark the man) to which our homage is paid, but to one of the strongest hearts and most gigantic minds of the age. I have known him for thirty years, and have seen him sitting among the wise and good in the councils of the nation. I myself have sat beside him and drunk in every word that fell from his almost inspired lips. I say before this assembly, and before the world, that if there is a patriotic heart that warms the bosom of any man, that heart is in the body of Daniel Webster. I have heard him discourse in private, at various times, on the subject of our public affairs, and I never heard him say a word that might be construed inimical to the interests of his country or his race, or that might not well have emanated from the heart of great and pure men. I have seen him engaged in the sports of the field with his gun upon his shoulder, following my own dogs; in short, whenever or wherever I have heard or seen him, he has always been the same great and generous man.

You need not then be surprised at my hesitation to speak on this occasion, or think my concern affected.

The exalted patriotism and great talents of your distinguished visitor are quite enough to disturb my poor abilities. But still I could not refuse your wish to hear me speak, or let the occasion pass without raising my feeble voice in welcome of your guest; nay, more, I am proud of the occasion, and rejoice in the opportunity to pay my fealty to exalted worth.

Mr. Webster has justly, and I believe truly, said that whenever he has crossed our territory and looked out on our fields the enthusiasm of patriotism was kindled in his breast to a greater degree than anywhere else. Mr. Webster is one of the few men who have studied the traditions of New Jersey, and I recommend them to the study of all my fellow-citizens. Her history has never yet been written. When it is truly written it will make some of the brightest pages in the history of our country, not only where it recounts the military exploits of the Revolution, but where it may tell of her steady perseverance in maintaining the institutions of the country in time of peace. A well-written history of the State of New Jersey will make the national heart leap with joy and pride. New Jersey has heretofore had too much dignity to boast of her achievements, and too much pride to complain of injustice. New Jersey has scarcely ever been heard to demand from the councils of the country her just and equal rights, but she has at last protested. The other day I, as your representative, called on the wisdom of the nation, then around me in the Capitol, to witness that New Jersey had suffered and sacrificed much for the country and the Union, that she had fought as valiantly and performed as important services to this nation as any of her sister States, and that she had received as few direct benefits from the General Government as any other State.

In the history of nations you can hardly find such an exhibition of self-dependence and moral grandeur as may be found in the annals of our State. New Jersey has proceeded on steadily in the path of patriotic duty and noble sacrifice, without complaint or yet remonstrance.

To estimate New Jersey by her own pretensions, you could scarcely imagine that she had ever made a sacrifice or fought a battle in the cause of Liberty or the Constitution. When you come, however, to examine her records, you will be amazed to see that she has accomplished so much for the public welfare, and astonished that she has received nothing worthy a name from the General Government. Her mineral resources appear to be inexhaustible, but they are buried in her mountains; her hills are filled with iron and copper, all useless, inactive, dead, in consequence of a constantly-fluctuating revenue system. I will never be a beggar at their doors, but I shall not be slow to tell them what our necessities require, and what, in my judgment, justice demands. I shall insist, because it is good Democratic doctrine. I shall insist upon dragging the iron out of our mountains down to the sea-coast. We want it for our national defences. I am aware that I tread upon delicate ground. I hope no one will see cause to be offended. I mean no offence. Why should not the operations of the General Government contribute to the development of our resources as it has done that of other States? I hope to get this matter of iron as well as of glass included in the next tariff bill. The tariff was heretofore a Democratic measure in the State of New Jersey.

The first resolutions on this subject, as well as I can recollect, were introduced in the Legislature of this State by Mr. James J. Wilson, a gentleman of eminence and worth. No one will dispute or doubt his Democracy. As a leader of the Democratic party, he was looked up to and much respected throughout the State.

Not many years after this, however, the party was rent asunder. One side took with them the thunder. It was all the thunder they had. They would not allow the matter to be settled, and thus it became a party question. How much more necessary a tariff is at this time, let experience and facts show. With an annual expenditure of fifty millions of dollars staring us in the face, can any thing be more ridiculous than to quarrel about the vagaries of free trade? This amount of expenditure will require an average duty of thirty-three per cent. on all our importations. We have no other resource for revenue of any consequence but the duties on imports. What folly then, I repeat, to be constantly wrangling about the doctrines of free trade! Fellow-citizens, my party robes do not hang very heavy on my shoulders when the welfare, the honour, or the interest, of my country are at stake.

I have passed my grand climacteric, and can have at best but few more years. I live now in and for my children. If I were to consult my interest alone or my ambition, I would concern myself but little about the constitution or the laws; I would not be much concerned at what might happen. I speak not for myself, but for my children's children.

Here, in this favoured land, is the last and best asylum of Liberty; drive her from these shores, and where will she find a resting-place?

Fellow-citizens, among the most important means of preserving our government in its strength and purity is a rigid economy in our public expenditures: they have increased during the last quarter of a century from thirteen to fifty millions of dollars; and if the augmentation of increase should be the same during the next twenty-five years, the cost of this Government will be carried up to the enormous amount of two hundred millions of dollars,—about three-fourths of the expenses of the British Empire, not including the payment of the interest on her public debt. If this prodigal and wasteful expenditure be not arrested, the country will be ruined.

If corruption, with its hydra head and its long train of evils, once begins to sap the foundations of the Republic, Freedom is clean gone forever.

I desire to see this Government brought back to the simplicity and economy of the days of Jefferson. Such sentiments may seem strange to some of my fellow citizens, but it must be borne in mind that I belong to the young and progressive school of Democracy. It is true I was brought up at the feet of Gamaliel, among the strictest sect of Federalists: my father was a Federalist; I was too young to take a part in the politics of those days. He was a compeer of Hamilton, of Washington, and other great men of those times; he loved them when they lived, and loved their memories when dead. It was his glory to follow where the footsteps of Washington led. If I had been old enough in those days, I would probably have been a Federalist. A purer band of patriots and more honest men never ruled the destinies of any country. They acted wisely in their day and generation.

THE END.

STEREOTYPED BY L. JOHNSON & CO.
PHILADELPHIA.

www.ingramcontent.com/pod-product-compliance
Lightning Source LLC
Chambersburg PA
CBHW032031090426
42733CB00029B/79